DAVID BOWIE

A PEOPLE'S HISTORY

Neil Cossar

All rights reserved. No part of this publication may be reproduced, stored in a retrieval system, or transmitted in any form or by any means, electronic, electrostatic, recording, magnetic tape, mechanical, photocopying or otherwise, without prior permission in writing from the publisher.

The publisher makes no representation, express or implied, with regard to the accuracy of the information contained in this publication and
cannot accept any responsibility in law for any errors or omissions.

The right of Neil Cossar to be identified as author of this Work has been asserted by him in accordance with sections 77 and 78 of the Copyright, Designs and Patents Act 1988.

No part of this book may be reproduced in any form without permission from the publisher except for the quotation of brief passages in reviews.

A catalogue record for this book is available from the British Library

This edition © Spenwood Books 2025

ISBN: 978-1-915858-46-7

Published by Spenwood Books Limited
1 Totnes Road, Manchester, M21 8XF
richard@spenwoodbooks.com

Photo credits (with thanks)
Bob Gruen, 4: George Underwood, 22: Dana Gillespie, 26: Morgan Fisher, 33: Vernon Dewhurst, 38: Keith Christmas, 47: © Peter Hince, 66, 148 & 149: Robin Mayhew, 86: John Hutchinson, 114: Brian Boardman, 95 & 122: Marc Riley, 178: Colin Murray, 209: Bruce Butler, 210 & 418: Carinthia West, Hanging Out Archive, 216: Judy Totton, 259 & 271: Andrea Mastroeni, 290: Pete Mitchell, 319: Alexis Rowell, 339: Michael Lavine, 348: Rob McHarg, 331, 386, 397, 399 & 397: Lisa Nelson Brown, 415.

Contents

1958 – 1969

Best Friends 1958 – 1969
21
Bromley

Clarks College
24
Bromley

The Konrads
27
June 1963

Manish Boys
29
1964

Stockton ABC Globe Cinema
30
Stockton – 4 December 1964

Blue Moon Club
31
Cheltenham – 4 September 1965

The Marquee Club
32
Soho – 1966

Britannia Pier
36
Great Yarmouth – 27 June 1966

Clareville Grove
37
South Kensington, West London

The New Musical Express Talent Contest
39
Hammersmith Palais, London

Space Oddity
39
London – 2 February 1969

The Three Tuns
41
Beckenham

The Magic Village
42
Manchester – 21 February 1969

Free Trade Hall
42
Manchester – 22 February 1969

The Magic Village
43
Manchester – 22 February 1969

Philharmonic Hall
44
Liverpool – 1 March 1969

Three HorseShoes
45
Hampstead, London – May 1969

Rolling Stones free concert
46
Hyde Park – 5 July 1969

The London Hospital Medical College
47
Whitechapel – September 1969

The Odeon
48
Manchester – 25 October 1969

Bonnyrigg Regal
53
Edinburgh – 9 November 1969

Electric Garden
53
Glasgow – 10 November 1969

Albert Hall
54
Stirling – 11 November 1969

Music Hall
54
Aberdeen – 12 November 1969

Fillmore North, Locarno Ballroom
55
Sunderland – 13 March 1970

1970

Poco-a-Poco
58
Stockport, Manchester – 27 April 1970

Glastonbury Fair
61
Worthy Farm, Pilton – 23 June 1971

Friars, Borough Assembly Hall
63
Aylesbury – 25 September 1971

Country Club
65
Haverstock, Hampstead – November 1971

1972-1973

Friars, Borough Assembly Hall
67
Aylesbury – 29 January 1972

The Toby Jug
80
Tolworth, London – 10 February 1972

Birmingham Town Hall
83
Birmingham – 17 March 1972

Free Trade Hall
83
Manchester – 21 April 1972

Pavilion
85
Hemel Hempstead, London – 7 May 1972

Assembly Hall
88
Worthing – 11 May 1972

Polytechnic of Central London
88
London – 12 May 1972

Slough Technical College
90
Slough – 13 May 1972

Ebbisham
91
Epsom – 27 May 1972

Liverpool Stadium
91
Liverpool – 3 June 1972

Dunstable, Civic Hall
92
Dunstable – 21 June 1972

Civic Hall
93
Guildford – August 1972

Rainbow Theatre
95
London, – 19 August 1972

Bristol Locarno
98
Bristol – 27 August 1972

Music Hall
101
Cleveland, Ohio – 22 September 1972

Ellis Auditorium
102
Memphis, Tennessee – 24 September 1972

Carnegie Hall
102
New York City – 28 September 1972

Fisher Theater
102
Detroit, Michigan – 8 October 1972

Santa Monica Civic Auditorium
104
California – 20 October 1972

Winterland Auditorium
104
San Francisco – 27 October 1972

HardRock
107
Manchester – 28 & 29 December 1972

Empire Theatre
109
Edinburgh – 6 January 1973

Radio City Music Hall
110
New York City – 14 February 1973

Long Beach Arena
114
Long Beach, California – 10 March 1973

Shibuya Kokaido
114
Tokyo – 20 April 1973

Earls Court
117
London – 12 May 1973

Caird Hall
118
Dundee – 17 May 1973

Greens Playhouse
123
Glasgow – 18 May 1973

King George's Hall
124
Blackburn – 31 May 1973

Free Trade Hall
131
Manchester – 7 June 1973

Empire Theatre
131
Liverpool – 10 June 1973

De Montfort Hall
137
Leicester – 11 June 1973

City Hall
139
Salisbury – 14 June 1973

Town Hall
139
Birmingham – 21 June 1973

Top Rank Suite
140
Doncaster – 27 June 1973

Hammersmith Odeon
141
London – 2 July 1973

Hammersmith Odeon
145
London – 3 July 1973

1974

Rochester Community War Memorial
152
Rochester, New York – 17 June 1974

Municipal Auditorium
154
Nashville, Tennessee – 29 June 1974

Tower Theater
154
Upper Darby, Philadelphia – 8 – 13 July 1974

Madison Square Garden
156
New York City – 19 July 1974

Universal Amphitheatre
157
Los Angeles – 2 – 8 September 1974

Indiana Convention Center
157
Indianapolis – 8 October 1974

Michigan Palace Theater
159
Detroit – 15 – 20 October 1974

The Spectrum
160
Philadelphia – 18 November 1974

CONTENTS

1976

Seattle Center Coliseum
161
Washington - 3 February 1976

Arizona Veterans Memorial Coliseum
162
Phoenix - 15 Feb 1976

McNichols Sports Arena
162
Denver, Colorado - 17 February 1976

Mecca Arena
163
Milwaukee - 20 February 1976

Wings Stadium
164
Kalamazoo, Michigan - 21 February 1976

Riverfront Coliseum
165
Cincinnati - 23 February 1976

Montreal Forum
165
Montreal, Canada - 25 February 1976

Mid-South Coliseum
166
Memphis, Tennessee - 6 March 1976

Omni Coliseum
167
Atlanta - 8 March 1976

Civic Arena
167
Pittsburgh - 11 March 1976

Norfolk Scope
168
Norfolk, Virginia - 12 March 1976

Capital Centre
168
Landover, Maryland - 13 March 1976

Springfield Civic Center
169
Springfield, MA - 21 March 1976

New Haven Coliseum
169
Connecticut - 22 March 1976

Madison Square Garden
170
New York - 26 March 1976

UKK Hall
171
Helsinki, Finland - 24 April 1976

The Royal Tennishall
172
Stockholm, Sweden - 26 April 1976

Scandinavium
174
Gothenburg, Sweden - 28 April 1976

Empire Pool
177
London - 3 - 8 May 1976

1977

Le Plateau Auditorium
187
Montreal, Canada - 13 March 1977

Masonic Temple
187
Detroit - 25 March 1977

1978

Cobo Arena
188
Detroit, Michigan - 20 April 1978

Kungliga Tennishallen
189
Stockholm, Sweden - 2 June 1978

The Apollo
190
Glasgow - 19, 20, 21 & 22 June 1978

New Bingley Hall
192
Stafford - 24, 25 & 26 June 1978

Earl's Court
195
London - 29, 30 June, 1 July 1978

Adelaide Oval
205
Adelaide, Australia - 11 November 1978

Melbourne Cricket Ground
208
Melbourne, Australia - 18 November 1978

Lang Park
211
Brisbane, Australia - 21 November 1978

RAS Showgrounds
211
Sydney, Australia - 24 & 25 November 1978

Western Springs Stadium
212
Auckland, New Zealand - 2 December 1978

1980s

Mountain Studios
213
Montreux - July 1981

St Germans
213
Cornwall - Summer 1981

Warwickshire
218
England - Summer 1981

Power Station
218
Manhattan, New York City - December 1982

Sydney Australia
219
March 1983

Cannes Film Festival
220
Cannes, France - May 1983

1983

Palais des Sports de Gerland
224
Lyon, France – 24 May 1983

Wembley Arena
224
London – 2, 3 & 4 June 1983

National Exhibition Centre
225
Birmingham – 5 & 6 June 1983

Bieberer Berg Stadion
226
Offenbach am Main, Germany – 24 June 1983

Stadion Feijenoord
227
Rotterdam, Netherlands – 25 June 1983

Murrayfield Stadium
228
Edinburgh – 28 June 1983

Milton Keynes Bowl
231
Milton Keynes – 1, 2 & 3 July 1983

Hartford Civic Center
235
Hartford, Connecticut – 15 July 1983

The Spectrum
235
Philadelphia – 18 – 21 July 1983

Carrier Dome
236
Syracuse, New York – 23 July 1983

Madison Square Garden
238
New York City – 25 July 1983

Joe Louis Arena
240
Detroit, Michigan – 30 July 1983

Commonwealth Stadium
240
Edmonton, Alberta, Canada – 7 August 1983

BC Place
240
Vancouver, Canada – 9 August 1983

Reunion Arena
241
Dallas, Texas – 19 August 1983

Scope Cultural and Convention Center
242
Norfolk, Virginia – 24 August 1983

Sullivan Stadium
242
Foxborough, Massachusetts – 31 August 1983

Anaheim Stadium
244
California – 9 September 1983

Pacific National Exhibition Coliseum
245
Vancouver, Canada – 12 September 1983

Winnipeg Stadium
246
Winnipeg, Canada – 14 September 1983

Perth Entertainment Centre
247
Perth, Australia – 4, 5 & 6 November 1983

VFL Stadium
247
Melbourne, Australia – 12 November 1983

Sydney Showground
248
Sydney Australia, 19 November 1983

Athletic Park
248
Wellington, New Zealand – 24 November 1983

Western Springs Stadium
249
Auckland, New Zealand – 26 November 1983

Thai Army Sports Stadium
252
Bangkok, Thailand – 5 December 1983

Live Aid
254
Wembley Stadium, London – 13 July 1985

1987

Rock Werchter
260
Werchter, Belgium – 2 June 1987

Platz der Republik
260
Berlin, Germany – 6 June 1987

Stadio Flaminio
264
Rome, Italy – 15 June 1987

Roker Park
265
Sunderland – 23 June 1987

Prater-Stadium
265
Vienna, Austria – 1 July 1987

Stadium Municipal
268
Toulouse, France – 4 July 1987

Maine Road
270
Manchester – 14 – 15 July 1987

Veterans Stadium
273
Philadelphia – 30 July 1987

Anaheim Stadium
275
Anaheim, California – 8 August 1987

BC Place Stadium
277
Vancouver, Canada – 15 August 1987

CONTENTS

Commonwealth Stadium 278
Edmonton, Canada – 17 August 1987

Canadian National Exhibition Stadium 279
Ontario, Canada – 24 August 1987

Olympic Stadium 281
Montreal, Quebec – 30 August 1987

Sullivan Stadium 281
Foxborough, Massachusetts – 3 September 1987

Marcus Amphitheater 282
Milwaukee, Wisconsin – 10 September 1987

Pontiac Silverdome 282
Pontiac, Michigan – 12 September 1987

Miami Orange Bowl 282
Miami, Florida – 18 September 1987

Omni Coliseum 283
Atlanta – 21 September 1987

Louisiana Superdome 284
New Orleans, Louisiana – 6 October 1987

Sydney Entertainment Centre 285
Sydney, Australia – 3 – 14 November 1987

Western Springs Stadium 286
Auckland, New Zealand – 28 November 1987

1989

National Ballroom 289
Kilburn, London – 29 June 1989
289

1990

Skydome 291
Toronto, Canada – 7 March 1990

Northlands Coliseum 291
Edmonton, Canada – 12 March 1990

Royal Highland Show Exhibition Centre 293
Edinburgh – 23 & 24 March 1990

Docklands Arena 294
London – 28 March 1990

Sportpaleis Ahoy 294
Rotterdam, Netherlands – 30 March 1990

PalaEur 296
Rome, Italy – 17 April 1990

Miami Arena 298
Miami – 27 April 1990

Florida Suncoast Dome 298
St. Petersburg, Florida – 4 May 1990

Los Angeles Memorial Sports Arena 298
California – 23 May 1990

Dodger Stadium 299
Los Angeles – 26 May 1990

Marcus Amphitheater 300
Milwaukee – 13 June 1990

The Spectrum 300
Philadelphia – 10 July 1990

Milton Keynes Bowl 301
Milton Keynes – 4 – 5 August 1990

Maine Road Football Ground 304
Manchester – 7 August 1990

Stadion de Goffert 307
Nijmegen, Netherlands – 18 August 1990

Linzer Stadium 308
Linz, Austria – 29 Aug 1990

Festa de l'Unità 308
Modena, Italy – 8 September 1990

River Plate Stadium 311
Buenos Aires, Argentina – 29 September 1990

1991

Teatro Brancaccio 312
Rome, Italy – 9 October 1991

Zirkus Krone 315
Munich, Germany – 12 October 1991

Cirkus 316
Stockholm, Sweden – 21 October 1991

International II 317
Manchester – 3 November 1991

Mayfair 319
Newcastle upon Tyne – 5 November 1991

Orpheum Theater 320
Boston, Massachusetts – 25 Nov 1991

La Brique
320
Montreal, Quebec, Canada
– 1 December 1991

The Concert Hall
321
Toronto, Ontario – 3 December 1991

1992

Wembley Stadium
323
London – 20 April 1992

Black Tie White Noise
329
Recording sessions – June 1992

1995-1996

SkyDome
332
Toronto, Canada – 20 September 1995

Nissan Pavilion
333
Bristow, Virginia – 6 October 1995

King's Hall
334
Belfast, Northern Ireland – 5 Dec 1995

The Big Twix Mix Show
335
NEC Arena, Birmingham – 13 December 1995

Prins Van Oranjehall
336
Utrecht, Netherlands – 28 January 1996

Kremlin Palace Concert Hall
339
Moscow – 18 June 1996

P.A.O. Stadium
340
Athens, Greece – 1 July 1996

Park HaYarkon
340
Tel Aviv, Israel – 3 July

1996

The Phoenix Festival
342
Stratford upon Avon – 18 July 1996

Madison Square Garden
347
New York City – 9 January 1997

1997

Sommer Arena
350
Vienna, Austria – 24 June 1997

Pistoia Blues Festival
352
Piazza Duomo, Pistoia, Italy – 2 July 1997

Phoenix Festival
353
Stratford upon Avon – 20 July 1997

Barrowlands
356
Glasgow – 22 July 1997

Manchester Academy
357
Manchester – 23 July 1997

The Que Club
361
Birmingham – 1 August 1997

Riverside
363
Newcastle upon Tyne – 3 August 1997

Rock City
363
Nottingham – 5 August 1997

Olympia Theatre
369
Dublin, Ireland – 8 August 1997

Shepherd's Bush Empire
369
London – 11 August 1997

Chili Pepper
372
Ft. Lauderdale, Florida – 7 October 1990

Foro Sol
374
Mexico City, Mexico – 23 October 1997

1999

Burlington Arcade
375
London – January 1999

Manhattan Center
375
New York City – 23 August 1999

Astoria Theatre
378
London – 2 Dec 1999

Alcatraz
379
Milan, Italy – 4 December 1999

2000

Glastonbury Festival
381
Pilton – 25 June 2000

2002

The Quart Festival
387
Kristiansand, Norway – 3 July 2002

Summer Festival
389
Lucca, Italy – 15 July 2002

Maida Vale
392
London – 18 September 2002

Max-Schmeling-Halle
392
Berlin, Germany – 22 September 2002

Le Zénith, Paris
395
France – 24 September

CONTENTS

2002

**Carling Apollo
396**
Hammersmith, London – 2 October 2002

2003-2004

**Hartwall Areena
404**
Helsinki, Finland – 10 October 2003

**Forum di Assago
404**
Milan, Italy – 23 October 2003

**Hallenstadion
406**
Zürich, Switzerland – 24 October 2003

**Kölnarena
407**
Cologne, Germany – 31 October 2003

**Manchester Arena
408**
Manchester – 17 November 2003

**NEC LG Arena
410**
Birmingham – 19 - 20 November 2003

**Wembley Arena
410**
London – 25 November 2003

**CSU Convocation Center
412**
Cleveland, Ohio – 7 January 2004

**Pengrowth Saddledome
413**
Calgary, Canada – 21 January 2004

**Sydney Entertainment Centre
414**
Sydney, Australia – 20 Feb 2004

**Rod Laver Arena
417**
Melbourne, Australia – 26 - 27 February 2004

**Supreme Court Gardens
418**
Perth, Australia – 1 March 2004

**Rose Garden Arena
419**
Portland, Oregon – 13 April 2004

**Greek Theatre
420**
Los Angeles – 22 April 2004

**James L. Knight Center
421**
Miami, Florida – 6 May 2004

**The MARK of the Quad Cities
421**
Moline, Illinois – 22 May 2004

**Shea's Performing Arts Center
422**
Buffalo, New York – 25 May 2004

**Borgata Event Center
422**
Atlantic City – 30 May 2004

**Frognerparken
424**
Oslo, Norway – 18 June 2004

**T-Mobile Arena
425**
Prague, Czech Republic – 23 June 2004

**Royal Albert Hall
426**
London – 29 May 2006

2006 429

2010-2012 429

2015 430

**Stars are out tonight
436**

David and backing singer/companion Ava Cherry with Chris Charlesworth, then US Editor of Melody Maker, at a party following Todd Rundgren's Carnegie Hall gig on April 19, 1974

INTRODUCTION

BY CHRIS CHARLESWORTH

David Bowie was the most charismatic popular musician of his generation, a cultural polymath and style icon whose artistic breadth also took in theatre, film, video, fashion, mime, fine art criticism and prose writing. Though hugely admired by vast numbers of fans throughout the world, he often seemed uncomfortable with mainstream recognition and throughout his long career made a habit of stepping back to experiment with genres of music and cultural expression unlikely to find commercial acceptance. By refusing to rest on his laurels and – apart from a misstep in the Eighties when he courted the mass market to excess – recording a series of peerless albums at various times in his life, he maintained a consistent level of critical acclaim enjoyed by very few of his contemporaries.

Born David Robert Jones in Brixton in 1947, Bowie paid his dues in a number of groups and guises until his breakthrough in 1969 with the hit single 'Space Oddity', perfectly timed to coincide with the American moon landing that same year. The song's theme of alienation and impending doom would be a recurrent motif of Bowie's work, alongside a sense of otherworldliness on the part of its creator, as if David Bowie really was from another world, an alien being on a higher astral plane than mere mortals, someone who simply knew more than the rest of us.

The new decade brought a change in his business affairs with Bowie, perhaps frustrated by his lack of progress after two early albums, abandoning his dependable but old school manager Kenneth Pitt in favour of the more flamboyant but slightly Machiavellian Tony DeFries. Together they founded a company called MainMan and staffed it with colourful characters whose loyalty to David was never in doubt but whose spending habits would later come back to haunt him. DeFries encouraged his new client to act like a star before he actually was one, thus creating an illusion around Bowie that he was happy to go along with so long as it advanced his career. It turned out to be a Faustian pact but for the time being everyone was delighted with the new arrangement and, if nothing else, the MainMan crew certainly enlivened the London rock scene.

Nevertheless, Bowie's rise to stardom was not immediate. Though acclaimed by critics, his 1971 albums *The Man Who Sold The World*, the cover of which saw him in a 'man's dress', and *Hunky Dory* sold respectably if not spectacularly. An instinctive rather than virtuoso musician, Bowie played saxophone, guitar and keyboards but his greatest skill was in composition and finding the right collaborators to help realise his vision. During the making of these records he recruited a key early ally in guitarist Mick Ronson who joined his stage group shortly before Bowie renamed them The Spiders from Mars, its leader now restyled as Ziggy Stardust, the ensemble designed to perform his 1972 album named after themselves. This saw lift-off with Bowie as Ziggy, presenting himself in concert as an androgynous being, his spikey hair carrot red, his clothes more and more colourful, outré and revealing, his whole demeanour screaming 'star' from the highest pinnacle.

Ushering in glam rock but always maintaining a rather aloof presence above the genre's less cerebral acts like Slade, Sweet and his friend Marc Bolan's T. Rex, Bowie's elaborate costumes were all part of the same package, in hindsight a work of art in itself. Consciously or not, everything he did from that point onwards became part of his art and his life as an artist. Amongst his greatest achievements, therefore, was what he saw, when he looked at himself in the mirror.

Crucially, he represented the outsider, positioning himself on the side of those ill-suited for conventional society. His lyrics, often elliptical, spoke to misfits and loners, the timid and the disconnected, enabling them to cast off inhibitions and paving the way for a less macho style of rock performer and performance. A skilled interviewee, he was quick to realise that absolute truth was of less significance that the effect his words might carry. When he did speak to the press he usually made headlines, not least in January 1972 when he announced, without foundation, that he was gay or, at the very least, bisexual. Similarly, on a musical level he positioned himself outside the tried and tested blues rock formula typified by The Rolling Stones or more supercharged contemporaries like Led Zeppelin, his chief rival during the Seventies. While songs such as 'The Jean Genie', 'Suffragette City' and 'Rebel Rebel' certainly rocked with the best of glam's full-tilt explosions, others, like 'Changes', 'Life On Mars?' and 'Starman', reflected a more ethereal quality, the latter borrowing Harold Arlen's octave climb from 'Somewhere Over The Rainbow' to startling effect. Ziggy Stardust itself, of course, was assumed to be autobiographical.

By the end of 1972 Bowie was the biggest solo rock star in the UK, not to mention the most visually striking and controversial, and though

America's ingrained conservatism resisted him at first, the US fell the following year. He even found time to revive the careers of Lou Reed, Iggy Pop and Mott The Hoople. *Aladdin Sane* (1973) attracted advance orders of 100,000 in the UK and was in many ways Ziggy Part II, another huge success, its striking cover of Bowie as Ziggy with a blue thunderbolt etched across his face solidifying his surreal image. Then, just as it seemed as if Bowie would eclipse all before him, he abandoned Ziggy completely, memorably making the announcement from the stage at Hammersmith Odeon, shocking fans and, so word had it, even his own group, and returned to the drawing board. It would not be the first time that Bowie would abruptly change tack, a career strategy that he maintained until the very end.

The patchy covers album *Pin Ups* (1973) was a holding manoeuvre but with *Diamond Dogs* (1974), and perhaps more importantly its concurrent stage show, Bowie invented rock theatre, a style of presentation that paid no lip service whatsoever to conventional rock concerts and instead relied purely on dramatic effect and elaborate stage props. The following year he discovered blue-eyed soul with *Young Americans*, its funked-up US No.1 hit single 'Fame' a collaboration with John Lennon that savaged his relationship with manager Tony DeFries. He then stepped back from music to appear in Nicolas Roeg's sci-fi film *The Man Who Fell To Earth*. It was astute casting, Bowie's starring role as an extra-terrestrial sent to earth to save his own planet serving only to ramp up the impression of Bowie as a creature from beyond the stratosphere.

Bowie was on a roll though by his own volition it wasn't to last. *Station to Station* (1976), which merged black funk with the emerging European electronic school, is widely regarded as his best album ever, as timeless as it is flawless; yet, after a thrillingly successful world arena tour, it would presage Bowie's second retreat from the commercial sphere. Destabilized by a financially calamitous fall out with DeFries – henceforth he would largely manage his own business affairs in tandem with lawyers and personal assistant Corinne 'Coco' Schwab – and an enervating cocaine habit, he wisely relocated to Berlin to work with producer/auteur Brian Eno on a trilogy of introverted experimental

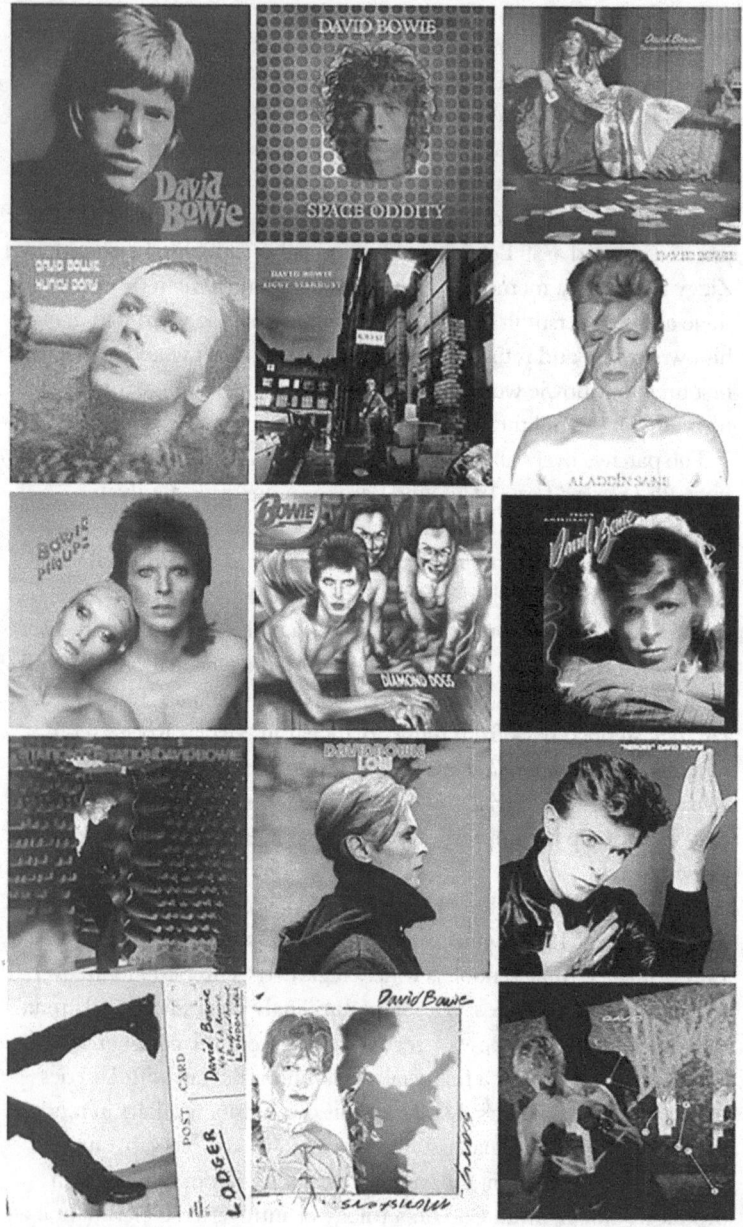

INTRODUCTION 15

During his career David Bowie released 25 studio albums, 10 live albums, 51 compilation albums, eight extended plays (EPs), 128 singles, including five UK number-one singles, and four soundtracks

albums, thus not only avoiding the need to compete with punk rock but setting himself up as a genuine innovator. Although many tracks on these now highly acclaimed records were instrumental in character and perversely un-commercial, the Berlin period produced the stirring majesty of 'Heroes', a meditation on the futility of the Berlin Wall that is arguably the finest song he ever wrote and certainly the most popular.

After emerging from his German retreat for another arena tour, *Scary Monsters* (1980) saw Bowie move to more conventional ground, its most affecting track 'Ashes To Ashes' a revision of the Major Tom saga from 'Space Oddity'. By this time videos – short films to promote singles – had arrived and few benefited more from this development than Bowie whose acting experience gave him the jump on less imaginative fellow travellers. The video for 'Ashes To Ashes', with Bowie in Pierrot costume, not only lit the touch paper beneath the New Romantic movement, but ushered in an era when he consistently led the field in this new art form. As if to prove the point, his next move, again unexpected, was to appear on stage – bravely and with distinction – in Chicago and on Broadway in New York as the severely deformed John Merrick in *The Elephant Man*, a role that required him to contort his frame throughout the play's duration.

A switch of record labels then saw Bowie pocket a reputed $17 million advance and move back into the musical mainstream, this time on his own terms. With EMI's promotional muscle behind him, *Let's Dance* (1983), produced by Nile Rodgers, became his best-selling album ever, its funk-driven title track a big hit with an even bigger hook. He was looking different now too, more mature and smartly turned out in stylish pastel suits, business-like yet as attractive as ever, his neatly coiffured blond hair and easy smile as appealing as the sheen of *Let's Dance* tracks like 'Modern Love' and 'China Girl'. The Serious Moonlight Tour that followed saw Bowie ever more accomplished on stage, his gift for presentation now executed with effortless panache, a crowd-pleasing spectacle of light, sound, movement and mime, all to accompany a catalogue of wonderful songs played by top class musicians led by guitarist Carlos Alomar. It was this vision of Bowie that in 1985 seduced a worldwide audience of millions at Live Aid, his four-song set during Bob Geldof's all-star charity extravaganza a highlight of the event and a triumph of mass communication.

The momentum, however, was not to last. *Tonight* (1984) failed to match the sparkle of *Let's Dance*, presaging an artistic decline that lasted for almost a decade, exacerbated by the disappointing *Never Let Me Down* (1987), which in the fullness of time Bowie himself would resoundingly disparage. The global success of the new 'normal' Bowie, and the less-than-radical musical soundtrack that accompanied this new model, proved to be his undoing. In distancing himself from the cutting edge, he fell between two stools, alienating both the new and less critical post *Let's Dance* audience that recoiled at his theatricality while at the same time disaffecting the more discerning long-term fans who were drawn to his visionary zeal. Matters weren't helped by contractual obligations to a hungry new record label.

Bowie's solution to this dilemma was to form a group, Tin Machine, in which he would claim to be 'just another member', an optimistic prospect to say the least. If nothing else the two heavy-handed Tin Machine albums in 1989 and 1991 and subsequent live recording a year later moved Bowie away from the spotlight to lick his wounds. His commercial stock was now at its lowest point since before the Ziggy era but he surprised the world again, not with music but by marrying the Somalian model Iman Mohamed Abdulmajid. Iman clearly inspired the romanticism of *Black Tie White Noise* (1993) and seemed to finally settle Bowie's restless spirit and curb his occasional lapses into hedonism.

Thereafter Bowie's muse would fluctuate across a series of thoughtful, occasionally acclaimed albums that were never quite as illustrious as those that preceded them but at the same time restored his reputation and sustained it for two further decades.

There were tours in which he was never less than immaculately turned out, with favourite songs from the past judiciously blended with newer material and, like many of his peers, he made announcements to the effect that he would no longer play the hits, only to renege on the pledge a year or two later. How could he not perform songs that had become touchstones in so many lives? Some of these later records, *Earthling* (1997) in particular, were on the experimental side while others, notably *Hours* (1999) and the enjoyable *Heathen* (2002), were designed for mass consumption, as was the less successful *Reality* (2003).

To promote *Reality* Bowie undertook a huge world tour that stretched from 2003 into 2004 but in June of 2004 was abruptly cancelled when he suffered heart problems at Scheeßel in Germany. It is understood that he underwent a heart bypass operation. After surgery, Bowie returned to New York, his home for the past decade and where he would continue to live in relative seclusion for the remainder of his life.

From that point on the public was told very little about what was happening in the world of David Bowie. He stopped giving interviews around 2006 and his official website remained silent for extended periods. It was reported that he had declined a knighthood. Although he made occasional guest appearances, notably with Arcade Fire, he was entering a long period of privacy during which rumours about his failing health – he'd been a heavy smoker for most of his life – proliferated. In the words of the noted music critic Charles Shaar Murray, we no longer knew who David Bowie was any more, even if we ever did.

Since presentation was so crucial to Bowie's craft it is safe to assume that the reason the world henceforth saw so little of him was because he could no longer present himself on stage or elsewhere in the manner he would prefer. Bowie would no sooner appear as a shadow of his former self than reassume the character of Ziggy Stardust so, rather than appear as someone who no longer resembled the David Bowie that was universally adored, he chose not to appear at all. Age, it seemed, was the great leveller, even for David Bowie. Nevertheless, his absence created a vacuum in which his star continued to shine brightly: the exhibition of his stage outfits and other memorabilia at London's Victoria & Albert Museum in 2013 attracted record crowds and would tour the world.

That same year Bowie's silence was broken dramatically with the unexpected release of *The Next Day*, which took fans and everyone else completely by surprise. In what in hindsight can be seen as another superb piece of media manipulation, as impressive as any in his entire career, its unheralded arrival was a front-page news story in itself, Bowie deriving more publicity by doing absolutely nothing than top flight acts receive from the massive advance promotion that is the norm in the 21st Century. A reflective, carefully crafted work, *The Next Day* won

European city locations were used to announce Bowies twenty-fourth studio album The Next Day

Bowie the Best British Male Solo Artist at the 2014 *Brit Awards*. The model Kate Moss, wearing one of Bowie's original Ziggy costumes, picked up the award on his behalf while an enlarged 1973 photo of the real thing, in the identical costume, looked on beautifully.

Two years later, on January 8, his 69th birthday came the elegiac brooding, *Blackstar* – a recording, which in hindsight, seems to have been deliberately designed as a requiem. With lyrics that vaguely referenced his rapidly approaching demise, it will remain a moving, emotional epitaph, intentional in design, a unique and strangely appropriate climax to an extraordinary life.

David Bowie passed away from cancer of the liver two days later. He'd evidently been diagnosed 18 months earlier and only a tight circle of family and friends knew the extent of his illness. Remarkably, it remained a close secret, so the announcement came as a profound shock to the world and inspired tributes from the high and mighty, fellow musicians and – most notably – multitudes of fans for whom David Bowie represented much more than simply a great rock star but an ideal, a way of life, an incentive to live as you choose and not be cowed by convention. Within hours of the news, these fans, many of them with thunderbolts painted on their faces, gathered in their thousands to sing his songs at locations associated with Bowie's life and career where hastily erected shrines spoke far more about his impact on this world than any of the clichés uttered by the great and the good.

In the second decade of the 21st Century, when performers from rock and roll's pioneering era seem to pass away with the inevitability of the changing seasons, the loss of David Bowie can be compared only to the deaths of Elvis Presley and John Lennon. 'I am not a rock star,' he would repeatedly tell journalists. He was right. He was much more than that; untouchable, perhaps comparable to stars in the old Hollywood sense of the term, perhaps in his daring and ambition beyond compare, shining as brightly as any star on a cloudless night, truly one of the brightest we shall ever see. He's up there now, looking down on us, and maybe, if you glance skywards and catch a comet flashing across the heavens, you might see David Bowie riding its fiery slipstream, laughing, singing and waving bye-bye, the prettiest pop star of them all. 'If we sparkle he might land tonight…'

Chris Charlesworth

1958-1969

Bowie's debut live performance was in 1958, when, with his friend George Underwood, he played a few songs at the 18th Bromley Scout packs annual vacation, held on the Isle Of Wight, including a version of the Lonnie Donegan hit 'Puttin' On The Style', with David on ukulele.

During the early Sixties, the young David Jones went on to perform with the likes of The Konrads, The Hooker Brothers, Dave and the Bowmen, Davie Jones and The King Bees, Dave's Reds and Blues, The Manish Boys and The Lower Third.

In this period, these assorted line-ups worked mainly around London and the surrounding area, playing an assortment of blues covers mixed with original songs. One short tour in December 1963 saw Davie Jones and The Manish Boys opening for Gerry and the Pacemakers, along with The Kinks, Marianne Faithfull and Gene Pitney.

On 16 September 1965, David Jones' official stage name became David Bowie and live dates continued under the name of David Bowie & the Buzz, included many appearances at The Marquee Club, Soho, London and less glamorous venues such as Brands Hatch Racing Track, the Shoreline Club, Bognor Regis and Blackpool's South Pier.

By 1967, Bowie was on tour in a band called The Riot Squad, known for their theatrical live shows and were billed as, 'The complete musical entertainers'. At the end of 1967, Bowie was appearing in his first stage show, *Pierrot In Turquoise,* in London theatres.

Also during 1967 Bowie recorded his first session at the BBC for the *Top Gear* show, recording five tracks and a further two more BBC radio session by the end of the Sixties.

BEST FRIENDS

1956-1969 BROMLEY

I WAS THERE: GEORGE UNDERWOOD

I met David in 1956. We were both enrolling into the 18th Bromley Cub Scouts and soon discovered we had similar tastes in music and wanted to be in a skiffle group.

14 year olds David Bowie and George Underwood making a visit to the American Embassy in London 1961.

David went through various 'fads' at that time which I did as well – hairstyles, American football, baseball, Davy Crockett – mostly things American.

The 'eye' incident was over a girl called Carol. It has been documented many times over the years, sometimes wrongly. I did punch David when we were 15-years old. Afterwards his pupil would not dilate and gave the illusion of different coloured eyes. Before that, his eyes were both blue. He did say to me many years later that I did him a favour.

He did show me a fan letter when we were in America in 1972 – it read something like – 'I am an alien from another planet and I know you are from the same planet.'

When we formed The King Bees in 1964, David wrote to John Bloom who was a rich entrepreneur at the time, saying 'Brian Epstein has got The Beatles – you need us!' Strangely enough he got a reply by telegram to ring Lesley Conn who became our manager and we got to make a record, so that letter did work.

My cousin, Keith, who went to Bromley Grammar school, used to hang out with a group of bikers in Bromley. I used to sneak out and go with them to various coffee bars on the back of my cousin's bike. Although they were a few years older than me, I got away with it. Brian Gill, nicknamed Gilly, was the leader, if you like, of this little gang. He got expelled from Bromley Grammar for telling the headmaster to 'fuck off' when asked to shave off his sideburns.

I told David about this and he was suitably impressed to include 'Gilly' if only by name as a member of David's gang – the spiders from mars.

I think I may have inspired David to write 'Jean Jeanie'. Let me explain – we were touring around the States in 1972. David didn't fly, so we went by train, car and sometimes in a Greyhound bus.

It was in the bus one time that I was strumming on a guitar that was being passed around to while away the time. Anyway, I was playing this riff, which was similar to a John Lee Hooker type thing. David, who was sitting right at the back, asked me to send the guitar over. He took that riff and within about 15 minutes had turned it into

The local press inform us that George Underwood's dad is a greengrocer

'Jean Jeanie'.

That 1972 US tour was amazing. We went with David and Angie by QE2 first class. David wore one of his Ziggy suits to dinner on the first night but decided it brought him too much attention. Surprise surprise! It was funny watching the people's expressions – eyes popping out of their heads. Very funny. Unpredictable is a word that comes to mind. One time in a hotel room with quite a few people around, David disappeared to the loo. When he reappeared he had shaved his eyebrows off! Never a dull moment with David around.

CLARKS COLLEGE

1962-1963 BROMLEY

I WAS THERE: JIM MILROY

I went to Clarks College in Bromley on the corner of Masons Hill and Hayes Lane. It was 1962 – 63. We were aged 15, 16. Next door was another school and next-door but one was the grammar school. David Jones was going to the grammar school.

A few of us used to meet up and have a smoke in an old army pillbox at the crossroads that was put there to stop Hitler invading in the Forties. There was a shop just down the road where you could buy Weights or Woodbines cigarettes one at a time. The shopkeeper would split packets for needy schoolboys and we used to meet up and have a smoke. Some of the times I don't think there was a lot of tobacco in them. There might have been one or two other substances!

There were three schools literally next door to each other and there was a working man's cafe on the corner of Shortlands Road, the road that went down to Bickley, and we used to meet up in there. Although we went to different schools, there was no animosity because, sports wise or other wise, our paths didn't cross. Everybody used to get chatting and put a bit of music on the juke box, anybody who had some spare coins, and we'd sit there with a coffee or, if we'd managed to acquire some cigarettes, we'd end up in the old pillbox.

He was in bands and trying to get bands started even then. We all tried to peroxide our hair back then. I over peroxided mine and it went green, which caused a bit of merriment.

They pulled the other schools down but David's school is still there. It's called Ravens Wood School or something now.

I WAS THERE: DANA GILLESPIE

I met David in 1962 when I was 14 at the Marquee Club in London, and he asked to come home with me. He was probably my first boyfriend, and used to walk me home from school, and carry my ballet shoes. He was incredibly kind and supportive and would always encourage my songwriting.

I lived in a fantastic, wild basement flat underneath my parents house in Kensington, West London, and every musician in the world landed up on this place. There would be evenings of him and Marc Bolan just writing songs and hanging out. It was this whole music world.

David always had this determination and was always wonderfully dressed in these outfits – I never saw him in a pair of old jeans and a T-shirt.

When he was living at Haddon Hall he was always scribbling on scraps of paper and often he would play his new stuff on acoustic guitar. He once rang me up to say that he'd written a new song and that he

14 year-old singer songwriter Dana Gillespie and cuddly friend in London, England

would be round at my place in 30 minutes, and he arrived and sat down to play 'Space Oddity'. I often heard his new songs and he always encouraged me to play my new stuff to him and he often sang what could be a good bass line or a drum groove and also gave me his bass guitar.

I went with him to the first ever Glastonbury and then stayed with him and Angie in their hotel room in New York for months, which was a bit of a wild time. But they were fantastic times and I'm so pleased I lived through them.

Years later I saw the Diamond Dogs Tour many times in USA, which was fabulous and it was a shame it was never seen in UK. I did see quite a few shows but I was also working myself, doing gigs or musicals, so I can't recall where and when. Most of my time spent with him was on our free time, so gigs weren't top of our list of time spent together.

Once he was permanently in America our paths didn't really cross and also he was getting over the legal mess that we were both in regarding MainMan. This whole breakup of what had been a family for us was too painful so really from the late Seventies I didn't see him again except at the Freddie Mercury Tribute concert at Wembley Stadium in 1992.

THE KONRADS

JUNE 1963

I WAS THERE: ALAN DODDS

We were just 16 and 17-year-old school friends and we needed a lead singer so we advertised in the local paper. David, who was still David Jones then, was 16 and he came along. He was the obvious choice – although I'm not sure if he was the only choice!

David had a fantastic stage presence, which was the reason we took him on. He could command an audience instantly.

In those days he used to play the saxophone. I remember he picked up a plastic alto saxophone and could play it reasonably well within a couple of weeks. He was very talented in that way and was always popular with the girls.

We played at schools, dances and church halls, it was just before disco and we did a lot of Beatles, Dave Clark Five music. Our repertoire was basically standard rock 'n' roll tunes and rhythm and blues.

We played all over the South East. We recorded a single for Decca called 'I Never Dreamed' which I wrote. Decca declined to offer us a contract and all we were left with was an acetate recording. We disbanded after about a year.

I WAS THERE: ROGER FERRIS

The Konrads had a gig at the Green Man pub in Blackheath in 1963. I stepped on the bottom of a broken pint glass and it went right into my foot just as I was changing to go on stage. There

BIOGRAPHY
──────── DECCA GROUP RECORDS

| DAVID BOWIE | DERAM |

D for December, D for David, D for Deram — December 2nd is D-day all round, for that's when Deram launches its exciting new contract star DAVID BOWIE singing his own outstanding song "RUBBER BAND".

David not only wrote the song, he scored the arrangement and produced the master recording.

"RUBBER BAND" is probably as near as David will ever get to moon and June. A love story without a happy ending, it is pathos set to tubas. A happening song.

On the 'B' side is "THE LONDON BOYS", David Bowie's partly autobiographical cameo of the brave and defiant little mod racing up-hill along Wardour Street to an empty Paradise.

was blood everywhere. It was pretty nasty. A doctor drove me to hospital and they did the gig without me. David went on as the front man that night. I was a better singer, but I had nowhere near his personality or charisma on stage.

The Manish Boys formed, (without Bowie), in Maidstone, and moved to London in 1964, where Leslie Conn became their agent. Conn was also Bowie's first manager, and when Bowie left the King Bees in mid-1964, Conn introduced the singer to The Manish Boys. Like The King Bees, The Manish Boys played R&B and like the Rolling Stones, named themselves after a Muddy Waters song.
The Manish Boys recorded just one single, 'I Pity the Fool'/ 'Take My Tip', released in March 1965. It was produced by Shel Talmy, who was also handling The Kinks and The Who at that time.

THE MANISH BOYS

1964

I WAS THERE: BOB SOLLY

We formed The Manish Boys, without Bowie of course, Bowie was an afterthought. We had a contact with Dick James, which was Northern Songs, and we went to see Dick James who lined us up along a wall and said 'look lads, one thing, no booze and no girls, I won't tolerate it.' We were then told to go and see Leslie Conn who was a manager in another office, and he said, 'I've got a great thing lined up for you, I'm glad I've met you all, because I've got a singer who's ideal

Released in 1965 'I Pity The Fool' featured a guitar solo by Jimmy Page

for you, his name is Davy Jones' and we said 'No more singers!' We all sang ourselves. And he said, 'well, he's made a record and he's very, very good, plays the saxophone. I'll come down with him at the weekend and you can give him a trial'.

So we did. He came down, one summer weekend, he came in the back door with Leslie, and we all thought wow! He had long hair and buckskin and everything and we thought, 'He'll do,' we'll make a place for him in the band. But we really didn't want him at first, we didn't want anyone else.

I WAS THERE: MIKE WHITEHEAD

We knew when we saw him he had star quality. What impressed us is that he was never normal in terms of sound, and he was determined to make a go of it and he wanted to get on and make it big. He was a very friendly, normal, guy – much like anybody on the street, it's amazing really. I don't think he ever put on any airs and graces, put it that way.

We went everywhere. We played up north, in London, Folkestone, Deal and in Maidstone and even got on TV which was great.

The Manish Boys were battling to make it big and we were booked to appear on the BBC2 show *Gadzooks! It's All Happening Now*, when the producers said we could only appear if young Davy got a haircut. There was an outcry from the fans, so the producer relented and we appeared on the show, live, playing our record 'Take My Tip'.

STOCKTON ABC GLOBE CINEMA

4 DECEMBER 1964 STOCKTON

I WAS THERE: RAY MURPHY

I had gone with a friend to see Marianne Faithfull and we were hanging around the stage door waiting for her to come out and Davie Jones and some of the other band members came out. We hadn't heard of him before and he wasn't even on the programme. He'd played bluesy music, which me and my mate were into, and we thought they were better than Gerry and the Pacemakers.

Davie Jones stopped to chat and I got his autograph. I was 15 then, and I was impressed by his style – I was just starting to grow my hair but his hair was long and blond and soft. I remember thinking 'I want to look like you', but I got a job in a bank after that.

It was only a very brief chat and then Marianne Faithful came out, so I ditched him and went to talk to her. The Kinks closed the first half of the show and they were very good. They played 'Waterloo Sunset' but changed the lyrics to 'Thornaby sunset' (an area nearby), which I thought was quite cool.

BLUE MOON CLUB

4 SEPTEMBER 1965 CHELTENHAM

I WAS THERE: MICHAEL WILLIAMS

David Bowie appeared at the Cheltenham Blue Moon Club, first on 4 September 1965 under his real name Davy Jones and the Lower Third (he later changed his name to Bowie to avoid confusion with Davy Jones of The Monkees!) and he played at the Moon again on 9 July 1966 as David Bowie & The Buzz!

Myself and friends saw his first gig as Davy Jones when we had never heard of him and his strange quirky music style, plus outrageous clothes caused us to get bored as we were more used to Soul, Tamla Motown and Blues music.

There was only a small crowd there and as the club didn't have an alcoholic drinks licence, we decided to leave the club and go out to the pub a couple of doors down. They put a luminous stamp on your hands so that you could go back in without paying twice.

We were a bit unkind to Bowie and his band and started to boo and jeer, calling him rubbish! Anyway, after about 20 minutes we returned to the club having consumed a few drinks and some strange tablets (which we later found out were 'purple hearts – amphetamines – blues pills', designed to boost your energy and senses levels), and it wasn't long before we were at the front of the stage cheering and raving about Bowie (Jones) and his

David checks the morning paper for any reviews whilst hanging out in Manchester Square, London

group and saying how brilliant they were. A complete contrast to around half an hour earlier! Of course, had we known then what we know now, we would have been worshippers and, 'over the *moon*' so to speak.

THE MARQUEE CLUB

1966 SOHO

I WAS THERE: MORGAN FISHER

In 1966, when I was 16, I first saw David Bowie play in the tatty old Marquee Club in London's Soho. He played there 15 times that year,

Future Mott The Hoople member Morgan Fisher

billed as David Bowie & The Buzz. I saw him at least three of those times, and after the initial impact, I made sure I'd get there earlier next time so as to be nearer the front and get a closer look at this charismatic being with piled-up blond hair and impossibly wide belts. I'd rush straight from school, still in uniform, this timid little lad who hadn't even become a mod yet (that happened a year later). The Marquee didn't have a drink license yet (only Coca-Cola was served), so I didn't need to lie about my age to get in.

Fifty years on, it is the sound of his voice that stays with me even now, echoing through a cheap PA system, and yet it thrilled me. The song from that era that lingers the most is 'The London Boys' – a surprisingly mature, compassionate ode written by 19-year-old Bowie, about young lads who moved up to London and got into the pill-taking scene, bought flash clothes and realized how hollow it all was. I didn't understand the lyrics much then, but the repeating refrain – 'The London boys, the London boys' – gave me goose pimples and echoed in my mind on the Tube ride back home.

Melodrama or magic? It felt like the latter to me.

Three years on, in 1969, by now a fairly successful musician, I was drinking one night in The Speakeasy – a secluded London hideaway for rockers where, over the years, I bumped into icons from Hendrix to Tiny Tim to Sid Vicious. On my way out in the small hours, having imbibed, as usual, several Scotch-and-Cokes, a record company exec I knew thrust a 7-inch promo record into my hand, saying, 'Here – you might like this. It's a new single by an interesting singer-songwriter.'

'Ah, OK, whatever,' I replied.

The next day, after a bleary breakfast, I played the single, not expecting much, and was immediately transported into a shimmering other world. I hadn't even looked at the label, but there was That Voice again. It was Bowie.

The song was 'Space Oddity,' released just a year after Kubrick's epic *2001: A Space Odyssey*. The opening words 'Ground control to Major Tom' in that edgy baritone voice gave me the familiar shivers, and I tried not to spill my tea on the sofa. Then the arrangement – still one of his best – held me open-mouthed for the entire five minutes of the song (very long for a single). I played it again and again, awed by the evolving blend of guitars, vibes, Stylophone and Mellotron. There was no *YouTube* in those days, and precious little exposure on TV. It was the *sound* of an artist that grabbed us music lovers 99 percent of the time. And grab me this did.

Jump forward four years and I am out of work and about to experience a major change in my life, directly due to Mr Bowie. Famously, he rescued a band called Mott The Hoople from splitting up, by giving them one of the best songs he ever wrote – 'All The Young Dudes.' It gave them their first hit (No. 3 in the U.K.) and steered them in a new direction, away from the Dylan/Stones blend of rock they had been wowing audiences nationwide with (but without the accompanying boom in record sales – hence their decision to split). Bowie then produced their album of the same name. Their keyboard player didn't much like the new direction they were going in and left the band.

Through an audition, I got the job (with Mott The Hoople), in the summer of 1973. A whirlwind of US/Europe tours and recordings followed, culminating on December 14 in a sold-out show at what was then Hammersmith Odeon, with a new young band called Queen as opening act. Throughout the afternoon rehearsals, the gossip was going around backstage that not only Bowie but Mick Jagger (with whom it was rumoured he had been having an affair) would attend. It was on, it was off, they would be coming, they won't make it – all through the afternoon conflicting calls were received, doubtless from some hapless secretary egged on by the giggling duo. Finally, just before showtime, they strode smiling into our seedy old dressing room. I handed them paper cups of cheapo wine – this is what gigging musicians are used to anywhere. They went into a huddle with our singer Ian Hunter, teasing him as he got dressed, saying, 'Ooh, getting ready for our audience, are we...?'

Once we started the show I, seated stage right behind my grand piano, sensed some movement behind me. It was the dynamic duo, arm-in-arm in the wings, dancing to our music with daft grins on their faces. They kept it up for the whole show, keeping me on my toes, playing the best I could for these two leaping legends just a couple of yards behind me. Then they slipped away sneakily before the encore, and that was the last time I saw David Bowie.

I kept in close touch with his music throughout the Seventies, buying every album, always moved and impressed by the multifarious ways he could sing. *Station to Station* was an LP I played constantly during one US tour, on my portable record player. The long opening sound of a steam train leading a full three minutes later into the shiveringly haunting words, 'The Ret-u-u-u-rn of the Thin White Duke, throwing darts in lovers' eyes' had me enthralled every time. There is no question in my mind that without *That Voice*, Bowie's career would have come to naught. It is the essence and soul of a deeply passionate, deeply creative artist.

That Voice still emotes and exhilarates as richly in his swansong (the *Blackstar* album) as it did that evening when a shy young schoolboy, on his own, watched an almost equally young singer in a tatty rock club all those years ago.

Steve Dunn and his band The Mi££ionaires who supported The Buzz

BRITANNIA PIER

27 JUNE 1966 GREAT YARMOUTH

I WAS THERE: STEVE DUNN

Unlike other artists, The Mi££ionaires appeared with on the Britannia Pier Sunday Shows (Tom Jones, Donovan, Dana, The Who etc), David Bowie was a relatively unknown quantity at the time, other than the huge following he had in Bromley and Greater London.

Compared to the other stars, and budding stars like us, I remember in particular that David didn't mix with the rest of us, preferring his own company instead. In this respect he presented quite a bizarre kind of guy bordering on mysterious, special, and willingly aloof. This gave the impression he was in some way out of place in the pop/rock type of environment we were all in, but of course even at this very early age he was manifesting a rather avant-garde way of expressing himself, which was to become his special trade mark as he evolved throughout his career.

Although there were enormous differences between him and Donovan for example, Bowie, like Donovan Leitch was in a category all on his own. Both would probably have been more comfortable at a poetry/drama convention or at a more intellectual University gig.

Watching him from the wings backstage at the 'Brit', it was clear that although he was appearing with his group, The Buzz, Bowie was very much a solo artist, in the catalyst stage of eventually branching out on his own. In watching him I remember thinking how much his style and voice resembled that of Anthony Newley, a mega star of the Fifties and early Sixties, who later it was revealed he idolised in his early years.

Later on of course he developed his own musical genre, to the extent that we all have a bit of Ziggy Stardust in us thanks to the wonderful music and self-created stage, and off-stage characters he created for us all.

In hindsight, in the Sixties, I wasn't ready for Bowie. Today like the rest of us, he has left his indelible mark, not only on me, but on the extensive musical and cultural world he has so expertly created.

CLAREVILLE GROVE

SOUTH KENSINGTON, WEST LONDON

I WAS THERE: VERNON DEWHURST

I met David Bowie late 1967 or early 68 when I lived in a shared house in Clareville Grove, South Kensington, West London, where there were about four or 5 of us sharing. David had the room on the top floor with Hermione, his girlfriend. I would often pop up for a smoke and glass of wine and to hear his latest songs and it was there I first heard 'Space Oddity'.

He was the guy into music and mime at the time, very creative and full of ideas. I remember him as a very friendly guy with a great sense of humour, able to laugh at himself too! I brought him an LP back from the States of a yodeling cowboy for a joke and I can remember his hilarious impression of the guy... he was an excellent mimic.

Photographer Vernon Dewhurst took the earliest known colour photos of Bowie when he was performing live at the Arts Lab and created this montage (also featured in colour in this book)

David invited me to his Arts Lab in Beckenham, and I photographed him playing there. They are, I believe, the earliest colour pictures of him performing live. When he saw the photographs, he asked me to meet with Calvin Mark Lee at Mercury Records to talk about the cover to his second LP. They both had this idea of David's head appearing out of a Vasarely-inspired op art background, but weren't sure if it could be done. I told them it could. David came to my studio in St. Michael Street, Paddington, and there we photographed the head shot – about three rolls of Ektachrome on a Hasselblad did it. David was a natural model, confident, relaxed, and fun to work with. I finally managed to create the finished montage after a few abortive attempts. It would have been so much easier now with Photoshop!

THE NEW MUSICAL EXPRESS TALENT CONTEST

HAMMERSMITH PALAIS, LONDON

I WAS THERE: GISELA OAKES NEE STRACH

My friend Betty Moloney and I met when we both began our teacher training, in 1967, at Newbold Revel, which was midway between Rugby and Coventry. After our first year we were asked to become Social Secretaries and organise dances, etc. at our college, which were usually held every Sunday night.

In the early part of 1968, *The New Musical Express* organised a talent contest at The Hammersmith Palais to which Social Secretaries from colleges and universities all over the country were invited.

Gisela Oakes saw Bowie in 1968

It was an all night affair and David Bowie sang right at the end of the proceedings, at 6.00am. At that time he was not at all famous and was introduced as plain Davie Jones. I remember he sat on a chair to the left of the stage, playing his guitar and singing, 'Space Oddity' being one of the songs he sang. I believe that became a hit in July of 1968, so his career obviously took off after we'd seen him.

SPACE ODDITY

2 FEBRUARY 1969 LONDON

I WAS THERE: JOHN HUTCHINSON, GUITARIST

It was a song always intended to be sung by a duo – by 'Ground Control' and 'Major Tom'. That was always clear enough, it was two people

communicating by radio across open space and in this case it was me playing 'Ground Control' and David playing 'Major Tom'.

We had recorded our first demo of 'Space Oddity' as well as some other originals of David's on his reel-to-reel 'Revox' tape recorder at the Clareville Grove flat.

For 'Space Oddity' I had borrowed David's battered Gibson 11 string guitar and David had played his Stylophone. This was a joke instrument, a battery-powered toy which had been advertised extensively by the (at the time family favourite) Rolf Harris, and it made a horrible buzzing noise, the pitch of the buzz being selected by an attached 'stylus'. David, a child at heart, liked stuff like that.

Some of the other songs on the Revox demo had also been the result of our collaboration, and though the song idea, melody, basic chords and the lyrics were always David's, we would work together so that the final shape of the song, and some of its chord inversions and licks, were mutually developed. I was the better guitarist, and I knew more chords than David, but the songs were his alone.

David was however still dependant to an extent on my skills

as guitarist and collaborator and now he seemed to see us as England's answer to Simon and Garfunkel.

For my part I was happy with this but I also can see the same imbalance of talent in the duo that possibly Art Garfunkel might have seen in his situation working with Paul Simon.

The title of the new song was a joke of course, a piss-take of Stanley Kubrick's *2001 – A Space Odyssey*, but David was I believe saying something valid about the emptiness of infinite space, the loneliness of the long distance spaceman, etc., and I liked the idea. The style of the song was pure Bee Gees and we had certainly both been impressed with the Aussies' bleatingly folky harmonies on their early records. The theory that I have read about more than once, the idea that the lyrics were about drugs, or specifically about a heroin trip, is nonsense.

THE THREE TUNS

BECKENHAM

I WAS THERE: JAN WILLIAMS

I used to go to the Three Tuns in the back room when I was about 16 to see David Bowie. I lived down the road in Penge. We thought he was amazing then. I remember the day he got married (to Angie in March 1970), and my friends and I were so upset because of course we all thought we'd have a chance of marrying him ourselves!

We also went to the Free Festival in Beckenham Rec in August 1969 – we thought we

Jan Williams was a regular at the Three Tuns and hoped to one day marry David Bowie

were at Woodstock! It was such a lovely day – the sun was shining and as we lived near and we were teenagers we knew lots of people in the park. We dressed in our best flower power gear and thought we were the bee's knees, with the icing on the cake being David Bowie performing on the bandstand. We always knew he was a star!

Three of my friends went to primary school with him and they used to have birthday parties with him.

THE MAGIC VILLAGE

21 FEBRUARY 1969 MANCHESTER

I WAS THERE: JOHN CONSTANTINE

David Bowie made a visit to the Magic Village (as he was playing in Manchester the following evening) I was on the cloakroom and charged him sixpence to hang his coat up.

I knocked on the office door to inform the manager Roger Eagle that Mr Bowie was in the club and he rushed out to greet him. I recall Bowie playing a great acoustic set to about 30 people in the bar, just for the fun of it, and as a warm-up for his concert at the Free Trade Hall the following night opening for Tyrannosaurus Rex. It was fantastic!

FREE TRADE HALL

22 FEBRUARY 1969 MANCHESTER

I WAS THERE: CHRIS PHILLIPS

I saw Bowie a few times. The first was at the Free Trade Hall supporting Tyrannosaurus Rex (as part of a 6-date tour). Tyrannosaurus Rex at this time were the duo of Marc Bolan and Steve Peregrin Took and had released two albums *My People Were Fair and Had Sky in Their Hair... But Now They're Content to Wear Stars on Their Brows* and *Prophets, Seers & Sages: The Angels of the Ages*.

Bowie was bottom of the bill as a mime artist, BBC DJ John

Peel was the compere and also appearing was sitar player Vytas Serelis. I had the programme and Bowie was mentioned on the front as 'Mime Artist'. I remember him sitting on this little stool on the stage performing a mime based on China's invasion of Tibet and moving his arms about.

THE MAGIC VILLAGE

22 FEBRUARY 1969 MANCHESTER

I WAS THERE: NIGEL HAND

I was outside the Magic Village talking to my very good friend, the late lamented Steve Gee (RIP), who was on the cash desk, when this guy comes walking up to me and says 'Hi, I'm David Bowie and I've just played a show here in town for the teenyboppers (he'd played the Free Trade Hall) and I'd like to play some music for the real people.' All this was directed at me. Steve Gee said 'What, THE David Bowie? Wait there.' He ran inside to tell Roger Eagle (the manager), and they both came running out of the club, grabbed Bowie and dragged him inside.

When Steve reappeared, I stayed outside chatting (he still had to attend to the cash desk). Some minutes later there was an almighty row between Roger and the artist who was supposed to play that night, someone from Bolton, I seem to remember. In those days they'd have a local act on a Friday and a big name on a Saturday and it was obviously this guy's big chance and he wasn't going to give it up without a fuss. Roger paid the guy off and Bowie did a show, which I missed because I stayed outside talking to Steve Gee.

PHILHARMONIC HALL

1 MARCH 1969 LIVERPOOL

I WAS THERE: TREFOR JONES

I only ever saw David Bowie once and that was March 1st 1969 at the Liverpool Philharmonic Hall. My mate Alan Wall and I were into Tyrannosaurus Rex.

We travelled from Ellesmere Port but nearly missed the show, because on arriving at Liverpool, we tried to get a taxi from Lime Street Railway station to the gig, but the drivers refused due to them waiting for passengers from a London train.

Tyrannosaurus Rex fan Trefor Jones

Next thing a ticket collector asked for our train tickets saying we had got off the Euston train, and called a transport cop. He didn't believe our story either, stating it was only a 5 minute walk to the Philharmonic. He accused us of fare dodging. Eventually we got to the show on time.

I was aware of David Bowie's mime act because it had been written about in the music press. I also remembered him from 1964 with the single 'Liza Jane', which I loved back then when I was 16. My first thought as he appeared on the stage was he had some guts doing this gig. He was impressive though and got some laughs with his actions involving rolling and smoking a joint. I don't really remember if any of the audience displayed a negative response. Obviously everyone was there for Marc Bolan and Steve Peregrin Took. However 'Space Oddity' was only a few months away in 1969. Bowie's music has stayed with me from the Sixties into my Sixties.

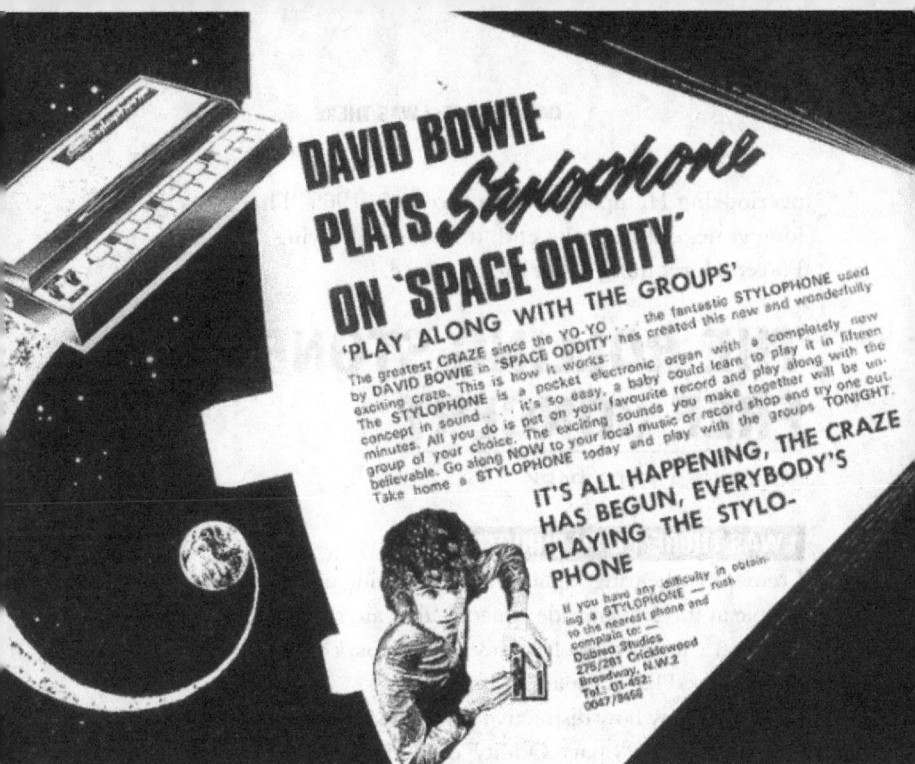

THREE HORSESHOES

MAY 1969 HAMPSTEAD, LONDON

I WAS THERE: JEZ LOWE

There used to be a folk club at the Three Horseshoes in Hampstead, where the organiser booked an unknown singer called David Bowie back in the late 1960s. A few weeks before the gig, the organiser suddenly saw that young David was riding high in the pop-charts with a song called 'Space Oddity', and so naturally assumed that he'd be too busy and famous to turn up to play at a little folk club on a chilly wednesday night in North London.

In fact, despite his new-found fame and fortune, David showed up, chatted to the regulars, listened to the resident singers, and then performed – on his blue acoustic guitar – in what was possibly his last ever solo gig, there in that dusty upstairs room overlooking Hampstead High Street, in 1969. That folk club is long gone, but until the end, it had a sign saying 'David Bowie Played Here' hung up at the entrance.

THE ROLLING STONES FREE CONCERT

5 JULY 1969 HYDE PARK

I WAS THERE: KEITH CHRISTMAS

I remember hearing 'Space Oddity' playing on the PA (to 250,000 people at this free outside concert), that afternoon before anybody came on – it was a lovely sunny day, the park was absolutely packed and it played like a dream.

People know how distinctive his sound and voice were but the moment I heard 'Space Oddity' on that day it struck me how clear the lyrics and production sound were.

It also sounded like a massive hit – at that point I'm not even sure it had got any radio play, so getting it on the playlist that day was a real coup for somebody or just jolly good luck.

Later in the year, because of the gigs I played as the main act at the Beckenham Arts Lab, then run by a rising star called David Bowie, I was asked to play the acoustic guitar on David's first album *Space Oddity*.

I played a Fender Palomino acoustic guitar while David played his

Some cat hanging out with singer songwriter Keith Christmas who played guitar on Bowie's Space Oddity album

12-string on 'Letter to Hermione', 'God Knows I'm Good' and 'An Occasional Dream'.

Tony Visconti reckons I played on four tracks and he should know, but I can only remember three of them. David was very nervous and the budget for that album was pretty tight, hence the fact that some of them were just me, and him playing.

We sat down on two chairs opposite each other in this cavernous studio that had all the atmosphere of an aircraft hanger and he played the songs to me for the first time and I had to think up what to play on the fly.

Today there would have been endless pre-session run-throughs but then it was much more undisciplined – typical 1969, really...

So I just made it up as we went along, the tapes rolled and that was that.

THE LONDON HOSPITAL MEDICAL COLLEGE

SEPTEMBER 1969 WHITECHAPEL

I WAS THERE: BOB HARRIS

I first saw David in a folky act called Feathers. He was very polite and surprisingly 'English'.

It was a fantastic, creative time. I lived with a mobile DJ and he'd double-booked himself, so I took David with me to a gig (The London Hospital Medical College) and introduced him on stage. He played 'Space Oddity' and they started slow handclapping. I was so angry I took the microphone and said, 'Remember this name: David Bowie. He's going to be a star and you'll remember the day you booed him off stage.'

Even then it struck me that, while on the surface David was very warm and exciting, he was closed off. He went behind some kind of mask: the make-up, the Lindsay Kemp mime thing. I counted him as one of the closest people in my life, but once he became successful,

Bowie was featured in the UK music weekly Disc & Music Echo *in October 1969*

he was unreachable. I think to get to that level of stardom, you've got to have a very high degree of self-absorption.

A few years back when I was involved with the Sound & Vision charity for cancer research, David immediately donated something. He can be very distant, but on this occasion he really wasn't.

THE ODEON

25 OCTOBER 1969 MANCHESTER

I WAS THERE: STEVE BERNING

I saw David Bowie three times between 1969 and 1973. With the benefit of hindsight they were all very different and historically significant.

The first time was as part of the Humble Pie package tour, on 25 October 1969, at the Odeon, Manchester. He did a short acoustic solo set, which featured 'Space Oddity'. This had been a minor hit a few months earlier and I think I considered him a 'one hit wonder'. Got that one wrong. The second time was 2 September 1972 at the Hardrock, Manchester. The Ziggy Stardust album had been released six weeks earlier, but my recollection is that the crowd was anything but 'glam rock' – in fact they were very hippyish and began the concert sitting cross-legged on the floor. I remember being most impressed by the Spiders, who were unbelievably tight.

The final concert was 7 June 1973 at the Free Trade Hall, Manchester. This was, I think, one of the last gigs before the 'final' Ziggy gigs at the Hammersmith Odeon, London. By this time the audience were possessed by full glam hysteria, which took some of the enjoyment off the gig. The addition of Mike Garson's jazz tinged keyboards made me yearn for the much rockier sound at the Hardrock, less than a year earlier.

I WAS THERE: JOHN HALL

I was 12 years old. I first heard the Small Faces 'Itchycoo Park ' in late 1967 on a big teak radiogram in the ballroom of the country house – Mottram Hall – we used to go to every season, I was hooked.

My sisters had The Beatles, Stones, Donovan and Brass Bands.

The Small Faces were mine. Then my much older (14 years old) cousin Linda's *FAB 208* announced the Small Faces had split up – I was devastated, but I got into *Are You Experienced*, Soul and Tamla Motown and 1968 and the Sixties slum clearances continued in Oldham, Lancashire.

Then the *NME* plastered on the front page – 'Supergroup Humble Pie have formed' with my hero Steve Marriott and 'The Face of 68' Peter Frampton ...I was intrigued. Rod Stewart walked off with Steve's band – but Steve walked off with the lovely Jenny – Rod's 'love of his life' apparently. 'Natural Born Bugie' blasted onto *Top of the Pops* and I fell for Humble Pie, hook, line and sinker.

Steve had turned down Led Zeppelin and went on to turn down the Stones for his 'own' bag, with his mate Peter – whose dad had taught a young David Bowie.

He desperately wanted to get away from the screams, mod hysteria, novelty songs, concept albums, hype and downright criminality of how he had been treated in the Small Faces.

I grabbed the first Pie album *As Safe as Yesterday Is* as soon as it came out and I loved the wacky box in a brown wrapper cover devoured every word on the inside sheet and wore the needle down with constant plays.

I started a (eventually massive three volume) Humble Pie scrapbook from pictures from Linda's 'girl magazines'.

'Humble Pie to do a 10 date tour' proclaimed the *NME* – I HAD to go – so I, presumably, nagged and cried to my parents until they eventually agreed to let Linda (the much older, at 14, responsible one) and I to go to the Manchester Odeon.

I couldn't sleep properly until the gig. My dad took us down early and I bought my 'Changes 69' programme and a lolly and settled into my seat. The lights went down and a handsome, curly haired guy with a crooked, quirky smile and bare chest (I think) came on with a battered acoustic guitar and did six songs under one spotlight.

'Wild Eyed Boy from Freecloud' and, especially, 'Space Oddity' shattered me (I rushed to buy the single the next day). Vulnerable yet strong, quiet yet powerful, unsure yet determined, ...revolutionary – how I dream of hearing that night's sweet music again.

'Thank – you, I'm David Bowie, goodnight.' I was mesmerised and whispered to Linda 'I'm going to meet him.' Unaware of backstage security protocols, I sailed past the ice cream lady. David was leaning against a door, alone and looking pensive.

'I really liked you...er, would you please sign my programme' I stuttered. 'What's your name?' said David. 'John' I replied. 'To John, love David Bowie' he wrote over his programme picture.

Now I'd like to think I suggested he form a pretend band called The Snakes from Uranus but I probably nodded nervous, almost

> Vulnerable yet strong, quiet yet powerful, unsure yet determined, ...revolutionary – how I dream of hearing that night's sweet music again

catatonic, as he chatted.

Then Humble Pie strolled past – I couldn't miss the chance of meeting my gods. So I turned and said 'Er, thanks' and left David leaning alone and downcast as I rushed to get my programme signed by The Pie.

I subsequently read Bowie was heckled with coins and cigs thrown at him at other Pie gigs, so I hope my fawning cheered him up a bit. Of course running off to 'someone more important' maybe didn't help.

Again I can't remember what I said to my heroes either but it wasn't much, so I ran back to my seat, waving cheerfully to Bowie... still leaning... alone.

I now ponder on how many records Bowie, Frampton and Marriott subsequently sold, obviously many millions around the world. Two years later Frampton went solo on *Comes Alive* to make the biggest selling live album of all time. Humble Pie cleaned up in the USA until Marriott's evil 'twin' 'Stan' took him over and made him incredibly hard to deal with.

I flopped down in my seat with Linda glaring and worried (she thought I'd been abducted by an alien race – which of course I had), then 'BANG' Dave Edmunds struck up the guitar wail of 'Sabre Dance' and Love Sculpture blasted my head with brain grinding, ear shattering, guitar riffarama.

I turned to Linda and smiled. I didn't realise then that I had changed my life forever and nothing would ever be the same again.

Humble Pie were amazing – I remember a short acoustic set mid way through – however it was strong, hard driving guitar boogie that impressed me... and strong melodic harmonies that got my head and heart racing. Of course I couldn't stop jabbering when my Dad picked us up. I was bitten by the music bug and was determined to see more live energy driven music.

Since seeing Bowie in 1969, I've been to over 6,000 gigs and still go to about three gigs a week (sometimes three gigs a night), and have a YouTube channel (mancmusic) which now has thousands of live videos and 1.5 million viewers.

Sadly I didn't see the Ziggy tour as it was a choice between that and saving for my new heroes Genesis, because being cool I said 'Oh I've seen Bowie, I wanna see somebody new.'

I saw him again at *Live Aid* when he was already a global superstar. I loved it.

Steve Marriott was a broken man by then, playing in the Packet of Three in pubs. Thankfully I met and saw Steve again a few months before he died at the Band on the Wall in Manchester in 1991. He smiled as he signed my scrapbook and my *Ogdens' Nut Gone Flake* CD.

The last time I saw Bowie was, ironically with Peter Frampton on my 30th birthday, at Maine Road, Manchester City's ex ground on a hot sunny happy day. The Glass Spider Tour was a wild theatrical showpiece with huge spiders, a world away from just him, a spotlight and a guitar. But I will never forget my first gig and meeting with probably the most influential star of the Seventies, Eighties and beyond.

BONNYRIGG REGAL

9 NOVEMBER 1969 EDINBURGH

I WAS THERE: SARA SANDERSON

My mum, Valerie Jubb, and her flatmates went to Bonnyrigg Regal, just outside Edinburgh, on a Friday night to see him play. The band didn't show up as they got lost en route from Perth. My mum and her friends waited in the bar to hitch a ride back to Edinburgh. The band showed up late and they got talking.

Mum and her flatmates thought 'what the hell' and invited them to let off fireworks and for dinner. The band was staying in nearby Broughton and they accepted (her flat was on nearby Northumberland St). Mum pulled out all the stops with a Fray Bentos pie. She says David ate very little and none of the pie – it may have been her cooking apparently! Then they let off fireworks in the garden.

'Space Oddity' had just been a hit single that summer I believe. She always said he was incredibly polite but also distant. Got the impression he was coming to terms with impending stardom.

ELECTRIC GARDEN

10 NOVEMBER 1969 GLASGOW

I WAS THERE: LINDA COLLINS

I remember in 1969 seeing David Bowie at the Electric Garden in Sauchiehall Street, Glasgow. There were only about 50 people there, we sat on the floor to listen to him. He was dressed in a silver suit with silver boots and he sat on a stool and played the

Linda Collins was just one of around 50 people who saw Bowie at The Electric Garden

guitar. The only song we remember was 'Space Oddity'. It was all very laid back with people sitting on the floor and clapping at the end. Later in the cafe/bar he came in and sat down with his friends for coffee.

ALBERT HALL

11 NOVEMBER 1969 STIRLING

I WAS THERE: KATRINA MACLEAN

In 1969 when I was in my second year at the High School of Stirling, there was news that David Bowie was doing a gig at the Albert Hall in Stirling following his success with 'Space Oddity'.

I had a lovely friend called Suzanne Shorthouse, who was eager to book us tickets for Bowie's concert. She went to Hay's music shop (the booking place in those days) and was actually the first person to pay and book tickets. Moreover, she was shown the map of the Albert Hall and picked the middle two seats in the front row which I commended her for. We were so excited about seeing David Bowie and were the envy of our peers who did not grasp the moment in getting a front row seat or a ticket.

Can you imagine our disappointment when the whole concert was withdrawn? When we approached the owner of Hay's music shop, who returned our money (think it was 50p each), we asked why the concert was not going ahead – his reply was that there was 'a lack of numbers'. Unbelievable, particularly as Bowie became such a universal icon. I remember my wee ticket was monochrome and his image showed his curly permed hair – the style he had in the late Sixties. I so wish I still had the ticket as it would be collectable and indeed very valuable in today's market.

MUSIC HALL

12 NOVEMBER 1969 ABERDEEN

I WAS THERE: BILL COWIE

In 1969, a little record shop just off the main street in Aberdeen was the main ticket agent for the Music Hall in Aberdeen. I knew the people who owned the store and

I was in the shop one day. David Bowie was booked to appear at the Music Hall the following night. It was very quiet in the shop at the time and I was standing near the counter when a guy came walking in and walked just past me and up to the counter to talk to the manager.

He had an Afro haircut and an Afghan coat. It was David Bowie. The shop manager was talking to him and they had quite a lengthy conversation. Then David left and the manager said to me 'it's disappointing because we were the agents for selling the tickets for his concert tomorrow night but we've had to cancel the concert.' David had had only one record out – 'Space Oddity' – and it had only just come out the week before.

The shop manager said 'we've sold hardly any tickets and not enough to justify going ahead.'

Nobody in Scotland had heard of this David Bowie.

FILLMORE NORTH, LOCARNO BALLROOM

13 MARCH 1970 SUNDERLAND

I WAS THERE: CHARLIE REAVLEY

I saw Bowie twice, once in early 1970 at the Mecca, Sunderland (aka Fillmore North) – post 'Space Oddity', tickets were ten shillings. I believe he may have been a support artist that night, (also on the bill was Principal Edwards), but the gig was pretty sparsely attended and not exactly memorable. I also saw him at Roker Park, where he did the unimaginable (if you happened to be a resident of Sunderland) by greeting the crowd with 'Good Evening Newcastle'. A supremely professional show though.

I WAS THERE: PHILLIP HALL

I was 16 and lived in Sunderland at the time, so didn't have to travel far for gigs. The Mecca on a Friday night was a regular place to go. We just turned up and watched whoever was on. As well as seeing Bowie we saw Pink Floyd, Free, Wishbone Ash, Tyrannosaurus Rex as they were in them days, Jethro Tull, Edgar Broughton, Nice, Pentangle, and many more. But of all of them, Bowie who we hadn't heard of before then was by far the most outrageous. He came on stage with a very tight superman style outfit on, with a huge outrageous collar and we just stood there and stared open-mouthed, an absolute fantastic performer.

1970 Having established himself as a solo artist with his UK top five hit 'Space Oddity', Bowie, underlined by his artistic rivalry with Marc Bolan, formed a band. John Cambridge, a drummer Bowie met at the Arts Lab, was joined by Tony Visconti on bass and Mick Ronson on electric guitar. Known as the Hype, the band mates created characters for themselves and wore elaborate costumes that prefigured the glam style of the Spiders from Mars.

David Bowie, alias 'Rainbowman' dressed in lurex tights, cape and pirate boots, Mick Ronson wore David Bowie's old 'Space Oddity' suit and became 'Gangsterman' Tony Visconti was Hypeman in a Superman suite but with an 'H' on it and John Cambridge wore a ten-gallon hat and became 'Cowboyman'.

After a disastrous opening gig at the London Roundhouse, they reverted to a configuration presenting Bowie as a solo artist. A heated disagreement between Bowie and Cambridge over the latter's drumming style saw Cambridge quit and was replaced by Mick Woodmansey. Not long after, Bowie fired his manager Ken Pitt and replaced him with Tony Defries

The studio sessions continued and resulted in Bowie's third album,

The Man Who Sold the World (1970), characterised by the heavy rock sound of his new backing band. It was a marked departure from the acoustic guitar and folk rock style established by 'Space Oddity'.

To promote Bowie in the US, Mercury Records financed a coast-to-coast publicity tour across America in which Bowie, between January and February 1971, was interviewed by radio stations and the media. Exploiting his androgynous appearance, the original cover of the UK version of the album depicted the singer wearing a dress: taking the garment with him, he wore it during interviews, to the approval of critics.

During the tour, Bowie's observation of two seminal American proto-punk artists led him to develop a concept that eventually found form in the Ziggy Stardust character: a melding of the persona of Iggy Pop with the music of Lou Reed. A girlfriend recalled his 'scrawling notes on a cocktail napkin about a crazy rock star named Iggy or Ziggy', and on his return to England he declared his intention to create a character 'who looks like he's landed from Mars'. The 'Stardust' surname was a tribute to the 'Legendary Stardust Cowboy', whose record he was given during the tour.

I WAS THERE: KEN SCOTT, STUDIO ENGINEER

I left Abbey Road and started working at a studio called Trident. I engineered a lot of David's first album there, which went under three titles - *David Bowie*, *Man of Words/Man of Music* and *Space Oddity*. I did a lot on that. I then did overdubs and mixed *The Man Who Sold the World*. These were both just as engineer; I worked with Tony Visconti on those.

Then one day I was working with David on something he was producing, and during one of the breaks I happened to say I wanted to move into production. He said he'd just signed a new management deal. He said he was going into the studio and was going to produce the album himself, but he didn't think he could do it. So I co-produced it with him, and that led to *Hunky Dory*.

I think there was a certain amount of fear when we started *Hunky Dory*, but as things started to come together, and it was obvious it was working, that fear started to disappear. From then on, he felt more and more sure and less and less fearful. That's why he could go from one genre to another. Most artists, if they're successful, they stick to that plan, because they're worried that they'll suddenly lose their fans. But David's attitude was always, 'I'm going to do what I want to do and hope they come along with me, but if they don't, they don't.' That's truly unique and totally courageous, especially in music. The whole thing with David was that, he was never in today, he was always in tomorrow.

David was the most amazing singer I've worked with; 95 percent of the vocals on the four albums I did with him as producer, they were first takes. I'd get a level at the beginning and we'd just go from beginning to end and that was it. No Auto-Tune, no punching in, nothing. Just complete takes.

POCO-A-POCO

27 APRIL 1970 STOCKPORT, MANCHESTER
I WAS THERE: DAVID MAYNARD

Everyone was very trusting in those days. I thought that I should be involved in promoting some gigs, how hard could that be? So I did in Stockport. The biggest of which was the multi-band gig at the Poco-a-Poco. David Bowie, High Tide, Barclay James Harvest, and the Purple Gang. Most were booked through Blackhill Enterprises (it would have been The Who as well, but they were just too expensive at £1,000 as I recall). I was 16 or 17 at the time so all the contracts that I signed were probably unenforceable. Happy days!

David was a really nice guy, I met him hours before the gig when he came to Stockport train station. I walked him up Manchester Road to the Fiveways Fish and Chip Shop where he bought and later consumed two meat pies. We then walked back to the Poco-a-Poco where he entertained me and a couple of mates by playing on some of Barclay James Harvest's equipment, singing some of his future hits. It has also been reported that David slept at Stockport Railway Station as he missed the train on the way back home after the gig.

> **Bowie**
>
> DAVID BOWIE: * The Prettiest Star (Mercury).
>
> A RATHER unexpected follow-up in that this is a complete contrast from "Space Oddity". There's none of the awe-inspiring grandeur or topicality of David's recent hit.
>
> This is, in fact, a thoroughly charming and wholly fascinating little song. Set to a relaxed jog-along rhythm, with a wowing guitar picking out the melody line behind David's subdued and sensitive vocal. The self-penned lyric is enchanting, if somewhat enigmatic — and the melody is haunting and hummable.
>
> It's a quiet, inoffensive disc, with a touch of mysticism that holds the listener in its spell. I like it immensely, and I reckon it could do very well indeed.
>
> *TIPPED FOR CHARTS
> †CHART POSSIBLE

DAVID BOWIE: The Prettiest Star

I WAS THERE: RICK WAKEMAN, MUSICIAN

I lived in a tiny little house in West Harrow and David called me up and said, 'Will you come and see me, I want to play you some songs.' So I went up and he opened his guitar case and took out this incredibly battered 12-string guitar and started playing these songs, one after the other, sensational songs, 'Changes', Life on Mars?' and other songs that eventually became *Hunky Dory*. He said, 'What do you think?' and I said 'These are sensational!'

Normally on an album you'd have one cracking song, maybe a couple of other good ones and a little bit of padding here and there, but it was just cracking song after cracking song. David asked me to make notes on each song for the piano, almost treat them as piano pieces; he said he wanted to come to this album from the piano point of view. So he said, 'What I want you to do, is to do what you really want to do and I'll get the rest of the guys to work around you'. Which has always been a bit embarrassing as people have said, 'You must have worked so hard to do those arrangements for 'Life on Mars?', but actually the truth is everyone had to work around me.

He was incredibly generous to musicians, he was playing and I was following along and you sort of settle into what you're doing and then suddenly he would play something and you would say, 'where did that come from? What are you doing?' He would suddenly do what I would call 'lead you up the garden path', when everything was nice and smooth and doing very logical chord changes and patterns and then he would do something completely off the wall. He did that in all of his pieces and that's what made him such a great writer.

People often ask me if I knew 'Life on Mars?' was going to be as huge as it was, and the answer is yes. I did loads and loads of sessions, maybe a couple of thousand of them over the years and the thing was, when something very special came out you really did know, and you always knew that *Hunky Dory* was going to be an iconic album that would live forever because of the songs on it and because how David approached making the album.

'Life on Mars?' is something I'm very proud to have been involved with, very proud to have been given the opportunity to play on it.

The phone you can hear ringing at the end of the track? At Trident the live room was downstairs and upstairs was the control room and I was told, if this is true or not, the phone rang up there and there was a door open and somehow it leaked downstairs onto a mic and for whatever reason, like a lot of quirky things on records, it was said, 'Lets leave it on!'

Later in the late Seventies – from 1976 until 1980 – I was living in Switzerland and David was living up the same mountain, everybody was living up mountains if you were living in Switzerland you didn't live on the flat. We used to meet regularly in a little club called the Museum Club, which is still there in Montreux, and put the world to rights. We got to know each other really well as friends.

GLASTONBURY FAYRE

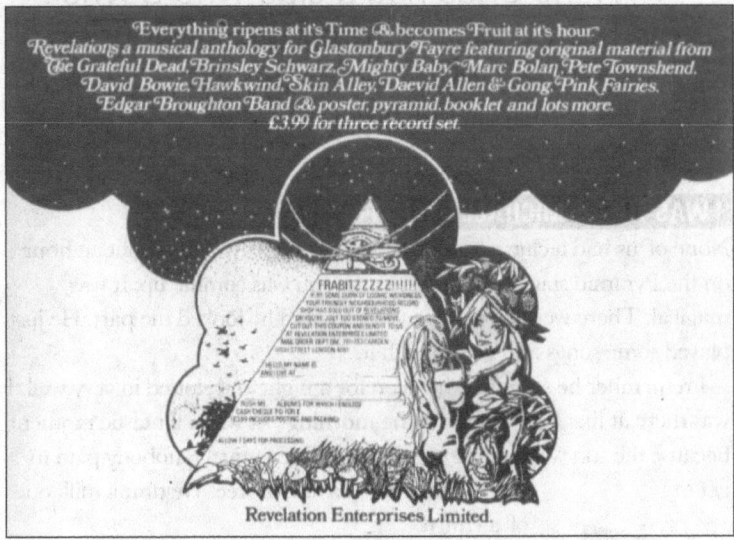

Advertisement for the triple album featuring the artists who appeared at the fayre

23 JUNE 1971 WORTHY FARM, PILTON

I WAS THERE: JULIEN TEMPLE, FILM & MUSIC VIDEO DIRECTOR

That first year (of Glastonbury), I was lucky enough to see some amazing music, Traffic were incredible. The highlight was this unknown character who was due to come on, and no-one knew who he was and no-one gave a shit, and everything was pushed back and back until eventually he came on at dawn, at four or 5 in the morning. We were all asleep in the tents and these guys were running around slapping our faces saying, 'Wake up, wake up, you got to see this guy', and this was a guy with a dress and a guitar, and it was David Bowie and it was the moment, or a moment, when everyone was turned on to what Bowie really was. He'd had

'Space Oddity' a few years before as a one-off, freak, novelty type hit, but he wasn't a star at all. And there he was in a dress, long hair, and just a guitar, sun coming up... it was magical.

> None of us had a clue who Bowie was but he played for about an hour on the Pyramid stage

I WAS THERE: MICHAEL EAVIS, FESTIVAL OWNER

None of us had a clue who Bowie was but he played for about an hour on the Pyramid stage at 4am just as the sun was coming up. It was magical. There were hippies everywhere and he looked the part. He just played some songs and got on with it.

I remember he stayed at the farm for a night and slotted in very well. I was there at first light at four in the morning – it was a fantastic moment because the sun was shining too. It was a free festival – nobody paid to get in and all the artists played for free. We drank milk out of a churn.

I kept trying to get Bowie to come back and it finally happened in 2000. He finished up with an encore of 'Heroes', which is the best song in the world as far as I'm concerned. That was a fantastic moment – I think maybe that was my best Glastonbury moment of all time. That was so brilliant. But he never came back again. We tried every year to persuade him to return to the Festival but a couple of years ago we were told he would never tour again.

Maybe they knew about his illness then. The thing with Bowie was that his songs were on a par with Sinatra and Presley – and the three of them are ahead of all the rest in terms of being all-time greats. Bowie's songs are absolutely bloody amazing, aren't they? I shook his hand and said thanks for coming back after his performance in 2000 but I didn't go for a drink with him – or even a smoke.

FRIARS, BOROUGH ASSEMBLY HALL

25 SEPTEMBER 1971 AYLESBURY

I WAS THERE: RICK PEARCE

Although it held little personal interest, the one thing the Moon landing was responsible for was the re-introduction of 'Space Oddity' to the charts. I had heard the single played by John Peel on BBC Radio 1, been hooked instantly and was delighted to see Bowie with perm and 12 string guitar appear on *Top of the Pops*, followed by... nothing. Occasionally I wondered when the silence would break, but other than 'The Prettiest Star' and 'Memory of a Free Festival', heard once each the following year on the radio, and then later the odd press report on Arnold Corns and 'men's dresses' it remained deafening (I must have been away when they broadcast the In Concerts). Occasional forays to the nearest town found a total absence of Bowie product in the only record shop. All in all, my sad little corner of middle England was pretty badly served.

Fast forward a year and I was attending FE College in Aylesbury and was running with a more sophisticated and musically aware crowd than the Trojan-v-Heavy Rock bunch of dichotomists whose company I'd had to suffer as a school kid. That spring, Friars, the local rock club run by the estimable David Stopps, had re-opened in Aylesbury after an enforced break, so at last I had regular access to diverse styles of live music. Also during the summer I'd encountered various tracks from *The Man Who Sold the World* sparking my interest again, so when Bowie's Sept 25th Friars gig was announced it was clearly an unmissable event.

Arriving at the Borough Assembly Hall on the night, I still

remember feeling a very real sense of occasion but having no idea of what would follow. Sitting on the wooden floor of the hall we heard that scheduled support band, America, would not be appearing. This seemed to bother a few people, two girls seated in front of us moaned constantly for most of the gig. Replacing the nameless nag riders we had Mick Softley who suffered from constant talking and ceaseless plaints from the 'America contingent'. He walked off briefly but was persuaded to return. 'Time Machine' with its soaring Roy Harper style vocals is the only song I remember. He was quickly followed by Lol Coxhill, who perched on a stool and entertained us with some freeform soprano sax extemporisations, which accompanied the two girls complaining rather well.

David Bowie and Mick Ronson came on as a duo. Bowie looked amazing in huge blue/black trousers, a beige, almost velvety, jacket and what looked like the red platform boots seen on the back of the 'Space Oddity' re-issue. He may have been wearing a large hat but I don't think it stayed on for too long. Ronson was wearing a grey smock thing like a schoolgirl's gymslip, white shirt, jeans and white Bolan style girls' shoes.

Not exactly your average beardy, shaggy rock 'n rollers.

With Ronno playing bass they created a magical, intimate atmosphere, covering Biff Rose songs before tackling 'Space Oddity'. After a while, beardy, shaggy Trevor Bolder and Woody Woodmansey were brought on, Ronno picked up his Gibson and they played 'The Supermen', the only *Man Who Sold The World* track of the night. By this time even the moaning girls had almost shut up and started to take notice.

The band played several songs from the forthcoming *Hunky Dory* album. 'Oh! You Pretty Things/Eight Line Poem', (the only time I ever saw them played that way), 'Changes' with ex Animal Tom Parker joining on piano, and the 'People Songs', (for Reed, Warhol and Dylan). They finished with a hurricane version of Chuck Berry's 'Around and Around', with Bowie by now topless, and encored to my delight, with 'Waiting For The Man' which I had recently discovered on the *Velvet Underground & Nico* album.

It's almost impossible to describe that night without resorting to hindsight, but the fact was we had no idea what was to come within only a few months. Almost everyone I knew at the time was there and we all became instant believers, but I do wonder if those girls ever stopped moaning and realised they'd witnessed history being made. And they'd only paid 50p for the privilege.

COUNTRY CLUB

NOVEMBER 1971 HAVERSTOCK, HAMPSTEAD

I WAS THERE: ROBIN MAYHEW

I first met David at the Country Club, Haverstock, Hampstead. I was the sound engineer for a band called Tucky Buzzard who were a heavy metal-type band and their stage volume was high. We performed first and then David and Mick Ronson did an acoustic set. Their sound was appalling with howl and feedback. We had to stay because we couldn't break our equipment down until the end of the show.

When David had finished, Angie Bowie came over to me and asked if I'd have a word with David. He was amazed that he could hear everything that Tucky Buzzard had played, even though their volume was so high. He said that he was preparing to take the Spiders from Mars out on the road and would I come to a rehearsal with the PA system we used to see how things would be? The venue was the Beckenham Rugby Club Hall.

The PA I was using was designed and built by Mike Turner (Turner Electronics) from Ealing, West London. Unlike the sound rigs of the early Seventies, which used separate bass horns, mid-range horns and tweeters, Turner's system used the 'wall of sound' concept, with multiple full-range speakers in reflex cabinets, each running at comparatively low output. The sheer number of cabinets gave a smooth, comfortable sound and moved a vast amount of air through the room/auditorium.

David was impressed by the fact that he could actually stand in front of the rig with his microphone without causing feedback. Obviously for larger arena type venues, which were bound to come,

Ziggy Stardust soundman Robin Mayhew (center) and Will Palin (on the right) wonder why Peter Hince isn't wearing his regulation Bowie T-shirt

long-range conventional horns had to be used, but for the early 2,000 to 3,000 seat venues, the Turner system was ideal for the Ziggy experience and this system was used at all the UK gigs. It definitely gave David an edge over other performers of the era and suited his more theatrical approach to rock music.

I was responsible for sound engineering all of his Ziggy Stardust concert performances around the world, between January 29 1972 and July 3 1973. I must credit Bowie for musically opening my eyes and influencing my life with his innovation and originality. We worked very closely before and while touring together for 18 months, during which we developed a close working and personal relationship.

David didn't break rules. He wrote new ones. His intelligence, creativity, innovation and courage effected a huge change in popular culture – change that endures to this very day. He just loved new inventions. If there were any new inventions, he would want to play with them. The video camera was just coming out, and he was fascinated by it. He was always looking for something different, and that was good for me because the PA system I was using was a bit different too – and wonderfully suitable for him. He was a very easy man to work with. Everybody played their part; everybody had their job, and we were all just one big team. There was nothing at all prima donna-ish about him. We were just all swept along on the crest of this wave, staying in the Beverly Hills Hotel, living in the lap of luxury, all room service, just young men together, and it was like everyone's dreams come true. It certainly was for Bowie. This was his breakthrough, the 512 days I worked with him I saw a man realise his ambition. He had done it.

1972-1973

The Ziggy Startdust Tour kicked off at the Borough Assembly Hall, Aylesbury, England, on Saturday evening, 29 January 1972. Tthe tour would be over six legs and saw Bowie and his band play 182 shows.

Ziggy Stardust was yet to be released, in fact as the tour started, Bowie was still spending time at Trident Studios, London, adding final touches to the Ziggy sessions. Some fans would hear Bowie in session on John Peel's *Sounds Of The Seventies* BBC Radio 1 show on the Friday before the tour started, when he played 'Hang On to Yourself', 'Ziggy Stardust', 'Queen Bitch', 'Waiting For The Man', and 'Lady Stardust'.

Bowie and photographer Brian Ward shot the cover for the Ziggy Stardust album in January. Originally shot in black and white, Ward tinted the photographs to achieve the ultra-real, storybook style of the album sleeve and telephone box back cover, reflecting the album's overtly British vaudeville pop and fantasy narrative.

FRIARS, BOROUGH ASSEMBLY HALL

29 JANUARY 1972 AYLESBURY

I WAS THERE: RICK PEARCE

With hindsight this would have been momentous, but back then we had no idea that this was the first ever show for a phenomenon that would take over our lives for the next eighteen months and remain a constant factor, in various forms, right up to the present.

Needless to say we got hold of our tickets as soon as they came out and on the night we piled into the Borough Assembly Hall full of eager anticipation. So fast in fact that Mick Ronson, still on stage fiddling with his pedals, had to exit rapidly as we staked out an area at the front and settled down to wait.

I shall pass over the true awfulness of support band Grand Canyon as they have been crucified very effectively elsewhere. Suffice to say they lived up to their name, a huge empty void signifying nothing.

Then it was showtime! I'm sure they were using Beethoven's Ninth by then although I'm not entirely certain. The band and Bowie strode on looking like a gang of haute couture Droogs/Wild Boys, streets ahead of Burgess, Burroughs or Kubrick's imaginations, and roared into that set.

The almost named Spiders looked a little uncomfortable in their new stage gear and bassist Trevor Bolder had yet to grow his sidies to their full silver sprayed garden gnome glory, but Bowie and band were tight and well rehearsed which was just as well with the teething problems that followed. It started with the pickup falling off Bowie's new guitar which was quickly gaffa taped on for the rest of the set, but worse was the intermittent fault that caused Ronno's guitar to keep cutting out. He had a brief respite when he switched to piano for 'Life on Mars?', but this gig was clearly full of frustrating moments for him.

I wouldn't describe the set as tentative by any means but this was the first time it had been performed in front of an audience and was understandably a little slower and more measured than the later gigs by which time they had reached the telepathic stage that comes to all bands after constant touring. There was a great deal more between song chat and much of the new material was named and introduced as part of the next album, which was to be called *The Rise and Fall of Ziggy Stardust and the Spiders from Mars*. This was the first time we'd heard its title, whether anyone else outside of the inner circle of band and management had at that point is anyone's guess.

Eventually Bowie and Ronno swapped amps, which seemed to solve the problem. An enduring memory comes from the end of the set during 'Waiting For The Man' with Ronno producing an uncharacteristically clean sound from his sanded down Les Paul, while Bowie, thrashing great fuzztoned washes of sonic chaos from his twelve string, thrust and gyrated the neck lewdly in the direction of his guitarist's hindquarters. All great stuff, and an amusing precursor to the 'electric blow job', which became a regular feature, after its debut at Oxford Town Hall that summer.

The set finished with 'Rock 'n' Roll Suicide' and I have a clear memory of seeing a magazine photo some time later, of my friend Jenny, instantly recognisable by her long blond hair and bright yellow floor length cardy, clutching Bowie's hands as he reached down from the stage.

After the gig, Jenny and Jackie, my girlfriend at the time, managed to blag their way backstage and met David Bowie. They were immensely and understandably pleased with themselves for weeks afterwards.

This was a huge leap forward for Bowie and a massive change made in only four months. Rebirth? Metamorphosis? Your choice. I know the hall was packed and this time nobody was sitting down. This was rock 'n' roll with serious attitude, coming at us for the first time, straight from the future. And so, unlike Yeats' rough beast slouching towards Bethlehem to be born, Ziggy came sashaying out of Beckenham fully formed and in the process made our little corner of the world a better brighter place.

Another memory from this period is 'Starman' on the July 6th *Top of the Pops*. I had no idea it was about to happen, phoned Jackie and had a conversation running along the lines of:

'Hi, are you watching...?'

'Yes I am, I can't believe it...etc.'

A true life if unintentional case of 'Hey that's far out so you heard him too' as Bowie sings the chorus with his arm round Ronno. Just imagine the scene in thousands of living rooms across the country...

I don't remember how we got hold of tickets for the July 15th 1972 Friars date but we did, somehow. Memories of the gig itself are a jumble of confused images and impressions:

A huge wave of energy and sound coming off the stage, 'Hang On to Yourself' hitting us like a bolt of lightning, it's the first time I've seen them in a small venue since they played here in January...blue lit but otherwise darkened stage for 'The Supermen'... total strobe disorientation and fragments of 'She Shook Me Cold' during the jam section of 'I Feel Free'... Ronno raising his arm to signal the end of 'White Light/White Heat' and Woody just keeps on drumming... Crushed against the PA by the crowd with Jackie, Jenny and her friend Tim and being deaf for days after... Bowie taking off his jacket towards the end of the show, ripping it to pieces, throwing rags to the crowd.

At the same time Stuey George and (probably) stage manager Peter Hunsley and sound man Robin Mayhew are hurling fliers from both sides of the stage, girls are fighting over bits of white satin and I'm wondering how it's possible to look cool in the middle of all of this, realising it's impossible and giving up on even trying... grabbing Ronno's guitar as he runs to the front of the stage and shoves it out into the audience... the surface of the guitar is rough, almost like sandpaper and the strings are very light gauge. Wondering if seeing The Beatles at The Cavern was anywhere near as good as this.

Eventually the band head offstage, the houselights come on and we are left hanging about feeling drained, deafened and stunned by the sheer intensity. Jackie, John and I leave the hall and end up in the bombsite, which passes for a car park beside the Borough Assembly Hall. There's a large crowd of people clustered round a limo parked by the stage door. Getting into my car we drive slowly out of the car park clearing a way through the crowd. The limo slots in behind us and we move forward, slowly clearing a path as we go.

Out in the Market Square we turn left and move slowly through the crowd spilling out of the passage leading from the venue and onto the street. Speeding up we head round the bottom of the square past the courts and into the tunnel under Friars Square. Indicating left, I pull the car over across the bus station entrance and the limo sails past hooting its horn. We hoot and wave as David Bowie, Mick Ronson and Angie pass by waving back and heading off into the night, the future and immortality. The last thing we see are the brake lights flashing as they slow to turn left and join the main road heading out of town…

After that things just got bigger, wilder and totally beyond control. David Bowie and the Spiders were no longer able to be just our band. The Universe, or at least America had taken them over and we would never get them back. Sadly that's how it works and the only choice we have is to live with it every time it happens or to become bitter, twisted, cynical and ultimately deadly boring.

On further consideration, there is no choice!

I WAS THERE: KRIS NEEDS

The buzz is that something magical is going to happen tonight, the anticipation building in Aylesbury's old Borough Assembly Hall rapidly approaching feverish. We know; Bowie promised after he played here the previous September.

Then he'd been a shy singer-songwriter, hiding beneath his long blond tresses, playing a rare solo gig. To test the water he attempted to get his career back on track after the one-hit wonderdom of 'Space Oddity' two years earlier. Surprised and buoyed by the enthusiastic response, Bowie had promised to come back with something completely different and amazing.

Four months later in front of double the audience (including future stars Queen), the lights dimmed while Walter Carlos' synthesised 'Ode to Joy' from *A Clockwork Orange* filled the hushed venue. Strobes exploded as the glacial chorale built to a climax, three band members in shiny jump-suits taking position as an unearthly figure appeared at the back. Then, freak out!

As the strobes drop to blinding light, Ziggy Stardust and the Spiders from Mars kick into 'Hang On to Yourself', before sealing their arrival with 'Ziggy Stardust', Bowie strutting and preening about in his diamond pattern blue-grey jumpsuit and red wrestling boots. The set traverses much of the as-yet-unheard Ziggy Stardust album and *Hunky Dory* items played on the previous visit, including a show-stopping 'Life on Mars?'.

A lengthy workout on Cream's 'I Feel Free' gives guitarist Mick

Ronson a chance to stretch out and Bowie the chance to change into a shiny white satin ensemble with black embroidery. The home stretch included Chuck Berry's 'Around And Around', a belting 'I'm Waiting For The Man' and showbiz finale of 'Rock 'n' Roll Suicide', which saw a few local girls submit to Bowie's request to give him their hands (but not enough for an Iggy-style crowd-supported walkabout).

Afterwards, a grinning Bowie sat in the small dressing room, engulfed in triumphant post-gig afterglow, while clamouring teenage sauce-pots asking why he wore makeup. 'Well, I don't want to go around looking like a dead bear,' he reasoned. The transformation into a rock 'n' roll star he sang about on 'Star' had started, set to increasingly dominate the next 18 months. At a little club in the Buckinghamshire countryside, Bowie's career (finally) had liftoff.

I say this whenever I'm called to talk or write about Bowie's most revolutionary creation; the unbridled shock and awe of clapping eyes on Ziggy Stardust for the first time in the androgynous, alien flesh remains one of the most vividly indelible, soul-detonating moments of my entire life. No one had experienced the full impact before then; it was

virgin territory. My own first impression was that Bowie had created Ziggy as a character, some kind of cartoon superhero version of a rock 'n' roll star, with concept and story-line already written to its dramatically inevitable climax.

In 1971, the 'real' rock icons were the likes of Jagger, the burgeoning Keef cult, newcomers such as Rod Stewart overtaking Mott The Hoople's underdog reality, while Marc Bolan was establishing a new breed of glamorous street urchin teen idol which seemed nearest to where Bowie was coming from. But there was no ultimate rock 'n' roll star to gaze at in the heavens, which is where Ziggy came in, a leper Messiah informed by US underground titans such as Lou Reed and Iggy Pop, colliding with old school Hollywood glamour; crucially, as was already happening in Andy Warhol's Factory, perhaps the biggest influence on Bowie at this time of rampantly-unfolding evolution.

The mythical doomed future pop star could have been a hackneyed concept but this was something else, a gift from the gods for a teenage Stones-Mott fan like me. Where the Stones had turned their new fans on to the likes of Muddy Waters and Chuck Berry, Bowie would do the same for his Warhol, Stooges and Velvets influences. There was nothing like Ziggy back then, except the recently banned *A Clockwork Orange* film. Once that particular influence was understood, Bowie's cold new world made more sense. Like the Stones, the shockwaves of his impact

Young Kris Needs was one of a select crowd who witnessed the live debut of Ziggy Stardust at Aylesbury's old Borough Assembly Hall

reverberated deeper than the music, invading image, culture and social taboos, sparking a new revolution for the kids while provoking an even more profound contempt from worried parents to homophobic council chiefs, even traditional rock fans. Just the fact that Bowie sported a new kind of short, spikey hair-style was startling at a time when barnet length still seemed to rule everything, inspiring many to prune their locks. No one knew that a direct lineage to punk rock was opening up but, at that moment in an age of denim, pop music was being invaded by a vision from the future, rock 'n' roll's sound and vision about to be changed forever in the most unlikely stratas.

Since Ziggy's initial ascension, the story has been endlessly retold and analysed, presented as anything from Bowie's great master-plan to the Second Coming, obviously minus the lifelong epiphany of witnessing it first hand. Ultimately, Ziggy's initial success was a flash flood of brilliance unleashed from Bowie's nuclear reactor brain which, in the early Seventies, seemed to be overheating with brainstormed ideas born out of the influences he was soaking up like a crazed sponge.

It's possible to trace the evolution of Ziggy by going back to the frustrating 1970 doldrums period when he couldn't follow the previous year's 'Space Oddity' with another hit, falling flat with outings like 'The Prettiest Star'.

One crucial element fell into place when he married Angela that March, who would prove to be a human dynamo behind the evolution into his next phase, from crystallising his whims to encouraging the anything goes, creatively-inspiring atmosphere at the couple's sprawling Haddon Hall residence in Beckenham, Kent.

Much of the material for that period's albums was worked up in the rehearsal room in the basement; finely-tuned melodic songs, shot with reaction against the hippie dream which had enveloped the country for the previous few years. To that end, November's *The Man Who Sold the World*, released in the UK the following April, remains the darkest, most overlooked album in Bowie's canon, an edgy, psychodramatic masterpiece which laid in place themes, and musical germs which he would pursue for the rest of the decade.

1971 was Bowie's year of transition, including the first two American trips where, sporting his Mr Fish man's dress, he would meet and become gripped by Lou Reed, Iggy Pop, Andy Warhol and his subterranean entourage; many he would take on board Ziggy's mothership once it got off the ground, including Cherry Vanilla, Leee Black Childers, Tony Zanetta and Wayne County, whose outrageous transexual-from-hell stage act would be a profound later influence.

When the whole company descended on London's Roundhouse that August for the XXX-rated production of *Pork*, Bowie was further tickled and galvanised, live-wire Angie never far from voicing her encouragement. Warhol's penchant for reinvention and knack for fabricating 'superstars' would also have a major bearing on Bowie's career.

That year also saw Tony Defries, a hard-nosed lawyer, who idolised Presley's Colonel Tom Parker, take over as manager, while Bowie went through a phase of writing and recording the lighter, more commercial fare which would appear on that December's *Hunky Dory* album.

It was at that point that the first Friars Aylesbury appearance, on September 25, occurred to plant the rocket beneath Bowie and ignite the motivation to make his next career phase a living, breathing rock 'n' roll stage phenomenon.

The club, which had started in 1969 and for which I designed flyers, had a reputation for its warm atmosphere and one of the best crowds in the country. Although Bowie was still struggling against one hit wonder syndrome, promoter David Stopps was willing to splash out £150 to book him for a one-off show to test the water. The hall was about half full, 400 hardcore regulars paying 50p to get in.

Bowie turned up in the afternoon and spent much of the pre-gig time shuffling about in his floppy hat, voluminous black culottes and red platform boots, looking nervous. At one point, he asked if we had a heater because he was cold, although that might have been a mask for his nervous shakes.

What happened next was basically the first live show by David Bowie and the Spiders from Mars, the set starting folky with Ronson, before the pair were joined by drummer Woody Woodmansey and bassist Trevor Bolder. Bowie played songs from the recently-completed *Hunky Dory*, including 'Oh! You Pretty Thing' and next single 'Changes'. The band and crowd had warmed up dramatically by the Lou Reed-inspired 'Queen Bitch', Chuck Berry's 'Around And Around' and the Velvets' 'I'm Waiting For The Man'.

From my vantage point behind Ronno's amp, I could see relief and elation lighting up Bowie's face. Afterwards, sitting in the little dressing room, he now seemed brimming with a new confidence, which he took away and harnessed into the gestating Ziggy Stardust project. 'That was great and next time you see me I'm going to be totally different,' he beamed.

In short, he simply went off and, in the four months before that return, wrote and recorded the *Ziggy* album, and created the character. Bowie had already written songs such as 'Moonage Daydream' and 'Star', while constructing his new persona from components including Iggy (although the Ziggy name was also inspired by a clothes shop he spotted on a train journey), and obscure outsider nutter the Legendary Stardust Cowboy, whose dementedly cacophonic 'Paralyzed' single he had picked up in the US. Another major influence was old rocker Vince Taylor, who enjoyed Elvis-status in France before freaking out in the late Sixties, believing he was either from outer space or Jesus Christ (The Clash later covered his 'Brand New Cadillac').

Throw in Japanese designer Kansai Yamamoto coming up with the new hair-style, *A Clockwork Orange* for the Spiders' stage jump-suits (hated with a passion by the Spiders from Hull), elements of

Kabuki theatre, and Ziggy would be ready for that January unveiling, but possibly Bowie's greatest wheeze was coolly and calculatedly informing a *Melody Maker* journalist that he was gay, guaranteeing the front page and all kind of furore.

Bowie was effectively steaming in to clear the decks for a new kind of superstar: himself. Warhol had shown him the potential of outrage as a weapon to get noticed; Bowie distilled and diluted these elements into a *Clockwork Orange* style future package which foresaw the death of traditional rock 'n' roll stars. A new icon was needed and Ziggy Stardust would be the leper messiah beaming in to blow everyone's minds. 'Our new stage act will be outrageous…quite

> Bowie turned up in the afternoon and spent much of the pre-gig time shuffling about in his floppy hat, voluminous black culottes and red platform boots

different to anything anyone has tried to do before,' he declared in *Melody Maker*.

It's often reported that the first gig by David Bowie and the Spiders from Mars' first gig was at a Tolworth pub called the Toby Jug on February 10, 1972. That might have been the first show on the UK tour which lurched sporadically around the UK through the first months of that year, but the Borough Assembly Hall in Aylesbury Market Square, as immortalised in 'Five Years', was Ziggy's first landing spot, nearly two weeks earlier. Bowie was totally different from the nervous creature of a few months earlier. Although he gave me a cheeky kiss when he left, I could tell where this man's own sexual leanings were directed. It was all part of a very grand plan.

It was still early days. He didn't finish recording 'Starman', his perfectly constructed retort to the record company's request for a hit single, until the week after the Aylesbury gig and it wasn't released until April 28. 'Rock 'n' Roll Suicide' and 'Sufragette City' were also late additions to the *Ziggy* album, which at one time, was going to have 'Around And Around' as its title track.

Despite the shattering impact that Ziggy's first appearance had on many of the crowd that night, it escaped the national press, shockwaves taking a few more weeks to seep through from subsequent one-nighters. Ziggy was so shockingly new and different at that time, he couldn't be an overnight sensation (but when it did start to happen…).

Maybe unsurprisingly, Bowie's fan club was being run by an Aylesbury girl. I started helping out, designing the membership card. Me and my mates caught Bowie wherever we could through until June, including gigs at Dunstable and the memorable one at Oxford Town Hall where, apart from trading in the diamond jumpsuit for the red and green quilted number sported on the infamous *Top of the Pops* 'Starman' appearance, he went down on Ronson's guitar, providing photographer Mick Rock with one of his most abiding images.

We were always greeted warmly by Bowie, who didn't seem to believe how fast it was happening, but was always gracious and considerate to 'the boys and girls from Aylesbury'. Pretty soon, Tony DeFries cut him off, trying to create an untouchable legend but, for this short time, it was marvellous watching Ziggy's rise at close quarters. He returned to Friars on July 15, playing a showcase for a planeload of US journos and record company execs flown in to start the buzz for Ziggy's invasion of America.

Although I had managed to witness a Ziggy soundcheck in the afternoon, things had changed; the show was slicker and Bowie had gained a mean, black bodyguard called Stuey, who informed me after the gig that I would see his charge, 'over my dead body'.

Even if it's not his greatest album (the jury is always out), Ziggy Stardust remains Bowie's most important peak. Listening to it 40 years on, away from the surrounding hysteria and my own inner teenage rampage going on then, the album has lost none of its special magic, bathed in a warm glow of timeless immortality. Bolstered by extra clarity and presence from 21st century remastering technology, the record's finer points can be properly appreciated: from Ronson's sublime flair for arrangements to little touches like Bowie's throwaway mutter of 'Just watch me now' at the end of 'Star'. It's almost to himself but, in retrospect, maybe the most telling utterance on the whole album. How could even Ziggy Stardust have known that, 40 years later, we would still be doing just that?

THE TOBY JUG

10 FEBRUARY 1972 TOLWORTH, LONDON

I WAS THERE: STEPHEN KING

In February 1972 I was just a month away from my 18th birthday. I used to buy the *Melody Maker* music magazine every week, keeping abreast of the very latest trends and following my heroes. In the back pages of the *Melody Maker* were adverts for whatever gigs were going on that week. Venues such as the Marquee Club, the Greyhound, Golden Lion, Speakeasy and of course the Toby Jug were all featured. David Bowie would be playing at the Toby Jug on the 10 February and, as we now know this was to be the very first gig of his Ziggy Stardust UK Tour.

I had read the famous 'Oh You Pretty Thing!' David Bowie interview in *Melody Maker* from a few weeks earlier and had also caught his appearance on BBC TV's *The Old Grey Whistle Test*. And of course, I still remembered his 'Space Oddity' single, which had been a hit several years earlier but nothing prepared me for what I was about to experience on this day.

The Toby Jug Pub, Tolworth had for many years been a venue

for up and coming bands. Playing host to the likes of Traffic, Led Zeppelin, Jethro Tull, Ten Years After and King Crimson, it was well established as a local pub gig. I had persuaded a couple of friends from work to come along and check out this David Bowie who had suddenly appeared all over the media.

The pub itself was fairly small and the venue was just an ordinary function room. I don't recall having to queue for long to get in. We paid our entrance fee and got our hands stamped so that we could get out if we wanted and be re-admitted without hassle. There was no support group – just a DJ.

About 9pm the house lights were switched off. I think a taped introduction from *A Clockwork Orange* was played and Ziggy Stardust (with his trademark red hair) and The Spiders from Mars then took to the two-foot high stage. While he used a pianist later in his concerts – on this night it was just Bowie and The Spiders.

There were about 60 people in the room, mostly aged between 17 and 25, and we watched the concert standing. There were a few tables and chairs at the back of the room but people only used them to stand on for a better view. We were 10 feet away and the energy was just incredible. I had never seen or heard anything like it before.

I'm pretty sure he wore the very same combat outfit as on the Ziggy Stardust album cover and *The Old Grey Whistle Test*. I definitely remember him wearing the same knee high wrestling boots. I think he wore the same costume all through the set.

A very small lighting rig was used to incredible effect – often just a tight pin-spot on the 'Main Man' himself. The lighting was theatre style – not the usual rock flashing Par cans. Bowie had

brought theatre to a humble pub gig!

The sound was fantastic – so loud my ears were ringing for days afterwards. I can still remember feeling the sheer power of the opening chords of 'Ziggy Stardust'. Mick Ronson had a tremendous guitar sound.

The songs pounded into us thick and fast, interspersed by brief introductions from Bowie. About halfway through the show came the acoustic numbers. 'Port of Amsterdam', 'My Death', 'Wild Eyed Boy from Freecloud', 'Space Oddity' and 'Andy Warhol', seem to stick in my mind. Then it was time to crank it up again for 'Hang On to Yourself', 'Suffragette City' and 'Queen Bitch.' I can clearly recall the hairs on the back of my neck standing up during 'Queen Bitch.'

It all gets hazy here – I was oblivious to everything and everyone else in the room. I couldn't blink for fear of missing something. Nothing would ever be the same again. I knew one thing for sure – David Bowie was going to be huge!

The audience was enthusiastic and responded with rapturous applause, whistles and cheers. Bowie appeared to enjoy the show as well. The material was so fresh. After rehearsing the set without an audience it must have been great for him to finally get this response from the crowd. I don't remember anyone heckling. My reaction? I was completely blown away. I was just entranced by the entire performance. It was a heady combination of the best music I have ever heard, tremendous sound, very basic but so effective lighting. The concert finished around 11pm – a two-hour set.

I was so impressed with the gig that I dragged some more friends to the Wallington Public Hall gig the following week. Sadly nothing could compete with the Toby Jug gig and for me still hasn't to this day. The Wallington Public Hall was only about half full and lacked the intimacy of the Toby Jug. Still it was a great set there too – but I had now been spoiled! I later saw him at The Rainbow Theatre Concert on 19 August 1972 with Roxy Music supporting.

BIRMINGHAM TOWN HALL

17 MARCH 1972 BIRMINGHAM

I WAS THERE: MICK ROCK, PHOTOGRAPHER

When I first met David we swapped anecdotes; he wanted to hear about Syd Barrett and I wanted to know about Lou Reed and Iggy Pop. We talked about how Syd had had it all. Syd and David were similar in the way that neither of them sang like an American. At that time there was a big American influence on music, but Syd and David went against that and sang in a British way.

David was very aware of Syd; very interested in him. Of course, in 1973 David did a cover version of 'See Emily Play' for his *Pin Ups* album. There were many parallels between Syd and David early on, although clearly David had a much tougher psyche. David's 'The Man Who Sold The World' always makes me think of Syd. It's a perfect description of him.

FREE TRADE HALL

APRIL 21 1972 MANCHESTER

I WAS THERE: MARK DOYLE

I saw David at the Free Trade Hall, Manchester in April 72. He began with 'Hang On to Yourself' and 'Ziggy Stardust' and then explained to the audience that he'd spent the last week in rehearsals and that his vocal chords were sore. He could either play a short 'hard' set or a longer 'softer' set – which did we want? We opted for the long set and he proceeded to play all of Ziggy, several of his back catalogue, plus 'White Light/White Heat' and 'I Feel Free'. After about 90 minutes, the audience were ecstatic and David seemed pretty pleased with the reception too – enough to actually walk out onto the audience's hands at the front of the stage, and they did manage to keep him aloft (for a short while anyway!) Definitely one of the all time great gigs!'

I WAS THERE: TONY HUSBAND

I'd been following Bowie for some time. I'd seen him doing his mime show with Tyrannosaurus Rex, seen him at Glastonbury and prevented a greaser throwing a bottle at him at a Humble Pie gig (got thumped for my efforts). Anyway, I'd got *The Man Who Sold the World* and was totally knocked out by it. Ronson's thrilling guitar, Visconti's doom-laden bass and some of the heaviest songs ever recorded, so when the tour was announced I was brimming.

On the day the tickets were released I went to the ticket office at the Manchester Lewis department store at the back of the lingerie department, an old guy showed me the seating plan of the Free Trade Hall and said 'Take your pick, you're the first' (a moment I am still proud of). I had the entire hall to choose from and chose the circle front row, dead centre, a choice I was later to regret. I presumed it would be full so I would have the best view etc. Come the night, it wasn't full, I'd say about 200 to 400 or so dripped into the 3000-seat Free Trade Hall. I can't remember who the support bands were but I remember the Spiders entrance, dressed in glitter suits, stack heels,

fucking amazing. This was when I realised being in the circle was a shit place to be. Everyone rushed the stage and me, and the handful of circlellites sat watching the spectacle unfold.

> FREE TRADE HALL (Peter Street) MANCHESTER
> GEM MANAGEMENT presents...
> **DAVID BOWIE**
> IN CONCERT + Supporting Act
> FRIDAY, 21st APRIL, 1972
> at 7·30 p.m.
> STALLS — 40p (8/-)
> O
> 21

I can't remember what order the songs came in, or to be honest, what they were even, but I do remember a blistering gig. Bowie at his arrogant best, strutting the stage, Ronson darting around playing paint peeling guitar, and the solid rhythm of Bolder and Woodmansey.

I remember Bowie crowd surfing, the small knot of fans carrying him over their heads. I remember him passing an acoustic guitar into the crowd and I'm thinking 'what the fuck am I doing up here?' I remember Bowie stepping toward the microphone and it banging him in the mouth, through the show he kept feeling his tooth, strange what you remember. I looked to the side and some of the Free Trade Hall management were looking at this band of freaks, they were smirking and laughing, three guys in suits had never seen the like, neither had we. It was truly an awesome gig.

When David got bigger I went to see The Spiders at the Hardrock in Stretford with about 4,000 others. I didn't like the fact I had to share him and the band with 4,000 newcomers. I was at the Free Trade Hall with just 400 others months before, witnessing one of the all time great gigs by one of the all time great bands. I'm proud of that and it's burned into my memory forever.

PAVILION

7 MAY 1972 HEMEL HEMPSTEAD

I WAS THERE: NIGEL HERITAGE

In May 1972 I was 18 and a regular middle-class, suburban,

grammar school lad who had left school early and was working at London Zoo.

I had just been to my first Cup Final at Wembley; we lost. A non-footballing friend tried to cheer me up; did I want to go and see David Bowie at Hemel Hempstead Pavilion? On a Sunday? Not really; all I knew about David Bowie was 'Space Oddity', the cover of *Hunky Dory* and that he was gay. But I went. That Sunday night concert changed my life.

Afterwards I talked for 90 minutes non-stop about Bowie and

Ziggy s road crew: George Underwood (Illustrations), Peter Hunsley (Stage Equipment), Robin Mayhew (Sound), Bob See (Lighting)

Ziggy. He wasn't limp-wristed or weak and insipid (my naive image of a gay man), he was completely in control from the moment he strode onto stage and announced, 'My name is David Bowie, and these are the Spiders from Mars and this is some of our music.' He could do any kind of song, from fast-paced rock with the band to Jacques Brel acoustic on his own; he didn't just sing songs, he acted each one, his lyrics were brilliant and memorable – Dylan had a voice 'like sand and glue'; of course he did, the perfect description.

In the next seven months I saw him seven times. I became an instant adoring fan. I had made a banner for that Wembley Cup Final to salute my football hero Charlie George, so why not make one for my music hero Ziggy? WH Smith used to sell boxes of gold and silver stars and we had several old white sheets and some curtain material in the garage. I loved sewing anyway. I made what I think was one of the first banners for a pop star; 'Ziggy' in bold red lettering and 'Stardust' spelt out in stars.

The banner had its initial outing at the Royal Festival Hall in July 72, from a box. (My Bowie mate's parents were on the Festival Hall mailing list so we got in early.) The surprise guest was Lou Reed, dressed completely in black, while Bowie was completely in white in that shimmering butterfly-armed tunic. At the crescendo to 'Suffragette City', 'Aaaaah, wham bam thank you ma'am', handfuls of those WH Smiths stars rained down on the people below whilst the banner was waved furiously.

The closing date of the 1972 Ziggy Stardust Tour was a return to Friars in Aylesbury where the banner re-appeared. Being 6' 5', unusually tall in those days, I was already mindful of people behind me at concerts. As everyone stood at Friars (there were no seats), I kept the banner furled until Bowie came back on stage for the encore, by which time it was out, proud and raised

above my head. He saw it, looked straight at me – and smiled. I was in heaven.

When that gig was mentioned in *New Musical Express*, I felt I had become a small part of the Ziggy legend; 'The phantom waver of the Ziggy banner put in an appearance as well', it said. 'Phantom' because their photographer had tried to take my photo at the end of the gig, banner held aloft. I quickly took it down and turned away; after all, I was just a regular middle-class, suburban, grammar school lad. The banner was for Bowie, not for the world, and he'd seen it, and he'd smiled.

ASSEMBLY HALL

11 MAY 1972 WORTHING

I WAS THERE: ALAN EDWARDS

I remember him playing a gig at Worthing Town Hall in 1972. He got off stage and came into the admittedly small crowd on Mick Ronson's shoulders while continuing to sing. Ronson kept churning out the riffs despite being a long way from the stage. Very punky, in fact!

POLYTECHNIC OF CENTRAL LONDON

12 MAY 1972 LONDON

I WAS THERE: ROSALIND RUSSELL

David Bowie came home to his London public when playing at London Central and camped up his show outrageously. For the first part of his set, he wore his tightly fitted jumpsuit and his hair showed a fresh red rinse. For the second he wore a pair of impossibly tight white satin trousers and a glittery black and white top. He posed, postured and pouted for the audience and everybody loved it.

Bowie is undoubtedly beautiful, but he's not just a pretty face. His show is well worked out and the timing between David and his band is perfect. For such young musicians, he has them trained to suit his act with exact precision.

He did all the songs we thought he would do – 'Changes' from his *Hunky Dory* album and 'Andy Warhol' from the same. Particularly good was his version of 'Moonage Daydream' – a song he wrote and produced for the Spiders when they were called something else. Coloured lights flashed in conjunction with the music, and gave good effect to the short set the Spiders did without David.

The big surprise came when David and his lead guitarist Mick Ronson sat at the front of the stage, and David sang 'Space Oddity'. Even after an encore, it was a while before the audience would leave the hall, such was the success of the show.

SLOUGH TECHNICAL COLLEGE

13 MAY 1972 SLOUGH

I WAS THERE: SUSAN SMITH

I saw him at Slough College in 1972. He was in the 'Starman' phase, wearing a silver space suit and boots, as was Mick Ronson. The audience mainly students were very non-plussed about it all. I remember we were just hanging out in the corridors waiting for the show to start, no queues, no 'excitement' as you would have in later years. The show as I recall was good, my outstanding memory was the space suit garb!

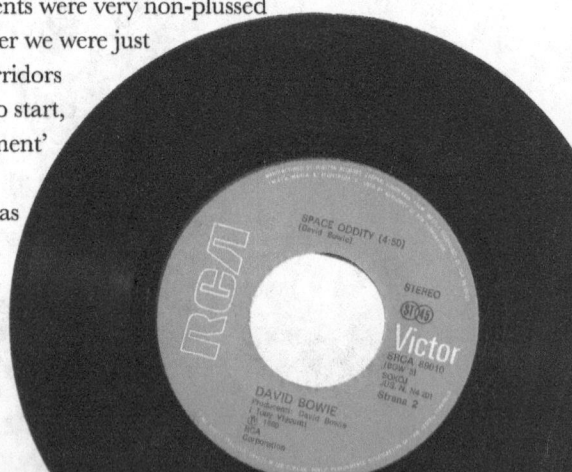

EBBISHAM

27 MAY 1972 EPSOM, SURREY

I WAS THERE: ROBIN MAYHEW, ZIGGY TOUR SOUND ENGINEER

This show was special to me as my second son Oliver was born at Epsom Hospital just round the corner from the gig. As soon as the last number had finished I shot round to see him delivered. David and Angie sent us flowers.

LIVERPOOL STADIUM

3 JUNE 1972 LIVERPOOL

I WAS THERE: JEFF CHEGWIN

It was summer of June 1972 and I was a young teenager in Liverpool. My sister Janice Long and I were meeting a friend from London who was visiting Liverpool. We stepped into the lift of The St George's Hotel to be joined by Ziggy Stardust – David Bowie in full Ziggy attire and red hair standing inches away from us and sharing our space.

He must have been staying at the hotel. No words were exchanged but this little gem of a historic moment in time will live in my mind forever. I went on to work with many music legends working in promotions, and my sister Janice became an iconic BBC music radio broadcaster. Just wished I had taken a photo!

Jeff Chegwin looks pleased with himself after sharing a lift with David Bowie

DUNSTABLE CIVIC HALL

21 JUNE 1972 DUNSTABLE

'He looked like Vogue's idea of what the well-dressed astronaut should be wearing. Dare it be said? A delicious space oddity'.

Melody Maker

All The Young Dudes

Bowie came into contact with Mott The Hoople's bassist Peter Watts and learned that the band was ready to split due to continued lack of commercial success after releasing four singles and albums, all of which failed to reach the Top 40. When the band rejected his first offer of, 'Suffragette City', Bowie wrote 'All The Young Dudes' especially for them, allegedly sitting cross-legged on the floor of a room in Regent Street, London, in front of the band's lead singer, Ian Hunter. Mott The Hoople released 'All The Young Dudes' on 27 July 1972.

CIVIC HALL
AUGUST 1972 GUILDFORD

I WAS THERE: PHILLIP ARTHUR CLONEY

David Bowie appeared in Guildford at a Mott The Hoople show at the Civic Hall in August 1972. I remember him coming on stage not really believing it was him. Amazing moment for 17-year old music fan. Mott had just done a full set and then announced that they were finishing with 'All The Young Dudes'. The stage went dark and David Bowie walked on, everyone was amazed that he had come to our town just for one song! The next day the town was full of the story that David Bowie had appeared.

He also later appeared in Guildford two other times and I was lucky to catch theses concerts.

I WAS THERE: RICHARD DIXON

Sadly I only saw David Bowie once and that came as a complete surprise. The year was 1972 at a Mott The Hoople concert in Guildford. I knew that David was associated with the band and that he had written 'All The Young Dudes' but never expected what was about to happen. In the middle of the concert the band struck up the opening chords of 'All The Young Dudes'. The notes reverberated around the auditorium and before Ian Hunter began singing a man clad in a white suit came onto the stage and there was David singing backing vocals. A great moment that is etched in my memory.

I WAS THERE: ROBIN MAYHEW, ZIGGY TOUR SOUND ENGINEER

On the very early gigs from the mixer position at the back of the hall and from the sides, myself and Peter Hunsley (the stage manager) would throw out handfuls of A4 pictures of David and the Spiders during the 'wham bam thank you ma'am' line in 'Suffragette City' to finish the show.

One day, when we were still in the Gem offices in Regent Street, I was asked to proof-read all the lyrics to *The Rise and Fall Of Ziggy Stardust and the Spiders from Mars* to make sure that they matched the sung words. They were all typed out and after listening over and over to the 'Ziggy Stardust' track, I swear that David sung 'like a leper messiah' – whereas the typed lyric sheet words were 'like a leather messiah' – so I changed them. Again in 'Rock 'n' Roll Suicide', I heard David singing 'wall to wall (as in carpet) is calling' not the 'waterwall is calling' as in the draft lyrics – so I changed them. If you look at any lyric sheet for the album you will see my words there. I never talked to David about it!! Maybe I'm responsible in some way for weird lyrics!

RAINBOW THEATRE

19 AUGUST 1972 LONDON

I WAS THERE: FRANK HENRY

In the early Seventies, myself and one of my oldest friends, John Condon, were lucky enough to have made it to university in Dublin. David Bowie's fourth studio album, *Hunky Dory*, had been released in December 1971 and was essential listening for most students living in 'bedsit land' at the time. The place to go, for Irish students at the time, was London, where during the summer months, there was an abundance of bar work available, mostly in Irish bars. In the summer of 1972, as we had done the previous years, John and myself found work in London. In June 1972, David Bowie had released his fifth studio album, *The Rise and Fall of Ziggy Stardust and the Spiders from*

Mars. Needless to say, a unique album title. If the near perfect *Hunky Dory* had been a wonderful, and a well received album, Ziggy Stardust was nothing less than a work of art.

Thus it was that on 19th August 1972, two long-haired and very naive Navan teenagers made their way to Finsbury Park, North London and the iconic Rainbow Theatre. I'm not certain how we both managed to obtain tickets for what turned out to be two sell-out concerts at the 3,000 seater venue, but we did.

A newly formed Roxy Music were, famously, the support act, but from the first moment, when the introductory *Clockwork Orange* ('Ode To Joy') theme heralded Bowie's arrival on stage, to the last strains of the final encore, 'Rock 'n' Roll Suicide', we were shocked, enthralled and gobsmacked in equal measure.

No musician had ever done before what Bowie did that night. From the costumes, including frequent costume changes, to the make-up, the multi-level stage achieved through extensive scaffolding and ladders, the dry ice, the mime artists (Lindsay Kemp and his dancers, The Astronettes), the screen on which hundreds of images and film clips were projected, this was not just a musical concert, this was absolutely groundbreaking multi-media theatre. And the music: Nineteen tracks played by Bowie and his band – including the late great Mick Ronson – almost faultlessly, but with incredible intensity, including 'Life on Mars?', 'Changes', 'Starman', 'Five Years', 'Suffragette City', as well as two Lou Reed tracks ('White Light/White Heat' and 'I'm Waiting for the Man'). This was music performed as never before.

We weren't to know at the time, but the audience included Mick Jagger, Rod Stewart, Alice Cooper and Elton John. The story goes that Lou Reed had to be led out, sobbing, by Andy Warhol, so overcome by the show was he.

My own personal favourite moment in the concert was when Bowie, for the first time ever, performed the haunting Jacques Brel song 'My Death', accompanied by his twelve string guitar. Absolutely chilling and, in hindsight, prophetic. Needless to say, we were 'on a high' for days afterwards, as I suspect were most of the audience.

I was not a fan of all of Bowie's subsequent offerings, but no one could ever deny his genius. In those halcyon summer days, we were truly fortunate to see some of the world's top acts at the peak of their powers, play London, including Led Zeppelin, The Beach Boys, The Eagles, Yes and Elton John.

For the past decade, I have been passionately interested in the life and music of Mozart. Occasionally, however, I listen to, or watch on YouTube, music from that golden era. Come what may, that night in North London is etched in my mind, for all time. David Bowie – a Wizard, a true Star. May he rest in peace.

I WAS THERE: CHRIS PHILLIPS

I was living in Suffolk at the time, but travelled to London quite a few times to see some of my favorite bands. Buying tickets in those days was easy. You would read about gigs in the *NME* or *Sounds*, and send a cheque or postal order to the venue with a stamped address envelope, and within a few days you would have the tickets delivered through your letter box. I saw Tom Waits, Joni Mitchell and Steely Dan like this.

This was the second time I had seen Bowie, and the first with a band, (first time was solo acoustic in 1969). He came out to the *Clockwork Orange* theme, entering the stage through some sort of scaffolding. I can't really remember much apart from that. I know it was sold out, and loads of fans were wearing makeup to look like Bowie. I do remember I had platform boots on.

Roxy Music with Brian Eno in all their glam outfits supported

Bowie. Sadly I sold the programme to this show on eBay recently.

BRISTOL LOCARNO

27 AUGUST 1972 BRISTOL

I WAS THERE: PAUL SHEPPARD

An air of expectation and a distinct hum in the crowd as the lights darken, the sombre tones of *Also Sprach Zarathustra* echo around the hall and then a flash of lights, the crash of guitars and there he was, 'Ziggy Stardust' aka David Bowie and his band, the Spiders from Mars. I'd bought the album a short while before after being introduced to his music in depth via *Hunky Dory*, so boy, was I looking forward to this! All the Ziggy elements were there, the camp poses, the simulated fellatio on Ronson's guitar, the glitter and the gold.

A strange place, The Locarno. It doubled both as an ice rink and a music venue. Having skated (well, sort of) there the year before, I was conscious throughout the show that there was ice beneath my feet. Would the floor hold as the crowd bopped, jigged and leapt up and down on it? Keeping my paranoia to myself I was in awe of the sheer electricity this guy and his band were creating on stage. In my lifetime, only Bob Marley (who I saw live four years later) had the same level of charisma, the magic glow of 'presence'.

Some of the music was unfamiliar to me not being a Velvet Underground fan but it all merged into one glorious noise. Mick Ronson was his usual on-stage effervescent self, an image and pose I found out later was a complete contradiction to his off-stage persona. The rhythm section did their thing but left the theatrics to Bowie and Ronson. Bowie had developed a stagecraft that allowed the crowd to feel not mere spectators but part of this glittery

Keen ice skater Paul Sheppard does his best cool pose

madness. And what a madness it was!

I was a Bowie fan before this show, a fan whilst in attendance and a die-hard fan since. His early death in 2016 therefore hit hard but I will always have my 'Ziggy' show as a golden memory of his golden years.

SET LIST
01. Hang On to Yourself
02. Queen Bitch
03. John, I'm Only Dancing
04. The Supermen
05. Ziggy Stardust
06. Moonage Daydream
07. Starman
08. This Boy (Beatles' cover)
09. The Width of a Circle
10. I'm Waiting for the Man (Velvet Underground cover)
11. White Light/White Heat (Velvet Underground cover)
12. Suffragette City

ENCORE:
13. Around and Around (Chuck Berry cover)

---

10 September 1972
After completing the first UK leg of his Ziggy Stardust Tour, David and Angie set sail on the Queen Elizabeth II, departing from Southampton, England for the weeklong voyage to New York City.

MUSIC HALL

22 SEPT 1972 CLEVELAND, OHIO

I WAS THERE: ROBERT LAMB

As luck would have it I grew up in Cleveland Ohio. It doesn't sound lucky but let me assure you, if you loved rock 'n' roll there was no better place on the planet to be for music. Born in the birth year of Rock 'n' roll, 1954 and lived in a house where music played on records and the radio all day and night exposed me to every kind of music. I started my own collection at the age of 8 and at 10 I attended my first concert to see The Beatles (in the third row), and that definitely changed everything. By my senior year in high school in 1972 I was heavily into the Stones, Joe Walsh, Allman Brothers and Clapton was god.

So on that night in September, nine of us had tickets to see this guy nobody knew anything about but we were in it for the drugs (mescaline and pot and booze) and the party. I was totally mesmerized by what I witnessed on stage, aliens dressed in some kind of futuristic drag playing the most kick ass rock 'n' roll ever produced... till this day... I just found and posted a video from that night and I had chills run up and down my spine watching it 40 years later. It changed everything for me... I even became a guitar player and now I play slide guitar everyday. And thank my lucky stars that I was there that night.

ELLIS AUDITORIUM

24 SEPTEMBER 1972 MEMPHIS, TENNESSEE

I WAS THERE: CELESTE PASLEY

I was a 16-year old Catholic schoolgirl trying to find my path. David Bowie created for me more questions than answers. I was transformed just as much as he was.

CARNEGIE HALL

28 SEPTEMBER 1972 NEW YORK CITY

I WAS THERE: DOUGLAS ROCK

The first time I saw David Bowic was in New York in the early Seventies, Ziggy Stardust and the Spiders from Mars. I later saw him in Montreal, Canada and then when he came back to the States and for the Young American tour. A great innovator in music and made history a better place with music that will always be timeless, a true legend. David Bowie was a great man and gave us hope through his music that our future was going to be awesome.

FISHER THEATER

8 OCTOBER 1972 DETROIT, MICHIGAN

I WAS THERE: JEANNE HILKO

Myself, and five of my High School friends, attended the David Bowie concert at the Fisher Theater, Detroit. This concert was one of my many 'firsts', and it happened to be David Bowie's Ziggy Stardust! We were all just 16-years old and just beginning our concert regime.

When David came out in his flamboyant costume, dressed with feathers and glitter from head to toe and finger nails, us Midwestern ladies were shocked (to say the least), but so excited to be watching

Willy Palin

SUITE M. McDonald + T. Defries
~~H. S. + H. S.~~ Ginsberg
Iggy Pop
Lee Black Childers
Gustl Bracur
A. Jones and W. Palin
C. Foxxx
Bob See + Jim Moody
Al Holtz + Steve Huston
Woodmansey + Bowlder
Mick Ronson
Tony Zanetta
Mick + Sheila Rock
B. Garson
Stu Ginsberg and Mrs Ginsberg
Sue Fessey
Dai Davies
Robin Mayhew + P. Huntsley
Tony Frost + S. George
SUITE Mr + Mrs Jones
Mr + Mrs Underwood
T. Juigens + M. Fremer
Mike Garson
Bus driver

REGIS HOTEL, DETROIT
OCT 8th.

Ziggy touring party for the Regis Hotel Detroit. Mr & Mrs Jones were in room 418 this 'crazy guy' all decked out in those high steppin boots with heels that went from Columbus to Detroit and back!!

He began to sing Ziggy, and we fell in love!! that was 'it'; he shook, rattled 'n' rolled our souls to music oblivion, which we will never ever forget. My one friend began dancing in the aisle to 'Suffragette City', that was to be her song forever more, and when I hear it, I always think of her (she laughs to this day).

My song, of course was 'Jean Genie.' Seems all of us had our attributed songs. We came away from that concert with ears ringing and hearts pounding, as we could not wait until he returned to Columbus once again. I of course have seen him many more times, but the one in High School, 44 years ago was to be the 'finest debut'.

SANTA MONICA CIVIC AUDITORIUM

20 OCTOBER 1972 CALIFORNIA

I WAS THERE: GAIL POWELL

I saw David Bowie at the Santa Monica Civic in 1972. It was brilliant. I remember 'Width of a Circle' and Mick Ronson was so incredible. Bowie was just so commanding of the stage. I was just 17-years old, it was such a special event. I'm glad I got to be a part of one of his first concerts.

WINTERLAND AUDITORIUM

27 OCTOBER 1972 SAN FRANCISCO

I WAS THERE: BOBBY ASEA

My story starts a week before I even heard of David Bowie. Living in the San Francisco Bay Area, I was fortunate enough to go to many concerts there. Winterland was a venue that hosted many big names in the business and I went to as many shows as possible. On October 13 1972, I went to see T. Rex there. On the same bill were Poco and the Doobie Brothers.

Like many of my peers back in those days, I was experimenting with all types of drugs. That night I decided to drop a psychedelic drug called mescaline. Mescaline is known for its hallucinogenic effects comparable to those of LSD and psilocybin. I remember that during the intermission between bands, I ventured out to the lobby to mingle with other concert goers and at that point I was feeling the full effect of the drug that I had taken. As I wandered through the

Bobby and friend dress in their best Halloween costumes for the Winterland concert

lobby, I happened to notice a poster, advertising the upcoming show for the following weekend. It featured a photo of what appeared to me, as some kind of alien looking creature. It looked like something that I had never laid my eyes on before. The photo was of David Bowie and all that I could do was stare at it and wonder if I was hallucinating from the mescaline. At the time, I was totally into the glitter movement that was happening and I thought to myself, 'This guy looks very strange and very cool. I have to come back next week to see him in person.'

Excited by the thought of seeing this new performer in a few days, I spent the whole next week preparing for the show. I immediately went out and bought the album and was blown away

how great it was. *Ziggy Stardust and the Spiders from Mars*! Wow!

Since the show was falling on Halloween weekend, I made sure to come up with some kind of freaky costume. It wasn't just any concert where I could dress up in costume with a lot of makeup. I knew this was going to be a very special show. Needless to say, the whole event lived up to my wildest expectations. Although the attendance was low, it was cool being amongst people who shared the same enthusiasm for this new band and who dressed up for the occasion.

The band performed songs from the latest album such as: 'Hang On To Yourself', 'Ziggy Stardust', 'Moonage Daydream', 'Rock 'n' Roll Suicide' etc. which I had just recently become familiar with, but also songs that I had never heard that were just as good. Songs like: 'Life on Mars?', 'Space Oddity' and 'Queen Bitch'. Bowie sounded and looked wonderful and I also remember how great his band was. They played fantastic and looked like they really came from Mars.

I followed David Bowie for most of his career and went to see him in concert for his Diamond Dogs, Station to Station, Serious Moonlight and Glass Spider Tours. They were all top-notch extravaganzas, but it is the Ziggy show that is my all-time favorite.

10 December 1972
The three shows at the Tower Theater, Upper Darby, Pennsylvania closed the first leg of the 26-date North American Ziggy Stardust Tour. Bowie returned to NYC where he boarded the Royal Hellenic Mail Ship Ellinis, and sailed home to England.

Bowie wrote 'Aladdin Sane' as he sailed back to the UK.

The subject matter was inspired by a book he was reading at the time, Evelyn Waugh's *Vile Bodies* (later filmed as *Bright Young Things*, a phrase that also appears in the song's lyrics).

HARDROCK

28 & 29 DECEMBER 1972 MANCHESTER

I WAS THERE: PHIL BRENNAN

My favourite musical memory from my youth came in December 1972 when I was just fourteen years old; it was one of the most enlightening nights of my life.

I had actually turned up without a ticket at The Free Trade Hall for David Bowie's gig in April of '72, I did eventually manage to sneak in but technically I didn't see the great man as he had already left the stage after the final song, although I did see the rest of the band taking their final bow.

Having missed out again on his gigs at The Hardrock in Manchester in September I made sure I was in the queue when tickets went on sale for his gigs at the same venue in December.

The two gigs fell between Christmas and New Year and having received some money for my birthday in October, I treated myself to a ticket for both nights. I handed over the princely sum of £2.50 and quickly put my tickets in my pocket before rushing home to put them away safely in my bedroom.

Every night for the next few weeks I would take the tickets out and just stare at them whilst listening to the albums *Space Oddity*, *The Man Who Sold the World*, *Hunky Dory* and his latest creation, *The Rise and Fall of Ziggy Stardust and the Spiders from Mars*.

That Thursday night in December I arrived at The Hardrock about three hours before the doors opened. I met up with a couple of lads from school and we chatted nervously about what we were about to witness.

Eventually we were in and before we knew it Bowie was there in front of us. He strode onto the stage in a glittery jacket and tight red knee-length pants, and bright red spiky hair, yelling out something about school kids and urging 'I believe in education – educate me!' before the band burst into life with their version of The Rolling Stones classic 'Let's Spend the Night Together'.

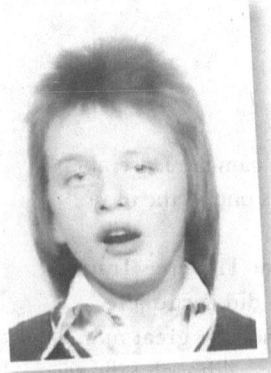

Phil was very pleased with his 'Ziggy' hair cut after a trip to the barbers

There was barely time to breathe before they stormed through 'Hang On to Yourself' and 'Ziggy Stardust'. The thing that struck me straight away was Mick Ronson's guitar playing, it was absolutely enthralling.

Bowie stalked the stage like a man who knew he had his audience in the palm of his hand, he slowed it down with 'The Supermen', 'Changes', 'Life on Mars?' and 'Five Years' before the mesmerising opening bars of 'The Width of a Circle' rang round the hall.

I had very quickly become a real fan of Bowie's album tracks, probably more so than his single releases in all honesty. I felt that there was so much more to the songs themselves and at this point in the gig I felt as if they were playing the song just for me as I sang along to every word.

Ronson had already made his mark on me but I felt that he really came into his own over the next few songs 'John, I'm Only Dancing', 'Moonage Daydream', 'The Jean Genie' and 'Suffragette City' before the band closed out with a superb version of 'Rock 'n' Roll Suicide'.

And that was it. The band left the stage, the lights came up and all I could see were a sea of people soaked in sweat, all wide eyed with excitement at what we had all just witnessed.

I listened to the chatter as we made our way to the doors. Several people were saying that they were going to return the next night to try and get tickets outside off the touts. I smiled to myself knowing that I would be here again tomorrow night to live through it all again. I had finally managed to attend a David Bowie gig and knowing that I was going to witness it all again the next night was a brilliant feeling!

EMPIRE THEATRE

6 JANUARY 1973 EDINBURGH

I WAS THERE: BRIAN BOARDMAN

During the early Seventies, a couple of pals and I used to travel through to Edinburgh for late-night gigs at the Empire Theatre (now the Festival Theatre) in Nicholson Street. At that time the theatre was used for bingo sessions during the evening and as a concert venue for late-night shows. I seem to remember that midweek concerts would start at 7:30pm, but most of the late-night gigs seemed to take place on a Saturday evening and the occasional Friday evening.

We would travel by train from Dundee to Edinburgh Waverley for concerts featuring some of the top-name bands of the day. The doors would open at 11:00pm and the concerts would usually commence at 11:30pm running into the early hours of the next day.

After the gigs we would board the London-Aberdeen overnight train at Waverley station at approximately 3:30-4:30am and arrive back in Dundee at about 5:30-6:30am. We would then normally walk home via the Tay Road Bridge to Newport-on-Tay and Wormit where we all stayed.

The supporting bands for the David Bowie gig on 6th January 1973 were Fumble and Stealer's Wheel. Tickets were priced at £1.00 each. Following this particular gig, I remember waiting at Waverley station for our train home with a group of fellow Bowie fans. They were all crowded around listening to some of the numbers, which I'd managed to capture at the concert on my cassette tape recorder for keepsake.

RADIO CITY MUSIC HALL

14 FEBRUARY 1973 NEW YORK CITY

I WAS THERE: RICK SALIERNO

I have seen David Bowie live many times. The first time was Valentine's Day 1973 at Radio City Music Hall in New York on the Ziggy Stardust Tour. The show was incredible, far beyond anything I had ever seen before. I was 18, and from then on I was totally devoted to Bowie. Among the many other times I saw him were The Diamond Dogs tour at MSG 1974, The Soul Tour at Radio City 1974, Station to Station Tour 1976, playing keyboards with Iggy Pop at the Palladium, New York City 1977, opening night of *The Elephant Man* on Broadway September 23, 1980, the warm up show for the Reality Tour at the Chance Theater in Poughkeepsie New York City 2003, as well as four other shows on the Reality Tour.

I had been hearing a lot of Bowie on WNEW FM in the early Seventies and was very into his new album, Ziggy Stardust. When I heard that he would be in New York I made sure I got tickets as soon as they went on sale. We drove in from New Jersey, and having just turned 18, it was the first time I ever drove into NYC. Seating was general admission and there was a long line when we got there, but luckily I saw a friend near the front of the line and he let us cut in. The show was amazing from the first sight of Bowie descending from the ceiling to the finale when he collapsed on stage. I left the concert in total awe at what I had just seen.

The next day I went to the record store and bought all the Bowie LPs that I didn't have. I bought all the rock magazines with articles about him and became a total fan. I somehow obtained the direct phone number for the MainMan offices in New York and called at least once a week to see if any more shows were coming up.

Rick Salierno shows off his Bowie record collection

The next one I attended in 1974 was the Diamond Dogs tour at Madison Square Garden. We had excellent seats on the floor and the show was amazing, with the giant sets and special effects. Only a few months later, Bowie re-appeared in New York at Radio City in his new persona, transitioning to his Young Americans faze. I was expecting more of the Diamond Dogs type show, but was pleasantly surprised with the new 'soul' sound.

I continued to closely follow all of Bowie's activities, and saw him next during the Station to Station tour in 1976 again at Madison Square Garden. This was the first Bowie show I took my future wife to. Again it was a very impressive show. As I was always keeping up with Bowie's appearances, I was able to get good seats for the Iggy Pop show at the Palladium in 1977, with Blondie as the opening act. Bowie was very laid back, playing keyboards in the background and leaving the singing to Iggy.

Word had started spreading that Bowie would be appearing in Broadway in *The Elephant Man*. Through my diligence; I was able to secure two tickets to the opening night at the Booth Theatre, September 23, 1980. David put on a very impressive performance and received a standing ovation.

My next Bowie concert was at the Serious Moonlight Tour in July 1976 at Madison Square Garden. My wife was pregnant with twins at the time, so I attended this show alone. I had a seat behind the stage, but was very close and had an excellent view of Bowie and the entire band, although from the back. Another great show.

A few years later I saw Bowie at Giants Stadium on the Glass Spider Tour. Another show with great special effects and Peter Frampton on guitar. The only drawback was that it was raining for part of the show.

During this time, from 1981 to about 1986 I had been publishing a newsletter called the Bowie Bulletin, which reported on all the new records, VHS tapes, concerts and all other things Bowie. This was long before the internet had this information readily available.

For a time I had lost some interest in Bowie, being busy with a family and career. I had missed the Tin Machine, Nine Inch Nails and Earthling Tours, but in 2002, I saw an article about the 5 boroughs tour of New York City, and scored tickets to the Beacon Theatre. The Bowie magic was still there and rekindled my devotion. By now the BowieNet website was the place for news about the man, with members getting certain perks. I checked the site every day and was astonished that he would be playing a small club called the Chance in Poughkeepsie, New York as a warm up show for the upcoming Reality tour. Being a member of BowieNet, I was able to get tickets and the show was very intimate and rocking. Iman was sitting in a booth right behind me. That set the stage for the Reality Tour and I attended the shows in Philadelphia, New York City and Atlantic City NJ.

After that and Bowie's heart attack scare, his appearances were few and far between. However in January 2016, his old band mates Woody Woodmansey and Tony Visconti formed a group called Holy Holy to play the entire *Man Who Sold The World* album live. My tickets were for January 8, Bowie's birthday. There was chatter about Bowie making a guest appearance, but that was not to be. Tony Visconti did call Bowie from the stage and the crowd sang Happy Birthday to the man. The next day we went to see Lazarus with Michael C Hall, 2nd row center. An excellent show great performances and all Bowie songs. We called this our Bowie weekend, and were shocked to find out the next night that Bowie had died. It was a great shock. But Bowie's music and influence in the arts will live on forever.

I WAS THERE: KANSAI YAMAMOTO, DESIGNER

There's a 13-hour time difference between Tokyo and New York, but a good friend of mine there phoned me several times in the middle of the night, saying, 'There's this very interesting person here called David Bowie, you've got to see him. Fly over now!'

If someone calls at 4am telling you to get on a plane, it must be for something pretty interesting. So I had my secretary cancel all my plans for that week, and I went to New York.

I went straight from JFK airport to the Radio City Music Hall, and was shown to the front row just as the show was about to start. I'd never seen a performance like it. Bowie came down from the ceiling, wearing my clothes. My designs have been influenced by kabuki theatre, as was his show. There's a movement used in kabuki called hikinuki, where one costume is dramatically stripped off, revealing a different outfit underneath.

At first Bowie was wearing all black, then suddenly he was in full colour. The audience was so impressed they all rose to their feet.

To me, it was the beginning of a new age. We met afterwards, and I felt we had the same energy. I've never gone for wabi-sabi – the austere elegance that people admire about Japan. I like bright colours, and I like to stand out in a crowd. So I had real empathy with Bowie. He's from the West, I'm from the East, but we had the same crazy energy in our hearts. We inspired each other, and pushed each other to another level.

When the tour came to Japan later that year, we went out for dinner with Tamasaburo, who is one of the great kabuki actors. Bowie's young son – now the film director Duncan Jones – would come and play with my family.

LONG BEACH ARENA

10 MARCH 1973 LONG BEACH, CALIFORNIA

I WAS THERE: MARILYN MORWBRACHET

Ziggy Stardust, I was 18-years old, and I dressed for the occasion in short shorts, satin halter top, sparkly stockings, and of course super high platform shoes and lots of glitter make-up. What a trip it was, with the help of a little window pane! 'Give me your hands, cause you're wonderful...' then, 'Thank you, goodnight!'

SHIBUYA KOKAIDO

20 APRIL 1973 TOKYO

I WAS THERE: LEWIS MELVIN

I saw the David Bowie and Spiders from Mars tour of Japan in 1973. It was the last show of the Japan Tour in Shibuya Kokaido, Tokyo and I was 15-years-old at the time. I remember vividly the concert was a near riot at the end! Bowie was running around the stage wearing only a red jock strap! I think the last song they played was 'Around & Around' by Chuck Berry. Then they ran off stage!

I WAS THERE: JOHN HUTCHINSON, TOUR RHYTHM GUITARIST

The final gig in Tokyo was a riot. No really, I mean it *was a riot*. In the estimation of the attended Tokyo police it was anyway.

The gig had certainly almost predictably been a triumphant end to the Japanese tour. David usually took three encores, and the very last one which was some old rock 'n' roll song most probably Chuck Berry's 'Around and Around' because it was a favourite of David's, was delayed for fifteen minutes whilst the crowd went even wilder. The kids rushed the stage before we had finished the song.

Mick Ronson yelled at me and the saxophone section 'Geoff, fucking run for it!' as he made for the exit stage-right at a gallop in his high heels. I was right behind Mick. We had no time to unplug our guitars, and amplifiers crashed over behind us on-stage as guitar leads were torn out of jack sockets. The 'wings' of the stage very luckily for us had solid hinged doors, and everyone in the band got safely behind them without any injury. But it had been a close thing. The theatre was in pandemonium, policeman

Ziggy acoustic guitarist John Hutchinson on stage with Bowie

grappled with screaming girls on the stage and in the auditorium. The road crew struggled to extricate kids, frozen by panic from the crush, and Angie Bowie who had been out front and enjoying the frenzy, was now caught up in the fracas, and was helping youngsters who had become trapped under their seats which had toppled over, row after row like dominoes.

The police were furious, and there were claims that some 'westerners' in the crowd, allegedly Angie Bowie and Tony Zanetta, had incited the near riot by swinging some chairs around the heads when they had decided that the show was a little dull and needed a boost. Tony and Angie had in fact encouraged the kids to rush to the front to make for a better finale.

The Tokyo Police complained to the RCA office in Tokyo and demanded the RCA identify and handover for questioning the people who had incited the riot. The next morning, believing that warrants had already been issued for their arrest, Angie, along with little Zowie were rushed to Tokyo airport. There they discovered that the Tokyo police were watching all departures for London and San Francisco, ready with warrants for the arrest of Angie. Improvising with commendable speed and ingenuity one of the crew bought new tickets and put the fugitives on the next flight to Honolulu.

21 April 1973
Due to his fear of flying, Bowie had decided before accepting the Japanese tour that he would return to England by land and sea across Siberia. Traveling with his

childhood friend and backup singer Geoff MacCormack, they left Japan on Saturday, April 21, sailing from the port of Yokohama aboard the SS Felix Dzerzhinsky.

This journey would take them 600 miles across sea to the Port of Nakhodka on the south easternmost coast of Russia. The voyage was a long one and Bowie was able to rest on the boat. During part of the sailing, Bowie played an impromptu set of a few songs one evening during the cabaret including 'Space Oddity' and 'Port of Amsterdam' while MacCormack played the congas.

They then took the Trans-Siberian railway from Vladivostok to Moscow, crossing seven time zones, and taking almost a week to travel. During this part of the journey, Bowie and MacCormack stayed for three days in Moscow, watching the May Day parade, checking out the GUM department store and visiting the Kremlin.

In an extract from one of Bowie's letters written during this journey he said. 'Siberia was incredibly impressive. All day long, we were travelling along the majestic forests, rivers and wide plains. I could not have imagined that there are still spaces in the world filled by such virgin wilderness.'

EARL'S COURT

12 MAY 1973 LONDON

I WAS THERE: GEOFF SMITH

I was 17 years old when I went to see Bowie at Earl's Court with my lifelong friend Seamus O'Connel. The big memory that I have is of the crowd who in the absence of modern day security measures mostly crowded in to the front of stage area irrespective of where their seat was. The show was temporarily halted to allow people to return to their seats and to try and establish order.

I remember the track 'Time' from *Aladdin Sane* as a highlight. Something about a 'grown up' singing 'falls wanking to the floor' seemed incredibly saucy to a young kid. It was the first time I'd seen David Bowie although not the last. I remember other shows at

Wembley, both indoor and outdoor and another, which I think was at Earl's Court (although I maybe wrong about the venue). This would have been around the time of the Station to Station Tour and I remember that I sat near to the Bromley punk crowd which included the Vivienne Westwood's model and scene person, Jordan.

CAIRD HALL

17 MAY 1973 DUNDEE

I WAS THERE: BRIAN MULREANY

I saw Bowie for the first time on 17th May 1973 when he played the Caird Hall, Dundee. I was almost 16 at the time. I remember lots about the day including the funeral of our parish priest Father Murphy and in the afternoon I sat my O Grade Metalwork exam. I was a big fan of the Ziggy Stardust album and I also knew 'John I'm Only Dancing' and 'Space Oddity' so this was a gig I was so looking forward to.

16 year old Scottish fan Brian Mulreany – Prince of Wales baggy trousers, red socks and platform shoes not in view

I actually remember what I wore on the evening, a horizontally striped tank top with a red shirt underneath with round collar tips, grey Prince of Wales baggy trousers, red socks and platform shoes.

When I arrived at the venue a queue had formed where I met two school pals who teased me that they had seen Bowie in a nearby pub scooping pints with Mick Ronson. I believed them at first, how gullible I was back then!

The gig blew me away; lights dimmed then the Beethoven 'Ode to Joy' intro then straight into 'Hang On to Yourself.' Forty-four years later I still remember the vivid red stage lights, the piercing strobe light and the mime Bowie did during 'The Width of a Circle.'

During 'Space Oddity' the venue sparkled with lights that resembled the stars of the universe. The encore included 'Rock 'n' Roll Suicide'. I think it was during the encore that Bowie was perched on top of a rack of speakers, which tumbled when he was atop. He almost came a cropper.

When the gig started we had been in the balcony at the back of the hall but we soon made our way down to the front of the stalls to see the action close up. I had a little camera with me and managed to get some close up photographs from the front rows.

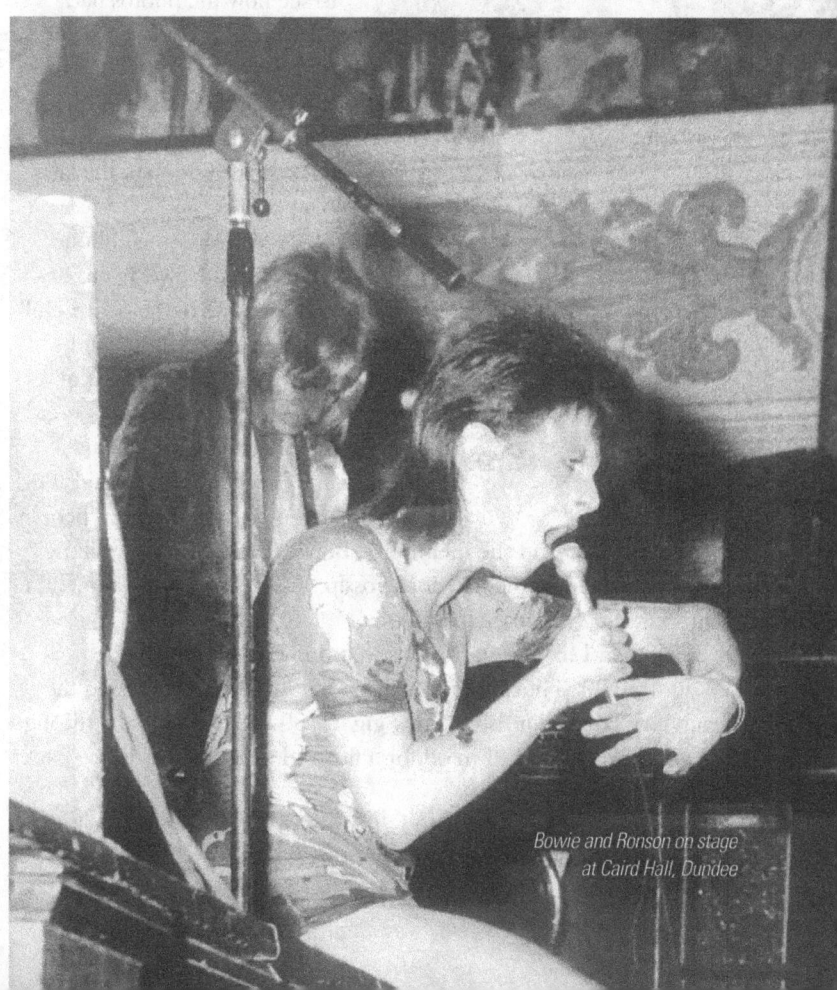

Bowie and Ronson on stage at Caird Hall, Dundee

Shortly after the gig I met a guy who lived in my street and he mentioned he had seen me at the gig. I told him I had some undeveloped photographs and I was overjoyed when he told me he was going out with a girl who worked in a photo developing lab in Dundee, and he offered to get the photographs developed for free for me. I duly handed over the roll of film. Weeks later I knocked on his door desperate to see how the photos had turned out. I could have laid him flat when he told me he was no longer going out with the girl and anyway she had packed up her job at the lab. No photographs!

William White before he was chased out of The Caird Hall, Dundee after taking Bowie's harmonica

My next-door neighbour chauffeured Bowie from the Angus Hotel to the Caird Hall and back to the hotel and a few years later a client of mine told me she had been a chambermaid in the Angus in the Seventies, and said she had met lots of famous people. I asked her who and she mentioned Bowie. I asked her to spill the beans hoping for some salacious gossip but she said, 'Oh I remember him well, such a nice, polite man'.

Since then I have seen Bowie seven times, the last being in Glasgow in 2003 during the Reality Tour and I also witnessed the legendary Barrowlands Glasgow gig in 1997 when, half way through the gig Bowie told us, 'I'm off for a fag and a cup of tea. I'll be back in ten minutes'.

My daughters are age 28 and 26 and I'm proud as punch when they play a Bowie song when we get together.

I WAS THERE: WILLIAM WHITE

So the day finally came. Bowie was in the middle of his Ziggy Stardust Tour, we were massive fans and we were shown our seats. We were four rows from the front, and with no heavy security or barriers, we were extremely close to our idols! The show was our first concert ever, and of course we were blown away, especially at the end when the crowd surged forward and we could nearly touch Mick Ronson! My other memory was of David climbing up to the top of the speaker stack to sing to the folk on the balcony and then jumping back down!

But more fun was to come. We drove round to the Angus Hotel as we knew Bowie was staying there. After pleading to get in, his then wife Angie came down to speak to us. She thanked us for coming but sadly told us David wouldn't becoming to see us.

Undeterred we returned to the Caird Hall. Entering the back doors we found ourselves able to wander around the backstage areas and artists dressing rooms, fascinated to see Bowie's make-up left there!

We were initially chased out, but amazingly returned and this time we were on the stage where the roadies were packing up. We asked if they wanted a hand and they were very friendly and let us take broken drumsticks and even the mouth organ Bowie had used during 'Jean Jeanie'. There was a pile of the iconic *Aladdin Sane* posters, and we were invited to take what we wanted!

Bizarrely I always remember there being a big basket of fruit on the stage. I don't think any of us took any. I'm not sure healthy eating had reached our part of Scotland in the Seventies! Sadly I no longer have any of the 'souvenirs' we acquired that night, but maybe some of my former school pals do.

I have of course remained a huge fan, and was lucky enough to see him perform several times since, and I even dragged my wife to see his apartment building when we were in New York in 2014.

I WAS THERE: IAN DOBSON

The concert was on the back of the release of the *Aladdin Sane* album and covered the Ziggy Stardust numbers as well. I wasn't a Bowie fan as such as, in my opinion, he was a bit glam at the time but nevertheless I went along. The audience was largely made up of young ladies screaming and waving Bowie 'football scarves' which were being sold outside the venue for a quid. Seeing the audience I had more of a sense of attending an Osmonds show rather than a serious rock concert and had low expectations of what was to come.

The concert turned out to be one of the highlights of my music spectating life, absolutely awesome. I've no particular amusing or interesting story to tell which might be of interest, but my memory of the show is still clear and stands out as one of the best I've ever been to. The main things I remember were Bowie's presence and command of the stage, his showmanship as he undertook six costume changes during the show, and the raw power of the Spiders pumping out the backing. Mick Ronson was some guitar player and he and Bowie really camped it up on stage. Great music and great performance.

I'm not sure if the concert was what the young scarf waving ladies expected but it was certainly a million miles from The Osmonds show I feared might take place. True rock 'n' roll royalty.

I WAS THERE: BRIAN BOARDMAN

I saw David Bowie perform live on three occasions. The first time was at the Rainbow Theatre, London, 30th August 1972. The second time was a late night gig (11.00pm) at the Empire Theatre (now the Festival Theatre), Edinburgh, 6th January 1973 and the third time was at the Caird Hall, Dundee, 17th May 1973.

I attended the gig with a friend of mine, the late David Fenton, and afterwards we went along to the Angus Hotel where Bowie and his Spiders from Mars band were staying overnight. Staff allowed us into the foyer to meet him and let me take a photograph, which I still have to this day. I remember distinctly

Bowie was chatting with keyboard player Mike Garson, when a staff member unlocked the door to let us in. I recall walking over to him, as he turned towards me. He was wearing bright blue dungarees in total contrast to his sparkling red hair. I introduced myself and asked if I could take a photo. He obliged and was most polite. Next day, we travelled down to London to see Pink Floyd at Earl's Court Arena on Friday 18th May, and then attended the England versus Scotland home international football match at Wembley Stadium on Saturday 19th May, a match England won 1-0. However, we didn't allow that to spoil what was a terrific weekend!

GREEN'S PLAYHOUSE

18 MAY 1973 GLASGOW

I WAS THERE: BOAB BELL

I saw him at Green's Playhouse in Glasgow. He climbed up the speakers while singing 'Ziggy' and tripped on the mic wire on the way down. Bowie never fell, he just stumbled, but I got to shake his hand first before he went back down.

I WAS THERE: MARIE FOWLER

I saw him at Green's Playhouse Glasgow and I'm sure it was 1973, when I was 14 or 15. I queued for hours for my ticket and just before the concert my mum threw it out accidentally. I persuaded the girl next door for 50p to help me go through the rubbish bin. We managed to find it and it was all tea bag stains and bean juice stains. I remember standing on the backs of the seats at the concert and coming home feeling like I was walking on air.

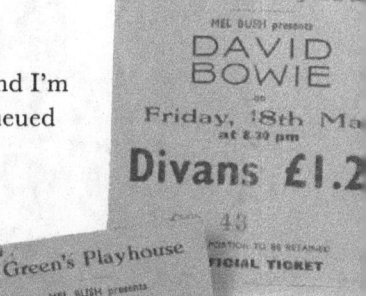

KING GEORGE'S HALL

31 MAY 1973 BLACKBURN

I WAS THERE: JIM WILKINSON

I was on the drabbest caravan site imaginable somewhere on Lancashire's Fylde Coast. No one in my family can even remember where it was. I was 14 years old, a tubby little schoolboy stuck in the middle of a mundane family holiday in the middle of nowhere.

But the night that followed that endless day changed my life.

It was May 31, 1973 and the biggest sensation in pop since The Beatles was about to be beamed down into my hometown. David Bowie and The Spiders from Mars brought the Aladdin Sane Tour to the stage of King George's Hall in previously grey, depressing, drab, dismal, monochrome cotton town Blackburn. It actually might have been quite a bright, sunny day to be honest.

It was my first live gig and in another four decades there would

Jim Wilkinson and his girlfriend Christine Wilson who went to the Stafford 78 concert

never be another to send my head into a whirl and my insides feeling like they were revolving around my body at Formula 1 speed for two hours. If you had been allowed those years of hindsight, you would have chosen that band, that frontman, that time to see rock'n'roll for the very first time.

Let's set the scene. Ours wasn't a particularly hip household. We had a record player – one of those suitcase Dansettes on legs – and by the end of my third year at school I had a collection of singles and a handful of albums. But Bolan and The Jackson 5 had to vie with Jack Jones and Helen Reddy for turntable time.

I'd been to a couple of those end-of-pier shows and perhaps the biggest names I'd seen to that point in terms of chart action were Dana and Frank Ifield. Even at 12 and 13 you knew that wasn't where it was at.

One of those same summers I'd sat in the TV lounge of a bed and breakfast in Scarborough and seen Marc Bolan on *Top of the Pops* have a strange, unspoken effect on a bunch of slightly older holidaying teenage girls, that I didn't quite understand. I knew it was a direction you'd probably like to go in but hadn't a clue how to set off, never mind arrive there. It certainly wasn't any reaction a middle-aged guy singing 'I Remember You' in a suit provoked.

But the only time I'd ever sat in the stalls at King George's Hall before that night was at tedious, interminable school speech nights, a mandatory but utterly dreaded annual event.

I was only allowed to go to the Bowie gig because an adult was taking me. Fortunately it wasn't my dad, who might have been utterly outraged by the spectacle. His workmate John, it had emerged, was a huge fan, which at least lent my pre-occupation with Ziggy some adult-endorsed credibility. I had bought the Ziggy album after an unexpected windfall. After seeing the Bolan effect and placing a personal ad in 'Disco Songwords' or some such publication, stating 'Boy, 13, into T. Rex, wants girl penfriend', I received about 400 replies. With almost more bags of letters from pre-pubescent females than the beleaguered postman could carry, I launched the one entrepreneurial success of my life and sold them for 2p a time at school.

The *Rise and Fall of Ziggy Stardust and The Spiders from Mars* cost me £2.18 from Reidy's in Blackburn. I still have it with the sticker on somewhere. But dad came home one night with some sage advice: 'John at work reckons you should get an LP called *Hunky Dory*. Says it's even better.' My letter-selling profits allowed for that and that Christmas of '72 I got the *Space Oddity* and *Man Who Sold The World* re-issues, and by the time *Aladdin Sane* came out in April of 1973 – delivered to my house by an RCA rep at tea-time on release day in a van, after insufficient copies were available to satisfy pre-orders – I was in a frenzy over the fact that Bowie was playing not one but two Lancashire dates.

John had bought his wife and myself tickets for both shows and consented to take me, to allay any parental fears that I would be whisked away from the venue by a make-up wearing gay cult who sang lyrics like 'I've got eyes in my backside that see electric tomatoes' ('Go on then, what on earth does that mean?' I was regularly quizzed) never to return. He was a cool guy, John. Maybe about 30 then, beautiful wife, great house, posh car and the most fabulous huge stereo system I'd ever seen in the huge modernised cottage I waited in, having been transported from Knott End or wherever, to be taken to the show. I wish I could remember the journey there and the crowd but the next thing I can remember is sitting in the front row balcony waiting for the lights to go out.

They eventually did and Beethoven's 'Ode To Joy' as distorted through *A Clockwork Orange* (which of course I hadn't seen or read) played... Here's the best thing. There was no support act that night. No hammy pub-rock band in jeans and T-shirts cranking out blues licks or Chuck Berry licks. No Fumble or Stealers Wheel or any such. As the hall darkened and 'Ode' came to mad climax, strobe lights – something else I'd never seen – flashed and momentarily illuminated figures walked across the stage with great coloured Ziggy/Aladdin flashes briefly visible then invisible on the backdrop behind.

Two of the first three guys I saw walk on that stage, Mick Ronson and Trevor Bolder, are no longer with us, but along with Woody Woodmansey there could have been no more striking, futuristic prelude to the drama to come as a maelstrom of spangly tights, stack heels, hair spikey or platinum and enormous Dickensian sideburns flashed in and out of vision in a blur of white light and bacofoil costumes.

Ducks Deluxe sauntering on an hour and a half before the main act just wouldn't have been the same.

A nano-second of silence and darkness and then...

'Bam-bam-ba-ba-ba-ba-ba-ba-ba-ba-ba-Bam-Bam....' Ronno thrashed the intro to 'Hang On to Yourself' out on his Les Paul, all billowy blouse and black sparkly matador pants and your eyes turned to centre stage where Bowie stood in a Japanese costume practically impossible to move in, bright orange barnet and pale face, arms extended...

'Well she's a tongue-twisting storm...'

Of course, what I can actually recollect is mixed up with what I've seen many times from the Hammersmith film by Don Pennebaker, which was basically the same show.

But what I can remember is the gulping, gasping slack-jawed feeling of awe to be in the moment, the presence, the time. A pair of girls – future Mrs Ronson and Bowie hairstyle creator Suzi Fussey one of them – came out in black cat type costumes and pulled from either side to reveal that the ensemble was velcroed together down the front and suddenly Bowie was posed there in a silky white tunic with matching thigh-length boots. It was often said that hitherto macho/straight builders fancied him and though not many would have admitted it in 1972 East Lancashire at that juncture, it's still possible to imagine why.

'Ziggy Stardust' was freed from his Yansai Kamamoto wardrobe restrictions and free to gyrate as he wished in a series of numbers which even today in display cases at the V and A museum people are paying good money to gaze in wonder at. By the fourth number, 'Wild Eyed Boy from Freecloud' (segued into 'All The Young Dudes' and 'Oh! You Pretty Things'), I had got my breath back and recall the astonished wonderment of seeing these songs I knew so well played by the people who created them in the same bloody room I was sat in!

The mirror ball shimmering as David strummed the 12-string intro to 'Space Oddity'... I hadn't noticed that at school prize night....the strobey guitar fight with Ronno in 'Width Of a Circle'... the mimed 'gap in the wall' routine... myriad costume changes while Mick played his solo... Garson's insane jazz stylings... 'Suffragette City' practically blowing the roof off... the closing 'Gimme your hands' set-piece of 'Rock 'n' Roll Suicide'. Incredible. Simply incredible to see that at 14, before you saw any other live band in the whole wide world.

(I was quite lucky – the first support band I ever had to 'sit through' later that year in the same hall was a London-based quartet who had been hired to warm up for Mott The Hoople. You may have heard of Queen and their singer Freddie Mercury. They had obviously had about twice as much spent on presenting their act as the headliners!)

Watching that Hammersmith DVD there was nothing particularly ground-breaking or avant-garde about the music Bowie and The Spiders were presenting live. Some of the subtler, stranger, quiter, deeper moments from *Hunky*, *Ziggy* and *Aladdin* were absent (there was no 'Starman', 'Life on Mars?', 'Drive-In Saturday' that night, and certainly no 'Quicksand' or 'Bewlay Brothers').

But Bowie was taking the tired, beery, jeans-and-beards-and-T-shirts lumpen, leaden version of 1970's rock'n'roll – itself as an art form less than 20 years old – and filtering it through a dazzling prism of glamour and edginess and sex and androgyny into the town halls and public concert venues of suburban Britain, to present a spectacle more exotic and out there than had previously been hinted at down the two decades since Elvis shook the hips.

The night before the Blackburn gig and the night of it the Bowie entourage stayed at the Charnock Richard Motor Lodge. Imagine that! There would be sales executives such as my dad was or 70's 'Life on Mars?' style bobbies like my wife's father sat there as this carnival of the weird trooped in and out for a couple of days!

About ten days later at Preston Guildhall, where the stage as some of you may know is barely elevated above the audience, Bowie halted a stomping 'Jean Genie' and unleashed the passions and madness of the fired-up, frenzied youth by insisting that some roughhouse security fellas, brutally over-zealously chucking fans off the stage, retreat from its environs before continuing.

The ensuing 'Let's Spend The Night Together' almost threw the building into utter chaos and anarchy – three more years, mark, until the concept was fashionable – before the pace slowed down a little.

I used to be able to reel off the set lists, which were slightly different – from both shows. But I've been to many, many gigs since. Epic gigs, historic ones, bands at the very height of their power and glory.

I've been to a good few wonderful Bowie gigs since...Stafford Bingley Hall, Milton Keynes Bowl, Roker Park, Maine Road.

But it was never, ever, again, like that first time. And for even someone as anal-retentive as I, small details fade.

A few weeks later Bowie made his fabled, 'this is the last show we'll ever do' speech on the Hammersmith stage.

I remember reading about it in the *NME* waiting for a bus outside Blackburn Mecca just a couple of hundred yards from King George's. Bowie had 'retired' it said.

Life was over. Retired? It couldn't be, could it? What was there to live for? (Bear in mind I hadn't even had a girlfriend at that stage I don't think). Of course my life had barely begun. Bowie's ascent as an artist had only just done so. But I'm so grateful that our paths collided briefly that day, that month.

This is the bit where I'd like to say life was never the same because I decided that being in a band was the only thing for it, went out and formed one and...you know the rest goes, Ian McCulloch, Marc Almond, Gary Numan all that lot.

Not me. I flunked a few O levels because I no longer cared about getting my homework done if there was an album to listen to, or a lyric sheet to pore over. After that concert it was music first, football second and anything else we'll take it from there.

I became the Lancastrian equivalent of what was once brilliantly described as the archetypal *NME* reader, 'The accounts clerk in Middlesbrough who considers himself a bit hipper than his workmates.'

John, who took me to those two gigs, he was a real hero to me too. Rugby captain at Blackburn. Great big bear of a man. Mr Oozed Success. He was probably what I wanted to be, what I could realistically aspire to I guess, without any discernible gifts for the arts, even more so than Bowie. He and Sue took me to Stafford in 1978, with a girl of my own then too.

Last time I saw him we were both walking down to Ewood Park for football. He was with his two lads. 'I feel it's my civic duty,' he smiled. I knew what he meant. He was right about *Hunky Dory* too.

I think a lot about him whenever I remember that night, the kindness of the guy allowing that little boy to be there, waiting to see his idol, get his first shot of live rock'n'roll.

Trevor, Ronno, John... I guess many of the people who were there that night aren't here any more.

Those who are, well, we're different people now aren't we? Time isn't kind to many of us but still being here is enough to be thankful for.

But experience like that, it can't have a value put on it.

FREE TRADE HALL

7 JUNE 1973 MANCHESTER

I WAS THERE: CHRIS COLLINS

I saw David Bowie at the Free Trade Hall in '73 (£1.35 a ticket – teatime show!) Great show. I remember the rush for the front when he told the bouncers to stand down, 'If I wanted security, I'd have brought my own', but also remember people queuing up along the end of the balcony to try and jump on the stage and one of the roadies bashing them on the legs with a broom handle to get them to climb back!

EMPIRE THEATRE

10 JUNE 1973 LIVERPOOL

I WAS THERE: KARL PARSONS

I can't remember the day but it was hot, although the weather and the show were the last thing on my mind as my train pulled into Liverpool.

First up I had to navigate my way out of Lime Street Station from the hoards of 'Scotty Road' skinheads, all of whom enjoyed nothing better than beating the living daylights out of anyone looking vaguely 'weird'. Oh the joys of being a fan of David Bowie in the early years. How did I survive?

My mum stumped up the money for the ticket, much to my dad's annoyance. His observations of Marc Bolan and Ziggy Stardust need to remain confined to history, especially when *Top of the Pops* featured either/or. Maybe he wasn't that anti narcissistic after all, as I recently was caught slagging off Kanye West, much to the dismay of my daughter!

Anyway, back to the show. My ticket was for the matinee event. It was all the rage in those days. Me, in collaboration with hundreds of other likeminded kids, all of who were very inexperienced gig goers like myself, waited patiently for something to happen.

As the lights go down...

Hysteria breaks out, in unison with the opening chords of 'Hang On to Yourself', delivered by someone who I was not overly aware of, but turned out to be the one and only Mick Ronson. As it happens I recently met his daughter in a recording studio and bored her with this same story, so you're not on your own!

My overriding thoughts were how loud the sound was, with Bowie smashing out the high notes, and how much flaming colour there was literally everywhere.

I've always been into fashion, but boy the clothing and costumes were simply from a different planet. I studied the clothing in detail, just as I lost myself in the emotion of the music mix and lighting energy.

I can't remember a set list. It didn't occur to me at the time to do so. But I do remember 'Width of a Circle' which remains today one of my most favoured tunes – notably because as Bowie broke into the first verse our eyes met and fixed. Ever since that moment, every time the song is within earshot I'm taken back to my seat of 1973.

My only other recollection, and I may be wrong here, but I think the band played a Stones cover. Then it dawned on me, as the crowd began to chant for encores I had soon to run the gauntlet to the train station and back home.

I survived to tell the tale.

I WAS THERE: KATE RIGBY

I grew up listening to the charts. I remember 'Space Oddity' in the charts in 1969 when I was ten. Bowie's songs were becoming big hits for other people: 'Oh! You Pretty Things' for Peter Noone, and 'All The Young Dudes' for Mott The Hoople, which he wrote to save their ailing career – still one of my favourite ever songs. But it wasn't until Bowie appeared on *Top of the Pops* in 1972, playing 'Starman' that something turned on inside me. I didn't realize then that others would report, years later, that this appearance had been life-changing for them too. But to me, as a not-quite-thirteen-year-old, Bowie made a lasting impression, with his spiky hair and androgyny; his unworldly eyes – each a different colour. And the song was wonderful.

I became a big fan. When my family moved back to the outskirts of Liverpool later that year, my sister Ann and I developed our character-inventions. 'Our people' we called them, though we started out acting real characters, like David Bowie and Alice Cooper – another of our heroes – before inventing our own.

I remember seeing my brother ready to go out somewhere, one night, with my oldest sister, and I asked him where he was going. He said he was going to see David Bowie. I was so jealous. I wanted to go too! Nowadays we can check it all online and I see that the date was in 1972, September 4th at the Top Rank, Liverpool. I had to wait until the following summer in 1973 to see David Bowie at the Liverpool Empire. My first ever concert.

In September 1972 I went to a new school and met new friends. One of my friends, Sharon, was a Marc Bolan fan, but also a fan of Bowie. She knew things. Like the date he was coming to the Liverpool Empire, and sometime that spring we took the bus into town to buy tickets. I remember us sitting upstairs on the bus, excited with anticipation, and we bought three tickets, one each for us and one for my sister Ann.

That concert was on June 10th 1973. I didn't need to check on the internet because it's indelibly written on my mind as is the fact that he did two performances, though when I checked the internet it was of course confirmed. I just wish there was some footage somewhere. Maybe some will be unearthed some day. We had no cameras in those days, well few did, not like today's kids with their iPhones, ready to document every note, every chord, every flaunt and swagger. We went to the later performance on that date and could hear his first

Kate Rigby and her sister Ann dance in the garden while waiting for their Ziggy concert clothes to dry

performance from outside. To think he was just on the other side of those bricks, that side entrance.

There were denim-clad and dyed-hair kids buzzing with anticipation. It was just over a week to my fourteenth birthday. I didn't have a great selection of clothes, I wore an orange T-shirt, one discarded by my oldest sister, maroon loons, and love beads – all the rage then. They cost about 10 pence but they broke during the concert. Some scattered off the thread and I threw the rest of them at Bowie. We were so near the front we were crushed against the bar of the pit. We didn't care. We don't at that age. I was so mesmerised by Bowie, I reached a trance-like state as he delighted us with his songs and his change of outfits, all ostentatious and outrageous and camp.

At one point, when he was singing 'Starman', the bit where it goes 'I had to phone someone so I picked on you-oo-oo', as he did the 'you-oo-oo' he pointed to three different people at the front. One of them was me! Was I the second one he pointed to? Maybe if we could play these things back we would find it wasn't as we thought.

It is all a blur now but at the time, I knew I was a hundred per cent certain I was one of those he pointed at and 'had to phone'. For Bowie it was just another concert, just part of what he did, night after night, but for me? I don't remember whether that was before or after my resolve, but somewhere in that concert I decided it wasn't enough just to watch him. I had to be up there with him – just for one second, so that he would know of me, that I existed, and it would be just me and David, for that one second.

But something went wrong. I jostled in an effort to carry out this resolve. Ann must have moved too. Sharon last seen trying to make her way across one of the bars in the pit and being thwarted by a bouncer. I think I wanted to head to the stage door, hopeless and naive and the star struck teen that I was.

But we were jammed packed like sardines, and there were some horrid opportunistic young boys – well, we assumed they were young, all the people at the front were adolescents – who from behind jabbed their fingers down our pants (mine and Ann's), taking advantage of our enforced restriction. We couldn't even bat them off because there was no room to swing an arm. God how they jabbed. It was excruciating. But we couldn't even see their arms, let alone their faces. We'd not come for this, but this was the Seventies for you. I guess we'd already invaded each other's space so the vile boys thought they could trespass some more. I'm sure we tried to move but they moved with us in the scrum and, if we had been able to turn, a scuffle would have ensued and we'd have lost our place. I didn't feel my body violated so much as my enjoyment. How dare they? What were they doing there if they just wanted to finger girls? But I don't want to dwell on that, except to say that by the end of the evening my bra was torn and Ann's handbag was stolen along with her make-up. Or it may have been her handbag was emptied of its contents. The whole place was a wreck. The seats were all ripped up and Ann was most upset about her handbag.

Sharon gave Ann a bit of her make-up on the bus home and earlier a kind bloke helped Ann look for her bag or its missing contents and gave her his programme of the concert as a sort of consolation, which we still have somewhere. We come across it from time to time when moving house or searching the boxes in the cupboard. I wish I could locate it easily along with one or two other things, like that picture I did of Bowie all in dots.

But through the years I have been determined not to let those scumbags ruin my memory of what was an otherwise magical experience.

I bought the Ziggy Stardust album not long after the concert. It was my first album, and as with any firsts, you always remember and treasure it. I played it to death. I got my hair cut that autumn and somebody told me I looked like David Bowie with it short, where previously it had been straggling to my shoulders, thick like a mop.

I went on to buy *Hunky Dory* and *The Man Who Sold the World*, which enjoyed a revival, as did *Space Oddity*, which Ann bought. She also bought *Aladdin Sane*. They were our favourites. Ann picked up *The World of David Bowie*, one of his earliest recordings where he was likened to Anthony Newley, for a few pence. It is probably worth a few bob now. The hits kept coming. After 'Starman', there was 'The

Jean Genie', 'Drive-In Saturday', 'Life on Mars?', 'Sorrow'. In 1974, when David had already moved on from his Ziggy era, I had a Bowie cut, or an attempted one. It didn't quite work as his did but I have a few passport mementoes from that time. I confess to being quite obsessed with Bowie.

In our shoplifting phase, I think it was my friend Ann who nicked a book called *The David Bowie Story* from a Liverpool store. It wasn't expensive but we didn't have much money and we read it from cover to cover, devoured the pictures and the details about his background. Another memento lost over the years to mildew or a charity shop or even the cupboard!

At the beginning of 1975 we watched *Cracked Actor*, a documentary about his life so far. I was very interested in masks and personas and mental illness then. He said something about, 'I'm glad I'm me now', like he felt Ziggy was taking over and he no longer knew where he ended and Bowie began. That's why he killed him off. I wrote something about having a new understanding about why he'd done that, because now I was all of 15, and so I was starting to get it, why he needed to change, evolve, kill off Ziggy. I started to get why he didn't want to be stuck, typecast, stereotyped! It made sense to me all of a sudden. He'd done something very clever, quit while at his height. Only a few people can pull it off. But he did it not only for his sanity. But because he was ready for the next challenge.

I liked *Young Amercians*. I liked the funkiness of 'Fame'. I wasn't so keen on the stuff he was doing in the mid and late Seventies but I admired him for it. People have always said he was a master of reinvention; it's become a cliché, but it's true. I went to see *The Man Who Fell To Earth* at the pictures and later watched *Elephant Man* on TV as well as other plays featuring David.

For years I have included many of my characters in my writing. Nowadays everyone unashamedly acts out characters in everyday life – people adopt personas on social media all the time!

After the Ziggy era Ann and I got into the next big exciting thing in music – punk, new wave, the colour and theatre of the New Romantics. Would these have happened if it weren't for Bowie? So much that we now take for granted can be traced back to him and his innovation. He was at the cutting edge with his gender fluidity and his appetite for change.

I saw him again in 1987 with my friend Jacky as part of the Glass Spider Tour. He played at Wembley Stadium on June 19th that year, the day after my 28th birthday. I was in bed the day before with a stinking cold. The cold was still heavy on the 19th but I wanted to go so we travelled by train from Bournemouth. Jacky bought me a brandy or something. It will be in my 1987 diary. We went to an art gallery first but I just sat in a daze. The evening came and Big Country were on first in the pouring rain. Then Bowie came on. Wembley Stadium is a far cry from Liverpool Empire. We only had a distant view of the stage, so they had screens up, only our screen wasn't working. So we missed all the theatrics, except for the odd couple of minutes we caught of Bowie courtesy of the people in front who lent us their binoculars once or twice.

DE MONTFORT HALL

11 JUNE 1973 LEICESTER

I WAS THERE: BRUCE PEGG

I think my mum stood in line at the de Mont box office to get the David Bowie tickets, as I would have been in school when they went on sale. I remember they sold out immediately, and I couldn't believe my luck that I was actually going to see one of my idols.

Ever the showman, Bowie knew how to wind up an audience before he even set foot on stage. There was no warm-up act, and the 8 o'clock

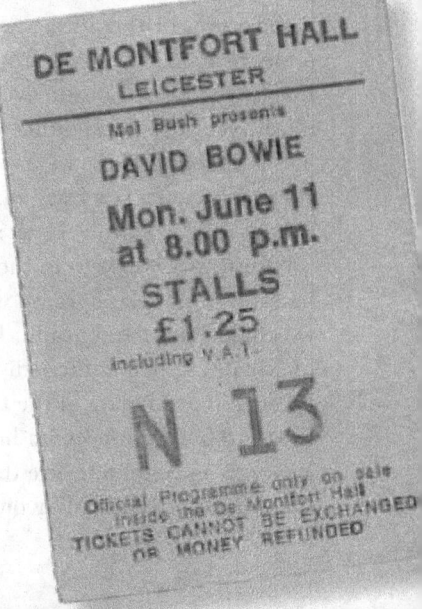

start time came and went. By 8:15, the crowd was getting very restless, and by 8:30 you could positively feel the tension. I was with my friend Mal West, sitting in the stalls somewhere under the balcony, when the houselights finally went off; the band broke into 'Hang On to Yourself' and a mad charge for the stage took place. The chairs in the stalls, that had been in orderly rows just seconds before went flying, and people just started scrambling for the best vantage points.

Instinctively, Mal and I ran down the centre aisle and got to about row G or so when the crush of people got so thick we couldn't move any further forward. All the chairs in front of us had been destroyed or kicked to the side of the hall by then, but we found a couple that were still intact and stood on them for the entire show. We figured that no jobsworth would come anywhere near us and tell us to sit down after that little melee.

To the best of my recollection, that was the last time the de Mont put seats in the stalls during the Seventies for anything they deemed to be a rock concert.

What followed was close to two hours of rock and roll perfection. The costume changes, the mime routines, the sheer power of the music—everything deliberately calculated to overwhelm the senses. Toward the end, during 'Jean Genie,' Bowie and Mick Ronson even simulated sex on stage, and though my 13-year-old mind didn't know exactly what was going on, I had a pretty good idea.

I was gobsmacked by it all. It was just about the coolest bloody thing I ever saw or ever will see again.

Afterwards, we went to the backstage door. There were only a handful of people there, so we stuck around for a while to see if we could get an autograph. But all we got was a fleeting glimpse of Mr Bowie being hurriedly escorted into a waiting Rolls-Royce. I remember thinking at the time that it wouldn't have killed him to spend five minutes with his fans. But this was at the height of Ziggy mania, so I am sure that there were plenty of crazies out there that he wanted to avoid.

I WAS THERE: JULIE AYRES

I was 15 years old when my friends and I went to see David Bowie in his Ziggy Stardust Tour. After the concert we dashed to the Holiday Inn, Leicester where David was staying. I jumped into the lift and went up to the floor David was on and he was in the corridor. He walked past me and I said, 'Hello David!' He just turned and smiled at me as he walked past. I will never forget that sideward look and smile. He was a beautiful man and I could hardly believe I was so close to him. Mick Ronson was not so far behind him and he spoke to me. He asked me if I enjoyed the concert and I told him yes I did. I was such a young girl and so excited. Then a bouncer guy quietly told me it was time for me to go and I left on a cloud!

CITY HALL

14 JUNE 1973 SALISBURY

I WAS THERE: ROBIN MAYHEW, SOUND ENGINEER

We were using a brand new radio microphone, which David was delighted with. During the show, David jumped off part of the PA stack and twisted his ankle, so he was unable to do much moving about on stage. All we could find was a small school kids chair for him to sit on and rest his ankle. He made an announcement that his performance would be less active and he came off stage and walked slowly right through the audience to the back and joined me by the mixing desk and using the radio microphone sang the rest of the show from there. After the show David turned to me and said, 'We sound pretty good, don't we?'

TOWN HALL

21 JUNE 1973 BIRMINGHAM

I WAS THERE: CARRIE WHITE

Aged 17 and at college, I went to see David Bowie at the

Birmingham Town Hall in 1973. Bowie played twice that day, and I attended the evening show. Standout songs were 'Jean Genie' and 'Space Oddity', complete with lights dimmed and a mirror ball shining over the whole arena. Costume changes a plenty and a near sell out. I remember Bowie wasn't in a very good mood that night and threw the microphone stand across the stage at one point!

P.S. I met and 'kissed' his wife Angie a few years later, plus at a huge rave in 1997 (Tribal Gathering, Luton, England), he stood in front of us shaking hands with fans while we watched Orbital.

TOP RANK SUITE

27 JUNE 1973 DONCASTER

I WAS THERE: REX DAVIES

Maybe it was during 'Hang On to Yourself' or possibly 'Moonage Daydream', but me and Clive are right up the front, dead centre, smacking our hands on the stage in time to the music. Mick Ronson, resplendent in gold lame jumpsuit, is strutting around in his platforms as Bowie, barefoot in his asymmetric unitard, consummate showman that he is, connects with the crowd jammed all the way to the back of the Top Rank on the evening of 27th June 1973.

Clive is the skinhead boyfriend of Delphine, elder sister of my sixth-form school-pal Cynth. Arriving at the back of the room earlier he has expressed disappointment at the restricted views and, whilst the girls take to the balcony, Clive has ploughed through the crowd with me following in his wake until we could not get any closer.

Ronno's strut turns to a stomp and his foot narrowly misses my outstretched fingers. I wave my hand disapprovingly at him and catching my eye he misunderstands and concludes I'd like to join in the fun, dropping to a crouch and thrusting his guitar at me. I manage one strum, bare-fingered, before arms shoot round and over my head as everyone else tries to do the same.

Rex Davies (center) with Jim Collins and Paul Heaven discuss how it felt for Rex to strum Mick Ronson's guitar

I don't remember how we got back, what else happened that night or indeed much else from that whole period. At the time Bowie was just the latest in a long line of thrills we were obliged to try and fill our days with. I think it was Wishbone Ash at Sheffield City Hall the following week. Only rock and roll, but we liked it. Over the years of course, it's become a good story to tell. Obscure but not especially impressive. Detailed in one respect but a bit vague in others. For real Bowie freaks only. Sole Love?

HAMMERSMITH ODEON

2 JULY 1973 LONDON

I WAS THERE: PAUL BRADLEY

The show that I remember the most clearly was my very first one in July 1973 when I was 14 years old. I lived on an estate just to the rear of what was then the Hammersmith Odeon, and from my group of friends at the time, three of us used to listen to LPs in each others' bedrooms. Ziggy Stardust was foremost amongst these so when it was announced that Bowie would be playing the Odeon we decided that we would get tickets. This was my first ever concert and several weeks saving pocket money ensued. These were the days before personal computers, mobile phones, Ticketmaster and Seatwave, etc. The way then to obtain tickets was to queue up at the box office.

I remember that tickets went on sale on a chilly, gloomy Saturday, several weeks before the concert date and we decided to meet up at 9.00am. By the time we got to the back gate of our estate on Queen Caroline Street the queue already stretched back to it, but quickly extended up the street much further towards the river. It was the most interesting group of people I had ever seen all in one place. There was a smattering of ordinary looking kids like us but the majority, both boys and girls, were clearly Ziggy inspired in the way they dressed and were getting lots of attention from passers by.

We queued for a couple of hours and someone was giving out orange posters that had the words to Don McLean's 'American Pie' written on them. The song was in the charts at that time. Oddly the poster had little cartoon drawings of Ziggy in the margins. I could never work out the connection.

When we finally arrived at the box office it was possible to chat to the staff to negotiate exactly what seats you wanted. We were told that four shows were planned, two matinees and two evening shows. Luckily we did not buy any matinee tickets as these were later cancelled. Purely due to how close we could get to the front, we ended up buying tickets for the 2 July, which turned out to be the night before the Ziggy retirement show. We got seats about a third of the way back from the front, in the centre of the stalls.

When the big day arrived I remember coming home from school and it was very hot and sunny. My walk home from the bus stop in Fulham Palace Road took me past the rear of the Odeon and I could hear the sound check going on. It was the distinctive bass line of 'Aladdin Sane' that I remember most clearly.

There was a really palpable sense of excitement outside the Odeon as we approached on the evening. A BBC film crew was doing interviews and loads of older kids had really dressed up for the occasion. I remember when we got inside there was a long delay before the show started and then there was a kind of false start as Mike Garson came on and ran through piano versions of some Bowie songs. It was relatively calm at that point and I noticed the film cameras positioned at the front of the stage with their little monitors glowing. I was totally unprepared for what happened next.

It all seemed to happen in a blur as Bowie was loudly announced, the lights went out and the *Clockwork Orange* version of 'Beethoven's Ninth' blared from the PA. Simultaneously, everyone rushed to the front and within seconds there was a mound of bodies climbing on seats and on each other at the front of the stalls circling the stage. Luckily I was a pretty tall 14-year old, so I had a reasonably good view. Two things have remained with me from the start of the show, as it was my first ever concert. The roar of the band ripping into 'Hang On to Yourself' was the first thing. The second was the image of Ziggy, arms out wide at shoulder height, having his silver cloak ripped in two down the centre by two girls who rushed on from the wings.

From there on, it is all impressionistic fragments of memory for me. Bowie dropping from one knee to the other then standing back up in time with the line from 'Watch That Man', 'When the reverend alabaster danced on his knee'. The thousands of reflected lights from a mirrorball suddenly blazing in increased intensity as 'Space Oddity' reached its first crescendo after the spoken countdown following the lyric, 'May god's love be with you'.

The glass wall mime during 'Width Of a Circle' and the extended guitar duel between Mick Ronson and Trevor Bolder, seemingly conducted in stop motion under the strobe lights. The whole audience punching the air and shouting the word, 'Buddy' as Bowie sang it in the chorus of 'Drive-In Saturday'. The startling costume change before Bowie sang 'Time' and the dramatic pause where all that could be heard was his breathing in the middle of the song.

The change of pace as Bowie was picked out by a spotlight at the front of the stage filled the auditorium with his voice and 12 string on 'My Death'. The sea of hands reaching out as he sang, 'Gimme Your Hands' at the end of 'Rock 'n' Roll Suicide'. Then it was all over and we filed out of the theatre.

There were vendors on the street with Ziggy posters spread out on the pavement. I bought a couple on the short walk home.

The next evening I listened from my open bedroom window as the final Ziggy show went on. It was another warm evening and the vents at the side of the Odeon were open so I could hear the show and even the screams and shouts of the audience.

On my way home from school the following day, after the Ziggy circus had left town, I took a detour off the Fulham Palace Road and down an alleyway by the Duke Of Cornwall Pub. I often took this alternative route home. It led round the back of the Odeon and is not accessible to the public now. Back then it was always open and as I walked through I saw lying there a pile of the stage props from the show, the banners with lightning flashes and the little music stands used by the brass section of the band, all similarly adorned with the lightning flashes and just dumped there. I will always regret not taking a few items as souvenirs. I suppose at 14 you always think there will be other opportunities.

All in all, though, that is the only tiny regret from what was otherwise a once in a lifetime opportunity gratefully taken and still the greatest concert that I have ever seen.

HAMMERSMITH ODEON

3 JULY 1973 LONDON

I WAS THERE: KAREN ROCHE

I saw him at the Hammersmith Odeon, London – the concert at which he announced that Ziggy Stardust was finished. I still have my ticket with his then wife's autograph on the back.

I WAS THERE: DAVID CRONIN

Let's begin by saying that I had been a David Bowie fan since the Sixties. In fact the first album of his (that I still own I might add), is *David Bowie* on the Deram label, so by 1973 I was well into David and his music. The 3rd July 1973 was my 17th birthday and at the time I was a sailor in the Royal Navy, and the ship I was serving on was docked in Portsmouth, England. My friend who I went to school with named Peter Tape was also a huge Bowie fan, so we decided to get tickets for the gig, even though it was on a Tuesday night and I didn't know where I would be at the time. When the day arrived, the ship was still alongside so I traveled up to London to see the show.

Outside the Hammersmith Odeon the atmosphere was electric, with many people dressed in 'David' style. My mate Peter had long hair in the style of Mick Ronson, whereas I had a military length style, although I did have jeans and a satin jacket on!

When that first chord

boomed out from the stage the crowd went wild by the time those immortal words 'Ziggy played guitar' filled the room he had everybody mesmerized. Then I remember him coming to the front of the stage to play 'My Death', a track I had not heard before. Little did we know how poignant those lyrics were to be. Then it was back to the magic and diversity of his set list, the brilliant cover of the Stones' 'Let's Spend The Night Together' followed by a blistering couple of tracks with Jeff Beck, including the fantastic 'Jean Genie'. What happened next nobody expected, not even the band if my memory serves me correctly.

Just before the final song, 'Rock 'n' Roll Suicide', he said something like, 'We will remember this show not just because it's the end of the tour but it's the last show we will ever do!' The audience fell into a stunned silence for a moment with people crying and shouted out things like 'no, David, no,' then the haunting words of 'Rock 'n' Roll Suicide' filled the whole place. Outside the crowd seemed numbed by the whole experience. Whether it was the sheer brilliance of the show or the bombshell news, I think you would have to ask each individual, and of course it wasn't his last performance, just the last in the guise of Ziggy.

As for me and Peter, he made his way back home to the east end of London and I went to Waterloo to catch my train back to Portsmouth. Waylaid by a couple of beers, I missed the last train out and had to catch the first one out the next morning. I knew I would be late getting back but thought I would be able to swing it with my chief (petty officer) as it was my birthday.

Walking through the dockyard heading for the jetty that my ship was tied up alongside, I looked up to see a space where this great big grey hulk should have been. Now in somewhat of a slight panic I went to the regulating office (navy police) only to be informed the ship had sailed at 0700 hours that morning and I was now under arrest for being AWOL. It was ascertained that my ship was heading for Rosyth in Scotland and they decided to put me on a train to meet it there, which I did.

A few days later I was in front of the Captain for punishment. 'What was my excuse for missing the ship?' I was asked. 'Well, Sir, it was my birthday and I went up to London to see a few friends and have a couple of beers when right at the end of the night we found out that a very close friend had died and that we would never see him again'.

Whilst he could understand my grief the Captain said nevertheless I had been absent without leave whilst a serving member of the Royal Navy and gave me a punishment of three days loss of pay.

Three days loss of leave! Worth every penny of every minute! Thank you David for the memories. RIP.

I WAS THERE: GRAHAM RICHARDS YEATES

I was at the Hammersmith Odeon final Ziggy concert on July 3rd 1973. I was near the back as the friend I was with was afraid the crowd would spoil his hair! Jonathan was the friend's name. He was the campest man I've ever known. We both moved to London from South Wales in 1972, as being gay in South Wales then was torturous. Jonathan's hair was his obsession. I can see him now panicking and holding his hair as people were crowding in! At least he dragged me along to the Hammersmith Odeon that night. I'm eternally grateful to him.

After seeing Ziggy I came out and returned to South Wales with a lime green Ziggy haircut and a rebellious pride in being gay. Watching the film recently, brought so many memories back of being young and gay in Earl's Court in the early Seventies. I'm proud to have been one of the London Boys.

I WAS THERE: PETER HINCE, ROAD CREW

I was young, just about 18 and the rookie of the crew. I don't have one particular memory of working with David back then, but it was great fun, a huge adventure. It was an exciting, ground-breaking era. I remember seeing velcro for the first time, which David would use on his stage costume. The wardrobe girls would come on stage in the blackout, one on either side, and pull at his costume, which was

Ziggy tour crew Peter Hince and Mark Fussey pose after fitting all that gear in the back of the van for the 179th time

Velcroed together, to reveal something extravagant he was wearing underneath. It was very slick and professional.

I also remember how hard we worked. The Ziggy Tour, was 180 shows or something, with very few days off and with the matinee shows we were doing two shows a day, then pack up, move on and do the same the next day. There was no crew catering, someone would go out to get food. There was no McDonalds back then, so we had a Wimpy burger, or bacon sandwiches. We were all young and fit, and just got on with it!

David was not particularly withdrawn, but quite measured. He never screamed or shouted, or had tantrums. He respected the band, and the crew, but it was his project – he was always very much his own man.

After he 'retired' at Hammersmith, David was recording *Diamond Dogs* in Olympic Studios. I was there in case anything was needed, and he wanted a tambourine, so I was sent out to get one. Instead of playing the tambourine with his hand, David was banging it on the front of an acoustic guitar to get a different type of sound. On the Ziggy tour he used a Mellotron on stage. It was like an early synthesiser, which worked with tapes. He always wanted to push the boundaries.

Mick Ronson was such a nice guy, and as a musician just phenomenal. When things went wrong, he understood and there were never any issues, he was a pleasure to work for. Woody and Trevor were more restrained kind of guys; a solid rhythm unit. I know The Spiders weren't very comfortable at first with wearing eye-make-up and all that went with the glam-rock look. They were three regular guys from up north in Hull!

I WAS THERE: ROBIN MAYHEW

My last Ziggy concert working as the soundman was the Hammersmith Odeon gig when David broke up the band. Mick Ronson and Peter Hunsley were the only ones who knew it was going to happen. Peter told me that David was going to 'break up the band' over the intercom just before the last show began.

1974

Puerto Rican-American guitarist Carlos Alomar worked with David Bowie from the mid-1970s to the early 2000s, having played on more Bowie albums than any other musician (other than pianist Mike Garson). During a six-week break from his tour in mid-1974, Bowie recorded a series of songs for a new album in Sigma Sound Studios with Alomar. Most of the material for the *Young Americans* album was recorded during these sessions, and Alomar joined Bowie for the second leg of the Diamond Dogs tour

I WAS THERE: CARLOS ALOMAR

I met David while we were doing tracks for Lulu at RCA Studios. Everybody thinks I met David when we started doing the *Young Americans* album, but it was really when he came to America to work with Lulu that I met him.

He was her producer and I was a contracted session musician. But we connected on a personal level, because he was really thin, and I said, 'Man, you need to eat!' I thought, 'He's a Brit. He's away from home. Why don't I just invite him to the house, and we'll sit down and have a meal?'

We started talking and he was very curious about my group The Main Ingredient, my work with James Brown, and all the R&B acts I'd played with. In those conversations I realized the Brits had studied American soul music and American jazz. This guy knew his black people, more than most Americans, as regrettable as that might be. And I really found him so interesting. I didn't know anything about the Spiders from Mars or any of that stuff.

I could tell when we first met that David had ideas about where he wanted to go with his music. But he didn't say anything at first. Then I got a phone call asking if I could do some work on this album, which later I found out was *Diamond Dogs*. But I was making $800 a week with my group The Main Ingredient and they were nowhere near that money. I was 22 and newly married, so I couldn't give up a sure thing for the money they were talking about. So I went back to tour with The Main Ingredient.

Time went on, and the next time David was in town we got

together and really had a good time. We went to the theater. And I took him to the Apollo Theater to see Richard Pryor. Then, later on, I get another phone call. 'Carlos, I'm going to be in Philadelphia. I got some of the guys from TSOP.' He was so excited about tackling this whole sound and the soulfulness and everything he'd been talking about that he really wanted to do. I could hear it in his voice, because we had talked about it a lot. I knew it was one of those life dreams he wanted to fulfill. I told him, 'I want to do this, but you're going to have to take care of the money.' He said he'd take care of everything. And don't you know? Boom, done deal! So I was contracted, went out to do the Philly stuff, and that ended up being *Young Americans*.

When I got to Philadelphia, I called my wife Robin, who's an amazing singer, and said, 'Come see me in Philadelphia'. She asked if she could bring Luther Vandross, because we were all really tight. I said, 'Of course!' Luther showed up to the session and, as always, Robin and Luther were just having a good time, ad-libbing a few things here and there. They couldn't help themselves. That's all we did. All we did was harmonize, all the time.

As singers, what else are you supposed to do? We were trained at the Apollo Theater. We knew how to take advantage of every opportunity. You never know when an opportunity will come up – that's what I always tell young musicians – and sure enough David said, 'That's great. I want you guys to do all the background vocals.' That's why all of those background vocals on *Young Americans* had Luther's thumbprints all over them.

I've heard people say that David just took my band and sang over us. But you cannot negate the fact that when it came to the vocals, he was above the background. Yes, like any good rhythm section or background vocals, we did our job just fine, but nobody was really listening to the band. Everybody was listening to the lead vocal. And this man was a crooner. This man was a singer. This man was stepping up to plate with all the soul singers that were there, and he wasn't backing down. So nobody was paying attention to anybody else. In hindsight, even if we were good, we were supposed to be good!

1974 – Diamond Dogs Tour

The Diamond Dogs North America tour was to promote the studio album *Diamond Dogs*. The end of the tour was also called *The Soul Tour*, which included some songs from the forthcoming album *Young Americans*.

The set for the theatrical Diamond Dogs Tour was designed by Mark Ravitz, who would go on to design set for Bowie's 1987 Glass Spider Tour. The set was built to resemble a city (called 'Hunger City'), weighed over six tons and included a variety of props (such as streetlamps, chairs and catwalks).

Bowie recalled the difficulties faced by the show, saying; 'It was good fun and dangerous, with the equipment breaking down and the bridges falling apart on stage. I kept getting stuck out over the audience's heads, on the hydraulic cherry picker, after the finish of 'Space Oddity'.

The show in Tampa, Florida, was performed without any of the stage props because the truck driver driving those components ended up in a highway ditch after being stung by a bee.

Bowie arrived in NYC on the SS France on 11 April, travelling as a first-class passenger. Towards the end of the journey, Bowie heard some of the crew were disappointed that he hadn't performed during the sailing, so he turned up in the canteen with an acoustic guitar where he played 10 songs including 'Space Oddity'. A few crew members took instruments and jammed along with him.

ROCHESTER COMMUNITY WAR MEMORIAL

17 JUNE 1974 ROCHESTER, NEW YORK

I WAS THERE: JOE POLIFRONI

The first time was I believe 1974 in Rochester, NY, Diamond Dogs Tour. Amazing, almost every song had a Broadway production feel. It was like watching *MTV* videos live, but there was no *MTV* yet.

I am originally from Syracuse, NY but was living in Jacksonville, Florida. I had gone home for a visit and heard that David Bowie was

playing Rochester. I called a cousin and off we went on the 90 mile excursion to Rochester.

I already had some Bowie albums at the time (*Hunky Dory,* Ziggy Stardust, *Space Oddity* and *Diamond Dogs*) but my cousin had just recently heard of him. Neither of us knew what to expect from a David Bowie concert. We had assumed it would be a rock concert like most concerts we had been to. It was nothing like any rock concert we had been to! I was 22 and been going to concerts regularly since my first at 13 in 1965 with the Rolling Stones in Syracuse. I had to beg and plead with my parents to let me go. It is still special because it was my first and was five guys on stage playing their asses off, but that's it (useless trivia, the following year after the concert, the Stones were detained by Syracuse police because Brian Jones was accused of dragging the American flag across the floor).

The first thing I noticed after we grabbed our seats was the band being way off to the side of the stage. Almost hidden really. Another unexpected thing were male dancers. It was 1974 after all.

The stage set was a city skyline and all much like NYC or Boston. When he started to sing 'Space Oddity' you saw nothing but the set and heard nothing but David singing 'Major Tom to ground control.' Doors and panels eventually opened on the city set and David Bowie was sitting in a customized cherry picker singing/talking into what looked like the old Princess phone (which was a microphone). He was floating in a most peculiar way over the audience for a good part of the song. Maybe all of it, I can't remember. At one point a boxing ring appeared with two dancers dressed like boxers in the ring. This was for the song 'Panic in Detroit'. Unfortunately the rest of the show is not so vivid. I seem remember a glass room or something he sang 'Big Boy' in. For the song 'Time' I think he was sitting on a giant hand or palm of a hand.

MUNICIPAL AUDITORIUM

29 JUNE 1974 NASHVILLE, TENNESSEE

I WAS THERE: MARK YURT

The first tour as the Thin White Duke. It was the *Diamond Dogs* Tour. David Sanborn on sax. Earl Slick on guitar. It was the tour that his *David Live* album was made from, (recorded just over a week later during six nights at the Tower Theater in Upper Darby, Pennsylvania). It was a fantastic show. I bought the live album as soon as it was released four months later.

TOWER THEATRE

8-13 JULY 1974 UPPER DARBY, PHILADELPHIA

I WAS THERE: MARIBETH DEPAULIS

I remember it like it was yesterday. I was 14 years old in 1974 when he came to the Tower Theatre, in Philadelphia for seven shows in one week and we saw six of them. My friends and I had all bought at least one ticket for one of the shows but were able to sneak in to the theatre for the others. We even got a chance to sneak in to watch him and the band practice. Seeing him rehearse was awesome. I think that's what did it for me. He came out in his Jeff hat and jeans and just seemed so friendly, he was joking around with the guys (that was for the Ziggy show), and then that night he came out as Ziggy, which was the first time I ever saw someone like that but it wasn't intimidating - it was memorising.

We lived in the neighborhood and the theatre used to show movies, so we knew how to get in. There was a back door and we would wade in knee high trash in a corridor to get to a loft that had a huge fan in it. We thought we were being very clever hiding in the loft, where we would wait and then go down to the floor. There is no way no-one ever saw us up there, but no-one ever told on us. It was great – it changed my interest in music forever and I've been a big Bowie fan ever since then. One of my friends even got a kiss from David and a feather from his boa while he was on stage. We were all extremely jealous of her.

If I had to pick one song that stuck out it was 'Rock 'n' Roll Suicide'. We knew the show was ending and we would run down to the stage. He would reach out to everyone and it felt like he was reaching out to you. Also, when they would come out and rip off his clothes about the third or fourth song into the show. And then the next show he would open with 'Space Oddity' and come out over the stage in a chair.

We were able to see several shows that weekend and got to go down to the stage and look into his eyes. I know this sounds crazy but it always felt like he was looking back and smiling. Before and after every show we would wait outside for him to arrive and leave and he would always wave and smile at us. I have seen him every time he was in Philadelphia and always manage to get to the stage and that same friendly face always smiled back. I am a huge Bowie fan, but not just for his music but the person he seemed to be. The more I read about him, it was the person he was.

MADISON SQUARE GARDEN

19 JULY 1974 NEW YORK CITY

I WAS THERE: RALPH CATANIA

It was his first show ever at the Garden and the final two shows of the first part of the tour. I was 15 years old and had already been to six rock shows. In 1973 Slade was my first show ever, followed by Mountain, Deep Purple, Ten Years After, Mott The Hoople and The Who. Now I was going to see David Bowie!

By this time I was already a huge fan. I had the new album *Diamond Dogs* along with *Pin-Ups*, *Aladdin Sane*, *Ziggy Stardust* and *Hunky Dory*. I could sing each and every song from those albums word for word just walking down the street, no music needed.

Four of us were going that night and we had seats in the 108 section, row 15, a nice view at MSG. We all lived in Lodi, New Jersey and took the bus into Manhattan as we had done before - not a long trip.

The show was amazing. I remember it opened with '1984'. My personal highlights were 'All the Young Dudes' as I was a HUGE Mott The Hoople fan and Bowie gave that tune to them to get them back on track, Along with 'Rock 'n Roll With Me' and 'Space Oddity' in which he hovered over the first few rows in a huge cherry picker crane. 'Diamond Dogs', 'The Jean Genie' - it was just an amazing night. Still one of the best shows I've been to.

UNIVERSAL AMPHITHEATRE

2-8 SEPTEMBER 1974 LOS ANGELES

I WAS THERE: ANNIE ESPINOZA

I was 23 years old and it was the Diamond Dogs tour at the Universal Amphitheatre at Universal Studios. We had seats on the floor and he was so awesome. I was with my two best friends and we were all dressed up. When the encores started we made our way down to the edge of the stage – wow, he was beautiful. My friend got so excited she threw her mink stole up on the stage and some other girl grabbed it and she never saw it again.

23 year-old Ralph Catania who saw The Diamond Dogs tour in Los Angeles

We heard he was supposed to show up at Rodney Bingenheimer's English pub on Melrose in Hollywood, so we headed over there. No such luck. He didn't show but we had a blast talking with a famous male groupie named Chuckie Star. I saw the same tour not long after that in Anaheim. We also went to the Station to Station tour at the Forum in Los Angeles and the last time I saw him was the Serious Moonlight Tour at the Forum. I miss him.

INDIANA CONVENTION CENTER

8 OCTOBER 1974 INDIANAPOLIS

I WAS THERE: DEBORAH McCORKLE

The vibe at the venue was close to 'anything goes'. Although I was too young to be experimenting with marijuana, drugs or alcohol, they were present in spades. This was before purses were checked by security and there were no body searches at the ticket entrances yet. Ticket takers smiled and said "enjoy the show", back then. They looked at your ticket (you got to keep) and welcomed you to the show. Once inside they left you alone unless violence erupted... which didn't happen in this crowd.

Though we were far from New York, this was a long awaited concert where Mid-Western kids could rise above and really enjoy themselves. Remember this was a time in history where segregation was still an issue. Very uptight socially, in small cities like Indianapolis. Bussing was going on at local high schools.

The Diamond Dogs tour was like bringing a wish or a dream to many young people. It was an opportunity to get away from many oppressing social, home or school behaviors and be free for a few hours. You saw races mix, sexes mix openly. Many fans sported exotic androgynous style in clothing, attitude, and communication. There was a lot of love and indiscreet sexual innuendo in full view. The local culture here was small town. We had no black people living in the suburbs or certain parts of the city. One Asian family was the extent of the diversity that year in my small town. But the concert... wow!

Every race in an entourage following the Diamond Dogs tour came to our venue. There was a guy the size of a football player in the front row, a gorgeous and extremely handsome black man milling about. He was dressed with a flamboyant pink boa. I was smitten.

The Convention Center was festival seating. People all excitedly mixed and mingled in an excited and close fresh new feeling. It was a sensation.

I experienced heavy flirting from both sexes and actually had my first open physical encounter with the same sex here. I was shocked by the open advances initially. Don't get me wrong it wasn't a Green Door (Las Vegas) scene... just heavy flirting, and light 'clothed' petting.. but orgy vibe style. Compliments flew and comments on appearance were popular. The whole crowd was into a party atmosphere. Like we were at a David Bowie theater as actors really.

The environment though concrete was warmed by the happy souls.

Part 1 – the music. When David finally took the stage...the stage was just a large wooden platform to lift David two or three feet above the crowd. He did include 'Young Americans' in the set, which was a magical moment for the Indy show. I think he opened with 'Changes'.

MICHIGAN PALACE THEATER

15-20 OCTOBER 1974 MICHIGAN

I WAS THERE: GARY DILLIOTT

A friend and I saw David Bowie on October 16 1974 at Michigan Palace in Detroit, a 4,000-seat theatre. I had just turned 16. I'd have to call it my first 'big' concert. We had premium tickets that cost $10. Cheap seats were $7. I was already a huge fan. The first thing I was struck by upon entering the theatre was the Ziggy Stardust and Aladdin Sane costumes, some really serious efforts here. That of course was just the beginning. We sat in the second or third row on the balcony, pretty close to centre, so the view and the sound were really great. Bowie played a great selection of songs. We were feeling pretty good thanks to a few of the people sitting around us. It felt like the entire audience was in perfect sync with the band.

How we got the tickets and got there was unusual. We lived over an hour from the box office and across the US border; we were 15 at the time and couldn't drive. I called information and got them to give me the mailing address of the box office and wrote them a letter requesting two premium tickets and included a money order. I wasn't even sure they would send us the tickets doing it this way but it was our only chance to get there. Brilliant, right! Except once we got the tickets I realized I should have gotten three or four tickets so that we could bribe someone into driving us. Fortunately, a few days before the show my friend's parents asked us if we had a ride yet and offered to drive us to the show and they would pick us up later. It all worked out and it's a great memory.

THE SPECTRUM

18 NOVEMBER 1974 PHILADELPHIA

I WAS THERE: KRISTA PURSELL WALTERS

I was 14 and it was my first concert. It was magical! But as great as the concert was, the fact that we all snuck out and slept out for tickets for the show was just as great. We met so many wonderful people and all night long we talked Bowie, listened to Bowie and sang Bowie. (And never got caught sneaking out). That was it – I was hooked. After that I was lucky enough to see him live 20 more times and once on Broadway in *The Elephant Man*. And the love affair lives on.

1976 The David Bowie Isolar Tour was in support of the album *Station to Station* and opened on 2 February 1976 at the Pacific Coliseum, Vancouver, and continued through North America and Europe. The tour is commonly referred to as Thin White Duke Tour, The Station to Station Tour, and The White Light Tour.

The performances began with a projected sequence of surrealist images, depicting a razor blade cutting into an eyeball, from the 1928 film *Un Chien Andalou*, by Luis Buñuel and Salvador Dalí. The visual element of the performances incorporated banks of fluorescent white light set against black backdrops creating a stark spectacle on a stage largely devoid of props or other visual distractions.

SEATTLE CENTER COLISEUM

3 FEBRUARY 1976 WASHINGTON

I WAS THERE: JEROME EVANSON

We were both 25 years old at the time of the Young Americans tour, (the first official date with my then girlfriend now wife). We drove about 5 hours round trip from Bellingham to Seattle Washington. As a big John Lennon fan, the two songs that stood out for me were 'Across the Universe' and 'Fame'. The latter included supporting vocals from John on the album. For the *Let's Dance* tour we traveled approximately three hours round trip from Seattle to Tacoma, Washington for the Tacoma Dome concert.

Favourite songs: 'Let's Dance' ('Under the moonlight, the serious moonlight..' - classic lyric) and 'Without You'. The colours of the stage production were brilliant. As was the giant glass spider being lowered to the stage during the performance. Great fun.

ARIZONA VETERANS MEMORIAL COLISEUM

15 FEBRUARY 1976 PHOENIX

I WAS THERE: DAN MARLEY

The one and only time I saw David Bowie was on 15 February 1976 at the Phoenix Veterans Memorial Coliseum for the Isolar Tour. It was the second concert I ever went to, and I wish I had a better memory of it. I do remember the opening act was the Dali/Bunuel film, *Un Chien Andalou*. And I wish I still had my programme that was a newspaper.

McNICHOLS SPORTS ARENA

17 FEBRUARY 1976 DENVER, COLORADO

I WAS THERE: HARLEY GRIFFITH LOFTON III

I was a senior in college in South Central Nebraska. I had been a follower of Bowie for several years and a friend and I jumped in his car and drove 360 miles (about five hours) to Denver the morning of the concert. We got there and picked up our tickets.

Unlike most concerts I went to at that time, I decided I wanted to be cold stone sober for the event. I knew that this tour and show was different from other shows that he had staged before, and I had read nothing about other performances on the tour and was totally unprepared for what would take place.

On entry into the arena the stage was placed at dead center of the auditorium. Equipment standing on stage, there was no scenery and no props. Clearly this was a departure from what I had seen of his shows before in magazines and film clips.

The albums *Young Americans* and *Station to Station* were going in a new direction and fans were curious where he would go next. The stage and auditorium went black. A screen came down and the silent, black and white film by Bunuel/Dali *Un Chien Andalou* began to play.

In the darkness as the film played the musicians took the stage... the slow methodical beat and cacophony of sound that begins 'Station to Station' began to pulse relentlessly like a coke driven kind of bolero building and building. The lighting all white above, in the back and in the front pulsed like lightning in waves visually crashing and at times almost blinding. And as the song built to its crescendo spotlights zoomed in on Bowie as he intoned, 'The return of the thin white duke/Throwing darts in lovers eyes...' and we were swept off for the rest of the ride.

At this distance in time it is really hard to recall many details, but I remember especially the rendition of The Velvet Underground's 'I'm Waiting for the Man' and 'Panic in Detroit' which was extended musically and so much more powerful than the studio version. There was an encore and I believe the show ended with 'The Jean Genie', and this part may have been only in my mind. But I believe this is what I saw.

On the last chord at the end of the song the lights behind and above the stage flashed like a blinding explosion, and the auditorium lights went up. As our eyes adjusted the stage was empty as if Bowie and the band had just disappeared into thin air. There were no more bows and it was finished. I followed the herd to the nearest exit and I wandered the streets of Denver in a daze for the rest of the night. Feeling like I had reached a peak experience. I would have the same feeling after seeing Dylan in 1978, Lou Reed's awesome Street Hassle tour, also in 1978, and Patti Smith in 1979.

I had always wanted to see Bowie again but the opportunity just never came. But I did get to see him once, and for me that is all that matters.

MECCA ARENA

20 FEBRUARY 1976 MILWAUKEE

I WAS THERE: PATRICIA COOKIE DOMINGUEZ

I had just turned 17 and was sitting in the eighth row. It was a different concert than anything I had seen before as the opening act was the scene from the 1928 surrealist movie *Un Chien Andalou* wrapping up with a razor blade slicing into an eyeball. The screen went up and the band started with the wails of 'Station to Station', talk about dramatic! Bowie didn't appear on stage until the song began. The return of the Thin White Duke, throwing darts in lovers' eyes, thin he was, black vest, pants, white shirt, hair slicked back looking like a 1920's silent screen star. Jaw dropping gorgeous. That show was the first of my many Bowie shows, and in some ways the best.

WINGS STADIUM

21 FEBRUARY 1976 KALAMAZOO, MICHIGAN

I WAS THERE: KATE MACDONALD

I had met one of my life long friends by playing David Bowie the day I moved into the dorms. I was in my third year of college at a small alternative college, part of a cluster of colleges, in Allendale, outside Grand Rapids, Michigan, when Bowie was touring close enough to see him. I believe I was the only active Bowie fan of the crowd I went with – there were boas involved and glam and men in make up. Not by me, but that was fine.

Kalamazoo, home of Western Michigan University, was about an hour's drive south. It was a large crowd. All of us were poor so we had nose bleed seats, way up and to the right where the acoustics were

Kate Mcdonald

not the best. We didn't have a very good view of the stage being so far off to the side. The concert started with the Dali/eyeball film, which horrified me. My friends were disappointed because it wasn't Ziggy or Aladdin Sane and were rather distracted.

I was just fascinated by how the crowd was responding to Bowie. He would step forward and the crowd would surge, move his arm and they would ripple. I contemplated that level of power for most of the concert: it pissed me off, fans as sheep. But when I realized that was what Ziggy was about and that he didn't want to relate that way anymore, even if he couldn't help that power, I just fell in love again.

The ride home was me listening to my friends complain. They didn't know the music and they didn't like the show. I came home and bought *Station to Station* and then *Young Americans*. I got different friends. It was profound.

RIVERFRONT COLISEUM

23 FEBRUARY 1976 CINCINNATI

I WAS THERE: MICHAEL GROUSE

I saw Ziggy at the Hollywood Palladium in 1973. I Saw the Diamond Dogs Tour in Dayton, Ohio and the Thin White Duke Tour in Cincinnati, Ohio front row and my friend caught a Gitane cigarette that he used as a prop on stage without lighting it. And I saw the Reality Tour in Indianapolis, Indiana. I Wish I could have seen more, he was always spectacular.

MONTREAL FORUM

25 FEBRUARY 1976 MONTREAL, CANADA

I WAS THERE: SANDI TAYLOR

I saw Bowie on February 25, 1976 at the Montreal Forum. It was the tour to support *Station to Station*. It Opened with the surreal black and white movie. We had excellent seats and it was awesome concert.

Helene Thian and her boyfriend Greg who took them to meet Bowie at Del Lago's

MID-SOUTH COLISEUM

6 MARCH 1976 MEMPHIS, TENNESSEE

I WAS THERE: HELENE MARIE THIAN

I always knew that I wanted to focus on David Bowie's style and become a fashion historian. It all began in New Orleans, Louisiana, my hometown, from where I drove as a teenager for nine hours all the way to Memphis (Bowie-authored, Mott The Hoople song reference intended) to see him in concert for the Isolar Tour in 1976.

Two years later, in 1978, I met David when I was 19. I was an undergraduate at university. My then-boyfriend asked me to go to a concert with him, but I had no idea that he had reserved special seats for us to see Bowie as he worked for a major rock concert promoter. After the show in Baton Rouge and on the way home to New Orleans, he told me to stop the car at a bar and disco called Del Lago's. We went in, and David and his band were all sitting there with no one else in the bar! My boyfriend had arranged the private gathering. We ended up dancing, talking and drinking all night. Bowie then said in the wee hours that he knew I had a Mercedes parked outside (how he knew, I didn't ask!), and asked if I could give him a lift back to his hotel. It was just Bowie, his bodyguard, my boyfriend and I in my burgundy Benz. Unforgettable, to say the least.

OMNI COLISEUM

8 MARCH 1976 ATLANTA

I WAS THERE: CLOYD MOLL

I was doing afternoon drive, at the time on WQXI-FM in Atlanta, Georgia in the mid-Seventies. I was 21 years old. The RCA records rep invited me to the show. I declined saying I wouldn't be interested in a weird sexual type show. He told me it's not that at all so I went to the show. Much to my surprise Mr Bowie was sitting on a bar stool wearing a thousand dollar lawyer's suit with the greatest band on the planet behind him. I was totally amazed. It didn't take long to realize this Bowie guy is a genius. It was a great night that I will never forget: RIP: David Bowie.

CIVIC ARENA

11 MARCH 1976 PITTSBURGH

I WAS THERE: BILL PARKISON

I was thirteen years old and had a very progressive mother who took me to see David Bowie in 1976; it was the Station to Station Tour.

The year before, David Bowie performed the entire 1984 floorshow on the *Midnight Special*. We couldn't tell if he was a guy or girl. We were hooked. Our first album purchased was *Pin-Ups*, then *Ziggy*, *Diamond Dogs* and *Station to Station*.

The concert opened with a bizarre Andy Warhol film and then out came Bowie as the Thin White Duke, black pants, vest and white shirt. The concert was straight forward; not artsy at all. Three interesting points; during 'Fame', Bowie counted the stage lights during the speed reduction sequence of the repeated 'Fame-Fame-Fame', and his drummer had an interesting strobe light sequence during the solo. So the faster the beat the more regular the lights would respond until they looked like static stage lighting. Pretty cool stuff to a 13-year old boy.

David was handed flowers, with which he walked to the other side of the stage and tossed into the crowd. He should have kept them!

Bowie received another gift, a VERY nice painting of himself in the cover photo for the *Young Americans* album. The artist took a bit of creative license on style and it worked. Bowie was very impressed with it and set it aside on stage.

At the concert's end, Bowie returned to the stage alone and applauded the audience. It was a 100% class act. At no time did he ever play the 'rock star'. It was a great first concert.

Side note: 1976 was a time when every concert hall smelled of marijuana. Everyone around us tried passing a joint over to us. Mom wasn't up for that, so the people around us would just blow the smoke around and between us. Needless to say mom was stoned, slap happy, giggly and craving French fries! A mini road trip to McDonalds was 'a must'. A great concert and Mom out performed Bowie. Just don't let her know I said that.

David Bowie: the embodiment of artist.

NORFOLK SCOPE
12 MARCH 1976 NORFOLK, VIRGINIA
I WAS THERE: MIKE DEE

I was very excited to be able to see Bowie in concert. I was 22 years old and traveled from Langley Air Force Base to the Richmond and Norfolk Virginia concerts. I discovered him a year prior to that. He played many songs from *Ziggy Stardust* and *Diamond Dogs* and *Station to Station*. What a band! I've never seen so many transvestites! Everyone got along and they played for three hours! I was up all night... I partied until dawn. What an experience!

CAPITAL CENTRE
13 MARCH 1976 LANDOVER, MARYLAND
I WAS THERE: KATHY INGRAM

I think I was 17 and it was my first experience of dropping acid when I saw him at the Capital Center in Maryland around 1976.

He was dressed in a black and white 1940s type of suit, with one spotlight, which was especially unusual for those times, which made it even trippier! In those days concerts were usually full of wild colors, flashing lights and exotic costumes, so it was actually quite trippy to see this contrast!

SPRINGFIELD CIVIC CENTER

21 MARCH 1976 SPRINGFIELD, MA

I WAS THERE: LAURIN HEMINGWAY

I saw David live at the Springfield Civic Center in Springfield hours after his arrest in Rochester, New York, (Bowie, Iggy Pop and two friends were arrested at the Americana Rochester Hotel on marijuana charges). If I was like most fans, we expected a far different experience and although he arrived late, his arrival did not disappoint. David did not miss a beat and enthralled me during 'Station to Station', a far cry from the Ziggy persona that had become familiar. That was the essence of him. He always surprised and challenged constructs. A true artist in my opinion!

NEW HAVEN COLISEUM

22 MARCH 1976 NEW HAVEN, CONNECTICUT

I WAS THERE: BARBARA CARPENTER

I saw David for the first time on March 22, 1976 at the New Haven Coliseum in New Haven, Connecticut. I was 15 years old and it was my first rock concert. I had been a Bowie fan for four years at that point. 'Fan' was an understatement – Bowie was my obsession.

I was nervous and excited at the same time because my friends and I weren't seated together and I was going to be sitting amongst strangers. I remember Kraftwerk's 'Radioactivity' playing as I made my way to my seat on the floor. There was a lot of smoke and an odor I had never smelled before… pot! Alcohol was being passed around. It was an eye opener for sure for a 15-year old shy, nerdy kid who didn't even smoke cigarettes. And then, finally, the lights went out and a screen came down and *Un Chien Andalou* was shown.

I remember sitting on the edge of my seat with such anticipation. I just couldn't wait for Bowie to walk out onto that stage... my dream of seeing Bowie live was finally coming true. Though time has dimmed my memory of the actual show, what I remember most was the feeling of anticipation, sheer joy and excitement, the wonder of it all, the experience. I've seen Bowie many, many times over the years and it was always thrilling. But that first Bowie concert, my first rock concert, was something very, very special.

MADISON SQUARE GARDEN

26 MARCH 1976 NEW YORK

I WAS THERE: STEVE MYRA

I've seen Bowie six times (if I remember correctly), the first being at Madison Square Garden, Station to Station tour. I was never more excited for a show leading up to that...seeing Bowie LIVE !!!

Several friends took the train in from Jersey. I remember the excitement outside the garden, still some people dressing in Ziggy garb. Awesome. Watching that French movie (the name escapes me), where they slit an eyeball with a razor (good clean fun), and then...the train !!! The opening to 'Station to Station'. Unbelievable, the band chugging away, Stacey Heydon wailing on guitar...until...there he was !!! Fucking Bowie. In the same room as us!! Stage all lit in white, Bowie in black slacks and vest, white shirt. 'The return of the thin white duke...' I will never forget...

UKK HALL

24 APRIL 1976 HELSINKI, FINLAND

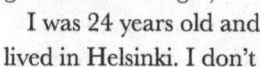

I saw David Bowie live in concert in Helsinki in April 1976. First we waited until it was dark and then we saw Luis Bunuel's and Salvador Dali's movie *Un Chien Andalou*. Bowie was dressed in a white suit like a character in that movie. Then we heard the rumour that Marc Bolan was here among the audience. And indeed he was (although he had gained some weight).

I was 24 years old and lived in Helsinki. I don't remember the songs, because it was so long ago. But I had been a David Bowie fan since 1968, when I first heard 'Space Oddity', and I loved 'Starman' and all those *Ziggy Stardust* songs.

After the concert I went to the rock club Natsa in Helsinki with my friends, among others Finnish rock journalist Mikko Montonen, (who has sadly now passed away). David Bowie came to the rock club with his company, including Marc Bolan and Iggy Pop. They seemed to have fun and enjoy themselves. Bowie even danced with one Finnish girl, but I don't know her name.

THE ROYAL TENNISHALL

26 APRIL 1976 STOCKHOLM, SWEDEN

I WAS THERE: MARIANNE STANGE

The first time I saw David live was in at The Royal Tennishall in Stockholm. I was 15 years old and a totally obsessed Bowie fan.

I remember standing outside the arena waiting to get in when suddenly a big, black limo drove up and there he was, the Thin White Duke, in the characteristic black leather coat, his bright orange and yellow hair in a tight back slick. He stepped out, followed by his then close companion Iggy Pop. My heart nearly stopped when they both passed us within a metre, David smiling shyly at the small crowd of fans standing there. He looked a bit confused; I think he took the wrong entrance. Every one of us there just froze, no one said a word. Time stood still. For me and for many other young teenage fans at the time, Bowie was almost looked upon as some sort of mythical godlike being and the moment felt unreal.

The concert was pure magic, and started with a sequence from Bunuel's *Un Chien Andalou*, then smoke filled the stage and the intro from 'Station to Station' began. It felt like I was in a dream, and when we were trying to get closer to the stage I remember my friend tore her pants when climbing over the seats.

I was very determined to meet Bowie one way or another, so I wrote a letter, making up a story that I was a (very) young, struggling artist in Sweden who was trying to get a record deal. The problem, I wrote, was that the record companies in Sweden weren't ready for 'the androgynous image' yet... so could he please help me with my career in London?

The thing was I couldn't really sing or play guitar but that was a minor problem, if it didn't work out my plan B was maybe being a

Struggling 13 year-old Swedish singer-songwriter Marianne Stange

nanny to Zowie..ha ha. Nothing wrong with my self-confidence in those days!

I took a sewing class, made this suit and posed for this photo at our summer-house (my sister was the photographer) and intended to attach it with the letter.

But my courage failed me in the end and I never sent the letter which I've kept somewhere, but it's impossible to find amongst all my things in my basement. I remember I wrote it with a green marker pen in a rather childish handwriting.

As you can see the picture is full of 'wrinkles' and it is torn. That's because I kept it in the plastic case on the back of my bus card so I could show it to my friends.

Over the years I saw him live six more times between 1978 and 2003. Even if all these concerts were great experiences, that first time stayed with me as something very special.

David Bowie changed my life. He brought colour into a black and white world. I immediately felt such a strong connection to him, which is so hard to explain to anyone else but another Bowie fan, and there are many of us. I'm still, one year later, trying to process the fact that he's not with us anymore, but his extraordinary beauty, talent, charisma and wisdom will stay with us forever.

SCANDINAVIUM

28 APRIL 1976 GOTHENBURG, SWEDEN

I WAS THERE: KATARINA PERSSON

On Wednesday April 28th, 1976 I caught the 8.15 morning train from Grums to Gothenburg to see David Bowie perform later that night on his Station to Station tour. I was 16-years old and had been a huge fan since 1973 when I listened to *Ziggy Stardust* for the very first time at the library in Grums. I'm eternally thankful to the foresighted librarian, who introduced such quality music to the inhabitants of this godforsaken village to which I had moved in 1972.

I was accompanied by a classmate, whose grandmother lived in Gothenburg and where we stayed the night. As we were not allowed to walk on our own in the city late in the evening, we ordered a cab to the Scandinavium Arena and back again after the concert. We entered the arena at 6.40pm and before we stepped inside I bought some Bowie stuff and a copy of the nowadays much coveted Isolar Tour programme.

We found our seats some 40 metres in front of the big black stage. I was thrilled and excited and got totally absorbed by the amazing sound that came out of the huge loudspeakers, which I later found out was Kraftwerk's 'Autobahn'. At 7.45 a film screen was rolled out from the top of the stage, which showed Lois Buñuel and Salvador Dali´s film *Un Chien Andalou* from 1929. Most surreal, I must admit, but as it was David Bowie's choice of film, I tried to look at it in an adult kind of cultural way and decided it must be great art!

Almost immediately after the film ended, the intro to 'Station to

Station' started and David Bowie calmly walked onto the stage from the right wings towards the microphone and began to sing. I couldn't believe that the elegant Thin White Duke was actually there in person in his white shirt, black baggy trousers and waistcoat. That dark voice of his gave me shivers down my spine!

As he entered the stage people started running forward in the aisle, and so did we. I supposed we got as near as 10 metres from the stage and could actually see his facial expressions. I'd written down the set list, which contained 15 songs, and noted that I liked 'Five Years', the most that evening. Dennis Davies' spectacular drum solo in the middle of 'Panic in Detroit' seemed to last forever, and I started worrying if Bowie had disappeared, but fortunately he came back. After 'Diamond Dogs' he presented the band and finally said, 'And my name is David Bowie'. The audience went wild while the Thin White Duke himself bowed three times and got off the stage! My god, was that it?

Luckily he was clapped back on and performed 'The Jean Genie' and 'Rebel Rebel' as the last number.

On our way home the taxi driver drove past Park Aveny Hotel, where a lot of people had gathered outside the entrance. We guessed that it was where David Bowie stayed, so we went there the next day. About seven or eight youngsters waited stoically outside the hotel, and as we had plenty of time before we were going to catch the train back to Grums, we waited as well, just in case David would show up. The staff of the hotel denied that he stayed there, of course, but when a black limo eventually drove up and Coco Schwab came out of the door in sunglasses, dressed in a trench coat and high black leather boots, we knew he was there for sure.

Two hours after we had arrived, both entrance doors flung open at the same time and in the middle of two racks of clothes came David Bowie escorted by his driver and bodyguard Tony Mascia. I managed to get a shot of him just before he entered the backseat of the limo. He was smiling and looked very elegant in a hat, dark blue coat, a purple scarf and light coloured trousers. He was also carrying a leather handbag and had a glove of a dog doll on his right hand. That doll, Moje, was popular in a children's TV-programme in Sweden at the time (Misse och Moje), but I was still surprised to see him with it. Maybe someone had given it to him and he would bring it back home to his son?

I guess I was starstruck, even if the word wasn't invented then, but I still managed to take two more photos, with my instamatic camera, as he seated himself inside the limo. I urgently felt the need of getting his attention so I said, 'Hello, David', which was about all I could utter in English in those days. He said nothing, only politely smiled before someone closed the door and the limo drove away.

In my notebook I have scribbled down that his luggage also contained three gold records and his long black leather coat. I still can't believe how lucky I was to experience this. As expected no one in the godforsaken village took any notice when I told them about my adventures in Gothenburg. They still can't spell the word 'quality'.

EMPIRE POOL

LONDON – 3 – 8 MAY 1976

I WAS THERE: MARC RILEY

When Ziggy announced his 'retirement' in the July of 1973 I was convinced that that was it!! I'd never get to be in the same room as the man who changed my life so remarkably, just one year earlier. I was besotted by Bowie and as unexpected as his arrival was, so too his 'end game'. Of course Bowie didn't retire but he did something almost as bad. He decamped to America for the next stage of his career and all I could do was watch from afar via the *NME* and *Melody Maker*. It was torture. Alan Yentob's BBC Documentary *Cracked Actor* in many ways made it even worse! Seeing what David was doing for the Americans without giving us so much as a second thought was hard to swallow.

When the Wembley Empire Pool 'Station to Station' dates were announced I was now a grown man… aged 15. I begged my parents to let me go to London on a National Express coach…and with this permission I sent off a postal order for my ticket. I could barely believe the day would come…I'd really get to see David Bowie in the flesh. The truth of the matter is I could barely see him at all come the day. I had almost the worst ticket in the 10,000 seater house. The only consolation I got was the fact that world famous boxer John Conteh was sat one row behind me! I now realise that the White Light shows were amongst the best that Bowie would ever do but at the time the fact that db was half a mile away AND he didn't engage in ANY theatrics whatsoever left me feeling just a slight disappointment. Don't be too harsh on me. Not yet turned 16 and desperate to see the same kind of extravaganza he'd staged in the USA...but all I got was a sharp suit and white fluorescent light strips.

My love for Bowie never wavered though Punk (and joining The Fall) did keep me busy for the next few years.

In 1995 I got to meet David for the first time. Mark Radcliffe and I were invited to New York City to record a two-hour special with him. He was the most playful and generous of men. He could tell both Radcliffe and I were in awe of him but he ploughed through our fear and dissipated it. I went on to meet db a further 8 or 9 times. He was always a gent. Funny and intelligent. The last time I saw him was just a few weeks before his last ever full show when I interviewed him in a London hotel room for Bowie day on BBC 6Music in 2004. It was hilarious. He wasn't interested in talking about himself or plugging his tour...he wanted to talk about the fact that seahorses had recently been found in the Thames for the first time in decades. That excited him.

I'd always dreaded the day Bowie would die. I selfishly hoped I wouldn't be on air that day and have to face my loss with an audience listening in. Of course this proved to be the case. One of the hardest shows I've ever had to do... but I'm glad I did it. I couldn't have anyone else sat in MY chair talking about MY hero on THAT day.

There's an oft used cliche that goes 'Never meet your Heroes'... don't believe a word.

I WAS THERE: PETER LEIGHTON

I am now 57 years old and come from and still live in Stourbridge in the West Midlands. David Bowie had always been my passion since I saw him on *Top of the Pops* as Ziggy (with my dad in the background hooting 'who the bloody hell is that?') He had just come back from the USA and I remember a bit of controversy about a salute at Waterloo station? And he announced five nights at what was the Empire Pool, Wembley. I just had to go, but was only 16. Luckily my friend Rich Griffin was a big fan also. Secretly we sent off for tickets and managed to get them for the, (I think) the Tuesday show.

I later produced the tickets and my Mom went mad and said I couldn't go because I was too young to travel to London (I eventually got to go with my friend who was 18 years old).

I have a very vivid memory of him singing 'Word On a Wing'. It imprinted itself on my memory and will do until my dying day. I was awestruck. I remember the black and white horror film before the show with some classical music. He struck off with 'Station to Station'. The long intro seemed to go on forever, and then he was there and my dream was fulfilled.

I WAS THERE: IAN SMITH

I first saw Bowie on 5 May 1976 at Wembley Empire Pool (now the Arena). My mum wasn't too pleased as she had queued for hours in the pouring rain in Leicester to get tickets for me to see Elton John on the same date. I had applied for Bowie tickets but hadn't received any so assumed they had sold out and had resigned myself to seeing Elton instead. When the Bowie tickets arrived they were for limited view but the decision was easy. The Elton tickets were sold! My mate and I bought several vinyl bootlegs after that gig which we still have today.

The concerts were full of fans with their red hair and lightning bolt across their faces. The lights went up and Bowie appeared in a suit and blond hair. I can still hear the gasp of shock from the audience to this day. It was quite amusing.

The 1990 Greatest Hits tour gig at the Milton Keynes Bowl sold out in 14 minutes and I couldn't get tickets, until I called my sister in London who knew an agent in Shaftesbury Avenue. He said he had some for a later gig at the same venue, which hadn't been announced yet! He sent me two and me and my mate had the first tickets for that gig before they even went on sale to the public. It proved that these so called 'added extra dates' are already arranged.

I WAS THERE: CHRIS ROBERTS

When the Station to Station Tour played LA, the audience included Elton John, Rod Stewart, Ringo Starr, Christopher Isherwood and

David Hockney. When it reached London, the audience included myself, and two friends, having been driven all the way down from North Wales by a heavily bribed dad. To go to a city was exciting enough. To enter Wembley and wait for David Bowie to walk onstage – about 10 yards away, as blind luck would have it – was foreplay.

With time it's been rightly recognised as one of the best shows ever toured. With a great band (Carlos Alomar prominent), and inspired lighting (searchlights, follow-spots) drawn from German Expressionism, it was astounding. The Thin White Duke had slicked-back hair like a vampiric cabaret artiste, black waistcoat, all the cold charisma in the world. Opening with the train sound-effects from *Station to Station*, the set focused on latter work, but also slipped in 'Life on Mars?', 'Panic in Detroit', 'Fame' and 'Rebel Rebel'.

I WAS THERE: KEV McDEMPSTER

Like so many of my generation, my first experience of David Bowie was that appearance on *Top of the Pops*; all bright red/orange hair, make up and jump suit, lasciviously slinging his arm around the shoulder of his sidekick, Mick Ronson, performing 'Starman' and terrifying parents nationwide. I loved it.

So it was that *Ziggy Stardust* and the *Spiders from Mars* came into my life and has stayed close to my heart and ears ever since.

Bowie toured the UK extensively in 1973 in support of Ziggy companion and follow up *Aladdin Sane*. Sadly, my gig wings hadn't fully

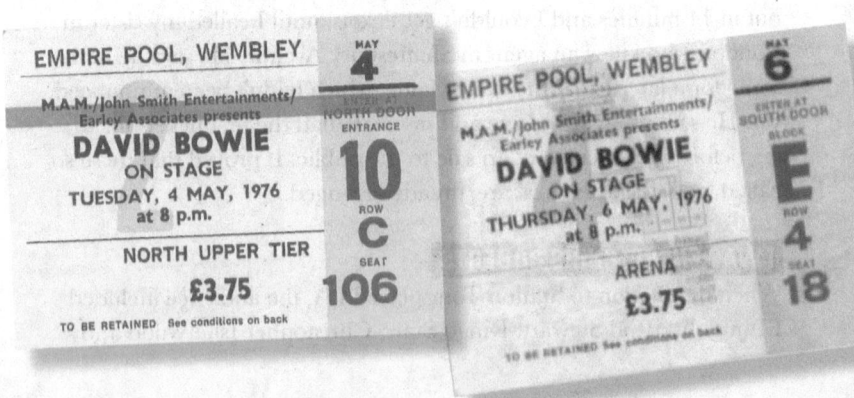

developed and so I missed out on the opportunity to see my heroes. I swore I'd definitely see Bowie and The Spiders, next time.

Except, there wasn't a next time.

I (almost) wept when the newsman told us The Spiders had really died in Hammersmith. Seriously, I was devastated to acknowledge I'd never see Ziggy and crew ever again. However, I managed to console myself with the thought that at the very least there'd be a chance to see him and my guitar God Ronno again, next time. They were inseparable, surely.

Except they weren't. And there wasn't a next time. Again.

I bought *Diamond Dogs* on the day of release and on first listen thought it was OK, idly perusing the cover as I listened. One thing I did notice was the guitar sound. It was… different. So I checked the credits.

Where was Mick Ronson's name? I checked again. Still I couldn't see it. There was no Mick Ronson. How could he? No Woody, no Trevor and no wobbly piano man was bad enough, but no Ronno?

To this day I've never listened to the *Diamond Dogs* album again (should do, really) and utterly loathed *Young Americans* ('Fame' aside. Well, it had John on it, after all). I was a rocker and David just didn't rock anymore and there was still no Ronno, so…

That changed upon the release of *Station to Station*. Bowie had ch-ch-ch-ch-changed (again).

The first few seconds of the title track alone rekindled my interest. The feedback guitar, the chugging rhythm. It may not have been rock 'n' roll as we knew it but the blue eyed soul of 'Americans' had been mainly jettisoned. 'Golden Years' was a great pop single. I enjoyed the album and so my mind was made up, set in stone.

Next time, this time, I would see him when he toured, whichever Bowie it was.

Except he didn't, well, not really. It was London or nowhere. Therefore, myself, and my buddies Ted, Tom and Graham (by now, a hardened and experienced gig going troupe in our mid-teens) planned our trip to see the Thin White Duke in the great metropolis.

We'd undertaken the same trip the previous year to see Led Zeppelin at Earl's Court but that's another story. This time we (a) had a better idea of what we were doing and (b) our parents knew we were going.

So it was that we took our places on Friday, May 7th 1976, in the enormous, ramshackle hangar of the Empire Pool, Wembley and we were waiting for the man.

After what seemed like an eternity of guitar and ominous, plonking piano notes under stark, white fluorescent tube lighting, on he came.

Fuck me, he was thin. A stick insect in a slick suit and white shirt, leading his accomplished new backing outfit as he got the musical journey under way, from 'Station to Station' to 'Suffragette City', 'Fame', even going way back to 'Queen Bitch' and 'Life on Mars?', although the older songs had been tweaked and altered (in some cases just a little too much for my liking), to bring them more into line alongside the likes of 'TVC15' and especially 'Stay', which was truly mighty when performed live.

Yes Bowie commanded the stage, albeit in that eerie, aloof manner of his then persona and yes the band were consummate professionals as they delivered the songs in a manner befitting such talented players. However, it was just a little too cold, a little too clinical. It was unarguably rock theatre, indisputably good and undoubtedly something to behold but as I left in all honestly, I didn't think I'd make such an effort to see Bowie again.

Years passed, albums and tours came and went and although I was aware that Bowie was still making music and releasing albums, some more interesting than others, I was taking no more than a passing interest in him playing shows in the UK on an irregular basis.

1976

The urge to witness what he was doing live had left me. I watched the various videos recorded on various tours and thought 'hmm...not bad... maybe...' but not enough to book those tickets and make that journey (Yes, Tin Machine came to my home town but, c'mon, be serious...).

So it remained until 2003, when Bowie unleashed *Reality* on an unsuspecting world. Well, an unsuspecting, lapsed fan, anyway.

In truth, I hadn't heard a note from the album until being persuaded to head over to the cinema to see the new album played in full, live, on the big screen as part of the pre-release promotion campaign.

Reality was a pinch of *Aladdin Sane* mixed with a helping of *Station to Station* mixed in with his uncanny knack of creating a catchy chorus and the Bowie persona had changed again. This was a warmer, more outgoing David then the distant diva of years ago. He smiled, he even told jokes and looked as happy as he had done in years and it shone through in the performance.

Looking and sounding better than he had in years, the music of *Reality* contained all of the elements that had drawn me to his music all those years ago. This band brought an edge to the songs, and in a now unshackled Earl Slick he had a guitar sidekick that once again brought the rock and the (almost) Ronson-ness back to the party.

Some thirty years later, I was hooked. Again. If he was taking this out on the road, I was gonna be there.

The A Reality Tour was announced shortly afterwards, taking in the usual indoor arenas in the UK late in 2003, arriving in Manchester on Monday 17th November. Sold out, fervent, vibrant, adoring and lapping up every song from every era of the Bowie oeuvre, faithful renditions of the hits and legendary album tracks mixed in with the best from the new album. Opening with a thumping 'Rebel Rebel', a smiling Bowie was the perfect front man and raconteur ('Stand up, sit down, we don't give a fuck what you do but you're in for a long night'), as he led the crowd through the galloping title track along with other selections from the new album such as the lead off single 'New Killer Star', 'Never Get Old' and the melancholy 'The Loneliest Guy' which all slotted in perfectly alongside cuts from the previous album '*Heathen*' such as 'Cactus', 'Afraid' and 'Sunday'.

Then of course there were the anthems and lifelong musical companions I'd loved from the Seventies, ('Changes', 'Life on Mars?' and 'The Man Who Sold the World' sounding just like the originals), as well as later gems such as 'Ashes To Ashes', 'China Girl' and 'Under Pressure' before closing with an anthemic, emotional 'Heroes'.

The encores came from *Ziggy*. 'Five Years', 'Suffragette City' and the legendary title track itself were all note perfect. Around two hours later I could have (almost) cried (again).

It was one of those shows you wished you could see again and again but tickets for the remainder of the tour were as rare as any rarity-related idiomatic expression you care to choose. It would just have to be committed to memory to be relived over and over again in the mind.

Then again, maybe not...

When the news came early in 2004 that Bowie, along with The Who and Stereophonics were to headline that year's Isle of Wight Festival, the pull was too great, the memory of that scintillating night in Manchester was still too fresh, too strong to resist.

Everything about the event was – is truly memorable. The island basked in glorious sunshine (no, really, it did). The atmosphere was friendly and joyous, as a magnificent long weekend from Friday to Sunday unfolded for the throng within Seaclose Park as the festivities gambolled toward Bowie's event-closing appearance on Sunday June 13th.

Once again 'Rebel Rebel' and 'Heroes' bookended the main set, a cover of The Pixies' 'Cactus', a vastly different proposition live when compared to its *Heathen* outing, with its D!-A!-V!-I!-D! chant (in the style of the T. Rex glitter bomb 'The Groover'), sitting comfortably alongside delightful surprises such as 'Quicksand' and the arm-waving singalong joy of 'All The Young Dudes' (despite Bowie's tongue in cheek request for everyone not to join in 'as we don't want to upset all the farmers, ok?' Some hope).

A handful of selections from *Reality*, 'New Killer Star', 'The Loneliest Guy' and the title track were liberally scattered throughout the evening. 'Sister Midnight', originally written for Iggy Pop's *The Idiot* album, slipped comfortably alongside a stomping funk-rock 'Fame' and a driving 'China Girl'. A hopping and popping 'Ashes To Ashes' prepared the way for a shuddering, near ten minute version of 'Station to Station', the howling guitars of Gerry Leonard and Earl Slick sending the train thundering down the tracks in a performance that simply dwarfed the rendition I'd witnessed so many years previously, itself preceding a coruscating, proto-nu metal rendition of 'I'm Afraid Of Americans'.

This was a man looking comfortable in his own skin as opposed to hiding behind a latest incarnation, looking every inch the rock star, his voice rich and full of all the mannerisms we'd become so accustomed to over the years, poking fun at footballer David Beckham who, immediately prior to Bowie taking the stage, had missed a penalty in the Euro 2004 match versus France ('unlike Beckham, this David's still got his balls!'), weaving happily through his expansive back catalogue and seeming set to stretch himself further in the future.

The title track from *Heathen*, 'Suffragette City' and 'Ziggy' closed out the night as the curfew closed in, the set having to be curtailed by the organiser's decision to show England's dismal football failure on the big screens (good job, guys). Regardless, the festival ended in a fusillade of fireworks and pyro as in excess of thirty thousand punters made their happy ways to the campsites and/or home and eventually mostly back to the mainland.

It was to be his last, full live performance in the UK.

Nowadays he may be a Heavenly Blackstar to many, if not most.

To me he's the Starman again, his arm draped once more across Ronno's shoulders.

1977 Arriving in New York after completing a six dates in England with the Vibrators as the opening act, Pop and Bowie flew to New York, where they met up with Mr and Mrs. David Johanssen and caught a performance by the Patti Smith Group. From there, they made their way across the border and into Montreal, Quebec, where the Iggy Pop – The Idiot Tour. kicked off on March 13, 1977, with Bowie on keyboards and backing vocals and Blondie as the support act.

The jaunt featured a band that included two future members of Tin Machine: Tony Sales on bass and Hunt Sales on drums.

Bowie carried on with the tour all the way through April 15, when it concluded with a performance at the Santa Monica Civic Auditorium.

Bowie later said, 'It was the first time I'd ever really put myself into a band since The Spiders. It was great not having the pressure of being the singer up front...Iggy would be preening himself before he went on and I'd be sitting there reading a book. 'That year the two also collaborated on Pop's second album, *Lust for Life*, which would become a long-awaited critical and commercial success.

LE PLATEAU AUDITORIUM

13 MARCH 1977 MONTREAL, CANADA

I WAS THERE: CHRIS STEIN – BLONDIE

We got into an RV after one of our shows and just drove up to Montreal for the first gig. We were very groggy and we walked into this hall and those guys are standing there. They were our complete heroes. The fact that he took a backset to Iggy during that tour was a huge deal because he was a big mega-star then. Bowie was totally gracious.

MASONIC TEMPLE

25 MARCH 1977 DETROIT

I WAS THERE: RICKIE WOODRING

My friend was a big Iggy Pop fan and he gave me a free ticket with the guarantee that David Bowie would join him on stage. We drove about 75 miles, from Grand Blanc Michigan to the Masonic Temple in Detroit. Debbie Harry came out dressed like a country singer, (Dolly Parton maybe), and the whole place started booing, and they would not stop. She threw her microphone down, and the drummer kicked his drums off the stage, and they left. This caused a very long, rowdy wait for Iggy and David Bowie. It was a long time ago, and my long-term memory is shot, but I remember an intense show. Iggy was back home in Detroit and he had Bowie with him. Even with Iggy's antics, my eyes, and I assume everyone else's; we're glued on David.

1978 The Isolar II –World Tour, more commonly known as The Low / Heroes World Tour or The Stage Tour, opened on 29 March 1978 at the San Diego Sports Arena, continuing through North America, Europe and Australia before reaching a conclusion at the Nippon Budokan in Japan on 12 December 1978.

Originally, Brian Eno planned to be a part of the band, but had to drop out due to health reasons. The band only had two weeks to rehearse for the tour and Carlos Alomar was the tour's bandleader, and drove the rehearsals.

The Australian leg of the tour included Bowie's first concerts down under and his first large-scale outdoor concerts.

COBO ARENA

20 APRIL 1978 DETROIT, MICHIGAN

I WAS THERE: MADONNA

David Bowie changed the course of my life forever. I never felt like I fit in growing up in Michigan. Like an oddball or a freak. I went to see him in concert at Cobo Arena in Detroit. It was the first concert I'd ever been to. I snuck out of the house with my girlfriend wearing a cape. We got caught after and I was grounded for the summer. I didn't care.

I already had many of his records and was so inspired by the way he played with gender confusion. He Was both masculine and feminine. Funny and serious. Clever and wise. His lyrics were witty ironic and

mysterious. At the time he was the Thin White Duke and he had mime artists on stage with him and very specific choreography, and I saw how he created a persona and used different art forms within the arena of rock and roll to create entertainment. I found him so inspiring and innovative.

Unique and provocative. A real genius. His music was always inspiring but seeing him live set me off on a journey that for me I hope will never end. His photographs are hanging all over my house today. He was so chic and beautiful and elegant. So ahead of his time. Thank you David Bowie. I owe you a lot.

KUNGLIGA TENNISHALLEN

2 JUNE 1978 STOCKHOLM, SWEDEN

I WAS THERE: LINDA SMEE

I was 20-years old in 1978, freshly and stupidly married and accompanying my new husband while he worked in Stockholm for a few months. I think the Bowie concert was in June, so not too cold. We got the train to the tennis hall from Lidingo where we were living. It was a sold out concert.]

Swedish audiences of the Seventies were a fairly sedate lot, but even they couldn't sit still and shut up for long. He did a few costume changes, all harem pants

with cropped jackets. When 'Station to Station' started the "ch ch ch ch ch" noise started. It was a guitar but sounded like a train going from one side of the huge hall to the other. The audience followed the sound with their heads just like at a tennis game, maybe that was his aim!

He sauntered on after a few minutes of the clever intro, burst into song...and the crowd went crazy. He wore a white harem pants suit.

It was 39 years ago but something I have never forgotten.

The world will miss you.

THE APOLLO

19, 20, 21 & 22 JUNE 1978 GLASGOW

I WAS THERE: RENATO LUCCHESI

I was 12-years old when I first saw Bowie on *Top of the Pops* and I was spellbound; it changed my life. Unlike almost everyone else of my generation, it wasn't 'Starman' for me it was 'The Jean Genie' in '73', (the footage which had thought to have been lost turned up recently thankfully to the cameraman that kept a video for his private collection). I heard he was playing Green's Playhouse in Glasgow and one of my friends' big sister offered to take me but regrettable my mum wouldn't let me go. I had to wait a further five years.

June 1978. I left my home town of Galston straight after work, took the bus to Kilmarnock and then the train into Glasgow, I couldn't believe I was finally going to see my hero. Hundreds of us queued outside the famous Glasgow Apollo

Renato Lucchesi meets former Bowie manager Ken Pitt backstage at The Apollo, Glasgow 1978

shaking with excitement and anticipation, dressed up to the nines.

I can't remember if there was a support band. I don't think there was but when the lights went down and the very first notes of 'Warzawa' and David walked on stage I stood in the stalls arms out stretched, tears rolling down my cheeks.

I've seen Bowie many times since but like your first kiss or your first car there is something special about your first time.

I WAS THERE: GARY HOPTON

I first started listening to David Bowie in 1975. I was 13 and the re-issue of the 'Space Oddity' single caught my attention. Wow, this is special, I thought and a bargain as well as it had two tracks on the B side, 'Velvet Goldmine' and 'Changes' which was unusual at the time!

This started me on my lifelong journey of being a David Bowie fan as I started collecting the albums but noticed no live dates had been in Scotland since 1973. Then, on that memorable day in 1978 when I read my *NME* and saw the headline, 'BOWIE WORLD TOUR'! This tour included Glasgow, which I was really excited about, however then reality sank in, how would I get tickets? How would I get there? Being only 16 at the time I had never really travelled further than Kirkcaldy (6 miles away) on my own!

My (then) brother in law saved the day. He worked in a bank in Dunfermline, and one of the guys there was going to get tickets. He asked me how many I would like and I replied three please, one for me, one for my friend, and one for a local girl who really liked Bowie.

When the tickets arrived I could not stop looking at them. I was going to see David Bowie!

When the time arrived, 19 June 1978, I was so excited I could not sleep for thinking about it, but I had a few obstacles to overcome to get there. I had to get a bus to Dunfermline, then a bus to Crossford (just outside Dunfermline) and then had to wait on a mini bus that was picking us up! What if the bus did not turn up? What if they forgot about us? All sorts of things were running through my head!

Thankfully, the bus arrived, (the girl I got the ticket for did not fancy it, so I sold her ticket at the venue). When I got on the bus we noticed it was only half full. The Dunfermline guys told us that a local band called The Skids were supposed to be travelling with us but they said they had got so big headed after the success of their new single 'Into The Valley' they decided to make their own way there!

One of the guys on the bus looked the spitting image of Bowie during his Cracked Actor phase. The rest, (including me) had Bowie t-shirts, etc. After the show back on the bus the Cracked Actor guy actually broke down and cried sobbing, the experience was that overwhelming for him.

From the opening song of 'Warszawa' to the closing song of 'Stay' from *Station to Station* I was mesmerised, I was actually watching David Bowie! The set list was amazing though I still think to this day 'Hang On to Yourself' was played too fast. It all went far too quickly and before long we were leaving the venue for the mini bus back home wondering when he would play again in Scotland. (It would be another five long years).

It was an unforgettable experience, and I went to every other Bowie gig since then. Murrayfield in 1983, Tin Machine at the Forum Livingston in 1989, Edinburgh Exhibition Centre in 1990, Tin Machine again Glasgow Barrowland, 1991, Outside Tour SECC Glasgow 1995, Earthling at Glasgow Barrowlands in 1997, and Reality at Glasgow SECC in 2003.

Memories that will last forever. Thank you David Bowie.

NEW BINGLEY HALL

24, 25 & 26 JUNE 1978 STAFFORD

I WAS THERE: STEVE DRAYTON

What with him being an other-worldly superstar, in 1978, a 17 year old scunny lad didn't go to see David Bowie. How could I ever inhabit his orbit? He was from outer space. I was from Lincolnshire. He belonged to me, but in a far-end-of-the-universe type of way. Then Mark McCubbin announced he had five tickets to see the Isolar 2 tour at Stafford Bingley Hall.

He would drive us in his Cortina. We stocked up on unfiltered Gauloises and Sobraine Cocktail's, that's what Dave smoked.

We dressed up. We queued in the freezing cold awaiting entry.

Having stood for hours, being packed tight way back, the show started, with 'Warszawa', then 'Heroes' then 'What In The World'. It all got a bit sweaty.

David was tiny, far, far away, I felt a clammy faint coming on, so pushed my way to the side of the crowd. 'Jean Genie'. I felt better.

I had a wander. The stage was about seven foot high, and because of this, there was a huge gap between audience and band. I'm six feet two inches so could see perfectly. For the rest of the gig David sang directly at me. He was huge now. We made eye contact. He held out his hand to me 'cause I was wonderful'. When 'Station to Station' began I almost exploded. How could they even begin to play something so complicated? The French and Russian fags were rank and I ended up swapping them all for 10 No. 6, much more palatable.

Not very David, but he wouldn't have minded. After all, we had made a connection.

I WAS THERE:

We were three 17-years old and in a band, called the Liggers. Our main purpose at that time was to gain access to as many gigs and parties that we could,

The Liggers with Donna Sullivan third from the left

especially gaining access to any after parties that were going, where we could lig free drink and any other substances we could get hold of.

We were going to see our idol, David Bowie. Unusually we couldn't blag any tickets for this, so had to stump up not only for the gig, but also, for travelling to Stafford and accommodation overnight. We were determined that we would gain access to the after party, where our hero would be in person, where he would be completely bewitched and bedazzled by our wit and repartee. Our conjectures on what may occur once we met David knew no bounds, and we spent many a happy hour discussing how this meeting could literally change our lives.

My first bubble burst when I realised that the accommodation my two amigos had booked was in a B&B with a landlady in attendance and an incredible small room for two. To save us some money it was decided that I was to sneak in and sleep on the floor, even though we were splitting the bill three ways! Their rationale was that we would be out most of the night, so would only be using it to get dressed and leave our gear. Plus, they had flipped a coin – as long as it was fair! We decided against getting any booze in for later for the same reason so off we tripped on our big adventure.

The gig seemed to be held in a massive space, like an aircraft hangar, although we were quite near the front and had a good view of Bowie on stage. His blond slicked back hair seemed luminous and he prowled the stage giving us renditions of 'Fame', 'Five Years' and my absolute favourite 'Station to Station'.

He was mesmerising. I had a cheap camera that I kept snapping – it wasn't until the film came back from the chemist that I realised I got more pictures of the audience's heads than I did of Bowie. At one point, there was an unexpected treat for the audience – Brian Eno was making an unscheduled appearance! Bowie introduced Eno on stage and then he took a break, walking to the side of the stage. He may have even been in the wings, although we could still see him. He slowly lit a cigarette and stood smoking and watching Eno playing. Poor Eno, he was brilliant but everyone's gaze had followed Bowie to the side of the stage, and were watching him, smoking and watching Eno – it was one of the coolest things I had ever seen.

At the end of the gig we were on a mission – looking for where the after show party was. We got wind that it was being held at another venue about a mile from where we were. So, off we went, with some other revelers (presumably the source of this information) – to find the party! After several hours and a lot of arguing we decided to give up – we had walked for miles, in what seemed to be mainly fields. Our dreams shattered we trudged back to town. To top it all it was so late, there was nowhere to get any booze. So once we had evaded the landlady and I was sneaked in to take my place on the uncomfortable floor, we had a very sobering post mortem on where we had gone wrong.

Not long after this a friend of ours had wangled her way into a post gig party when Iggy Pop had played Manchester. Whilst she was in his hotel room, he received a call from none other than David Bowie. She was as massive a fan as us and Iggy was chatting with Bowie and mentioned that he was hanging out with our friend, mentioning her by name. She told us later that all she could think was that David Bowie knew of her existence. We listened rapt – it was some comfort to know that someone we knew had been introduced to the great man himself! A vicarious thrill!

EARL'S COURT

29, 30 JUNE, 1 JULY 1978 LONDON

I WAS THERE: NED MALET DE CARTERET

I first saw him when I was 17 in 1978 at Earl's Court on his Isolar

11 world tour. It was either 29-30 June or 1st July, (whichever the Saturday was?) – it was truly awesome and I was rather star struck! The lights, the music, the man – he was just mesmerising – on reflection it was one of the greatest gigs that I have had the privilege to attend. 'Station to Station' was just awesome, all ten minutes of it! White lights, large strobes, black and grey very 'Heroes', Germanic – Carlos Alomar on guitar.

I WAS THERE: DAVE LEWIS

I had hoped to see the Station to Station tour in 1976 but missed out – so when this date was announced in the February of 1978, I made it a mission to get tickets. I went to this with my friends Dec Hickey, Yvonne Salim and Barry Farnsworth. This was the tour that would be chronicled on the *Stage* album. All sparse tubed lighting and lowkey spotlights. Of

course he was fantastic – it was actually the first ever rock show that I attended that had an interval. And what a return to the stage for the second half, six straight numbers from *Ziggy Stardust* and an encore of 'TVC15', 'Stay' and 'Rebel Rebel'. A truly wonderful night…and an ambition completed. I had finally seen David Bowie live on stage.

I WAS THERE: STEPHEN CARTER

Aged 14, we bunked off school to go with two of my mates, Sean from school and his mate also called Sean. We travelled from Guildford, Surrey. I don't think there was a support act but remember the DJ playing Iggy Pop's *Idiot* and *Lust for Life* albums before David came on. The most memorable part was the start of 'Station to Station'. It sounded like the screeching guitars swept from the back of the auditorium to the front like a train passing. The sound was immense.

I also went to the Milton Keynes show in 1983, and got stranded at Euston station after missing last train home. I was singing *Ziggy Stardust* cover to cover through the night.

I WAS THERE: BARRY CAIN

Wendy was 18 when I first asked her to dance in Tracy's during the winter of '74.

She had twisty hippy hair the colour of a hot summer night that dangled around a disarmingly pretty face shot with teenage anguish.

She loved music with a passion and had no confidence. I was 21, loved music with a passion and had no confidence. It was a good start. Fortunately, I could hide my lack of confidence thanks to a London backstreet upbringing. Most working-class people have no confidence. It's inbred.

Music was our common denominator and Wendy's favourite artist was David Bowie. I was a shade too old for the Bowie of the early Seventies. If I'd have been 18 then he

probably would've been my rock hero, but three years was a long time back then when it came to music. Hard rock and Motown were in my ears and in my eyes. Bowie was too poppy, too gimmicky, too effeminate for a 21-year-old. I liked my music with balls. Fucking big hairy ones. And also something you could dance to that shivered yer timbers and wrung the magic from your soul.

Tracy's was Gloucester's only night club then, but by the end of '74, the far larger Tiffany's had opened its lavish doors in the centre of town. I'd moved to Gloucester just three months before the night we first danced (wish I could remember the song) from the council flat I shared with mum and dad off Pentonville Road. I was living in a converted barn in Slad, where *Cider With Rosie* was set.

I'd landed a job as a trainee reporter on the evening paper – *The Citizen*. Life was sweet.

Wendy and I fell in love in the Neverland of the mid-Seventies. She was the kindest, gentlest, most generous person I'd ever met and I loved her dearly. When she smiled she lit up my life. She was so young and so innocent and so wonderfully alive and I was punching well above my weight.

She was, for want of a better word, posh. She lived with a posh father and a posh mother and a posh dog – a Cavalier King Charles. She had an even posher brother who worked in the city and is probably a gazillionaire now. She even had a horse called Posh. Just joshing. But she did have a horse.

I was out of my depth but they welcomed me with open arms – though I felt the brother needed persuading on the few occasions I met him. He was more circumspect, more protective of his sister and I respected him for it. They were a wonderfully happy family and it was an honour to be invited so cordially into their home.

When I became the resident pop-music writer with the weekly, appallingly named, *Pop Pourri* column, Wendy was impressed and that felt good. She had a habit of making me feel good about myself. That was her secret.

She was also impressed when we used to breeze to the front of long queues outside the two night clubs – the only guys standing in the great shadows of the city's cathedral after 11pm – and into the welcoming arms of the managers who knew how to look after a gentleman of the press. It was like being Henry Hill in *Goodfellas* and it felt good.

Outside both venues on Friday and Saturday nights the West

Country cider soul boys would gather, the velocity and spirit of Wigan Casino coursing through their pill-stained veins. Tracy's would occasionally feature a top-notch live act – we're talking Edwin Starr, KC and the Sunshine Band, and sad sweet dreamers Sweet Sensation – because the punters just loved to groove, their huge baggies billowing on the lager-sticky dance floor where their feet spun at the speed of light.

In 1975, Wendy and I went on holiday to Minorca where we danced endlessly, drunkenly, memorably to 'Lady Grinning Soul' in the Cova d'en Xoroi, a club carved out of a cave overlooking a Mediterranean splattered with moonlight.

When I moved back to London, Christmas '75, Wendy stayed behind. We both tried hard to wipe out a hundred miles with long telephone calls and occasional visits but we each had a hunch it might end in heartbreak.

I took her to The Who's Put The Boot In Charlton football stadium show in 76 after I started work on the South-East *London Mercury* and we sat out of the torrential rain in the VIP seats. She adored it and it made me feel good that I could do something special for her. She had the *Who's Next* album and 'Baba O'Riley' was always on the turntable.

One July afternoon in that long, sweltering '76 summer, I climbed into my newly purchased second-hand Cortina 2000 GXL which revved like the wind, and headed west to Gloucester to trade tongues and talk of love. I was still living at home with mum and dad and it was good to get away from work for a week.

I wound down the window as I hit the sun-drenched open road after leaving the M40, and Nils Lofgren eased into 'The Sun Hasn't Set On This Boy Yet'. A bunch of blackbirds shot out of a roadside bush and flew across the front of the car. It startled me for a moment but I forgot about it in the darkness of my Raybans and that exquisite Lofgren album.

I parked on the drive next to her dad's huge white Rover. The sun boomed as I walked up to the front door. I glanced back at my car and saw the carcasses of around five and twenty blackbirds baking against the radiator.

Her parents were out and Wendy looked beautiful.

I slept in her brother's room during my stay; he was recently married and lived in London. The temperatures soared into the high eighties and covered the glorious Gloucester green with golden sheets of heat. The soundtrack to those idyllic few days was the *Station to Station* album. My indifference to Bowie hadn't abated but even I realised upon hearing the album, that this was indeed a genius at work.

When I heard 'Wild Is The Wind' for the first time in Wendy's bedroom, I got one of those whisker away from heaven moments that had only happened a few times before on a first hearing – 'No Particular Place To Go', 'I Get Around', 'Good Vibrations', 'Reach Out I'll Be There', 'Hey Jude', 'I'm Not In Love', 'Bohemian Rhapsody'.

On my last night, Wendy and I met some friends and headed up the lazy River Severn on a disco cruise. We had a minor argument, it hurt to part again, and when we got back around 2am, we went to our rooms after a cursory kiss.

Around 5.30 that morning someone called my name in a dream. She kept calling and her voice grew louder, more intense, more emotional. I opened my eyes.

'Barry, come quick. I think he's dead!' I rolled over. Wendy's mum was at the door. She disappeared and I knew it was a dream.

Then I heard the screams. They were real.

I got up and checked out what was happening. Wendy and her mother were kneeling beside the bed, their arms flung across her father's motionless body. They begged me to do something, anything. They said the ambulance was on its way. No matter. He was cold. A massive haemorrhage had left a huge purple mark that spread across his neck like spilt wine.

He was well over six feet tall, strong, intelligent and healthy. He was also barely 50.

I watched the ambulance men carry him out on a stretcher. They struggled a little going down the stairs – he was no Twiggy. I'd known him for two years and now, having outlived him by some way, I can appreciate what a good-natured fellow he was. A thoroughly decent, wise man who would help anyone. He had a booming, infectious laugh that devoured a room and brought joy to everyone in it. I had a couple of minor disagreements with him, but I was a schmuck who knew jackshit and he was so right and I was so wrong. Indoctrination is a fucker to overcome. But overcome we must.

I felt duty bound to stay for the funeral and in the days leading up to it I lost touch with Wendy. My arms weren't strong enough to haul her from the slough of grief into which she'd fallen and her despondency was deep and dark. I fear I was of little comfort to her.

The following month we went on holiday together to Penzance. The sun was still burning and her heart was still breaking and my arms were still weak. I read Luke Rhinehart's *The Dice Man* during long sojourns under pub umbrellas sipping beer, smoking Peter Stuyvesant and sneaking looks at Wendy with her port and lemon and her tears. Yeah, I was great company. But what do you say to a girl who'd just lost her doting father about 30 years too early?

Plus, I wanted to finish *The Dice Man*. That thought alone made me realise I was far too young for all this. Someone whose dad had just died would usually be 50 or 60 and be better equipped to handle their emotions than a 21-year-old. We had the conversations of a middle-aged couple facing up to old age in the wake of death.

Another tearful goodbye in Gloucester. Driving back to London I vowed I'd pluck up the courage to ring her in a few days and say something 'cool' like, 'Why don't we stop foolin' ourselves? The game is over, over. Over.'

But within days I missed her like crazy and a month later she sat next to me on a frothy press coach heading back from Kempton Park racecourse after a jolly with Queen to celebrate the release of *A Day at the Races*. She watched me interview Brian May, she drank champagne alongside Freddie Mercury, she tripped the light fantastic for a whole day

It was inconceivable that she'd refuse the offer I was about to make.

'Listen,' I said. She smiled. Her smile was always open and honest and I loved her for it. 'Why don't you move down to London and we'll get a flat together?' My change of mind was based on two things – I missed that smile and the possibility of sex. I don't have a cheatin' heart.

'I can't.'

I was on auto – after all, she adored me and every time she saw me I impressed her more. Freddie Mercury? It wasn't like this in Tracy's. Let's face it, I was doing her a favour. It was an offer she couldn't refuse.

'You can't? What do you mean, 'you can't?''

'How can I leave my mother?' She didn't say 'Mum' very often. 'She'd be so alone if I left.'

'So you're saying you won't come?'

'I suppose I am.'

'Your mum can look after herself.' Her mother's face is frozen at 50 in my memory. She was an ex-gym teacher with tight hair and a warm heart and we really got on well. But Wendy was adamant. Leaving her mother was out of the question. I guess it ended there. We still saw each other occasionally, but we knew the game was up.

Funnily enough, Wendy did eventually move to London, but by then someone else had re-entered my stratosphere and was burning up. There hasn't been anybody else since.

In the summer of '78 I was freelancing at *Record Mirror's* offices above Covent Garden tube station and got offered a pair of press tickets for one of Bowie's Earls Court shows.

I hadn't seen Wendy for some time during which I'd proposed to someone else who I'd met before I went to Gloucester but that's another story from another planet (check out *'77 Sulphate Strip* and *57 Varieties of Talk Soup*) but I had her number and remembered her fondness for the Thin White Duke. So I called, as a friend. And she accepted my invitation, as a friend.

She was working in Harrods prior to taking a job in the costume department at the Royal Opera House and when we met that night she looked stunning in a grey, I think, man's suit complete with shirt and tie carried off gracefully with sharp heels and that hot summer night hair.

I was reviewing the show for Record Mirror and the only time I'd seen Bowie live was on the opening night of Iggy's Idiot tour the previous year at Friars, Aylesbury. Bowie was the keyboardist. He puffed long, flesh coloured cigarettes throughout the entire set and was noticeable only for his immobility.

I admit, I was a little excited at the prospect.

What's worried me over the years is did my snobby cynic critic stance ruin it for her? In short, was I a cunt?

And was I even more of a cunt when I told her, in the kitchen at home that night with my parents in the other room, that I'd proposed to another woman and she'd accepted?

What the fuck was I thinking? I didn't mean to hurt you, Wendy, I didn't mean to make you cry.

We did meet up again. Twice actually. Seven years after my marriage, I had a hankering for Gloucester and went on a pilgrimage. I drove around a few haunts, saw a few familiar faces and discovered Wendy had moved to Bath. A mutual friend called her. We spoke, it was so good to hear her sweet, sweet voice.

I drove to Bath that evening. We met in a bar, had a wonderful time and I ended up staying the night at her chic abode in the centre of Bath. She ran her own company making and designing a vast array of costumes for TV, films and the theatre and business was thriving.

We never even kissed. That part was a far-off memory in a far-off land. I slept in the spare room and she woke me in the morning with tea and biscuits. In return, I paid for a swanky lunch in a swanky hotel overlooking the city.

In the car on the way up to the hotel, 'Wild Is The Wind' crept out of the speakers like a dubious cat. I'd recorded it on the cassette years back and totally forgot it was on there.

'Remember Minorca?'

'But that was 'Lady Grinning Soul'.'

And for some inexplicable reason, we both laughed out loud.

'Those gigantic platform shoes you wore that made you seven feet tall.'

Shortchanging superstar?

BUT can Bowie bear Barry Cain's blowtorch critique?

DAVID BOWIE
Earls Court

WHAT price fame famE faME fAME FAMe FAMe fame now eh?

I love Bowie with all my indifference but that won't stop me from thinking he behaved badly, nay, criminally to the 17,000 that packed Earls Court on the second night of his travelling smile circus.

No doubt you read our Mr Lott's detailed review of the show a couple of weeks back so I won't bore you with another. Instead, let me explain my reasons for finding the whole thing slightly disappointing.

Firstly, the ludicrous entrance. Surely that's taking the desire not to be spotlighted too far. In fact it's the highest form of conceit to walk on while the houselights are still up lost amidst the boys in the band. The kids want a bang not a blank.

Secondly, instead of softening the blow by careering into an old meaty melody he slithers into the awful 'Waaaawa' from 'Low' and for five minutes a halfful of anticipation is swirled down a dromedrain.

Thirdly, the toothless toons from 'Low' and 'Heroes' are in the main just loose change. 'Heroes' itself is a classic and came across much better live than on vinyl. But where oh where was 'Sound And Vision'? The first half's standout was 'Fame' with a scorching finger pointing, light sublimated Bowie frozen on the final note. Magic.

Fourthly, the two numbers that could and should have destroyed the place — 'Jean Genie' and the final encore 'Rebel Rebel' — didn't because they were re-vamped. 'Genie' sounded flat and was saved by a magnificent duel between the incredible guitarist Adrian Below and violinist Simon House. 'Rebel' was a let down because the driving rocker we all know and love was metamorphosised into an almost Latin American rhythm. While watching Bowie's carry-on-camping dance routines one could be forgiven for thinking that his body has been taken over by an 'Ole Ola' screeching Rod Stewart.

Fifthly, Bowie should have made some concessions to his hysterical fans by giving them what they so much desired — 'Changes', 'Diamond Dogs', 'Life On Mars', 'Young Americans', 'Golden Years', 'Drive In Saturday', 'Rock 'n' Roll Suicide' even 'Space Oddity'. An artist of his stature can afford to indulge in his chameleon fantasies on record but surely live he ought to come across with the heavy goods. Most of these people may never get the chance to see him again.

On the credit side the presentation of the show was quite simply white light. Beautiful.

Bowie, so confident, so at ease, is probably the best mover you'll ever see on a rock 'n' roll stage.

The sound was superb (from my vantage point anyway). Maybe those at the back might just as well have been in Australia. And the assembled loved every white ice minute of it.

It was just the choice of material that was enough to make you puke. A thin white puke that is.

BARRY CAIN

Ah yes, I remembered them well. 'It was the fashion.'

And so we continued through lunch and into the late, balmy afternoon. As the day drew to a close, and it was time for us to part, I felt like David, the robot boy in the final scenes of A.I. Artificial Intelligence when he spent those precious last hours with his 'mum'. We knew we would never see each other again. Ever. It was death dressed up in memories.

Yet we met one final time. I think it was the following year and I know it was somewhere in the Cotswolds and we were in the company of some friends and it involved an overnight stay but honest to God, I don't remember a fucking thing. Yet I remember so much of my death dressed up in memories day. And I remember even more the night we danced together for the first time.

Because of Wendy, David Bowie has ingrained himself on my lady grinning, shrivelled soul. I've kept a certain smile in a safe deposit box and visit it occasionally. Past loves grow more beautiful with time.

For our love is like the wind...

ADELAIDE OVAL

11 NOVEMBER 1978 ADELAIDE, AUSTRALIA

I WAS THERE: FOTIS KAPETOPOULOS

It was a strange thing to be a Bowie fan as a Greek boy and in Adelaide in the Seventies, at least in the early stages of Bowie's personas. My Greek and Italian peers in skin-tight-black-jeans, into AC/DC and Black Sabbath, threatened me with death. Those into disco, with high-waisted, ball-squeezing satin pants and platforms also wanted to kill me. (Luckily the second could not run as fast in those platforms.)

Why? Anyone that liked the androgynous Bowie was a 'poof'. The slower, ultra-stoned Hawkwind, Pink Floyd, Santana and Led Zep guys looked down on Bowie. You just weren't that 'heavy'. Regardless that *The Man Who Sold the World* was one of the heaviest albums of the early Seventies. For many of the Aussies it was even simpler; a gay-looking wog needs a serious beating.

On the other hand we, the few black Bowie fans, knew how special we were. We were vague, experimental with drugs, some to their demise, and with sex, some never deciding. We were readers and talkers, lovers of theatre, cinema and weird funk, classical music and even obscure folk.

I wore eyeliner, sharp suits, and silk ties. I smoked Gitanes while others smoked Escort. As a hetro male my effete elegance also meant more girls, and cool ones. I grew a fringe and dyed it blond. Bowie was the world outside my flat, boring, suburban Adelaide. He was elegant, so much so that my mother and father even liked his sartorial European style. 'That's how men should dress,' my father said, looking at the cover of *Station to Station*.

Finally, in 1978 Bowie came to Australia. He began his tour in Perth and his second concert was in Adelaide at the Adelaide Oval as part of the Low/Heroes tour. I went with a few mates and my younger cousin who I had to 'take care' of according to my aunt.

I was wired with excitement and I shared a joint with my friends. I threatened my cousin if ever he talked about the joint I would 'never take him out again'. He never said a word to this day and he's now 50 years old.

The Angels as the support band were a testament to the bogan base of Australia. After they ended their one endless, stupid four-chord song, silence blanketed the Oval and 'Warszawa', the other worldly instrumental from *Low* began and Bowie appeared like the apparition.

The Thin White Duke was here. The computerised wall of fluorescent light created shadows and sharp reliefs of Bowie as he danced across them. The stark Germanic expressionism of that performance collided with many of the older *Aladdin Sane* fans. I remember thinking 'he is the New Wave, no one else', and with my peroxide-blond fringe, my younger 13-year-old cousin in tow and a few buddies, we were thus the New Wave, the blokes that don't fit.

I remember on the way home that night, in the back of my uncle's Ford Fairlane, longing to escape the grey flatness of Adelaide. My cousin was stunned; his young mind was unable to process it, all he could say was 'that was incredible…'

Back at my uncle's place, we lay back on the huge couch of my uncle's Seventies entertainment lounge and listened to the whole of *Low* on his massive Marantz speakers. It was our *Dark Side of The Moon*.

My uncle and father came in, said nothing, listened and after some time, instead of telling us to, 'Take that crap off', looked at each other and my old man said to my uncle, 'not bad'. That was ultimate confirmation for me from a man who thought anything that wasn't Theodorakis, Dalaras, Piaf or Mozart was not serious.

I saw Bowie again in 1983. I was 21 years old with a girlfriend and muscles. It was the Let's Dance tour, and I realised that a new and annoying fan base was there. The darkness had lifted. The cold fluorescent white lights, the Germanic experimentalism, the industrial jumpsuit and bomber jacket were replaced with a tan, gelato-coloured suits and Eighties dance funk.

I saw him again in Melbourne in the mid '00s as the natural man, the middle-aged and middle-class man – a great performer, a great musician but not the Thin White Duke. I loved Bowie, but few works after *Heroes* would seduce me as much, even though I did wait for his work and looked forward to one or two good pieces.

Until *Blackstar*, his death mask became a new watershed for me. A few days before his death I saw the clip to *Blackstar* and thought, 'this is dark, he's lamenting his youth, but he's not dead'. I wasn't sure if it was gratuitous narcissism. Now I know and when I look at the clip and hear 'Lazarus', I see my father wasting away from cancer in '92 and my mother gasping for air last year.

Lazarus does not rise, but the Blackstar is the final destination for all heroes.

I WAS THERE: COLIN MURRAY

As the light began to fade the support band, The Angels, who were playing to a home crowd, entertained, and were warmly welcomed.

It seemed an age between The Angels finishing and a group of musicians walking quietly on to stage and the opening bars of 'Warszawa' sounding. When you are young, there's a strong impact of seeing someone who has been admired in the flesh for the first time. They seem larger than life, almost magical. For me, that Adelaide concert on Saturday November 11 was magical.

I WAS THERE: GEORGE JANKOVIC

I was wiring under the stage. Bowie came down to introduce himself to me and we had a chat. He went out of his way to talk to a lot of people behind the scenes.

MELBOURNE CRICKET GROUND

18 NOVEMBER 1978 MELBOURNE, AUSTRALIA

I WAS THERE: BRUCE BUTLER

It was November 1978, my 20th birthday and David Bowie was arriving in Adelaide for his first ever Australian concert so my friend and I went to the airport to watch the planes arrive, (these were the days when you could walk out and watch the planes land). Finally Bowie's band got off the plane, and we ran down to the arrivals lounge. Bowie walked out, I'd written a gushing fan letter to him. I walked up and said, 'Hi David' and he was quite happy to stop and chat. I told him I'd come from Melbourne and how we'd been sleeping outside the MCG for two weeks to be sure we'd be up the front. He thought we were insane. He took the letter, got in his Mercedes and off he went. A week later I'm back in the queue in Melbourne for the concert and someone came down and said, 'Which one of you is Bruce? Mr Bowie sent me down to say thank you for the letter. He was really touched by what you said, he's grateful for your devotion,

and he wants me to give you a personal tour of the stage.' So we were taken inside the Melbourne Cricket Ground, given tour programmes and cups of tea and biscuits.

By the time of Bowie's next visit to Australia, in February 1983 to film the videos for 'Let's Dance' and 'China Girl', I was working in the music industry, at CBS Records in Sydney. One of the bands I was working with was The Psychedelic Furs, who were touring Australia on the back of their hit *Love My Way*. I knew Bowie was a fan so I left a message at the Sebel Town House saying I could get him tickets to a Psychedelic Furs show at the Coogee Bay Hotel.

I got a call, and it was his minder saying 'Mr Bowie would like to come to the show. What's the security like?' We hadn't even thought about security. So we got him to drive into the Coogee Bay bottle shop so we could sneak him through the back door into a private viewing area. He turned up with Geeling Ng, the girl in the 'China Girl' video and a bodyguard. He hung out backstage with us for a few hours, showed us what he'd learnt on the cello during his recent filming of *The Hunger* and even showed us how to to balance on an empty beer can without crushing it. He was in full party mood. He and Geeling Ng left about 5am to go down the beach and film that famous scene in 'China Girl' rolling around together naked in the sand and surf.

Top: Bruce Butler (with beard)
Bottom: Bruce Butler (drinking) outside the MCG who queued for tickets for a week in mid-September

LANG PARK

21 NOVEMBER 1978 BRISBANE, AUSTRALIA

I WAS THERE: RORY GIBSON

Never before have I sniffed so many armpits, been abused so frequently or been trodden on so freely. The concert was cramped and conditions were hot and humid. I had lost sight of my two friends, had my soft drink can knocked from my hand and half my meat roll was plastered on the back of some guy's shirt. To make conditions even more uncomfortable, gropers and bottom-pinchers had the time of their lives.

RAS SHOWGROUNDS

24 & 25 NOVEMBER 1978 SYDNEY, AUSTRALIA

I WAS THERE: JOHN LARKIN

I went to both of David Bowie's shows in Sydney that year. They were both excellent shows. However the show on the 25th November 1978 was brilliant. It was the last show of his Australian tour and Bowie was in excellent form. The encores were more spontaneous. Bowie and the band ended with 'Rebel Rebel' twice. Bowie thought that he and the band could do it better a second time around. He sang a few bars acapella from 'With A Little Help From My Friends' and he also sang a few lines from a beer commercial 'I Feel Like A Tooheys'. As the show concluded he grabbed anything he could from the stage and threw it out into the audience - towels, cups, etc.

After the Bowie concert at Lang Park, Brisbane on 21 November 1978, Russ Hinze, Queensland's minister from the newly-formed Noise Abatement Authority, told the press; 'These pop singers come out here to make a quick quid by disturbing our peace and tranquility. The Noise Abatement Authority will investigate complaints that last night's Bowie concert at Lang Park, Brisbane, disturbed the peace'. Hinze said there were thousands of complaints, but concert promoters said they only received eight. It was reported that the noise was loud enough to be heard 6 km away. Residents of the suburbs of Paddington, Barton and Milton described it as intolerable, but not everyone living in the area shared this perspective; some locals enjoyed the 'noise', taking advantage of a free concert and sitting on their verandas to listen.

WESTERN SPRINGS STADIUM

2 DECEMBER 1978 AUCKLAND, NEW ZEALAND

I WAS THERE: DAYLE ABBOTT

I was 23 and had been married since 1972 and went with friends up to Auckland to see David play in 1978. I had two young children and my husband who was a control freak said, 'No, you are not going'. I went and had the most amazing weekend.

However in all the concerts I have been to in my life including the three other shows of David's I saw here, nothing beats the magic, the charisma and beauty of seeing David Bowie live. Except as he sang 'Stay', some lowlife threw a flour bag at David and it hit him. It was at that concert David actually took photos of us all at Western Springs. I believe at the time it was one of the largest audiences he'd ever played to.

When I arrived back home in Wanganui at 9.30pm I found the sink, table and benches all piled up with dirty dishes ready for me to clean up!

1980s

Now living in New York, Bowie played Joseph Merrick in the Broadway theatre production *The Elephant Man*, which he undertook wearing no stage make-up, and which earned high praise for his expressive performance. He played the part 157 times between 1980 and 1981

Bowie released *Scary Monsters (And Super Creeps),* his fourteenth studio album in September 1980 on RCA Records. It was his final studio album on the label and his first following the so-called Berlin Trilogy of *Low, Heroes and Lodger*. As well as earning critical acclaim, (and producing the number-one hit 'Ashes to Ashes') the album peaked at No. 1 in the UK and restored Bowie's commercial standing in the US.

MOUNTAIN STUDIOS

JULY 1981 MONTREUX, SWITZERLAND

I WAS THERE: PETER HINCE, PHOTOGRAPHER

At this time I was working as head of Queen's road crew and was in the studio when Queen and David Bowie recorded 'Under Pressure' which was done very quickly. Drummer Roger Taylor invited David, who lived nearby in Vevey, into the studio and there was a genuine mutual admiration between all the musicians. The sessions were spontaneous, and done very quickly. There are various accounts of what happened, and that not all the members of Queen were happy with it. However, I was very close to John Deacon and he thought it was one of the best things Queen ever did. The original vocals were changed during mixing in New York, so there are other versions of the song, along with other material Queen recorded with Bowie that never got released.

Some original songs they did together, and also covers – they were just jamming in the studio, and it all got recorded: 'All The Young Dudes', 'All The Way From Memphis', and various rock classics. After 'Under Pressure' came out and went to No.1, people asked, 'is it Queen with David Bowie' or is it 'David Bowie and Queen?' Good question…

ST GERMANS

SUMMER 1981 CORNWALL

I WAS THERE: CARINTHIA WEST

Recently, on the train from Penzance to Paddington, as I passed the tiny station of St Germans, I looked back, and high over the estuary bathed in the searing dawn light, was a perfect rainbow stretching over the rolling green lawns of Port Eliot, ancestral home of the Earls of St Germans.

Port Eliot itself is not visible from the train, but so very visible in my mind's eye and my memories. It was here I introduced Peregrine St Germans, the owner of Port Eliot, to David Bowie, in 1981. It was on this lawn I photographed us all smiling and laughing in anticipation of a relaxed country weekend. David had a great love of Cornwall, its myths and its legends, so when I heard he was planning to take his son Joe (as he was then called) on a sojourn to the southwest, and knowing that my friend, Peregrine, was keen to have him play at his festival, the Elephant Fayre, I suggested a long weekend at an historic country house would give them the opportunity to discuss the possibility, plus a chance for me to catch up with my dear friend, Corinne Schwab, (known to friends as Coco), who was David's longtime PA, right hand, and trusted companion.

I had met David through my friendship with Coco in the late Seventies, and had shared many good times with them both. I'd travelled with them on a chartered boat up the Italian coast, watched David and his band perform at several concerts from the stage side wings, visited some of his film sets, hung out in homes in New York and Switzerland, and mine in Warwickshire, play Grandmother's Footsteps and Scrabble, and even be styled in London by David for my first model shoot with a then unknown photographer called Mario Testino. (David had seen my portfolio of photos and pronounced them all 'rubbish'. 'Rinthy', he said (his pet nickname for me), 'there's this young Peruvian guy who's just done some pictures for me – I think he's really good – will you let me arrange a shoot for you?' One of the attributes that David had, and I have not heard enough about in all the tributes and obituaries that poured in when the world woke up to the news of his tragic and untimely death, was that David was SO kind. He did not have to arrange anything for me, I was not his girlfriend, nor his protege, just a friend of his own best friend, Coco, and that was enough for him.

He was also very funny, with a wicked sense of humour. Once on the set of *The Hunger* a very old man approached me and said he was terribly sorry to bother me, but he was David's father and as David couldn't be on the set that day, he had been asked to look after me. It was only because everyone around us was sniggering, that I realised it was in fact David in full ageing Methuselah make-up. Later, when I left the modeling and acting world to be an unknown journalist in Los Angeles, he allowed me to do an interview with him in a music magazine. That interview put me on the journalistic map in America, and (in pre-internet days!) brought more commissions and just enough money to put the down payment on an apartment. He was always doing kind acts for people he liked, and the Testino shoot was just one. To my eternal regret, (and Mario's embarrassment) the negatives were lost at the lab, so David's hand at tweaking my Anthony Price dress, and Coco's assurances that my lipstick was not smudged, were lost forever, however the memory remains, and surely that is what matters in the end.

So we gathered at Port Eliot, David, Coco, myself, Joe (then about 10, and later to become the respected film maker Duncan Jones), and Marion, Joe's nanny and family friend. The weekend did not start auspiciously. Peregrine had some fixed views on children eating with grown ups and assumed that the four of us would sit down for dinner on Friday night (under the Rembrandt and drinking Leoville Barton) and Marion and Joe would 'eat in the nursery'. When I found out – minutes before their arrival – I was horrified. 'David is here on a family holiday – he's a post divorce dad, and the whole point is that he sees Joe as much as possible. Marion is an integral part of the family. There is no way that David will want to eat in separate rooms'. Peregrine was adamant and put on his best 'I am the 10th Earl of St Germans – this is my house so what I say goes' expression. 'I have lunch at one and dinner at eight, and a no-children under 15 rule at each'. I threatened to leave and take my friends with me to a nearby Cornwallian hotel, and grudgingly, Peregrine agreed, but the stage was definitely not set for the two men to bond. For all Peregrine's great charm and (much publicized) 'eccentric hippie lifestyle', he was in fact deeply old-fashioned in some ways, and as the weekend progressed, despite some interesting trips like a visit to a local arts and crafts house, David never did play the Elephant Fayre.

'Rinthy' said David conspiratorially to me, as Perry showed him the Robert Lenkowitz mural on his drawing room wall, and the maze with the bulls head buried at it's centre. 'I discovered the word 'Lucifer' scrawled in red on a mirror this morning. This place is too

Carinthia West in the Eighties – styled by Bowie, photo by Testino

weird, even for me!' To be fair this probably had nothing to do with Peregrine, as the mirror was in the rooms of the playwright Heathcote Williams, who at that time was lodging in a wing of the house.

So, as my London bound train glides over Brunel's aqueduct in 2017, I look back to Port Eliot's lawn in 1981 and I remember that I took a photograph of us all that weekend. I took it with the camera on a tripod, then whipped round to sit on the grass. There's David with Coco behind him, me shading my eyes from the sun, and Peregrine with his son Jago. I suppose it was an original 'Ussie'.

David died the week of his birthday, just before releasing his final album, *Lazarus*, and Peregrine died in August, just before his beloved Port Eliot Festival opened. Jago too had sadly died, a few years ago, much too young.

As the train pulls in to Plymouth, the rainbow recedes, and a whole bunch of cheerful yet rowdy football fans board, (deeply unconcerned with anything other than the beautiful game), my moment of reverie has passed. Putting on my headphones, I bed down in my seat and listen to *Lazarus*, David's last album, and the title song with the extraordinarily prescient lines 'Look up here, I'm in heaven, I've got scars that can't be seen, I've got drama can't be stolen, everybody knows me now', which, of course, is true.

They know the very public David, the multi-talented musician, singer, songwriter, actor, alchemist etc. His death caused a huge outpouring of tributes from fans. *Lazarus*, the play, opened in New York and London, and various pieces of his art collection were sold at Sotheby's, raising millions. His extraordinary legacy will live forever, but on the morning he died, so elegantly and quietly with not even some of his closest friends knowing, (how like David). When I heard the news on the radio like everyone else, apart from the shaft of pure sadness that shot through me like a spear at the loss of someone I had personally known, I thought (rather selfishly on reflection) 'no one will ever call me 'Rinthy' again'...

WARWICKSHIRE

SUMMER 1981 ENGLAND

I WAS THERE: CHARLIE DORE

I washed up and David dried the dishes after Sunday lunch one weekend at a Warwickshire house party in 1982 and he was friendly, humorous and very normal. Our host, Carinthia West's much older cousin James, a very nice but totally unreconstructed member of the land-owning classes, had genuinely never heard of David Bowie and said, 'Carinthia tells me you're in the pop music business. What exactly do you do?' Which David thought was hilarious. He took the question at face value and gave James a brief run-down.

POWER STATION

DECEMBER 1982 MANHATTAN, NEW YORK CITY

I WAS THERE: NILE RODGERS, MUSICIAN, PRODUCER

One night I went to an after hours club and I ran into David Bowie who was sitting all by himself, he was drinking an orange juice and I walked over to him and started talking. I knew about all of his people from *Young Americans* because they all lived in the same building, they were like really good friends, so we just started chatting about Luther Vandross, Carlos and everybody and at some point David and I agreed to make a record. And it was really that night; we just got on so well. It was actually really early in the morning, I met him around 5 or 6am.

He invited me over to Switzerland to work on pre- production and he had this thumbnail of a song, which would eventually be called 'Let's Dance'. It worked out so well, I wrote out the arrangements and did the parts and we got these jazz guys to do it in Switzerland and it just sounded phenomenal and David was thrilled and after that we ended up doing that album, which had 'China Girl', and 'Modern Love'. It was a huge record, the biggest in his career.

The music video for 'China Girl', featuring New Zealand model Geeling Ng, was directed by David Mallet and shot mainly in the Chinatown district of Sydney, Australia. Along with his previous single's video for 'Let's Dance' with the critique of racism in Australia, Bowie described the video as a 'very simple, very direct' statement against racism.

SYDNEY

MARCH 1983 AUSTRALIA

I WAS THERE: GEELING CHING

I've been a huge David Bowie fan my entire life. The first album I ever bought was *Ziggy Stardust and the Spiders from Mars*, so to actually meet the man in person, I was totally star struck and for once I just couldn't get any words out. It was quite amazing. Then when I was told I had got the part, I almost fell over, it was so exiting!

His initial thought was to come down to Australia and shoot the video for 'Let's Dance' and highlight the plight of the aboriginal people in Australia, and also to use the beautiful outback which is unique in the world. I was told by David Mallet the producer and director, that they thought if they could shoot 'China Girl' in Sydney, they'd do it at the same time as 'Let's Dance', and if they couldn't cast it they'd head up to Hong Kong on the way home and they'd shoot it in Hong Kong. But luckily I was there and the rest is history.

It's interesting, as when I was actually shooting the video I had no idea of the political statement that he was making. You know I was just (A), working with David Bowie, gosh! and (B) shooting a video and sort of all of the things that came along with that. I'd never done anything like it before in my life. So it wasn't until much, much later that I discovered the message he was trying to tell in the video and then looking at the video afterwards I could see that that message was actually quite clear.

Acting opposite David was terrifying, because he had a long history as a performer and I was a model and waitress. He was great to work with and I think because we had to have a relationship on screen, we were supposed to be lovers, he worked really hard to make sure that I felt comfortable with him, and he was a pleasure to work with.

The last time I saw David was when he toured New Zealand in 2004 and I went backstage to meet up with him.

People from the record company were gathering around him backstage to have their photo taken while my friend and myself stood off to the side. I was thinking, I hope I get to say 'Hi' to him or at least get a smile in or something, and then he looked up and smiled and came charging over and said, 'Hey, how are you. It's great to see you.' I was just blown away. It was just another example of how warm and friendly he really was.

I'm blessed to have been part of that incredible talent, with someone who has changed the world of music… not just music, but the face of fashion, makeup, everything.

CANNES FILM FESTIVAL

CANNES, FRANCE – MAY 1983

I WAS THERE: CHRIS PHIPPS, ASSISTANT PRODUCER, *THE TUBE*

My personal encounter with David was in 1983 when he agreed to be interviewed (for the UK TV show *The Tube*), at Cannes Film Festival.

Bowie was there promoting his new release *The Hunger*, a vampire flick co-starring Catherine Deneuve which was directed by North East movie maker, the late Tony Scott. He said he wouldn't talk about his music because he wanted to talk about his film. It was a huge coup to get him.

I will never forget being in the room with him. It was in a private apartment on the front in Cannes. His PR found me when he was ready and I knocked on the door with (the presenter) Jools Holland, and there he was. He started talking at length in a very relaxed way. And he was looking terribly relaxed, in a pair of chinos and a simple shirt.

I have to say he was the most charismatic person I've ever met.

There was something extraordinarily driven about him which appealed to people, and it appealed to me. I didn't feel inhibited by him. He talked to me about his enthusiasm for making short films for cinema. He thoroughly enjoyed being interviewed. He had great presence and I have met very few people with that presence. You could see he was creatively driven and I have always been fascinated by the greatest shape-shifter in music. Nobody every could categorise him. He had different influences and went from one to another so we never really found out about him.

I knew his first manager, Kenneth Pitt, quite well at a time when he was sort of doing an impersonation of Anthony Newley (Bowie recorded a tribute to the singer and actor in 1967). He was attempting to be an all-round entertainer. He made a novelty record called 'The Laughing Gnome'. The next minute he was androgynous, a visitor from another world – Ziggy Stardust; then he was soaking up electronic music and then he was in America soaking up soul music. And there was new wave romanticism in 'Ashes to Ashes'. It's just incredible. I think he was a musical dilettante. Visually, Bowie always kept things visually interesting too.

I WAS THERE: CHARLIE DORE, SINGER, SONGWRITER, ACTRESS

I was at the Cannes Film Festival promoting a film I played opposite Jonathan Pryce in *The Ploughman's Lunch*, written by Ian McEwan & directed by Richard Eyre – and was invited to a post show launch party for the Python's *The Meaning of Life*.

Our film was showing, but wasn't in competition and was very low key, compared to all

Singer, songwriter and actress Charlie Dore

the razzmatazz associated with the Python film. I was the only cast member there as the other leads were filming.

I was good friends with Eric Idle and knew a couple of the other Pythons – in fact they were the only people I actually knew at the party, but of course most of the time they were busy being interviewed, hosting the evening and generally being lionised so I found myself feeling a bit of a gooseberry and wondering when it would be polite to leave.

David Bowie was there too, sitting at a table surrounded by the glitterati, and he must have noticed me looking a bit lost as he waved me over and found me a chair. I said I was there promoting *Ploughman's Lunch* and a photographer started snapping away at David so I leaned out of shot but he put his arm around me said, 'Come on Charlie, do yourself a bit of good – let's get some photos!' and cheerfully invited the photographer to take some more. I didn't know where the photographer was from and wasn't sharp-elbowed enough to pursue him afterwards, so I never saw any copies (if they even survived) but I thought that was very generous-spirited of David, and from what I hear, not unusual.

1983 The Serious Moonlight Tour was Bowie's longest, largest and most successful concert tour. The tour opened at the Vorst Forest Nationaal, Brussels, on 18 May 1983 and ended in the Hong Kong Coliseum on 8 December 1983; 15 countries visited, 96 performances, and over 2.6 million tickets sold.

The tour, designed to support Bowie's latest album *Let's Dance*, was initially designed to be a smaller tour, playing to the likes of sub-10,000-seat indoor venues around the world, similar to previous Bowie tours. However, the success of *Let's Dance* caused unexpectedly high demand for tickets: there were 250,000 requests for 44,000 tickets at one show, for example, and as a result the tour was changed to instead play in a variety of larger outdoor and festival-style venues. The largest crowd for a single show during the tour was 80,000 in Auckland, New Zealand, while the largest crowd for a festival date was 300,000 at the US 83

Festival in California. The tour sold out at every venue it played. The November 26 show in Auckland became – at the time – the most attended concert in the Southern Hemisphere with over 80,000 people in attendance.

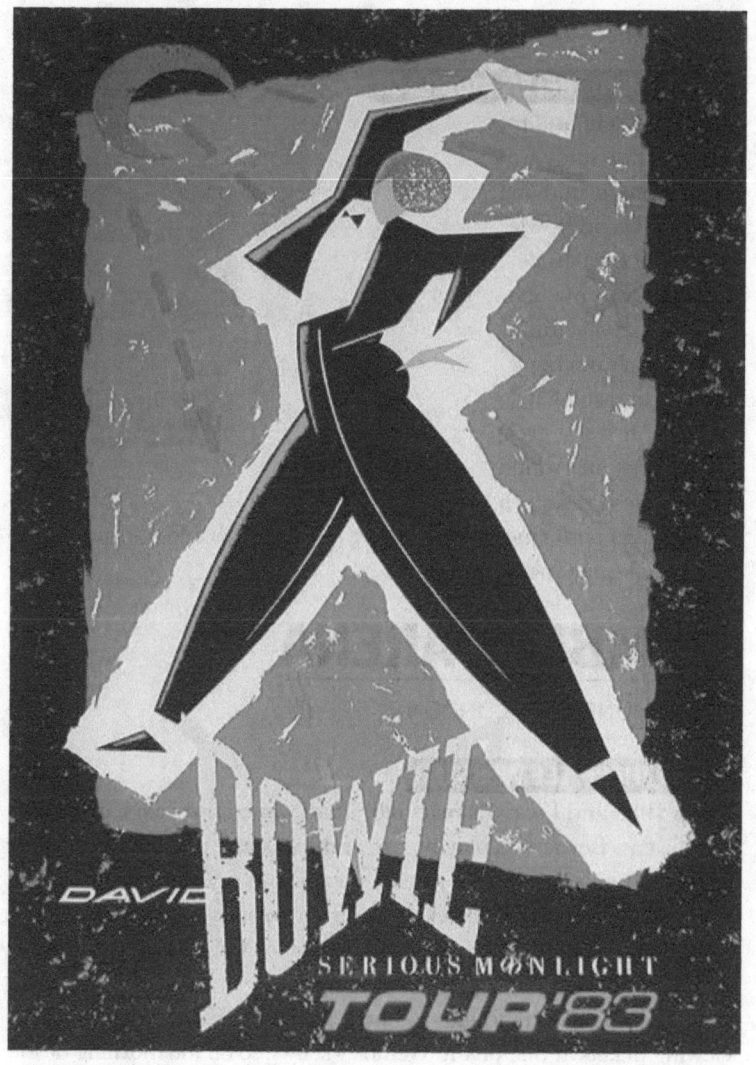

PALAIS DES SPORTS DE GERLAND

24 MAY 1983 LYON, FRANCE

I WAS THERE: HELEN MURDOCH

I was a student and my third year of study was a year abroad studying in Lyon. David Bowie came to the Palais de Sport – it was my first gig at a major stadium but it wasn't too big a venue – and still felt intimate. It was a great atmosphere and sound quality. He was superb

– wonderful performer and stunning to watch. It's a long time ago but it's left great memories!

WEMBLEY ARENA

2, 3 & 4 JUNE 1983 LONDON

I WAS THERE: LEE WEBSTER

It was 1983 and I was 19 years old. I had waited five years, ironically, for this day. Bowie was playing live and I was in a panic, as I had never seen him before. After much pleading to my Dad, he wrote a cheque, and I applied for tickets. After an anxious wait my tickets turned up but I only received them for two of the concerts at Milton Keynes Bowl.

Then somehow we found out there was going to be restricted viewing tickets at one of the Wembley shows, so on the morning of the sale two of my friends and myself headed to Wembley and arrived at six in the morning. We queued for 12 hours (we had nothing but biscuits to eat), and we had trouble with people trying to muscle in to get tickets to sell on later in the day.

That day remains one of the best memories of my life. I got to meet like-minded Bowie fans and saw my hero. The show was amazing and the view pretty good. It was worth every minute of the twelve-hour wait, and when I look back now, the waiting and meeting with other Bowie fans makes it even better

Thank you David. I'm a Blackstar.

NATIONAL EXHIBITION CENTRE

5 & 6 JUNE 1983 BIRMINGHAM

I WAS THERE: PETE CARROLL

I've seen Bowie several times, all of them memorable; but the show at the Birmingham NEC in the early **Eighties** was important because it was the moment he started reaching out to a larger, broader audience. The impact of 'Let's Dance' pushed him into large arenas demanding more focus on a bigger visual presentation. These were the early days when artists started to design stage sets to enhance their show. It's not surprising that Bowie was ahead of the game. It was an early example of a rock 'n' roll show removing the gap between stage and audience in a cavernous, soulless environment; a majestic widescreen union of sound and vision creating a shared experience. Images from the show still flash in my brain decades later.

BIEBERER BERG STADION

24 JUNE 1983 OFFENBACH AM MAIN, GERMANY

I WAS THERE: RIK STEWART

I saw David Bowie in concert at the soccer stadium in Offenbach, Germany. I was 19-years old and stationed in Germany with the USAF. It was the Serious Moonlight Tour and myself and several military friends went to the concert. The stadium in Offenbach held about 30,000 people in the stands and maybe 15,000 on the field and it was jam-packed.

Bowie came out to a roaring ovation just before 9pm and joined his enormous band in a yellow zoot suit with suspenders and matching yellow fedora. They played about two and a half hours straight and played a ton of great songs including, 'Heroes', 'Golden Years', 'Let's Dance', 'China Girl',

Rik Stewart and friend on stage

'Rebel Rebel', 'Space Oddity', 'Young Americans', 'Fame', 'Jean Jeanie' and the encore was 'Modern Love' (David played sax on that one and also sax on 'Golden Years'). It was a phenomenal show with Mr Bowie at the absolute top of his craft.

STADION FEIJENOORD

25 JUNE 1983 ROTTERDAM, NETHERLANDS

I WAS THERE: SONJA FENIJN

On Saturday 25th June 1983 I joined my brother to go to David Bowie's Serious Moonlight Tour in the Feijenoord Stadium (de Kuip) in Rotterdam. More than 50,000 fans had come to Rotterdam to see and hear Bowie. I felt butterflies in my belly as I waited excitedly for my hero to appear. I had been a fan since 1972.

The opening acts were a concert of their own, featuring UB40 and Ice House. During UB40's performance the crowd was really getting in the mood, and there were plenty of groups dancing and singing. Some of the dancers were even getting more attention than the performing band.

Then it was 9.30pm and a band comes on the podium, a voice announced; 'It has been five years'... and... Bowie appears with his golden locks over a fabulous blue costume and starts with 'Star' to launch his performance. The crowd in the stadium is a wave of enthusiastic fans; even those who don't know the whole song were screaming their lungs out. Many fans were dressed as Ziggy Stardust or one of his other alter egos. With the song 'China Girl' the fans went crazy when Bowie wrapped his arms around himself, secretly wishing they were his 'China Girl'.

He sang 21 numbers, but still no 'The Jean Genie', the song which started it all for me. But he made up for it in the encore, when he performed 'Stay', 'The Jean Genie', 'I Can't Explain' and ended the show with 'Modern Love'. On the way home in the car we strained our voices going through the whole repertoire, of course no way near as good as Bowie had performed. Now, 34 years later I still enjoy the concert DVD. Thank you Starman!!!

MURRAYFIELD STADIUM

28 JUNE 1983 EDINBURGH

I WAS THERE: JOHN MORRISON

I remember the first time I saw Bowie in concert like it was yesterday. It was the Serious Moonlight Tour at Murrayfield in Edinburgh. It was the first time I'd been outside of Glasgow for a gig and six of us crammed into my mate's dad's Ford Cortina. We left Paisley (outside of Glasgow) about 8am, as we were eager to get there.

I can't remember exactly when the doors opened, but we must have been standing outside that stadium for hours. We were one of the first to get in and I remember feeling totally gutted when our tickets were for as far from the stage as you could get. There was also a fence up so you couldn't get onto the pitch without a ticket. We were standing up at the fence when someone who had a pitch ticket came up and passed his ticket to me through the fence. Soon I was on the pitch along with my other five friends as the ticket went back and forth through the fence.

From being miles from the stage to being in the first ten rows couldn't get any better. Soon the support acts were on and off – Ice House and Thompson Twins. Then it was time for the man himself and he was worth the wait and then some. Bowie strutted on stage to 'Star' from *Ziggy Stardust* and the place erupted. The whole day went by in a flash and I can honestly say was one of the best days of my life. I was fortunate to see him another couple of times and there will never be another performer like him. Many thanks David for the music that got me through my years from ten years old first seeing you on *Top of the Pops*, ('The Jean Genie'), right up to the end.

I WAS THERE: PAUL GILLIE

I went to see David Bowie at the original Murrayfield Rugby Stadium in Edinburgh during his Serious Moonlight Tour in 1983. It was a Monday, it was raining all day and it was the very first concert to be held at the stadium (it has since been rebuilt). Icehouse and the Thompson Twins were the support acts. I was looking forward to Icehouse playing as I loved their single 'Hey Little Girl' but the Thompson Twins blew them away.

By the time the main man took to the stage everyone was soaked as the old stadium only had one stand covered at that time. The show was amazing with a great selection of songs. The south side of the stadium has a railway line running close to it and a train did an unscheduled stop directly opposite the stage, allowing passengers to get a taste of the concert! During one of the songs a large inflatable of the Earth was thrown out into the audience but went back to the stage deflated and David made a comment about Ronald Reagan, who was the US president at that time. All in all it was an amazing concert (even with the rain) and a bit of history for the stadium too. I had a four mile walk afterwards to the bus station in the rain, but I had more than a spring in my step.

I WAS THERE: GARETH WYNN VERNON

I had been a massive fan of Bowie since the age of 8 or 9, listening to his music on the radiogram, because we didn't own a television yet. I remember that I had emigrated away from the UK until 1983 when I boarded a plane in Detroit to come home and I could hear Bowie's 'Panic in Detroit' on the radio station WRIF. So many classic Bowie tunes marked different ages of my life and so when the tickets came out for Murrayfield, I was not going to miss him.

Pouring rain on the night, the Thin White Duke came on stage after the opening acts of Icehouse and the Thompson Twins who, by the way, were amazing. Dressed in a beige suit, Bowie played right through the pouring rain hitting almost all his great anthems and much of his latest offering *Let's Dance* to a huge crowd, who couldn't care less if it had been snowing or raining cats and dogs. I snuck in a half bottle of Black Heart rum and although drenched to the skin, felt warm inside, as I had seen one of my greatest musical heroes. Me and my girlfriend took the No.37 bus back to Falkirk with huge, beaming perma-smiles on our faces all the way.

I WAS THERE: HAZEL CATHERINE MORRIS

I was 20-years old when I went to Murrayfield Edinburgh with my friend Elaine Rennie. The Thomson Twins were support. My off duty rota was changed so I had to pull a sick day, my boss was two rows behind me. He had also pulled a sickie! Thank goodness no mobile phones then. I also saw Bowie in 1985 at the Live Aid Concert in Wembley, when 15 of us travelled down and lived in a transit van and a B&B. It was an amazing weekend from start to finish.

I WAS THERE: SANDRA TAYLOR

My friend introduced me to David Bowie when I was just 14 in the Eighties. What a breath of fresh air he was compared to what was masquerading as music in the charts at the time.

Bowie hadn't toured for some time, so we were delighted to hear the announcement about the Serious Moonlight Tour. We saved up our pocket money of £2 a week and anxiously waited for news of the upcoming gig. Some writer in the *Daily Record* said there would be no Scottish dates. We were devastated; being only fifteen at the time there was no way our parents were going to let us travel to London or Milton Keynes. We spent all our pocket money and consoled ourselves buying Bowie albums instead.

Well, as we all know he played Murrayfield on the 28th June and up we trailed and stood outside the stadium in the miserable weather. We listened to 'TVC 15' and got all maudlin and went home. To add insult to serious injury, we found out everybody that was standing outside was let in to hear the encore of 'Modern Love'. Grrrrrrrrr.

My Dad at the time however, knew a guy from work that was going and he organised a programme for me which I treasure to this day.

MILTON KEYNES BOWL

1, 2 & 3 JULY 1983 MILTON KEYNES

I WAS THERE: KAY DYSON

I've seen David 13 times in total. It Started in 1983 with the Serious Moonlight Tour at Milton Keynes bowl. Wow was it hot that day. I was 20 and had started listening to him around the release of *Scary Monsters*. I Was completely hooked and got tickets for him whenever I could including Tin Machine, the Freddie Mercury Tribute Concert and all the way up to the last time on the Reality Tour in Manchester. He was the master and I treasure my memories so much. I Will miss him forever.

I WAS THERE: JASMINE STORM

I was rather late coming to the party. When David Bowie sang 'Starman' to the *Top of the Pops* audience in 1972, I was completely unaware what *Top of the Pops* was. By 1975 when 'Space Oddity' reached the charts, I vaguely remember Pan's People dancing to it, but as a pre-teen my life was covered in tartan from the Bay City Rollers. However, starting secondary school in 1979 gave me a greater understanding of music to realise what a legend Bowie was. I bought my first album, *Ziggy Stardust and the Spiders from Mars*, from a boy in my class for £1.50, which was quite a lot of money to me back then, and fell head over heels in love. It was the start of a love affair that has continued throughout my life.

After *Ziggy*, I bought all the albums I could get my hands on with my limited budget from a paper round and Saturday job in Woolworths. I discovered the early Deram Sixties Bowie and rocking glam Seventies Bowie and loved it all. And although it's fair to say I liked some of *Scary Monsters*, I was very much stuck in the Seventies.

I spent hours listening over and over again to the brilliance of his words and music. I marveled at how clever 'Five Years' was – to tell a story with such emotion! I was intrigued at the cut-up technique used on 'Moonage Daydream'. I fell in love with 'Young Americans' and hoped one day to meet someone who would make me feel the way this album did. No other music really ever came close although I did have a soft spot for ABBA.

In 1983 all my dreams came true. I couldn't believe that not only was Bowie touring – but he was coming to my town. I may have been born in London but I no longer lived in a big city, so for Milton Keynes to be put on the map in this way was more than luck – it was fate. No matter what I would be there.

It wasn't easy to find people who loved him like I did, who would want to go to the concert, but because the gig was local, a couple of school friends came with me. I was still at school and only had a Saturday job so could only afford one ticket, which was for the first night – Friday. But a good friend offered me his ticket for the Sunday so I was able to go twice. Plans to meet in the pub on Saturday (yes I know I was only 16) to discuss all things Bowie meant the whole weekend would be a Bowie fest!

On that Friday morning I got up very early and caught a bus to The National Bowl. I had never been there before, I was too young to drive and had no idea where it was in relation to the rest of the town and where my home was. But I was first in line at 11am. The doors didn't open until 2pm and I knew he wouldn't be on until much later – but nothing could dampen my enthusiasm.

I knew we couldn't bring in water or food so I didn't bring any but I did hide my 110 compact camera in my bag as I really wanted a couple of photos of him. Rules on photography were strict back then, and cameras in general were not allowed. This was only the second gig I had ever been to, and the first on my own, but I knew it was significant and I was willing to take the risk. Once I was inside I ran to the front and secured my space. I had already lost my friends from school but didn't care. I also knew that meant I couldn't go to get food or go to the toilet or I might lose my place. Again, I didn't care.

The sun was shining and I was all in white – hoping to stand out in the crowd. I got chatting to a few people around me but no one seemed to love him like me. I don't say that lightly. I wanted to find someone who knew the album stuff – not just the singles. I wanted to say how much I loved some of the B-sides and have a soft spot for 'Amsterdam' (B-side to his single 'Sorrow'). Alas the people around me didn't want to talk that way. So I sat in the huge scooped out field with the sun shining down on me and listened to the music from the speakers. This was a perfect day. This was the day I get to meet David Bowie.

I sat through several groups – I vaguely remember The Beat and Icehouse - but to be honest none of them bothered me. I didn't care for them much. I couldn't wait for Bowie. The bouncers kept spraying the crowd with water. I wasn't very happy about this. I know they didn't want us to overheat but I didn't want my mascara to run the first time I meet him either!

Eventually it was time. I was so excited. I had butterflies in my stomach and the anticipation was tantalising. He came on and what a vision he was. I may have had my mouth open but I was in shock. Blond, a healthy looking tan and in a smart suit right in front of me, by only a few feet. My goodness I couldn't believe it. I felt

Jasmine Storm with her favourite poster boy

very emotional and had tears in my eyes but blinked them away as didn't want to cry because I wanted to capture and breathe in every moment. When he was at the back of the stage I couldn't even see him because I was right at the front and the stage was so high. I was transfixed by him. We sang along. We danced. It was truly a wonderful moment. 'Cracked Actor' came on and during those first few bars I looked around for someone in the crowd who would know it – and found a girl near me. We both sang it loudly whilst the rest of the crowd waited for another song they knew. It felt very special to know only the 'die-hards' knew it.

I wanted to stop time. I wanted to never let this moment end. But alas the concert did finish and the 60,000 people started to leave. There was a free shuttle bus service back to the city centre. I got on it and someone said to me, 'What happened to you?' I replied 'I was at the front!' I was in a daze, not looking so white anymore from being squashed in the crowd, clutching my programme that had got a bit damaged on one corner but none of that mattered. I was at the front and had seen him. And only 48 hours until the next time. Best night of my life? Absolutely!

Years later my mum was trying to understand my love of Bowie and said to me, 'Well if you love him why didn't you marry him?' I said to her, 'Mum – he didn't ask me!'

I WAS THERE: TOM BANKS

Having been a massive fan since 1969 I was uber excited to hear that the Serious Moonlight Tour was heading to Hong Kong (where I was living at the time) for a couple of nights in December 1983. Imagine my horror when I discovered that I was already booked on a flight to Vancouver the night before the first gig. It took me seven years to finally get to my first Bowie gig at the Milton Keynes Bowl. I endured a three-hour wait to get out of the car park at the end of the show – but totally worth it to get to see the man in the flesh.

HARTFORD CIVIC CENTER

15 JULY 1983 HARTFORD, CONNECTICUT

I WAS THERE: KAREN JUDD VALENCIA

I saw him in Hartford, Connecticut, when the balloons didn't come down from the ceiling. The next night they did drop. I also saw him at The Sting, a small venue in New Britain, Connecticut with Tin Machine when the It's My Life Tour played on 25 October 1991.

THE SPECTRUM

18-21 JULY 1983 PHILADELPHIA

I WAS THERE: JOE BUNTING

I saw David on July 20, 1983 on the third night of a five night stint at the Spectrum in Philadelphia. I was front row, center stage. I Got lucky getting the tickets. My buddy and I went to the Spectrum ticket window, expecting to get 'nose bleed seats' for the second show of the two dates originally advertised. We had no idea that they announced there would be a third, fourth, and fifth show added while we were on the way there. I knew we had good seats, but when the usher at the side of the stage said to me, 'Man, he's gonna be sweatin' on ya', it was like something straight out of a movie. I still remember being able to see his different colored eyes. Best show of my life.

I WAS THERE: STEVEN KAMINSKY

I was attending school at Bowman technical in Lancaster, Philadelphia at the time, so the drive to the stadium wasn't too far. It was one of my first concerts. I went with at least three other friends. We got there early enough to find a place on the field, (the bleachers were full). Bowie of course performed all of the tunes from his then newest album, and rifted through earlier hits from *Ziggy Stardust* and *Diamond Dogs*. If I remember correctly it was cold, we were all wearing coats. I would've been about 19 or 20 years old. Sadly that has become a long time ago, and I can't recall the exact date, but I think that was his only stop in Eastern PA. He was promoting his album *Let's Dance*. He brought the crowd to its feet when he performed 'Cat People (Putting Out Fire)' and the title track, 'Let's Dance' which I believe he opened with.

CARRIER DOME

23 JULY 1983 SYRACUSE, NEW YORK

HELEN LYON

I was introduced to Mr Bowie's genius during the *Ziggy Stardust* era. Friends and I spent many hours in 'altered states' listening to and appreciating what would become a life-long obsession of mine. We fantasized about what it would be like to spend a day inside his head, trying to wrap our minds

around his 'message'. He was so alien and so far from the norm of what was currently being shoved down our collective throats. With each new song, there seemed to be a world of limitless opportunities that had never occurred to us.

It took years for the opportunity to see him 'live'. We live in a rural part of New York State and it was not financially possible at that time for us to purchase concert tickets. By the time the Serious Moonlight Tour was announced we knew we just had to find a way.

Syracuse was only a three-hour drive away. So, two of my best friends and I decided to make it happen. The weeks leading up to the show were unbearable. It was all we could do to keep our concentration on our work and home lives. We worked a full eight- hour shift on the day of the show, punched out at quitting time, ran to our car in the lot, and hopped on the thruway to Syracuse. We checked into a motel just outside the city and prepared for what was to be a life-changing event.

The venue was the Carrier Dome and they were running shuttle buses from our hotel to the concert. They were great big city-like buses and each was filled to capacity with anxious fans. We could hardly contain our excitement. There was a buzz of unbridled expectation and wonderment at what we were all about to witness.

Our seats were section five floor seats, eleventh row.

The cavernous Carrier Dome was filled to capacity as we waited for the show to begin. There was a giant, glittering crescent moon suspended over the corner of the stage and shiny ethereal columns as set design. Carlos Alomar, and what I assumed to be his wife and a baby, casually strolled down our aisle. No one really recognized him. But, of course, I did. I was hurrying to find a pen in hopes of getting an autograph, but alas, he was gone by the time I got one.

As soon as Mr Bowie was announced, the venue erupted and everyone tried to rush forward to get as close as we could get.

That never happened. Security was extremely tight and admonished us to stay in our seats. We could stand either in front of or on our seats, but we were NOT to block the aisles! (something about a fire hazard).

The lights go down. The hum of an eager audience increased in volume and there he was! Brilliant blond hair, powder blue suit, and a smile that could melt the polar ice caps! I swear he looked as if he ascended from the heavens to grace us mortals with his presence. I immediately started crying and was just enthralled with what we were witnessing. I can't even tell you what the first song was. I didn't care at that point. All I knew was that he was finally in front of my face and I was going to take it all in. Years of wishing, hoping, fantasizing and longing had culminated in this moment.

When the show ended, it was such a hollow feeling. Almost like, 'Well, now what?' I truly did not want it to end. I received a taste and needed more. We reluctantly shuffled out of the Dome and fought our way to the jam-packed buses for the short ride back to our motel. Most people were oddly silent, as if they had witnessed the coming of the New Messiah. That experience changed my life in so many ways.

MADISON SQUARE GARDEN

25 JULY 1983 NEW YORK CITY

I WAS THERE: MICHAEL NAGLE

The first time I saw David Bowie live was on July 25, 1983. I was 18 years old and had worn out *Diamond Dogs* years earlier.

When I first listened to Bowie it wasn't cool to. His comments in the media about being bisexual didn't go over well at the time – even in Manhattan where I was born and raised. As a heterosexual male teen attending Catholic school, you wore uniforms every day so sporting a Bowie shirt wasn't an option anyway. My friends listened to pop stations but I had three older siblings who regularly played the classics including Led Zeppelin, Johnny and Edgar Winter, Black Sabbath, Alice Cooper, Leon Russell and many more.

When Bowie took the stage he looked sharp in a creamy yellow suit. He looked impeccable with JFK-like hair bouncing as he moved. I'd waited my whole life to see him. I felt like half the audience had no idea who it was they were seeing. If you'd only discovered Bowie with 'Let's Dance' you really had some homework to do. He opened with

'Star', which evoked the Brit-rock style that I was attracted to early on. Second track of the night was 'Heroes', which even then lifted you off the floor. The room almost swayed as the band played the music. Up until that instant, it was the single most amazing live performance of a song I had seen at any concert.

What I liked about the concert most was Bowie's alternating approach to the track list. You weren't disappointed if you were into Ziggy, Thin White Duke or any other stage of his career. He also did covers like 'White Light/White Heat', which felt good in New York City. It was almost like putting on *ChangesOneBowie* and having him come by to perform it personally and throw in bonus tracks. Still, it didn't feel like a 'greatest hits' performance.

The intimacy of songs like 'Life on Mars?' and 'Space Oddity' were right there locking out the thousands of fans sharing the experience with me.

The final song of the night was 'Modern Love' and the gold moon-shaped balloons were falling from the ceiling. It was an amazing experience and one I'll never forget. I saw Bowie two more times in my life but this one will always stand out since it was my first time seeing him. The best part now is that 34-years later my son Jack (now 14) auditioned for his high school talent show by singing 'Space Oddity'. He picked it entirely on his own and with zero influence from me aside from the occasional drives when he and I sing songs from the radio together. Jack also plays it on acoustic guitar and I can stop what I'm doing and appreciate still what an incredible song it is and artist Bowie was.

I WAS THERE: TROY MITCHELL OWENS

My mother knew one of Bowie's security men and he got me and my sister tickets about 20th row center on the floor at Madison Square Garden. The best seats I ever had. Bowie put on a great show. I remember the helium filled gold Mylar quarter moons falling from the ceiling.

JOE LOUIS ARENA

30 JULY 1983 DETROIT, MICHIGAN

I WAS THERE: KARA PERKINS

At the end of July 1983 at Joe Louis Arena in Detroit, Michigan, I loved every minute of David Bowie's Serious Moonlight Tour. I was young, free and loved to dance (still do!). I remember the lighting was perfect. He was beautifully dressed in a zoot suit. Every song was perfect. I still have the sleeveless sweatshirt from that night.

COMMONWEALTH STADIUM

7 AUGUST 1983 EDMONTON, ALBERTA, CANADA

I WAS THERE: LORI WOODHOUSE

It was the Serious Moonlight Tour 7 Aug 1983. It was hot and the concert was outdoors. We had a BBQ that day and all our friends attended. We were so high. When we parked, we couldn't close the door on my old car. Needless to say we didn't care. We just left the door open and hurried to the concert. Peter Gabriel and The Tubes opened for David Bowie. It was so amazing!! We played frisbee and danced all night. Seeing David Bowie was surreal. What a spectacular performance!! 'Let's Dance', 'China Girl', 'Heroes', 'Jean Genie'. I'll never forget that concert. I shared that moment in time with a dear friend who has since passed away. Oh yes, and the door on the car wouldn't shut because the seatbelt was hanging down!

BC PLACE

9 AUGUST 1983 VANCOUVER, CANADA

I WAS THERE: PAUL MOLUND

Although David Bowie put on a good show, acoustics for his

show were not great. Peter Gabriel preceded David Bowie, and acoustics were excellent, hearing every word perfectly. The soundman knew what he was doing, but it didn't seem to be the case for the Bowie segment of the concert.

The Bowie concert was well received though, as this was one of the first concerts in our new BC Place Stadium, (the stadium held 60,000 people in the stands and another 15,000, I believe, on the floor). And it was a sold out concert, as I recall. The venue has been completely rebuilt since 1983, for the 2010 Winter Olympics here.

REUNION ARENA

19 AUGUST 1983 DALLAS, TEXAS

I WAS THERE: PAUL LINDBERG

He did two sets, it was part of the Serious Moonlight Tour and it was amazing. My friends Roland Galvanin and Rik McDonald were with me. Our seats were up high behind the stage, so we were watching his back most of the time.

What impressed me was the professionalism of his band, how relaxed all the musicians were, and the quality of the sound. The band members were dressed up, not in costume but in suit and tie – almost Chicago Mob style but not quite. At one point he was singing a solo, so a few of the band members went to the back of the stage and mimicked playing a game of cards.

I've always liked how David Bowie used handclaps in his music ('Golden Years'), so I was watching to see how that would translate live. And he did it! Clapping into his vocal mic, again very relaxed and smooth, right on beat, just the right amount of effort.

I walked away from that show very impressed, and even with his back to us, I could still sense his charisma and showmanship.

One of the best concerts I've been to. It was an amazing show!

SCOPE CULTURAL AND CONVENTION CENTER

24 AUGUST 1983 NORFOLK, VIRGINIA

I WAS THERE: LES SHIFLER

I was in the Navy stationed at Norfolk, Virginia, from 1983-87. I saw many concerts in Norfolk, when my ship was not out at sea, at the Norfolk Scope, Hampton Roads, or Richmond in those years. I don't remember much else about the show, other than Bowie did play 'Let's Dance,' and 'Cat People (Putting Out Fire)', the theme from *Cat People*. Earl Slick was the guitar player, with most of his regular Eighties band, as I remember.

SULLIVAN STADIUM

31 AUGUST 1983 FOXBOROUGH, MASSACHUSETTS

I WAS THERE: DEANNA FRANCESCA FRONDUTO

I was blessed to see David Bowie perform in concert back in 1983, at the Sullivan Stadium (aka Gillette Stadium), Foxborough, Massachusetts. It was one of the best concerts of my life! I was 18 years old and remember the moment the beautiful blond haired Starman came out on the stage…the crowd went crazy!!! What a performance…OMG…incredible doesn't even begin to describe the impact of this memorable concert! The songs; each one brilliantly picked out and sung so perfectly in person, the electricity and magnetic waves as he moved across that floor as me and the others danced the night away.

A true showman who had so much vision beyond anyone's wildest dreams. Oh, and that smile!! Genuine. Nothing fake about that infectious smile that he transmitted across the audience with every song he sang.

Bright lights, full of energy, full of life, David Bowie had it all and made a statement to the world – to be who you are, dare to be different and comfortable inside, a man of the most intriguing and mind blowing fashion throughout the generation of time, determined in every aspect of the word - an artistic, creative musician who loved what he did. He owned that stage when he was on it and you could see that passion so clearly. I am Forever grateful to have seen this amazing, clever, brilliant artist perform, right in front of me.

I WAS THERE: CHRIS CONNOR

I won tickets for the Let's Dance show in Foxborough, but had to go to our local radio station WBCN in Boston to pick them up. We went on a double decker bus full of competition winners, after drinking at a bar outside the radio studio waiting for DJ Charles Laquidera to show up. I found my eight-month pregnant wife in the crowd and rocked the night away!

I WAS THERE: ROBERT WILLIAMS

It was the first and only time I had the pleasure to see him. I was 22 at the time and it was the Serious Moonlight Tour. It was incredible. I've played in bands since I was 14, first as a bass player, then guitarist singer. In 1980 my bands set list had 'Moonage Daydream', 'Soul Love', 'Ziggy Stardust' and 'Suffragette City' when we were playing the Boston scene.

At the concert there was a giant world balloon 15 or 20 feet in diameter that he threw out for the crowd to bounce all over the stadium. Every song sounded just like the recordings and that means everything to a musician. Beside a KISS show I saw in 1976 (my first concert), Bowie's was by far the best. He is as significant as John Lennon to me.

ANAHEIM STADIUM

9 SEPTEMBER 1983 CALIFORNIA

I WAS THERE: MICHAEL WACHS

I saw David Bowie in 1983 when he did the Serious Moonlight Tour at Anaheim Stadium, California. It was a festival type line-up that started around two in the afternoon with Madness, followed by The Go-Go's and headlining was David Bowie. I was in high school and went with some upperclassman and we had the time of our lives. We sat in the bleachers seats of Anaheim Stadium during Madness and the Go-Go's. I was so amazed at how many people were on the field. When David Bowie came out to perform he owned that stage, opening with 'Look Back In Anger'. He took the concert to another level and we were along for the ride. I still have the programme from the concert.

I WAS THERE: HEATHER MATTHEWS

Let me start by saying the early Eighties were a great time to see shows. We were lucky. Sir David Bowie, yes, I saw him in 1983. My parents first saw him in the Seventies, on the Ziggy Stardust Tour in upstate New York.

I was 15, and lived in Laguna Hills, California, 15 minutes away from Anaheim Stadium. My room was covered in Bowie posters walls to ceiling (seriously). But I almost wasn't able to go to the concert. My friend, who was in beauty college shaved the right side of my head (style back then, Cure-ish) and I came home to hear my mom freak out, and say I couldn't go to the Bowie concert the following day. I begged, kissed ass, pleaded... they let me go. My parents dropped my friend and I off. Her brother picked us up.

He came out in a fabulous yellow suit. I could not believe David Bowie was standing in front of us. Unbelievable. He sang: 'Fashion', 'Heroes', 'Let's Dance', 'Cat People', 'White Light/White Heat', 'Young Americans', 'Fame', 'Ashes to Ashes'. I'll never forget. 'Scary Monsters', 'Rebel Rebel', 'China Girl', sigh, electricity filled that air. Not kidding. The encore was: 'The Jean Genie' and 'Modern Love', and during the encore loads of balloons spilled out, all over. Everyone cheered, danced, sang.

There will never ever, never be anyone like him. It broke my heart when he passed. 2016 was brutal to the music industry. I have a Blackstar tattoo. Prince on my right wrist, Bowie on the left one.

PACIFIC NATIONAL EXHIBITION COLISEUM

12 SEPTEMBER 1983 VANCOUVER, CANADA

I WAS THERE: BRIAN R. WILSON

I was 23. It was the first date for me, and a beautiful lady I was wooing. She later became my fiancee, but in the end it didn't work out between her and I.

I remember being amazed by Bowie's colourful clothes and his moves. One of the guitarists likely had a Middle Eastern background, and he wore a hat that reminded me of something one would see in Turkey, which was certainly something different back then.

The backdrops of the stage were long and shimmering and reminded me of giant jellyfish. It's one of the best concerts I ever attended. My favourites were 'Fame', 'Fashion' and his newest hits like 'China Girl' and 'Let's Dance', but I gained new appreciation for some of his older hits like 'Golden Years' and 'Heroes'.

WINNIPEG STADIUM

14 SEPTEMBER 1983 WINNIPEG, CANADA

I WAS THERE: PAUL DOBSON

It was the first major outdoor concert at Winnipeg Stadium with over 35,000 in attendance. There was some serious moonlight on that Wednesday evening. There were 31 arrests for drug and liquor offences, and six people taken to hospital mainly suffering from injuries caused by crowd surging.

This concert blew the socks off my prairie city (home of Neil Young, and The Guess Who), it was the center of the world for us back then. That day is now my son's birthday and the tour finished up in my current home – Hong Kong, China! Thank you Mr Bowie for putting Winnipeg on the map and making the start of Grade 12 more memorable.

Bowie and his band were flying from gig to gig using a hired 707 jet charted from a company in Miami. Describe as 'a hotel on wings' it had a conference room, plush designer chairs, a kitchen, TV and movie screens, bars and a bedroom which David used at the back of the plane. After the show in Winnipeg, two female fans sneaked past security at the airport, ran across the runway and boarded the plane to try and meet David. They did and local TV news footage showed the girls talking to David at the top of the steps while he was eating a pack of peanuts. After signing autographs and receiving a kiss each from David the girls made their exit.

PERTH ENTERTAINMENT CENTRE

4, 5 & 6 NOVEMBER 1983 PERTH, AUSTRALIA

I WAS THERE: JO KING

I was so excited to be at a live Bowie show. He was larger than life, in fact breath-taking. Musically perfect. What an awesome gig. I'll never forget it!

VFL STADIUM

12 NOVEMBER 1983 MELBOURNE, AUSTRALIA

I WAS THERE: MICHELLE CULLEN

I was in stadium seating and Bowie looked like a dot on stage but we were also able to watch on the large screen. I went with friends from work. It was an amazing concert and Bowie certainly delivered. A wonderful memory. Bowie has always been my favourite artist and I am so glad I got to see him live.

SYDNEY SHOWGROUND

19 NOVEMBER 1983 SYDNEY, AUSTRALIA

I WAS THERE: SCOTT WILLIAMS

I saw the Serious Moonlight Tour at Sydney Cricket Ground. What a surprise for me to see Stevie Ray Vaughan on lead guitar. What a great show, treasured memories. 'Station to Station' was a standout. And Stevie's handiwork on 'Let's Dance'. I love that riff.

Bowie in New Zealand

After playing ten shows in Australia, Bowie arrived in Wellington (under the name David Jones on the passenger manifest), for two concerts, one with an anticipated crowd of 38,000 at Athletic Park in Wellington and the second at the Western Springs in Auckland, at the speedway stadium. Reports put the attendance figure for this show at 74,480, although there were people jumping the fence and other estimates put the crowd tally over 80,000.

The Auckland concert became the largest-ever for a single show in either Australia or New Zealand and made it into the *Guinness Book of Records* as the largest paying crowd per capita anywhere in the world. During the show, Bowie snapped photographs of the Auckland crowd, and at the end of the set, he spoke out against the nuclear arms race, which was dominating headlines around the world as the Cold War escalated. 'I wish our world leaders would stop their insane inability to recognise that we wish to live peacefully', Bowie said. Then, he released two white doves.

ATHLETIC PARK

24 NOVEMBER 1983 WELLINGTON, NEW ZEALAND

I WAS THERE: MANDY BRADSHAW

I was 17 years old and loved Bowie. Back then the local radio station would organise buses to take people down to Wellington for the concert. I was living in Napier, so it was a five hour trip in the bus to the show. A group of strangers all singing Bowie songs, super excited, and discussing what we thought it would like and hoped to see and hear.

I remember Bowie looking like a God. Handsome, he seemed so tall and thin. He was dressed to perfection in double-breasted suits, pants with braces (suspenders), undone bow tie hanging round his neck. 'Let's Dance' and 'China Girl' were pure magic. He had all the moves and owned the stage, the crowd, the night!

After the concert it would be straight back on the bus for another five hours. We would be singing again and chattering, still buzzing after the concert. Everyone would have bought T-shirts and programmes. After about an hour and half we would start to fall asleep, heads on strangers' shoulders but it didn't matter. We'd all seen Bowie, we were family for that one night!

WESTERN SPRINGS STADIUM

26 NOVEMBER 1983
AUCKLAND, NEW ZEALAND

I WAS THERE: ANGELA DOEGE HOCKING

I was 14 years old and it was the first concert I had ever been to. I was about, 15 rows from the front and Bowie winked at me! It was the best moment of my life then. It was recorded in *The Guinness Book of Records* as the largest crowd gathering per head of population anywhere in the world at 74,480, although officials believed it to be closer to 90,000. It still stands as the most amazing concert experience I have ever had. RIP to a true legend.

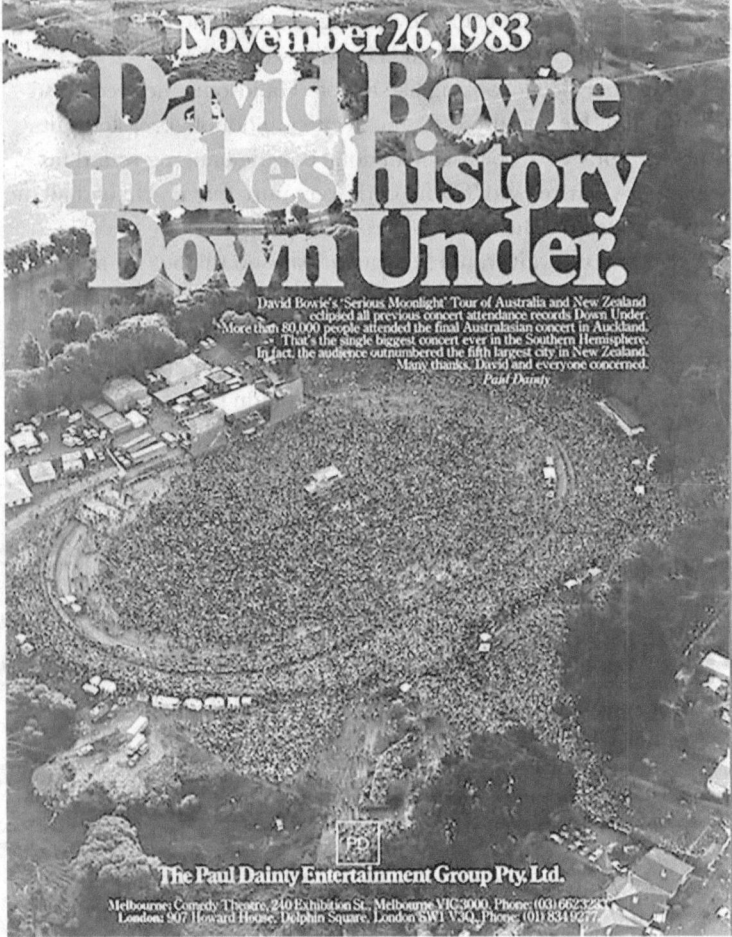

I WAS THERE: TREVOR BRYAN

It was my wife and myself at the time, and three friends. We borrowed mum's little Suzuki van and drove 100 miles to Western Springs. When we arrived it was packed. We shuffled along and it took us ages to get in. Once in we managed to push our way to nearly the front so we had a good view of the stage. I'm sorry to say I can't remember as much now as I would like, but the stand-out for me was Bowie singing a song to a human skull surrounded by long strips of plastic. It really blew my mind! The song he sung to the skull was 'Cracked Actor'.

Trying to get out afterwards was a nightmare, shuffling along, with my mate making bah bahhh bahing noises like a sheep and everyone around us laughing. It took us hours to get out of Auckland and we finally pulled over to the side of the road and waited until morning to go home. An Awesome concert and I'll never forget the experience.

I WAS THERE: KERI

My name is Keri, and it was my father and mother, that went to the David Bowie concert back in 1983. My daughter is nine now and has been in love with David Bowie since she was eight months old. Her father and myself played Guitar Hero which had 'Ziggy Stardust' on it and it was the first song she pulled herself up to stand against the couch and danced to!

When she was three years old, we went on a family holiday and with her spending money bought a vinyl album (I can't even remember which album it was as we didn't have a record player so it stays at her grandparents house so she can listen to it). At the age of four she sat outside our drive with an empty can to raise money to go visit David Bowie in England and cried because no one went past. She could sing 'Starman' word for word at the age of seven.

The day he died she was so devastated she couldn't believe it. We went to our local shopping center and bought *Black Star* and in two days she knew the 'Lazarus' lyrics off by heart. She has t-shirts and calendars. Her christmas present from her dad was four pins wrapped under the tree, then he pulled out a poster of a *Aladdin Sane*. Her jaw dropped more than a 16-year old getting a new iPhone.

Thailand

By December 1983 The Serious Moonlight Tour was nearing its end, with 96 shows played, 15 countries visited, over 2.6M tickets sold and just two more shows to go.

David Bowie's concert in Thailand on 5 Dec 1983, was not supposed to happen. With a price tag of US $1 million per show, a Bowie concert was too expensive for those who hoped to bring the tour to the country. Yet, in the end, Bowie took a huge pay cut simply so he could be in Bangkok and explore the city.

Although Bowie suffered a financial loss from his Bangkok concert, he apparently enjoyed every single minute he spent in the Thai capital. The promoters rented an old Mercedes limousine so he and three other members of his crew could do some sightseeing around Bangkok before the concert. During the day he travelled by boat along the Chao Phraya River, made a visit to a go-go bar in Bangkok and Bowie received a blessing from a Thai man, who spat what was apparently holy water from his mouth on Bowie's face.

The promoters became worried when by early evening David and his friends were very late arriving back at the venue. It turned out that the limousine broke down, and they all got out and hailed a cab, arriving only minutes before the show started.

THAI ARMY SPORTS STADIUM

5 DECEMBER 1983 BANGKOK, THAILAND

I WAS THERE: NOI NAMON

My knowledge of how great David Bowie was started from the popular radio station Nite Spot on FM 99 Bangkok. The DJ had been Bowie's number one fan. I was able to listen to her daytime programme regularly around 1979 when I was a freshman in university, since I didn't have to attend class all the time like when I was in high school. She played Bowie's songs from old albums at the end of every hour before a short newsbreak. She talked about his work, his films, and his life. I was hooked. She played 'When I Live My Dream' from the first LP. 'Space Oddity', 'The Man Who Sold the World', 'Starman', 'Suffragette City', 'The Jean Genie', 'Rock 'n' Roll Suicide', '1984' – all hits and non-hits. My favorite Bowie song at the time? 'Be My Wife', of course, as well as 'Sorrow', 'Fashion', 'Golden Years', and 'Life on Mars?'

Shortly after I had graduated from university and got my first job I learned that Bowie would be playing in Bangkok at the end of the year (1983) as part of the Serious Moonlight Tour. Was it real or just a rumour? We've had big names performing live in Bangkok before, such as Blondie (1978), The Pretenders (1978), Eric Clapton, The Doobie Brothers, (around 1981, the Michael McDonald era), America, Deep Purple, etc. Soon it was confirmed that David Bowie would have a concert in Bangkok.

The ticket was quite expensive for me because I'd just got out of college and had my first job. I couldn't miss it for the world. I asked my uncle (my mom's younger brother who was a big fan of Elvis Presley) to accompany me, because the venue – the Thai Army Stadium – was quite far from my home and it would be close to midnight when the concert was over. He agreed. Yeahhhhh.

Monday, the 5th of December 1983, the day of the concert. It was our King Bhumibol Adulyadej's birthday (a public holiday). We arrived at this open-aired stadium quite early to avoid the traffic. The stadium held 20,000 and had a single stand with covered seating on one side and terracing on three sides. It was hot that day so I decided to sit at one of the terraces waiting for the concert to start. People were arriving until the front of the stage was packed.

The concert was supposed to start at 8.30pm, but was a bit late. David Bowie walked to the front of the stage and the crowd just went wild. He calmed us down and then said, 'Happy Birthday to your King!' and put his hands together and bowed (in Thailand we call this gesture Wai, the gesture to show one's respect in this case). He didn't just ignore the occasion but was prepared to show his respect to our beloved king. This makes me adore him even more as a person. Then the concert started.

It was one of the most memorable moments in my entire life. My heart stopped when I heard the sound of drum and bass from 'Look Back in Anger' blaze over the stadium. After a while, I couldn't just stay at the terrace so I ran to the front of the stage to get closer to him. I left my uncle and my camera behind (big mistake, but it was too heavy for me to carry them on my neck all night to fully enjoyed the music). He sang all my favorite songs: 'Golden Years', 'Fashion', and 'Let's Dance'

back to back, I thought I would die. I was screaming so loud I lost my voice the next day.

Then 'Life on Mars?' and 'Sorrow'. His theatrical performance on stage was pure magic with guitarists Carlos Alomar and Earl Slick and the backup singers from the Simms Brothers. The experience was surreal to me. I was either screaming like mad or just standing there in disbelief trying to feel the whole thing from every fiber of my being. He closed the night with 'Modern Love'. I was so sad it had to end. The sight of him is still in my heart to this day.

Live Aid – 1985
On July 13, 1985, David Bowie would take the stage at Wembley Stadium as part of the Live Aid benefit concert. Bowie appeared at 7:20 p.m. in London, falling in between Queen (who had just ended their set with an incredible version of 'We Will Rock You'/We Are The Champions') and The Who. Bowie played 'TVC 15,' 'Rebel Rebel,' 'Modern Love' and 'Heroes' to nearly two billion people worldwide.

LIVE AID

13 JULY 1985 WEMBLEY STADIUM, LONDON

I WAS THERE: NED MALET DE CARTERET

I saw him at Wembley Stadium on 13th July 1985 at Live Aid (the third time I saw him live). I was in the left hand corner – upper terrace balcony – so really quite a good view – enough said! We saw Phil Collins on telly in Philadelphia when we got home, having seen him fly over the stadium in Concorde!

I WAS THERE: THOMAS DOLBY, MUSICIAN

We had about four days rehearsal, and we had to work after David had finished shooting each day where he was filming *Labyrinth* at Pinewood Studios. He kept changing his mind about what songs to do. He started off by saying he was going to promote his current single which I think was 'Loving The Alien', at the time but as he became more focused on the event he realised that he needed to play anthems really and we had played through each of the four songs before we went to Wembley, but we'd never played them back to back.

It was quite surreal, I remember that morning, walking around London, you would hear the pre-amble, everybody had their TV tuned to the show, so as you walked down the street, it was a hot day, you would hear it coming out of every open window, every time a car stopped at a traffic light you would hear it coming out, so the whole country was basically tuned to it.

I flew in on a helicopter from Wembley and whereas Bowie had been a perfect gentleman all through the rehearsal process and was very magnanimous and gracious, given his fear of flying in the helicopter he was the thin white duke all of a sudden with a hat pulled over his face! Chain smoking nervously he was saying 'When do we get there? How soon do we get there?'

I remember the pilot telling him he couldn't smoke.

We touched down a few blocks from Wembley and were transferred into a motorcade which drove through the streets at high speed, stopping inside the gates at Wembley, where we were surrounded by a

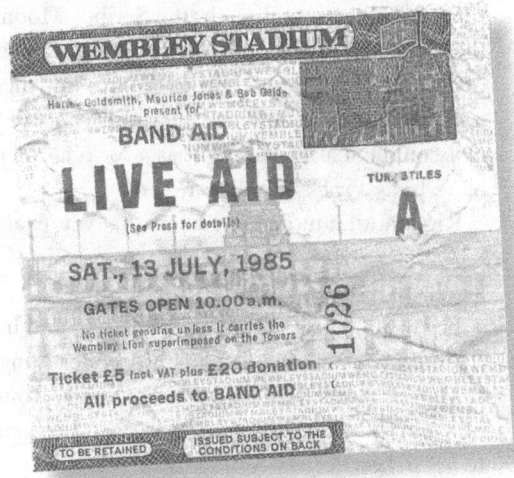

swarm of paparazzi who were all around the limo. Bowie was loving it, stepping out in front of the cameras, and by the time he'd finished posing for the press it was basically time to go on stage. We weren't even taken to the green room, we were taken straight to the side of the stage where we watched half a song of the previous band and then we were straight on stage and into it.

I was extremely nervous, but in a way I was channeling my teenage adulation, I sort of knew the songs intuitively rather than through practice. I looked out at the sea of people at Wembley and the songs just seemed to play themselves.

I WAS THERE: JULIAN LOWE

I was lucky enough to see Bowie perform live three times: twice at the Milton Keynes Bowl, on the Serious Moonlight tour in July 1983 and his Sound+Vision Tour in August 1990; but also at Wembley Stadium for his Live Aid performance on 13 July 1985.

The whole Live Aid concert was memorable simply for being the amazing event it was, but I clearly remember Bowie introducing his band during the outro of 'Heroes' and referring to 'the very brilliant Thomas Dolby', as well as him announcing one of the famine videos after his set with the words, 'Lest we forget why we're here...'

Out of the three, though, the Serious Moonlight show stands out a mile for me. I distinctly remember the hairs on my neck standing up on end when he came right to the front of the stage where we were and sang the last couple of lines to his encore 'Star':

'I could fall asleep at night as a rock 'n' roll star, I could fall in love all right as a rock 'n' roll star'.

Right at that moment, I knew that was exactly what Bowie was...

I WAS THERE: MARTYN CORNOCK

I Saw him at Live Aid when I was 16 and he totally blew me away, 'Heroes' has got to be one of the greatest songs ever. Then saw him at Cardiff Arms Park on the Glass Spider Tour. Also had the privilege of seeing Tin Machine play Newport, I remember queuing overnight to get tickets.

1987

Glass Spider Tour. Named after the album track 'Glass Spider', this 86-date tour was launched to support the album *Never Let Me Down*. Bowie wanted this tour to be 'ultra-theatrical', a combination of music, theater, and rock. Kicking off in May 1987, it was preceded by a two-week press tour that saw Bowie visit nine countries throughout Europe and North America.

The Glass Spider Tour was the first Bowie tour to visit Austria, Italy, Spain, Ireland and Wales and was also intended to visit Russia and South America, but these plans were later cancelled. The tour was, at this point, the longest and most expensive tour Bowie had embarked upon in his career.

Bowie conceived the tour as a theatrical show, and included spoken-word introductions to some songs, vignettes, and employed visuals including projected videos, theatrical lighting and stage props. On stage, Bowie, was joined by guitarist Peter Frampton, who he had known since their teen years, when they both attended Bromley Technical School, where Frampton's father was Bowie's art teacher. The show also featured a troupe of five dancers (choreographed by long-time Bowie collaborator Toni Basil).

The tour's set, described at the time as 'the largest touring set ever', was designed by Mark Ravitz, (who designed the set for the 1974 Diamond Dogs Tour). The giant spider was 60 feet (18.3m) high, 64 feet (19.5m) wide and included giant vacuumed tube legs that were lit from the inside with 20,000ft (6,096m) of color-changing lights. A single set took 43 trucks to move from show to show and the system required to run the show included two separate sound systems, 260 speaker cabinets, 1,000 lights and three computers.

The tour took a physical toll on Bowie. Not only did he grow noticeably thinner over the course of the tour, he found that he was exhausted before the tour even started.

Sadly Michael Clark, a lighting engineer, died at the Stadio Comunale in Florence, Italy on 9 June after falling from the scaffolding before the show commenced.

Other incidents include both shows in Rome (on 15 and 16 June) which saw riots as fans, that couldn't get tickets clashed with police.

On the second night, Bowie had to sing through tear gas and 50 people were arrested and 15 policemen were injured in the rioting. As the band's plane was leaving Rome after their show on 16 June, a bomb scare forced the plane to return the airport, only to discover that the local chief of police had used it as ruse to get Bowie's autograph.

I WAS THERE: PETER FRAMPTON, SINGER, GUITARIST

He called me up after the *Premonition* record. A dear friend for many years, we went to school together and he said, 'I love what you're playing. Would you come and do some of that on my album?' And then I went to Switzerland, and we went to dinner. He said, 'Wanna come on tour?' I said, 'Yep'. So that was it. That was the most re-invigorating thing I could have done. He gave me a gift on a silver platter. He reintroduced me in an arena that I couldn't fill throughout the world anymore. He reintroduced me as the musician, the guitar player. And I can never, ever - I'm getting chills right now - I can never, ever thank him enough, my dear friend.

I WAS THERE: JUDY TOTTON, PRESS OFFICER, GLASS SPIDER TOUR

The day we left London to work on the Glass Spider Tour I was creaking. I'd put my back out that week having just returned from a nine country/two week press conference trip with David and his band where we'd rushed across continents, stayed up late and generally been frantically busy. Consequently, when the tour itself arrived, I wasn't in the best of shape. So I took Carmine from my office with me. She carried the bags, we caught the flight and we duly embedded ourselves in the hotel.

Just as we were sorting out the paperwork (and there was a great deal of that on this tour, the requests never stopped coming) there was a knock on my bedroom door. Carmine opened it and there stood David. He came in, sat on the bed, had a cup of tea from the hotel teas-maid and generally chatted about what was to come. It was just utterly normal and down to earth. He gave me some notes to type up – I still have the original handwritten copy – an explanation of the show's theatrical themes and very vivid ideas.

It was the beginning of one of the most hectic tours I've ever been on what with royalty, film stars, pop stars and media all visiting, the two enormous giant spider sets leapfrogging from country to country and various memorable incidents along the way. But that first mental snapshot of David drinking tea on the bed in this rather dull hotel room will stay with me forever. It was so simple – but special. He truly was a very lovely man.

ROCK WERCHTER

2 JUNE 1987 WERCHTER, BELGIUM

I WAS THERE: LESLEY DE RIDDER

I was the first in line at the ticket office in Antwerp. I had never gotten out of bed so early in my teenage lifetime. I was 17 (almost 18 as my birthday is the 6th of June), and had been a fan since I was 14 years old. I got the tickets for me, my mother, sister and my friends, for the Glass Spider Tour at the outside festival venue of Werchter. On the day of the concert it was raining all day and I remember David kneeling down and his red suit was soaking wet when he got back up. I do believe there were some technical problems because of the rain. I saw the same concert later at an inside venue and there was more of a show and technical stuff going on then. But the magic of watching him on stage for the first time... I'll never forget...

On the way home we had a pretty serious car accident on the highway. But we all survived the minor injuries (whiplashes, concussions etc). Apparently we had a guardian angel, because a car hit our car really hard on this very busy highway.

Bowie is the one and only artist that has kept me fascinated. In every step he made. Yes, even the Tin Machine step.

PLATZ DER REPUBLIK

6 JUNE 1987 BERLIN, GERMANY

I WAS THERE: ROWAN GWILLIM

In summer 1987 I was just coming to the end of my year abroad which I had spent half in Russia and half in Germany (I was studying Modern Languages in Newcastle-upon-Tyne). I was living in Darmstadt (just south of Frankfurt) in a student flat, and my best friend there was a girl called Tine Hoefler.

At the time the Berlin Wall was up, of course, and although Darmstadt was a long way away (some 600 km), when we heard about the Concert for Berlin (part of the commemorations for the City's 750th anniversary), Tine and I decided to go.

We were both students and had very little money. Luckily tickets were subsidised by the West German Government, who couldn't afford (politically) for the concert to be a failure. So for the three days (other headliners were Eurythmics and Genesis) the ticket cost €15 Marks (which was about $7.50) We had nowhere to stay, so we borrowed a tent from my brother's then girlfriend (he was living in Heidelberg at the time).

Rowan Gwillim

We drove to Berlin along the famous 'corridor'. We drove through an East German checkpoint where the car details were taken and when we arrived in West Berlin, our details were taken again. This was in order to check our average speed to make sure that we had not made any unauthorised stops on the way, i.e. to pick up any extra passengers (escaping East Germany).

When we arrived in Berlin we knew no one. We had no idea of where to go, so we drove as close to where the concert was due to take place as we could, and pitched the tent alongside the River Spree with some other people who were also camped illegally.

That was the night before the concert, and I remember meeting our fellow campers and smoking a bit with them (we were young, we were foolish!). The skirt of the tent ended up with a cigarette burn and I remember my brother and his girlfriend were furious when we returned it to them later. It had been brand new. Oh,

and on the first morning a police boat came in close to us and told us in no uncertain terms to move our tent. We did not, of course! Ironic that on the other side of the Wall, such minor rebellion would have been severely punished!

The next day in the evening, along with tens of thousands of others, we crammed into a field in front of the Reicshtag. In 1990 I moved to Berlin for three years, but at the time this area was all completely unknown to me. The support act was a German guy called Rio Reiser, who was a huge star. Everyone was determined to have a great time, so although Reiser was given a good reception, when Bowie came on stage descending on a huge swing, the place went wild.

No comparison.

I was nowhere near the front, but the atmosphere was incredible. There was a huge illuminated spider around the stage, very intricate and impressive for an outside venue. There were some crazy dancers on stage and Bowie was looking dapper in a red suit. The crowd was singing along, determined, I think, to show Bowie how welcome he was. Perhaps people don't remember that the Glass Spider Tour had been given poor reviews, and Berlin was keen to show Bowie that he was still their God.

At the time we had very little

The concert site in Berlin the morning after

idea as to what was happening on the other side of the Wall. There were reports of unrest on the (West German) news, but of course we were in our tent for three more nights, so hadn't heard much about it. Celebrations were taking place in East Berlin too, of course, with each side determined to outdo the other. I think it was clear who won this round!

As mentioned, I subsequently lived in Berlin for three years, and Tine moved there for some time too. We both got to know people who had been smuggled out of East Berlin in the trunk of cars or escaped in incredibly daring ways. It was a different world, and one which Bowie was well acquainted with.

Tine and I are still friends and we have enjoyed indulging in nostalgia while piecing this together from our memories. It is strange that this concert is now the stuff of legend, and is often quoted as having contributed to the fall of the Berlin Wall and hence of East Germany, heralding the end of the Cold War.

I still love going to concerts, and although this often involves lots of effort (I live in rural France), travelling to Berlin during the Cold War to see Bowie is somewhere at the top of my list of memorable gigs!

STADIO FLAMINIO

15 JUNE 1987 ROME, ITALY

I WAS THERE: FRANCO BRIZI

Sometimes it's hard to remember the past. Things fades, other things changed. But sometimes, almost as magic, looking at a simple ticket 30 years old and kept as a treasure, images and thoughts come back to your mind. 15 June 1987, my first David Bowie show. I was thrilled, and a little bit confused.

At 10am outside the Stadio Flaminio there were many fans ticketless. It was a very mixed gathering: dark, younger fans, and old dogs like myself. At 16:00 we are on the grass, sitting, with the warm sun, which shone on the stage. Twilight comes and we are stunned: a giant Plexiglas spider tower above us all.

We wait for something we all know will be an unforgettable event. Background music fades. Adrenaline is in the air. You can smell it. Carlos Alomar is on the stage. He plays his guitar, with a thunderous solo. Then suddenly a voice from nowhere. 'Shut Up'. He stops. He's puzzled. But then goes back to playing. Two other times a voice will urge him to stop before dancers arrive almost from the sky itself, sliding down ropes. It's time for the intro of 'Up The Hill Backwards'. And from the spider's belly a red jeanie descends upon us, sitting on a silver lounge. It's him. It's finally here!

Screams, chorus, change or scenario. Songs, which hit us as hammer-fists, because they were hits in our life. It was a special and magical evening.

Later people said all kinds of things ('The show is gross' – 'Arrangements are crude!'), but nothing was able to change the magic that show left in our hearts. What stayed in our hearts and in our mind was a slow, languid version of 'Time'. It was magic, It was soul. It's David Bowie.

ROKER PARK

23 JUNE 1987 SUNDERLAND

I WAS THERE: STE CADDY

I was 15 and managed to get the day off school and went with my best friend at the time. I remember being nervous and excited. I remember the support bands were Big Country and The Screaming Blue Messiahs (who had the hit single 'I Wanna Be A Flintstone'), and then around 8pm, finally the main act.

He shouted 'Hello Newcastle' (we were in Sunderland!). The crowd surged forward and the noise level went up considerably. The show was fantastic and is still one of the best nights of my life. It took me at least 10 minutes to realise that the dancer in the black tights and make up was a guy! There was no encore from the top of the spider because it started to rain.

PRATER-STADIUM

1 JULY 1987 VIENNA, AUSTRIA

I WAS THERE: DAVID WINTERFELD

In the Viennese spring of 1987, posters and stickers in black on neon yellow simply announced, 'Bowie kommt' – Bowie is coming. Not much more advertising was needed. Bowie's concert in Vienna on the first of July 1987 during the Glass Spider Tour was only the second show Bowie ever played in Austria after his concert in the Stadthalle in 1978. This time, the chosen venue was the Praterstadion, Austria's

THE GLASS SPIDER TOUR

largest stadium, opened in 1931 in Vienna's huge park, the Prater. A roof above the ranks had been added in 1986. The first rock/pop act to play in the renovated stadium was Genesis, around two weeks prior to Bowie, and they faced severe sound problems which Bowie's sound crew hoped to avoid, using calculations done by a computer, as a news report said.

I was 15 years old at the time and couldn't care less about sound problems. I had become a Bowie fan in 1983, when I heard 'Let's

Dance' on the radio. At that time, my father bought *Ziggy Stardust* on LP and I was completely hooked (and never found a Bowie album I liked better afterwards). I was dreaming about seeing Bowie play in Munich in 1983, as Austrian music magazine *Rennbahn Express* organized a bus to the Olympiahalle, but obviously I was too young. But now, finally, the time to see David Bowie live had come.

I liked the new album and the prospect of a 'theatrical' rock show thrilled me, I even wanted to believe the news blurb that Bowie was going back to the raunchy sound of the early Seventies.

'The big day is here!' I wrote in ink into my red plastic binder where I kept a kind of Bowie-related diary, plus clipped pictures and reports from newspapers. At around noon I went to a meeting of TAABO – The Austrian Absolute Beginners Organisation, the Austrian fan club I had joined, but frankly, I could barely concentrate on the conversation, I was already so nervous.

By 6pm, the stadium was almost full. Newspaper reports indicated that 40,000 to 45,000 spectators wanted to see Bowie's Glass Spider Show – at the time, this was reported as Austria's second biggest crowd right after The Rolling Stones in 1982.

The heat was intense – a little relief was provided by water sprinklers, but they were on the opposite end of the stadium. I had no money left to buy myself a drink, as I bought the tour programme and the shirt, my most treasured piece of clothing for years to come (on the back, it wrongfully says that the show in Vienna was on June 30th, probably that was the initial date). At 7pm Nazz Nasko, an Austrian act signed by EMI, entered the stage. At 9 pm, finally, finally, Carlos Alomar started to play 'Purple Haze'.

Of course, 30 years later my memories are a little hazy themselves, and super-imposed with videos of the tour. But I still remember the things that impressed me the most. The throbbing of my heart when Bowie, seated in a throne, sang 'Glass Spider' into a telephone microphone while being lowered to the stage. The sheer spectacle of dancers, musicians, props and the spider stage itself, which was very effective once it got dark. The use of the background video screen during 'Heroes'. The goose bumps when birdman Bowie, in his third costume of the show, opened his wings while singing 'Time' on top of the giant spider. The joy of clapping and jumping madly to 'Modern Love', the last encore. I never waved bye-bye, because I didn't want it to end. I also remember that I hoped Bowie enjoyed himself and liked the audience response, in order for him to return to Austria (he did six more times).

Newspaper reviews at the time were mixed – while the yellow press applauded, a quality paper called the show 'superficial' and 'mediocre'. It is a fair bet to say that today the Glass Spider Tour is widely regarded as Bowie's worst effort on the road. At the time, I guess Bowie honestly believed in his material and in the show, at least when he started the European leg of the tour. And it wasnt all bad. We got pearls like 'All the Madmen', 'Time', 'Big Brother' and 'Sons of the Silent Age', and the best of Bowie's Eighties-period from 'Scary Monsters' to 'Absolute Beginners'.

For me, that hot day in July 1987 is unforgettable, one of the most important days in my entire life. It was my first David Bowie concert and it was also the first concert I attended by myself, which is kind of fun considering that the title song of the tour is (in parts) about children becoming self-reliant.

STADIUM MUNICIPAL

4 JULY 1987 TOULOUSE, FRANCE

I WAS THERE: CHARLOTTE MOUILLERAC

It was my first Bowie show, Toulouse, France, 4 July 1987. I was 17, and had been a fan a few years, since a cousin of mine told me about him. Before that I was into French oldies like Edith Piaf, Serge Reggiani, Brel, Barbara. I was a weird, shy and lonely kid. My first memory of hearing a Bowie song was when I was in a supermarket in 1985, when I heard 'This Is Not America'.

I must have made it clear it was a big deal for me, as my father agreed to drive me to Toulouse, 150km from home, which was really big coming from him. He is not into music at all. I don't remember the show itself, just that I loved it, and that I was very excited, it was almost like a sexual experience. So much so that I started flirting with a boy behind me (I was standing at the front) but then he became to intense, and I wanted to get out so I signalled the security guys that I wasn't feeling well so they took me out. I was taken to the infirmary and I must have seen the rest of the show from the rear after that.

That's all I remember. But it remains a day of the greatest importance for me.

I went to 24 Bowie shows in total, the last one being on the Reality tour on 15 November 2003 in Lyon.

I remember some locations, queues, running to get to the front, twisting my ankle, being tired, hotels. I was always in the front, often at the barrier, often on the left side (I don't know why I always ended up on the left). I remember being close to him and watching him intensely because it would be a year or more before the next tour. Feeling like a sailor's wife and so happy to see him. I remember his smile, the sensation he was happy there with us all. Ok, enough - I'm crying again. Miss him a lot.

I WAS THERE: MAGALI BOTUHA

I was 19 years old at the time, and I lived about 400km from the concert, so I took the train the day before and I stayed over in Toulouse with a friend. The day of the concert was fantastic. When it was time for the show, David Bowie appeared on his chair above the stage. My heart exploded when I saw him. I had been looking forward to seeing him in concert for a long time. I listen to him every day of my life. Sometimes I laugh, sometimes I cry.

MAINE ROAD

14-15 JULY 1987 MANCHESTER

I WAS THERE: TONY BRIGGS

My love affair with Bowie started when my sister came home with the 'Modern Love' single when I was 13. It wasn't the A-side that had me hooked, it was the live B-side that I played over and over again. My fascination started at this point and has resulted in a collection of Bowie records that is approximately 230 in number (luckily they even survived a house fire at our home).

I have always had a particular interest in live music, probably also started by the 'Modern Love' B-side. Indeed from the age of about 17, I used to undertake whole tours by bands, or at least as many dates as I could get to. I still enjoy this aspect of music but now I am getting older I need to do it in comfort. No more hitch hiking or sleeping under bridges etc. It is now driving and hotels. How age changes you!

The first Bowie concert I attended was on the Glass Spider Tour. This was at Manchester City Football ground at Maine Road, Manchester on 14 July 1987. I was seventeen at the time, turning 18 a couple of weeks after. I wasn't able to drive at the time and we bought tickets through a local travel agents, who had organised a coach trip, tickets included, to the concert. This was from Leicester. The coach got us to the venue around 4.15pm. Our seats were in the main stand (Gate 8) about a third of the way back from the stand about half way up the stand. I Couldn't complain really; didn't need to use the big screen to watch. Terence Trent D'Arby was the first support who came on about 5.15pm followed by Alison Moyet at 6.15pm. Bowie came on at about 8.00pm.

The most significant impact this concert made was to avoid these really large venues as two thirds of people are only really watching on the television. To this point in my life I have never again been to another stadium concert so I guess it had a lasting impact.

My significant memories of this concert are:

When Bowie got the girl out of the audience. I had no idea at this point that this was faked. I was totally sucked in by the moment.

The advantages of not having the internet and social media at the time meant it was hard to find out things like this quickly.

'Time'. This is such a magnificent song and I had the pleasure to hear it live. Additionally I was fortunate enough at Maine Road that the weather was kind enough to allow Bowie to perform this song from the large spider that towered above the stage.

I was also lucky as I quite like the *Never Let Me Down* album so I was able to hear a superb selection of 'old classics' along with the new songs that seemed to fall out of favour quite quickly, like most of the post *Let's Dance* songs I suppose. I also really enjoyed the theatrics. This was the first time this was used in this large scale way since the Diamond Dogs tour of the US in 1974. It kept the massive stadium stage busy and utilised it fully which I liked. I gather this ended up being considered a bit too 'overblown' in later years.

I WAS THERE: PHIL CHAPMAN

I saw David Bowie on the second of two dates at Maine Road, Manchester City FC's ground.

This wasn't really a conventional gig but a theatrical performance; I don't think I'd seen anything like it before. The stage had a huge spider looming over it, with long spindly glowing legs. The show

started with Bowie, in a bright red suit, descending from the belly of the spider; he was sitting in a chair, which looked as though it was suspended from a thread of web made by the spider. As he was lowered Bowie sang the song 'Glass Spider' into a telephone.

Most of the songs were performed with dancers and Bowie wore a head-mount wireless microphone so he could join in; the headset was quite big by modern standards and he fiddled with it a lot throughout the concert. The whole thing needed a bit of getting used to and it took the crowd a few songs to warm up. The band was great though and included Peter Frampton on guitar. Around halfway through the set Bowie left the stage for a costume change while his drummer, Alan Childs, played an extended solo. When Bowie returned to the stage we got a few more classic tracks, starting with 'Heroes'. The highlight for me was 'The Jean Genie', from my favourite Bowie period.

The main set finished with 'Let's Dance' and 'Fame' and I was looking forward to the encore; some friends who'd been at the previous night's show had told me it started with 'Time', from *Aladdin Sane*. Sadly he didn't play it and we got 'Blue Jean' followed by 'Modern Love' instead. I suspect my friends saw a better show the night before but this was still a highly entertaining, if unusual gig. But hey, this was David Bowie and one thing he was never guilty of was being ordinary.

VETERANS STADIUM

30 JULY 1987 PHILADELPHIA

I WAS THERE: CHRIS BRISBIN

I Saw him at Veterans Stadium in Philadelphia in September of 1987. Big show. Local band Tommy Conwell and Squeeze opened. Peter Frampton was his guitarist. It was like watching a Broadway show with all the dancers on stage. He did many of his classics like 'China Girl', 'Absolute Beginners', 'Modern Love', and 'Let's Dance'. The final part of the show was 'Jean Jeanie'. It was so cool to see the entire crowd of over 50,000 people dancing all at once to the song. Great show.

I WAS THERE: LISA-MARIE CARR

I saw him when I was seven years old, and had loved him since I was two. He was my first crush, he was my first concert. It was the Glass Spider Tour. I still remember it to this day.

My mother took me. It was my first act of rebellion as it was well after my bed-time, and she had informed me I could stand on my seat and dance. Ha ha! I will never forget when he came down from that glass spider, I just could not believe it was him, and he was actually real. Until that moment I truly thought he was fictional as my favorite video at the time was 'Blue Jean.' I still remember how he wiped the lipstick off of his face and how he moved, all of those dramatic gestures, how the light changed his face different colors and how very kind and handsome he was. It's not much of a story but it's a true testament of what an excellent performer he was in every way. I'm 36 and I still love all of his work. My mother and I, as well as countless friends old and new, have bonded over our love for David Bowie. He had the power to bring out so many sides of ourselves and many feelings. Most of all, his work, imagination, and wisdom have served as an immense inspiration, and a best friend through my entire life.

As a 7 year-old – Lisa-Marie Carr

I WAS THERE: BRIAN GALLAGHER

The first time I saw David Bowie live I was 18 years old during the Glass Spider Tour. It was the opening date of the North American leg of the tour, July 30, 1987, at the no longer existent Veterans Stadium in Philadelphia, PA (I was at all four Philly shows). On the opening night, Bowie and the band had finished performing 'Fame' and David said goodnight. Knowing there would be an encore, I started shouting 'Bowie! Bowie! Bowie!' The people around me quickly picked up on it. It spread from there and within less than a minute, about 65,000 Bowie fans were chanting in unison what I had started! Bowie returned with an amazing rendition of 'Time' (which obviously would have happened regardless of the chanting). Definitely a most memorable Bowie moment.

ANAHEIM STADIUM

8 AUGUST 1987 ANAHEIM, CALIFORNIA

I WAS THERE: DEREK MATTHEW RICH

I was extremely fortunate to see David Bowie live on three occasions, including my first-ever concert, waaaaaaay back in 1987.

Both of my parents adored the Thin White Duke, and his songs have been part of my life's soundtrack for as long as I can remember. I grew up weaned on *Station to Station, Hunky Dory*, and *Let's Dance* with listening sessions on my dad's turntable...as well as repeat viewings of *Labyrinth*. I dressed up as David, regardless if it was Halloween or not, and also spent hours upon hours drawing crude illustrations of him from a grainy, HBO 'Serious Moonlight' recording on VHS.

In the late summer of '87, my family had made the trek from Washington State down to Southern California to do one of those 'Grandparents & Disneyland' vacations. My birthday fell on July 28, and it would be my last celebration before leaving total carefree kiddie life and starting grade school. Roughly a week or so after my cake party, I was at the breakfast table with my Mom and Gramma, paging through the local newspaper. In the entertainment section, I stumbled upon a full-page article about (gasp) David Bowie's pair of upcoming Glass Spider Tour stops at Anaheim Stadium. My mind was blown even further when my mother divulged that, for my birthday, my Uncle Greg had purchased us tickets to the August 8th event. Total grade-school Bowie delirium ensued.

As for the show itself, I have more vivid memories of *that* night with David Bowie than most of gigs I've attended in my 20s and 30s. The stage was a massive, illuminated proscenium, in the form of the giant, titular 'glass spider' from the song of the same name (which appeared on 1987's *Never Let Me Down* album, which the tour was in support of). The spider's legs framed the edges of the stage, while its body and head took the place of where the familiar arch would be. The show began in total darkness (save for the illuminated spider) and was punctuated by Bowie's eerie, spoken word intro about the 'glass spider', during which he descended to the stage from the spider's maw, seated in a golden barbershop chair, and later began crooning into a golden telephone shaped microphone. It was, and still is, unlike everything I've ever seen.

Bowie himself had a handful of costume changes, but spent most of the night dancing around in a bright red jumpsuit, which contrasted brilliantly with his peroxided half-pompadour. I remember his backing band and dance troupe to be quite numerous and unrestrained, often roaming and weaving through each other dramatically around the stage, with the exception of the lead guitarist, who had his own, central platform? Why? Because Bowie's lead axeman this tour was none other than Peter Frampton, whom my mother and uncle kept raving about, yet I was totally clueless as to who he was.

Setlist wise, it was all pretty much Eighties Bowie. I remember most (if not all) of *Never Let Me Down* being performed, as it prompted me to beg my mother to buy me the vinyl record, so that I could listen to the 'new Bowie' at Gramma's house for the rest of our vacation (she obliged; I did). I assume that most of *Let's Dance* was played, as I can recall bouncing and singing along with her to 'China Girl' and 'Modern Love.'

I would see Bowie in California again two more times. In Irvine, with my friend Erica on the Moby-helmed Area2 tour, and at LA's fabulous Shine Auditorium for his A Reality Tour stop, with my old man. Both performances were memorable, in their own respects. The Irvine show featured some sweet Pixies and Neil Young covers, while the Shrine set list was this massive 'greatest hits' parade, which wonderfully made possible the treat of seeing my gin-filled old man tearfully belt out 'Rebel Rebel,' 'Ashes To Ashes' and 'All The Young Dudes', while giving me fatherly side-hugs.

However, despite this presence of a much-stronger set list (and the unmentionable added bonuses of 'adult-vs-kid' concert-going practices), it's impossible for the Shrine to match that first-time Anaheim magic. Before '87, David Bowie was the face on the TV and the voice coming from the speaker. My love for him, at that point, felt mostly observational and certainly *not* interactive, if you will. That crazy, six-year-old night with the Glass Spider changed the game. It was that first-ever, circuit-overloading taste of the sensation of singing the songs with their creator *right down there* (a few humble seating levels below), strutting around and bellowing them back at me. In more ways than I can count, it planted the seed that would bloom into the live music hobbies I would later pursue as both a teen and an adult. Thank you, David.

BC PLACE STADIUM

15 AUGUST 1987 VANCOUVER, CANADA

I WAS THERE: ALISA HARRISON

Duran Duran opened. I was seventh row centre. It was an incredible show; I will never forget the sets and choreography. The second time I saw Bowie was Sound + Vision, May 20, 1990, also at BC Place. I'd been sick in the hospital for nearly three months and saw this shortly after I got out. Life-affirming to say the least!

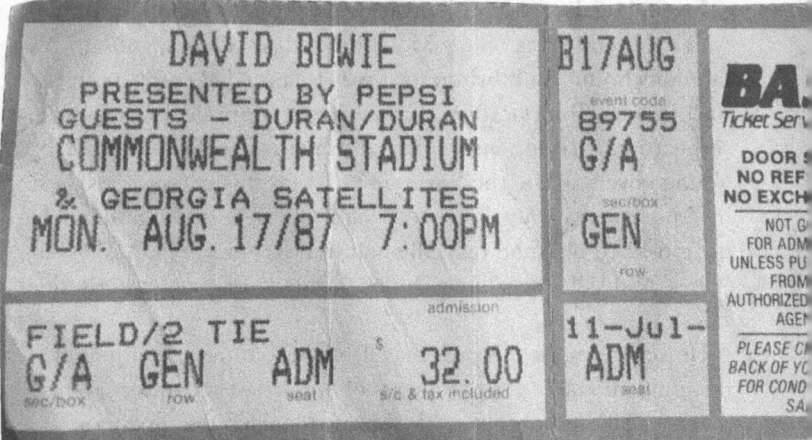

COMMONWEALTH STADIUM

17 AUGUST 1987 EDMONTON, CANADA

I WAS THERE: TRACY BEAUCHAMP

I was lucky enough to see his Glass Spider Tour in 1987 in Edmonton Alberta. The Georgia Satellites and Duran Duran opened up for him. I was living up north in Fort McMurray at the time. My brother who lived in Vancouver called me up and asked if I would like to go see Bowie in Vancouver with him. I of course, said yes, but my sister said I couldn't go, because she thought I wouldn't come back. She was probably right about that as well.

So since I didn't get go to the Vancouver show, I saw he was playing in Edmonton and I told her, 'I don't care what you say, I am going to see him play in Edmonton'. I got my way and I went. I was a little nervous since I didn't have a ticket for the show I had to buy it at the venue. When I went to buy the ticket, I asked how much it was, the person said $35. Was that for standing room only? No - general admission. HELL YA!!!!!!!!! I could get up close to the stage and see David sweat. I was soooooooo excited. I got to see a living legend and it was one of my best concerts. To this day, I have to give credit to my brother Brent for introducing me to Bowie at a very young age. David put on an amazing show and his singing was just as awesome. Thank you David for entertaining millions of us. You are still sadly missed.

I WAS THERE: CHERYL TOFFAN

I went to the Glass Spider Tour in Edmonton Alberta in 1987. It was about a three-hour drive from where I live in Calgary but we had a convoy of us going to the show. At that time and maybe even to date it was the craziest stage set up I had ever seen. Tickets for the whole show were $32.00!

Georgia Satellites and Duran Duran were back up for Bowie, (and were awesome too). Duran Duran remember were big in the Eighties.

It was an outdoor show and the spider stage to that point was the most amazing stage set up I had seen to date back in the Eighties. Peter Frampton played guitar as well at this show. I Have to say that was the most memorable show I'd been to and I go to a lot! I Saw him twice after in a smaller venue – the last was the best – when he came out on stage after not seeing him forever he looked awesome! I Got goose bumps! We purchased the concert DVD for that show.

CANADIAN NATIONAL EXHIBITION STADIUM

24 AUGUST 1987 ONTARIO, CANADA

I WAS THERE: HELEN LYON

This was the Glass Spider Tour. Duran Duran was the opening

act. Our seats were WAY, WAY in the back (so disappointing). The coolest part was, that since it is technically a stadium, the seating in our area were basically concrete benches. When the first chord was struck, it reverberated and vibrated our seats. All of these tiny spiders came out from nowhere. It kind of freaked us out, but excited us at the same time. It was a good show with great visuals...but definitely not my favorite.

I WAS THERE: PEGGY M RACE

I worked for Brockum selling T-shirts so we were at the venue early and were waiting inside the stadium for the T-shirts to arrive. Back then security was much laxer and we had all access passes, which meant we could be anywhere. We were sorting out the shirts when David Bowie came over to us. The thing that really stood out to me was how yellow David's teeth were, presumably from smoking. He bummed a smoke and joined our crowd and just starting talking. He was easygoing and so pleasant. He stayed with us for about 15 minutes, and said to stick around for the sound check telling us he was going to do 'In-A-Gadda-Da-Vida' (an Iron Butterfly song), and then got up, and walked away.

During the concert we took turns going to the front of the stage to watch. David had little paper Dixie cups on stage and he would fill them with water, take a sip, and then throw the cup into the crowd. The crowd would go wild trying to grab the cup. No one cared that water was being thrown at them.

And the song he played during the sound check, 'In-A-Gadda-Da-Vida', was friggin awesome. It was one of the best experiences of my life.

I WAS THERE: KIRSTY KING

I was 16 years old and it was my dream come true. I remember Duran Duran opened and I was so excited when David Bowie finally came out. He was lowered down on a chair and had the phone in hand. I thought the theatrics were amazing!

My boyfriend at the time was too tired to stay and wanted to leave (that should have been a sign!). I only saw half the show and could hear him starting to sing some of the great older tunes from the parking lot. I was beyond devastated! What I did see was fantastic though and I will never forget it. It was my one and only Bowie concert and one of my biggest regrets is I didn't get to see another.

I ended up marrying and divorcing said boyfriend. When we split up he took my entire Bowie collection, all the original albums, books, newspaper clippings and my one and only ticket stub. That is when I finally stood my ground! Best thing that ever happened and I got it all back.

OLYMPIC STADIUM

30 AUGUST 1987 MONTREAL, QUEBEC

I WAS THERE: JASON MONTO

I saw Bowie at the Montreal Olympic Stadium in '87 on his Glass Spider Tour. I remember Duran Duran opened up for him and they did a great show, which set the tone for the night. From the moment the show began, with Bowie descending to the stage from above as if lowered by a strand of web, to the last note of the encore, I was musically and visually in awe. One thing that comes to mind about that show was when he introduced his guitar player, Mr Peter Frampton, and then left the stage for about 15 minutes as Mr Frampton took over the spotlight doing what Frampton does best. Absolutely one of the best shows I have seen.

SULLIVAN STADIUM

3 SEPTEMBER 1987 FOXBOROUGH, MASSACHUSETTS

I WAS THERE: SARAH SADLER

It was Foxboro Massachusetts back when it was called Sullivan Stadium. David Bowie sang 'Time' from above the stage wearing this huge set of mechanical looking wings. Everything about it was spellbinding.

MARCUS AMPHITHEATER

10 SEPTEMBER 1987 MILWAUKEE, WISCONSIN

I WAS THERE: LISA PERRY

I was fortunate enough to meet Mr Bowie in 1987, backstage before his show here in Milwaukee on the Glass Spider Tour. He was very charming and warm. Shorter in person than I expected though. Fantastic memory!

PONTIAC SILVERDOME

12 SEPTEMBER 1987 PONTIAC, MICHIGAN

I WAS THERE: CHRISTOPHER SCOTT THOMPSON

The Glass Spider Tour was a four-hour show (roughly two and a half-hour set with a 45 minute break) These shows were awesome as the set lists increased dramatically. The shows were expensive but well worth the cost. David did all his good tunes from *Ziggy* all the way up to the album *Tonight*. I was lucky enough to be working to make the money to go which I did. Busted my butt to go as anything in life if you want it all you have to do is work, work, work.

MIAMI ORANGE BOWL

18 SEPTEMBER 1987 MIAMI, FLORIDA

I WAS THERE: BELYNDA MORRIS

After discovering David Bowie in 1972, when I was 12, with 'Space Oddity', for years I would run to the store to pick up a music magazine to see when he might be coming to Florida. For one reason or another, I always missed him until finally 1987's Glass Spider Tour! So I camped out in front of a record store with a bunch of other people, waiting for tickets to go on sale the next morning. Some girl brought a movie projector and showed a film of a portion of a

Belynda Morris camping out to buy Bowie tickets

Bowie concert. We were all a bit upset the next morning when they handed out random numbers that we drew from a hat, to show what place number we were in line for tickets, after we had camped out all night.

I had a crappy Kodak 110 camera that I smuggled into the Miami Orange Bowl and took pictures when he was on top of the spider, wearing golden wings, gold jacket, gold boots and singing 'Time'. I was so surprised when I realized that Peter Frampton was the one singing 'Sons of the Silent Age' I was finally at my very first David Bowie concert and what a show it was! Every thing I could have wanted, or imagined. Much anticipated and not disappointed in the slightest! My life was now complete!

OMNI COLISEUM

21 SEPTEMBER 1987 ATLANTA

I WAS THERE: BRUCE HALEY

I saw David Bowie about two weeks after graduating from the music trade school that I'd attended there in Atlanta. He was at the Omni arena downtown, and the place was pretty much full as I recall. It was the Glass Spider Tour, I think, although I remember that the album *Never Let Me Down* was out that year, featuring the hit single 'Day-In Day-Out'. The show was interesting in two ways. He had a whole dance theater 'troupe' on stage with the band, doing all manner of theatrics and acrobatics. And, he had Peter Frampton as his lead guitarist, which was a very welcome addition to an already great lineup. At one point, while soloing in the middle of a song (can't remember which one), Peter started playing the opening line of 'Do You Feel Like We Do', while his facial expression shown on the big screen portrayed him with a 'Hmmm, I know that song, what is that?' look on his face. This of course, drew laughter and applause. It was cool. I'm just thankful that I ever got to see David in concert. There have been far too many other groups and artists who I regret not seeing. I'm just thankful that he wasn't one of them. Truly a one-of-a kind musical mind, IMHO. RIP, David.

LOUISIANA SUPERDOME

6 OCTOBER 1987 NEW ORLEANS, LOUISIANA

I WAS THERE: DIANNE K. BENEFIELD

My cousin Jerry and I had tickets. Excited to finally see Bowie LIVE, we drove to the Superdome (we both live in New Orleans).

Our seats were in the bleachers about seven rows up, center stage, great view. Jerry and I had always loved David. One of my first singles was Bowie's 'Starman'. I loved that song. It was so visual, you could imagine a Starman up there in the skies! (Now I want to believe he really is up there!)

Anyway, Jerry and I were surprised at the crowd sitting around us. Clearly they were years younger than us. Me being 28, and Jerry 38 years old.

When David's band began the first riff of 'Jean Genie', we both leapt out of our seats and sang every word while dancing! Our youngster crowd looked at us kinda like, 'What the hell' because clearly this was not a song they recognized!!!

It was not clear to us that Frampton was on guitar, until David introduced him. That's all Jerry and I needed to hear to cheer even louder!

It was a magical night in our magical Superdome. A highlight of my life and now so happy to be able to say, 'Yes, I saw Bowie LIVE!'

SYDNEY ENTERTAINMENT CENTRE

3-14 NOVEMBER 1987 SYDNEY, AUSTRALIA

I WAS THERE: RHONDA DUNDAS

I was working in a record shop at the time, and we were also an agent for concert tours, so we sold tickets and ran buses to shows. I was asked to run a bus down to the David Bowie Glass Spider Tour with another work friend who was a big Bowie fan. As I was a lot younger, the only Bowie songs that I was familiar with were 'Ashes To Ashes' and the *Let's Dance* album. I remember when we were on the bus going there, I noticed that a number of people had their heads down and there was a funny smell. I asked my friend what they were doing and my friend informed me they were smoking pot. I said, 'Is that allowed? Should we say something?' My friend said, 'You can tell them to stop if you like'. I decided I wasn't going to say a word, I guess I had no idea really who David Bowie was, other than this artist I sold lots of CDs of. So I had no expectations.

I was in the mosh pit, not far from the stage, when this absolutely beautiful human being came down from the top of the stage, sitting on a red chair, singing into a telephone. I was gob smacked!! I had never seen a more charismatic performer in my life. I thought he was (and still is) the most amazing performer I have EVER seen live. From the very first song, I was blown away! His voice, his charisma, even his sex appeal. I think I actually fell in love with David Bowie that night. I was in AWE! We were close to the stage so I felt very close to him. The tracks that stood out to me, were The Stooges song, 'I Wanna Be Your Dog' with Charlie Sexton as a guest guitarist. I also loved 'Big Brother' and 'Up The Hill Backwards' and 'Never Let Me Down'. I loved every minute.

They were also filming that night. It's funny, but my 16-year old son discovered Bowie last year and is now a big fan. I had told him all about my experience of seeing him live, and that the night I went was filmed. He looked it up on YouTube and the two of us sat and watched it together. That was on the 8th of January 2016. Two days later Bowie was gone and my son and I mourned him together. It is a lovely memory I have, and I miss David Bowie terribly. But I still have the music and I am so thankful to the amazing David Bowie for his incredible gift.

WESTERN SPRINGS STADIUM

28 NOVEMBER 1987 AUCKLAND, NEW ZEALAND

I WAS THERE: DEAN WARDS

I was lucky enough to see David Bowie perform live 12 times between 1987 and 2003. One of my favourite shows was in November 1987, and the final night of the Glass Spider Tour in Western Springs, Auckland, with my sister Carole and best friend Malcolm.

I was 18 at the time and this was my first experience of going to a big gig. We were all big Bowie fans and there was no way we were going to miss the chance of seeing him perform live. A radio station in Christchurch advertised an organised trip to Auckland to see Bowie, with flights, hotel and tickets. The event was promoted six months in advance so we had to book our places and then wait patiently for the big day to arrive.

We flew Christchurch to Auckland on the Friday in a specially

charted a plane with the 'star' DJs who joined us for the event. The show was on Saturday and Auckland was buzzing on Friday evening with the news that Bowie was in town. The bars and clubs all had Bowie events. Shops all displayed Bowie memorabilia. Having such a big star come to New Zealand was a big deal.

Saturday was show day. We decided to get to the venue early and make a day of it, so a group of us caught a local bus to Western Springs, a big open air arena. We ended up at the park at around 3pm. The show wasn't due to start until 7pm! We ended up just sitting in the warm sun in front of the stage for hour after hour, watching the stage set-up happening. The elaborate stage set was already in place, in daylight the massive spider stage didn't seem that impressive, but as it grew darker and darker the stage came to life. By about 6pm the crowd had grown to a point where the shoving and pushing had begun. By the time Bowie appeared, coming down to the stage from high above, with very high hair, wearing a red suit and speaking into a telephone, the crowd went wild. 60,000 people all seemed to want to get to the front of the stage. The atmosphere was electric.

Bowie didn't disappoint and the show had a blend of old and new songs, and the sound was excellent. I had no clue what all the dancers were meant to be doing, but visually it was amazing, Bowie was chatty and in a fun mood. He said he was a little sad, as this was the last show of the tour.

At the end of the show purely by chance, I bumped into a former cricket pal who was doing security for the show. He invited me backstage to watch a special event. I had temporarily lost my sister in the crowd so went to look for her. When we returned to the security area, my pal had gone. Turns out the special event was Bowie setting fire to the Glass Spider! I only found out what happened years later. The next day we flew back to Christchurch having had the most amazing weekend.

1989 The Tin Machine Tour. The tour comprised 12 performances in six countries (USA, Denmark, Germany, France, Netherlands, United Kingdom) in venues with a capacity of 2,000 or less. Tin Machine performed the entirety of their Tin Machine album with the exception of 'Video Crime,' along with cover versions of songs from Bob Dylan ('Maggie's Farm') and Johnny Kidd and The Pirates ('Shakin' All Over').

NATIONAL BALLROOM

29 JUNE 1989 KILBURN, LONDON

I WAS THERE: SHAWN MARGARET COHEN

Many years ago I lived on Messina Avenue in West Hampstead, the NW6 area of London. I was coming home from somewhere at night and walked down my street from the Kilburn High Road where the rock venue, the National, was and as loud as you like I heard David Bowie singing. I looked around and realized something must be on at the National. I walked back to see the sign out in front, TIN MACHINE, and I smiled.

Here I am, this American, a long way from home, who grew up listening to David Bowie, as I was a teenager in high school from 1970-74, so 'Space Oddity' was big as well as 'Rebel, Rebel'. I just stood outside the venue and listened to Bowie sing his heart out! I had heard he had a band now called Tin Machine and nothing ever surprised me because he was always changing it up for his fans, what a trip though. So close yet so far. Loved every second of it too and as I wandered to my London digs at the bottom of the street, I could still hear him singing his next song. When I got into my flat, I opened the window and could still hear him! I didn't know he was at this venue or I would have gotten tickets, no internet then! But I was lucky. Right place at the right time!

1990

The Sound+Vision Tour was billed as a greatest hits tour in which Bowie would retire his back catalogue of hit songs from live performance. Spanning five continents in seven months, the tour surpassed Bowie's previous Serious Moonlight and Glass Spider Tours' statistics by visiting 27 countries with 108 performances.

In addition to the stark lighting and the backing 4-piece rock band, Bowie employed a new tool for this tour: a giant sixty-by-forty foot transparent gauze scrim. The scrim would occasionally be lowered in front of or behind Bowie, onto which images of Bowie and videos were projected.

The set was constructed by 80 workers who traveled with the tour, with the help of local workers who were hired in each city. A single set took 8 trucks to move (with an additional four buses for the workers), and required 9 hours to set up and four hours to load out each night.

SKYDOME

7 MARCH 1990 TORONTO, CANADA

I WAS THERE: RACHEL ANNE PENLON

Saw the Sound+Vision Tour in Toronto at what was then called SkyDome. Adrian Belew was musical director, lead guitar player and the rest of the band was Adrian's touring band. I live in Rochester, New York where David was arrested on a drug charge during the Diamond Dogs tour. Bowie swore he would never return here, he was found not guilty on the drug charge, but changed his mind and the Glass Spider Tour was booked here. The show was cancelled due to 'low ticket sales' but I think Bowie decided against coming back because of the old drug charge. The story goes that he was set up by two undercover female cops posing as groupies.

NORTHLANDS COLISEUM

12 MARCH 1990 EDMONTON, CANADA

I WAS THERE: ANDREW DONASS

I saw David Bowie in 1990 at the Edmonton Coliseum during his Sound+Vision Tour. It was purported to be the last tour where David Bowie would play his hits from the Seventies and Eighties.

The show employed images of the star dancer from the Montreal dance troupe La La La Human Steps being projected onto a screen. Sometimes the screen would be behind the band, showing the dancer dancing in synchronization to the music. At other times the screen was in front of the stage making it appear Bowie was dancing with the dancer. It was mesmerizing. I had never seen anything like it before. The music itself was outstanding. For me it was the first and

only time I saw the Thin White Duke; so just to see him perform his many hits was a thrill.

I will confess David Bowie was not the only reason I went to the show. I had heard a lot about La La La Human Steps, and a chance to see them perform beside someone of David Bowie's caliber was an opportunity I could not pass up. I was disappointed when it turned out to be only a projection of just one of the dancers, but that was not the case with Adrian Belew.

Belew was a guitarist I was familiar with from his work with King Crimson, a band I was seriously enamored with. I have always been a guitar music lover, and the chance to see Adrian Belew live was such a bonus. I must admit I went to this show more to see Adrian Belew than David Bowie. Make no mistake, it was a fabulous show. We are talking David Bowie. You cannot go wrong, but for me, personally, Adrian Belew on guitar made the show that much better.

I WAS THERE: DIANE HANNAH

I was 37 years old and was a fan but my 9-year old daughter idolized Bowie. I got tickets to take her, as this was her first concert. We lived in a small community outside Edmonton (Devon). Songs that stood out were 'China Girl' and 'Let's Dance'. Bowie wore a white suit through most of the concert. His hair was short and blond. Another memory for me was being amazed with his band. They were all excellent musicians.

ROYAL HIGHLAND SHOW EXHIBITION CENTRE

23 & 24 MARCH 1990 EDINBURGH

I WAS THERE: PHILIP HOPCROFT

I was married with two boys aged 9 and 6 – I know money was tight at the time and tickets would be about £20, so it was a bit of a 'treat' for me!! (Still married – coming up 37 years – so my extravagance wasn't that detrimental). I Went with a couple of mates and we stayed in Glenrothes which is about 30 miles away from Edinburgh so no real distance to travel.

It wasn't the most fan friendly venue – it was the Royal Highland Show Exhibition Centre – basically a large shed with a concrete floor normally used for cattle auctions. The stage wasn't very high so the view from about half way back wasn't the best. I'm about five feet ten and struggled a bit to get a decent view (I don't think my mate Graham Gillespie saw too much as he wasn't the tallest), but knowing the great man was on stage together with a pretty fantastic atmosphere and of course absolutely extraordinary music more than made up for the venues shortfalls.

I definitely recall 'Heroes', 'Ziggy Stardust', 'Life on Mars?' and 'China Girl' and pretty sure the encore was 'Jean Genie' as we were still singing that while we spent an hour waiting to get out the car park. It Must have been a midweek gig as I recall being at work next day probably still buzzing but feeling pretty knackered.

All in all a great experience!!

I WAS THERE: CHERIE BATTENSBY

He looked great but the sound quality wasn't, and he stopped a couple of songs mid-set as he couldn't hear himself sing. He also played 'Young Americans' without a sax.

DOCKLANDS ARENA

28 MARCH 1990 LONDON

I WAS THERE: DAVE LEWIS

The Sound+Vision Tour was a pure celebration of his catalogue – a greatest hits tour that tied in with a campaign for all his albums being reissued on CD by EMI – this commenced with a greatest hits album Sound + Vision. I made a big deal of this at the Our Price record store I managed at the time with window displays and an in store DJ playback – and the sales stacked up.

I was duly rewarded with a couple of tickets for the Docklands March 28 show and very welcomed they were too. The good lady Janet was pregnant and unable to go so I went with Denise Bibby, a colleague from work. Memories? Stunning use of the backdrop screen with silhouette images and a set list that lived up to the greatest hits billing. Bowie was on sale again…and on tour and it was like he had never been away…

SPORTPALEIS AHOY

30 MARCH 1990 ROTTERDAM, NETHERLANDS

I WAS THERE: PETER FREDERIKSEN

While hundreds of people gathered around the hall, an awful lot of fans turned up at the Hilton Hotel in the hope of getting a short glimpse of Bowie before he left for the sound check. After a few hours wait, the man came out to sign autographs in quite a hysterical atmosphere!

What the audience didn't get in London, it really got in Rotterdam. These guys are really incredible, and David knows it. During the years Bowie has performed so many great shows in this – surprisingly – rather small hall. It really became a magnificent show even in spite of my very high expectations.

'Thank you very much, thank you. Good evening' David says after 'Changes' and continues with 'la la la' in the intro to 'TVC15'. He seemed to be in a good mood. And indeed he was. He danced and smiled much more than in London, and – what was more important – his voice seemed so much better than in the London shows, but as the show went on it became weaker and weaker.

'This is a song I wrote in 1975, it's called 'Golden Years''. With two dates intermission it was great to hear this song again, with Bowie dancing a lot. After 'Be My Wife' they turned directly to a guitar intro I hadn't heard before, or...yes, indeed it was the intro to 'Ashes to Ashes', I'd heard in the London sound check a few days before. It was nice not to hear the very sudden keyboard intro as in previous shows. Again Bowie danced a lot to his own amusement and the crowd's enthusiasm. He had some problems with the microphone in the front of the stage, which clearly could be heard in 'Queen Bitch' and 'Ashes to Ashes', and after 'Fashion' – where David picked up a teddy bear thrown up on stage and sang with it in his hands. 'Thank you' Bowie says after a great version of 'Fashion'. 'OK, this is a love song, very romantic at the time, maybe still romantic, if my sore throat can get through it, it's called 'Life on Mars?''

When Bowie as usual ends 'Ashes to Ashes' with 'My mama said to get things done, you'd better not mess with Major Tom', together with the enthusiastic crowd, the audience wouldn't stop singing until the lights again spot David, who then sang the last verse again.

Particularly in the second part of the show he had a lot of

problems with the high notes and in many songs he spared his voice. After a little improvisation in 'Jean Genie' Bowie walked up to the front of the stage with his guitar and said, 'Okay, this's one I know you want us to do. I don't know if my voice can be there on the end of it, but if you know the words you can help me out' starting the opening chords to 'Rock 'n' Roll Suicide'.

For only the third time in Europe he plays this magnificent song, and indeed he has big problems doing it, but he puts all his feelings into it and sings it so emotionally. 'You are wonderful, thank you for a wonderful evening'

In retrospect, this still ranks as one of the very best shows on the tour.

PALAEUR

17 APRIL 1990 ROME, ITALY

I WAS THERE: FEDERICO GUGLIELMI

It's hard to believe, but the first time that David Bowie hit Rome wasn't until June 1987 for the Glass Spider Tour, but I unfortunately missed both the dates at the Stadio Flaminio because in those days I was out of town. Therefore, nothing could have stopped me from going to the next concert on April 17, 1990, the day before my thirtieth birthday: to admire the genius on stage of course, but also because the Sound+Vision

Tour was announced as a never-seen-before event, a 'greatest hits' show with dazzling lights, huge screens and hi-tech tricks. Too bad that PalaEur, a circular arena with about 12,000 seats built for the 1960 Olympic Games, had horrible acoustics, but... who cared? It was the price to pay to catch Him performing pieces of History like 'Space Oddity', 'Ziggy Stardust', 'Changes', 'Heroes', 'Life On Mars?' or 'Rock' 'n' Roll Suicide.

Yeah, I know... but because of my age the Bowie I love most is the Seventies' one. Tell me I'm crazy if you dare. The tracklist was fantastic and David Bowie seemed full of energy, just like the extraordinary band with Adrian Belew as terrific as I remembered him to be with the Talking Heads in the same venue a decade before. Twenty-seven years later, my memory keeps only some blurred flashes of images, colors, people screaming and singing, enjoying the astonishing sequence of music that will last until the end of times. I reached my thirties with 'Rock 'n' Roll Suicide' still echoing in my ears, and I couldn't ever think of a better 'happy birthday' than this.

MIAMI ARENA

27 APRIL 1990 MIAMI

I WAS THERE: BELYNDA MORRIS

We got to the Miami Arena in plenty of time, only for me to leave my glasses for seeing distance in the car. Realizing it after we got inside sitting in our seats, my wonderful boyfriend offered to run all the way back to the car where we parked in the well known but dangerous Liberty City. But I was afraid the arena would not let him back in so I sat there barely able to see but yet still in heaven listening to the wonderful music, with that incredible voice! I could still see, but not like I really wanted to.

FLORIDA SUNCOAST DOME

4 MAY 1990 ST. PETERSBURG, FLORIDA

I WAS THERE: RICHARD RODRIGUEZ

I was about 26 at the time and had to go to the local radio station to pick up the tickets. I got to a party for the other ticket winners before the show that was sponsored by Hooters. I also got the Sound + Vision boxed set. One song that stood out was 'Young Americans'. 40,000 plus people sang out 'Ain't there one damn song that can make me break down and cry'. Great show.

LOS ANGELES MEMORIAL SPORTS ARENA

23 MAY 1990 CALIFORNIA

I WAS THERE: MATT DIXON

Saw him on Sound+Vision Tour 1990 at the sports arena, University of North Carolina, Chapel Hill. There were only about 4,000 people there - the place was virtually empty. David chided the promoter to the small, enthusiastic crowd, and promised he'd give the 'Show of shows' to those in attendance. And he and the band delivered in spades.

DODGER STADIUM

26 MAY 1990   LOS ANGELES

I WAS THERE: ROB BARBATO

I decided to take my brother to his first concert. It was the David Bowie Sound+Vision Tour which was in LA Dodger Stadium. We lived in Orange County in Fullerton at the time so it wasn't a long drive. I remember Lenny Kravitz opened up for him, and after Lenny during the intermission. The DJs from KLOS Mark and Brian starting a big food fight with people in the stands.

When the concert first started a guy next to us opened up his cigarette pack and pulled out a joint and handed it to us. I remember my brother saying 'Do they do this shit at every concert?' My memories of Bowie's concert was that he had this huge mesh screen in front of the stage, which projected images on it during his show. It was awesome, especially being high! My favorite songs of his were 'Young Americans' and 'Changes'. It was a concert my brother and I would never forget.

MARCUS AMPHITHEATER

13 JUNE 1990 MILWAUKEE

I WAS THERE: JAMES WAGNER

Sound+Vision Tour: I was 29 at the time and drove 30 miles north to the show, which was at the Marcus Amphitheater right next to the lakefront of Lake Michigan. These grounds are also used for Milwaukee's Summerfest Music Festival.

I remember the mesh net covering the front of the stage. Then the 12 string strummed chords of 'Space Oddity'. Across the screen visions of Bowie as the countdown begins three, two, one. The screen drops and there stands the Thin White Duke. Adrian Belew on guitar and an amazing set of career spanning music.

If I recall he wanted to do a 'greatest hits' show to put these songs to rest before Tin Machine started. Really he was on top form. He did a great cover of 'Gloria'. He Played the well-known songs from *Let's Dance*. 'Ziggy Stardust', 'Suffragette City', 'Space Oddity' and 'Starman' were electric. I'm so fortunate to have seen such an iconic performer.

THE SPECTRUM

10 JULY 1990 PHILADELPHIA

I WAS THERE: JOHN GASS

Me and my brother's seats weren't that great so we snuck down to about 20 rows from the stage. He had Adrian Belew with him. It was a great show, Bowie classics with what was then newer songs (which are now classics). Also a few Velvet Underground covers, we had a great time. I Still can't believe he's gone.

MILTON KEYNES BOWL

4-5 AUGUST 1990 MILTON KEYNES

I WAS THERE: ROB PARSONS

I was 19 and this was my first ever 'proper' concert (not in a pub or local bandstand). I was a massive Queen fan in the Eighties and discovered Bowie through 'Under Pressure', and quickly bought all of his back catalogue, favourites being *Hunky Dory*, *Ziggy Stardust*, *Station to Station* and *Pinups* (from which I 'discovered' Springsteen, for which I will always be eternally grateful!)

A group of us from work managed to get tickets for Milton Keynes and I was blown away by the show, especially as it was basically a 'greatest hits' gig and one hit followed another! The one thing that really sticks in my mind was the huge video screen that came down across the front of the stage and projected images of dancers etc. I will always remember the huge David looking down on himself – I think it was during 'China Girl'. Our group had all managed to get separated so at the end my friend and I had no idea where to go or how to find the others. We walked up the big earth bank that surrounded the venue, ran down the other side and straight into the others! Amazing, considering how many people were there!

I WAS THERE: BILL DAY

This is still one of my favourite gigs ever – the heat and the holograms plus David looking like the coolest man on the planet! Also remember the fence getting trampled and reportedly 15,000 extra over capacity getting in!

I WAS THERE: JULIA JONES

This concert was advertised as his farewell tour – the last time he would ever play his past hits live. So of course I had to be there!! It took hours to drive from Wales to Milton Keynes and ages to get into the ground with 60,000 people. The atmosphere was electric throughout the afternoon as we absolutely melted in a blistering heat wave. It was an amazing concert but the thing I remember most was Bowie dancing with a giant version of himself on screen. It was very clever technology for 1990 and the crowd loved it. He was always at the cutting edge. That's why he blazed such an incredible trail that has gone down in history.

I WAS THERE: TOM BANKS

I grew up in Hong Kong at a time when all the big performers of the day used to bypass us on their way to Japan – so imagine my sheer joy when it was announced that David Bowie was bringing his Serious Moonlight Tour to the Hong Kong Coliseum for two shows on the 7 and 8 December 1983. My joy lasted for approximately 30 seconds when it dawned on me that I had another ticket sitting in a drawer in my flat – a non-changeable air ticket to Vancouver on 5th December – I was absolutely distraught that I was going to miss the show.

The gigs were awesome according to my friends – some of who even appeared in the concert footage knocking the huge inflatable globes around the venue. My pain was exacerbated when I learned that after one of the shows Bowie came down to the Causeway Bay nightclub called Rumours where I DJ'd – I could have perhaps met the man – I'll never know.

It was a seven year wait – but I managed to pick up four tickets for my (now ex) wife and two friends for the Sound+Vision Tour. Bowie had announced that this would be the last time he'd play tunes from his back catalogue – so I was ecstatic that I wasn't going to miss it.

The day didn't start well – a phone call just before we set off for Milton Keynes brought the news that our friends would not be making it due to a family tragedy – so we made the three hour drive to the MK Bowl on our own and sold their tickets to touts outside – so they at least got half their money back.

So I finally got to see one of the most iconic musicians of our time live – but the three hour wait to get out of the car-park put me off big stadium gigs for quite some time – well, for another seven years

anyway, until Michael Jackson played Wembley – but I went to that by train. I still have my ticket stub as a reminder of the day. I love the quote after Bowie died – along the lines of, 'The earth is millions of years old, so think yourself lucky that you were around at the same time as David Bowie'.

MAINE ROAD FOOTBALL GROUND

7 AUGUST 1990 MANCHESTER

I WAS THERE: JENNY KNOWLES

I was about eleven when I first saw Bowie play. I had my newly purchased *Ziggy Stardust* LP and I listened intently, pouring over the cover under the light from the street lamp outside my bedroom window. Thrust into a moonage daydream this was what life was about, what everything had been leading up to. He was so cool, I wanted to dress like him, go to the nightclubs my older sister was going to so I could smoke and bury my face in stylish make-up and lead that Bowie infused life that promised glamour and the true meaning of life. The best life.

He wasn't on TV that much in 1983 (just *Top of the Pops* '*Let's Dance*' era I think), but the images from the cover of the *Ziggy* album were concreted in my mind as the true Bowie.

When I got into secondary school I had his name written all over my wallpaper covered schoolbooks and had perfected signing my name as Jenny Bowie. It helped too that his spiky orange hair wasn't too different in colour (or style) to mine (startled hair!). I immediately became best friends with a new girl who sat next to me in a French lesson – the only person I'd ever met at school who knew who David Bowie was, I heaved a sigh of relief, I could've cried. She always said 'Life on Mars?' reminded her of me which I was ecstatic about, although no idea why.

Bowie was scheduled to play on the Friday night. Mum and Dad were out at Auntie Mary's and Uncle Danny's and he was due onstage with the Spiders at 9pm. I was beyond excited. He had never played Edgeley before (Stockport once).

1990

The lights were low (just one small one in the corner) and the venue was warm but intimate. Cigarette smoke (Senior Service naturally) hung in the air, like an unhealthy smoke machine. The cheers rang out and 'Five Years' began. It was 73 again and I was on the front row.

'Pushing through the market square
So many mothers sighing
News had just come over
We had five years left to cry in.'

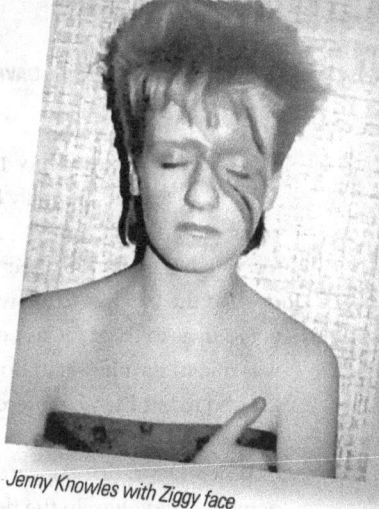
Jenny Knowles with Ziggy face

I was going to be David Bowie in female form. Slapped on make up and ginger hair- 'Five Years', 'Soul Love', 'Moonage Daydream' building up to 'Starman'. He was singing just for me. Front row, best seats in the house. 'It Aint Easy', 'Lady Stardust'. Then I heard a key in the door and my dad had come back. He'd forgotten his fags. And Bowie disappeared in a fug of smoke.

I never lost this idea which was why when I really saw Bowie in 1990, at the huge football stadium, Man City's Maine Road in Manchester, it was like being slapped with a wet, smelly fish, it was so impersonal. I should never have gone. I should have known any magic that I felt as a young girl couldn't be recaptured by a massive stadium where your idol is a pin-prick and you're surrounded by people not dressed in a Bowie style, including myself in shorts and T-shirt. A child's or teenager's imagination is much more powerful and just entirely amazing than a money making, pension building mass concert where it's just so you can say you went.

I WAS THERE: DIANE GASKELL

On August 7th 1990, David Bowie was playing a gig at Maine Road football ground in Manchester. I was 25 years old at the time. It was a lovely sunny day, when myself and another Bowie fan caught the coach in my hometown of Ashton-in-Makerfield to make the hour long journey to experience the genius of my idol.

I was so excited to finally be able to see David live. We got off the coach and didn't even bother to look whereabouts it had parked up. We queued up for what seemed like an eternity and when they finally opened the barriers to allow us onto the pitch we ran like the clappers to get as near to the stage as possible. I think it was about 4pm and Bowie was due to start his set at 8pm. Bowie's support band James came on around 6, but I wasn't interested in them, I just wanted them to get off then David could play.

When David first appeared on stage I couldn't believe that I was actually seeing him in the flesh, it was a magical moment. The noise from the crowd inside the stadium was deafening. It was my first ever concert and I had never experienced anything like it.

The songs, which stood out for me the most, were 'Rebel Rebel' and 'Station to Station' purely because of the intensity of the sound. The intro to 'Station to Station' was amazing, the bass beat was that loud that it felt like someone was punching me in the chest with each music beat. The atmosphere was electric and I remember alternating between jumping up and down and waving my arms around to some songs and to others particularly 'Stay' and 'Heroes' standing still and just listening to David's performance.

He sang all the classics but on reflection I would have loved to hear earlier songs such as 'God knows I'm Good'. The concert came to an end but nobody moved. Then he came back for an encore. The whole stadium went nuts. We were going to get another song. I didn't want it to ever end.

It took forever for us to leave the ground because everyone was chatting laughing and reliving the concert. I had already purchased my programme but decided that I wasn't leaving without a t-shirt. The queue was endless but I wasn't leaving without one.

We nearly missed the coach back home but I didn't care, I had experienced the best night of my life, watching David perform.

I am 51-years old now and to this day the memory of that day still makes me smile. David was a true visionary and a musical genius. His music is his legacy to all his fans worldwide and I am so glad to say I shared a small part of it with him.

STADION DE GOFFERT

18 AUGUST 1990 NIJMEGEN, NETHERLANDS

I WAS THERE: MARGRIET MENTING

When I was about 12-years old, I discovered Bowie through my older brother. He had just bought *Lodger* and I couldn't quite listen to it. So when *Scary Monsters* appeared, I bought it immediately and since then I am a great fan of him.

I saw him for the first time in 1990, in Nijmegen, The Netherlands. He played in the Goffertpark and Kim Wilde was the support act. I remember thinking 'Hmm, Kim Wilde, could be nice.' It wasn't. In fact, it was real bad! Bowie on the other hand was amazing! Of course, the first time you see your all time favourite singer perform live, is always great. The comments later in the papers were not that enthusiastic, but I thought he was fantastic! By that time I was 23-years old and I lived in Nijmegen so that came in pretty handy.

I saw Bowie another two times, in 1996 in Ahoy, Rotterdam and in

2004 in Amsterdam.

I went with my husband to the concert in Ahoy, Rotterdam. He didn't care too much for Bowie until he met me. I convinced him that Bowie was an amazing performer. He came with me and he agreed. In fact, he regretted he didn't visit the concert in Nijmegen in 1990 because Adrian Belew played with Bowie then and that's the favourite guitar player of my husband.

LINZER STADIUM

29 AUGUST 1990 LINZ, AUSTRIA

I WAS THERE: FLORIAN BAUER

I was 16, this was my third proper live concert (after 'Night of the guitars' and the Rolling Stones). I remember how exciting it was to travel to Linz by train from Vienna with my best friend David and his girlfriend. We were huge Bowie fans and felt quite superior than the masses who only knew the hits. The whole show was very stripped down, but I liked the black and white look and the versions very much! Bowie dedicated one song to Stevie Ray Vaughan, who had died in a helicopter crash a few days prior. At the end of 'Young Americans', Bowie wanted the audience to sing the remaining words 'Ain't there one damn song that can make me break down and cry', but after the reaction was too slow he collapsed to the floor and laid there restless, waiting. The tension was almost unbearable. We tried as best as we could to animate the people around us to sing. After more than half a minute of silence he started screaming 'Suffragette' and rocked into the next song. It was a very impressive scene and really stuck in my mind.

FESTA DE L'UNITÀ

8 SEPTEMBER 1990 MODENA, ITALY

I WAS THERE: ANDREA MASTROENI

In 1990, David Bowie came to my city, Modena. Not a big city, but that year in September there was a festival which lasted for three weeks, with restaurants, several initiatives and activities including shows and concerts (mostly Italian singers and bands) and it was completely open air. Usually a company provides everything, from the stage to the lights to the sound system, but these are not big concerts. Often the audience is about 10,000 people for the largest artists. In previous years Modena has welcomed several big rock stars like U2, Pink Floyd, Bob Dylan, Guns N' Roses and Prince but mostly these concerts were held at the stadium. So it wasn't a surprise that an artist like David Bowie was coming to Modena.

Andrea Mastroeni

Well... what I'm going to tell you is something bad that happened and that we're not used to at a concert that left me surprised and confused.

I was on holiday but I came home for that day. I had already atended the Bowie concert in Milan in April, where the show was fantastic but I couldn't not see this concert in my hometown.

The area for the concert was a field just beside the main area of the festival, and there were about 40,000 fans ready to see him.

Unfortunately it wasn't a good show. It was not the full stage that Bowie used on that tour, I was near the front, less than 10 metres. The acoustics were of very questionable quality; David himself stopped a couple of times to personally check the monitor in front

of him. He wasn't well, his voice that night wasn't at its best. But the worst came with 'Station to Station' when he stopped the band and threw his guitar on the ground in an annoyed angry way. He said something like, 'I'm gonna have to pick some easier songs, or we're never gonna get to the end.' He grabbed the microphone and said to the sound engineer, 'When I say I do not hear my voice you have to do your fucking job…you understand my words?' He left the stage and came back after maybe five or ten minutes and went on with the show, one song after the other, quickly, not a word. He just played his songs, as if he wanted to give his fans what they wanted then he left. The concert lasted around one hour 15 minutes, maybe one hour 30.

They said that his voice had gone and that he wasn't well. It could be, but really I don't remember that he lost his voice. A guy I know who worked for the festival told me that the problem was the sound system. It was good enough for an audience of 5,000 – 7,000 people, but not for 40,000. A couple of days before on the same stage, with the same sound system there was a concert of an Italian songwriter in front of about 2,000, different music, different audience, not a rock concert at all. Well, not the memory of a nice concert, but I'm glad I saw it.

RIVER PLATE STADIUM

29 SEPTEMBER 1990 BUENOS AIRES, ARGENTINA

I WAS THERE: ALEJANDRO ROMANO

I saw David when he toured in Argentina in 1990. I used to see a lot of local and international shows but this one marked me forever. I always remember that show. I taped it on VHS and I used to watch it over again. I went to the show with Richard, my partner at high school (we were both aged 15), and we were very big fans of Bowie. Richard used to say that one day he would record a cover of 'Heroes' when he made his own album, and he did it with his first band Friccion. I'm still in contact with Richard and we always have very good memories of that time listening to Bowie.

I WAS THERE: ALEX MONK

The first show of David in Argentina was September 29, 1990, the tour Sound + Vision, in the River Plate Stadium, with Bryan Adams as support artist. I was 36, and fortunately the stadium is about two miles from my home.

You know the Argentine fans are very noisy, but I can remember the night being very calm and the public very respectful. People were very amazed by the presence of the Thin White Duke on stage, that was what he passed onto the audience. Guitarist and band director at the time was Adrian Belew. It was a really short show, almost 15 songs, no more. Basically it consisted of a show with greatest hits: 'Ashes To Ashes', 'Blue Jean', 'Modern Love', 'China Girl', 'Fame', 'Heroes', 'Changes', 'Space Oddity', 'Life on Mars?' and 'Let's Dance', with all the audience dancing and singing. I remember that he sang a lovely version of 'Gloria', the song of Van Morrison.

David returned to Buenos Aires once more on November 7, 1997, for the Rock & Pop Festival (Rock & Pop was the most important radio station at the time). It took place in the Ferro Carril Oeste Stadium, another soccer stadium just in the geographic center of Buenos Aires city, three miles of my home. This time, he came to present *Earthling*. Also participating, Bush, No Doubt and some other local bands.

I can remember David with his haircut to the Mohican style.

At that moment, I was 41 years old. Of that show I can remember the outstanding participation of the girl on the bass: Gayle Ann Dorsey.

I WAS THERE: CRISS PAMPILLION

Seeing David Bowie in Buenos Aires (Argentina) was a dream come true. I discovered him when I was a teenager and loved him and his music immediately. The opening act was Bryan Adams. David and his band with Adrian Belew performed an amazing show full of energy. My eyes and ears couldn't believe it. Now I can't believe he isn't in this world. I'm still sad and cried when I knew about his death. He is a part of my personal story.

1991

The Tin Machine It's My Life Tour opened on October 5, 1991 after two warm-up shows in Dublin Ireland, a press show in Los Angeles, and three trade-industry shows in Minneapolis, Los Angeles and San Francisco.

A larger outing than the low-key Tin Machine Tour of 1989, this tour took in twelve countries and sixty-nine performances playing intimate venues of a few thousand seats or less. To start the show at some venues, an old TV was placed on stage, playing old sitcoms while the prelude to Wagner's *Tristan und Isolde* played over loudspeakers. Bowie claimed that the set list for the tour was made on the fly each night: 'We have no set list whatsoever. We have a complete list of all our songs on the floor of the stage and we yell it out as we feel it. If you catch us on a bad night, it can be one of the most disastrous shows you've ever seen. But on a good night – and fortunately with this band most nights have been good nights – it really happens'.

TEATRO BRANCACCIO

9 OCTOBER 1991 ROME, ITALY

I WAS THERE: FRANCESCO DONADIO

Yes, of course I was aware that Bowie *had* to change after the so-called Glass Spider debacle (which I was maybe alone in rating among the most spectacular coups of rock theatre of all times) but all the same I wasn't adequately prepared for the next Bowie reincarnation as the vocalist and guitarist of a noisy rock combo.

I had heard those Tin Machine records and didn't think much of them, but I went to see him anyway. I was a huge fan after all, and with Bowie in town it was a no brainer. So there I was, on the first of two nights, with my friend Alexandra, in two of the best seats of the old theatre. And there *he* was, in a lime green suit, short hair and an odd-looking perfect set of (new) teeth. But was this really David Bowie after all? In front of us, flanked by the ferocious Sales brothers and the bizarre Reeves Gabrels, was a fortyish quite anonymous rocker, shouting amidst the noise and smoking one cigarette after another *a' la* Keith Richards, just a working class member of the band.

So it happened that after about half an hour I exploded: 'I'm going', I suddenly said to Alexandra. She didn't seem to understand. 'This is it, I'm going. This is not Bowie!' I tried to get past her, but she stopped me, 'What are you blabbering? Look at him, look at how cool he is. He *is* David Bowie!' But I was having none of it, 'No, he's not, he is like…' 'He is like what?' 'He is… betraying himself!'. Well, to cut a long story short, she forced me to stay and endure the concert. I must admit that I kind of enjoyed 'Debaser', 'Go Now' and 'If There Is Something' (all covers, by the way) but on the whole I found it hard to digest. After this gig, I distanced myself from Bowie for a while, almost like a spurned lover. I wasn't very keen on his Nineties albums, didn't go to his concerts of the era and in 2002, when *Heathen* came out,

Francesco Donadio

I didn't even buy it. I only listened to it a couple of years later and I fell back in love with the artist immediately: *my* Bowie was finally back. Alas, it was too late to see him live again: after June 2004, he effectively retired from touring. So, that Tin Machine gig will forever remain my last Bowie sighting. He probably needed to do it to renew his confidence and maybe it *was* theatre after all: only now I realize that he was merely *playing the part* of the regular guy in a band. So now, thinking back to that autumnal night, I relish the memory and smile at my indignation: Bowie was human after all, and Earthlings are not supposed to be exceptional all the time (they're even allowed to play in Tin Machine – but only for a little while).

I WAS THERE: RENATO MASSACCESI

Renato Massaccesi

More than a quarter of a century has passed since my sister and I witnessed Bowie's umpteenth experiment in this historical theatre in Rome. I was 24 years old and my sister, five years younger than me, saw David the previous year during the Sound+Vision Tour (we are still great fans), but this time seemed to be a completely different question: Bowie had to be just a member of a band and not the greatest star with whom we had been in love since we were kids. Obviously we were wrong 'cause Bowie was the main actor and the others were just his band. I remember the disappointment that he did not play anything from his solo work (a cover from Roxy Music was the only song outside the Tin Machine repertoire, if I remember well) but this was compensated by a great performance and it was torture to have to stay seated.

Everything changed when before the encore we succeeded in going up to the stage where we could almost touch him. I can't say we were pogoing but something similar. I remember that sometimes during the show Bowie played his sax (the only time I listened to a sax solo of his was in a Lulu cover of 'The Man Who Sold The World'), and in another moment he took his shirt off as only the divine do (I still think he was a real God). Anyway, it was an extraordinary concert with great musicians and him, the greatest of all. After all, the Tin Machine discography, often mangled, was not so bad and especially their debut deserves to be among the ten most beautiful albums by David Bowie.

I don't know if you can say the same about the show, but all I know is that it will remain forever in the top ten of my heart. And, of course, my sister's heart.

ZIRKUS KRONE

12 OCTOBER 1991 MUNICH, GERMANY

I WAS THERE: FLORIAN BAUER

The whole Tin Machine project was very exciting for us die hard fans and to have the chance to see Bowie and the boys in this rather small venue was something we couldn't resist. So me, and my friend

David took the train to Munich which was a very special trip for us 17 – 18-year olds. I had to skip school the next day and was quite thrilled about this adventure. The Zirkus Krone is a tent-like building and you could get quite near to the stage. After seeing Bowie in a stadium with 40,000 people the year before I was really stoked to get so close! The audience was very wild and during 'Heaven's In Here' and 'Crack City', the surge to the stage and the pressure was really frightening. My friend grabbed Bowie's hand, when he reached for the audience.

Although Tin Machine is not so highly regarded now, I was happy to have seen Bowie in the band context!

CIRKUS

21 OCTOBER 1991 STOCKHOLM, SWEDEN

I WAS THERE: KATARINA PERSSON

I'm afraid I wasn't very fond of the Tin Machine concert at Cirkus in Stockholm on October 21st, 1991. One of the reasons for this was that the sound was painfully loud, in fact so loud I actually considered leaving my seat some times. Moreover I didn't like the songs very much, but I still had to go there and see David Bowie's new band.

In all this sheer cacophony, David Bowie was as elegant as usual, dressed in a neon green suit and a bright red t-shirt. Don't tell me how the other band members were dressed, probably in black. Elegant or not, after the show I was so disappointed I threw my ticket away as I didn't consider it to have been a proper David Bowie gig. Which I deeply regret today, of course!

In a review written by Stefan Malmqvist in Svenska Dagbladet on October 23rd 1991, he complained about David Bowie trying to be as an equitable member of Tin Machine as possible and let the other band members sing as well – and Hunt Sales even twice. He also wrote that the band was reinforced that very night with yet another guitarist, uncertain with whom, as he couldn't hear what David

Bowie was mumbling in the microphone. He also wrote that Tin Machine did their best to rattle and howl to prove it was heavy rock and nothing else that mattered.

Cirkus is an old and small venue, built as an amphitheater and according to a notice in Expressen a few years later; the audience consisted of 1,600 people that night. I wonder how many of these people went deaf after that sound explosion? When I'm listening to Tin Machine nowadays, I realize it isn't as bad as I thought it to be then. In fact I think the music is pretty awesome.

INTERNATIONAL II

3 NOVEMBER 1991 MANCHESTER

I WAS THERE: PETE MITCHELL

'You've Got A Habit of Leaving' by Davy Jones and The Lower Third, released in 1965 was one of my treasured Sixties 45 singles. I had a pristine promo copy on the Parlophone label. When released it sank without trace. The relatively unknown singer would soon change his surname to Bowie, avoiding confusion with actor/singer Davy Jones. Manchester born Jones, appeared on the same *Ed Sullivan Show* when The Beatles made their American live TV debut and became global superstars. The boys wanted to be John, Paul, George or Ringo and the girls wanted to marry them.

Observing the new phenomenon of Beatlemania, David Bowie would release his new single 'Can't Help Thinking About Me' in January 1966, it was another flop.

In September of that year Davy Jones would be seen on millions of TV screens around the world, starring in *The Monkees* TV Show. It was an instant hit. I was his paperboy, delivering the *Manchester Evening News* and the *Denton and Openshaw Reporter* to his parent's house; it was a pretty big deal. There was always a group of kids gathered outside and I would brush past them. Proudly and very carefully I would fold the paper and dutifully post the latest local news through the letterbox. *The Monkees* TV show would disappear from our screens in 1968 and by '69 they were falling apart. As the Beatles began to disintegrate in 1969 too, Bowie released 'Space Oddity', it would be his breakthrough recording landing at No 5 on the UK chart. To me this Jones v Jones was a two horse race.

Decades later I was having a pee next to Davy Jones in a London hotel when urged on by copious amounts of free alcohol, I blurt out 'I used to be your paperboy', and to prove it, I rattled off his parents house address. He told me to 'piss off', we both laughed. I would see him regularly when he returned to Manchester for a short while, he used to drink in my local. I think he drank bitter.

One Sunday I was playing my favourite Sixties Bowie track when Davy walked by my house pushing a baby in a buggy, he lived around the corner. He had returned home to pursue a career as a horse jockey, which didn't work out. I put my rare Bowie single back in its sleeve and left the house. I got in my little blue Ford Fiesta and headed out to the International 2, a cool modestly sized venue, which was about twenty minutes away. Armed with my precious vinyl, I went to the stage door and asked for Billy Coyle.

He welcomed me and I was ushered into a comfortable busy back stage area with sofas, bar, pool table and a dart-board. Sitting on one of the sofas, dressed in jeans and a black leather jacket smoking Gitanes cigarettes was David Bowie.

His record label EMI had arranged an interview with the Starman, who was in town with his band Tin Machine on their Its My Life tour. I had a show on my local station Piccadilly Radio. I hadn't slept a wink the night before. Hands are shaken, he is very relaxed and friendly. We chit chat about Manchester, the Hacienda and Oasis I seem to remember. David disappears for a little while and I play pool with Tony and Hunt Sayles, his bassist and drummer. They were in Iggy Pop's band, their father was a famous TV comedian who always ended up with a pie in his face. I also chat to the affable guitarist Reeves Gabriels, who now plays with the Cure. Bowie returns and we settle down to talk.

My memories of the interview are a little vague. We chat about

DJ Pete Mitchell looking well cheesed off after Bowie stole his mint condition copy of 'You've Got A Habit of Leaving'

his previous incarnations and I ask about fronting Tin Machine; 'I wasn't missing anything musically, I just wanted to front a rock and roll band like this. The only pressure is to have a good time'.

A couple of hours pass and he is required for the early evening sound check. I use this opportunity to show him my mint condition copy of 'You've Got A Habit of Leaving', with the intention of getting him to sign it. Immediately his eyes light up 'That's amazing. I've not got a copy of this, not even my Mum has one (she collected all her sons recordings). Thanks so much'. It was glued to his hand as he headed towards the stage. I didn't have the heart to wrestle the 45 back into my possession. It was gone forever. I often think about that afternoon and how surreal it was and of my brilliant Sixties Bowie single. Almost teary eyed, I think he is playing it on a portable record player, in an orbiting tin can, far above the World, whilst pulling on a Gitanes.

MAYFAIR

5 NOVEMBER 1991 NEWCASTLE UPON TYNE

I WAS THERE: ANDRE FANTARROW

I was there on 5th of November 1991 at the Newcastle Mayfair with his low-key band Tin Machine. After the show I walked round the back of the club hoping to see him. Waiting in the cold about 12am, drummer Hunt Sales came out for a smoke and saw me looking around the tour bus. He shouted at me, 'What's your name buddy?' I told him and he said 'Come over Andre it's cold'. Then he asked, 'Are you a big fan?' 'Hell, yeah', I said and then to my amazement he said come and meet some people. So I met the rest of the band, who were all very nice people, then I saw him (Bowie) about 20 feet away at the bar smoking with a very big bodyguard. I wasn't allowed near him but he did look towards me. Wow!

ORPHEUM THEATER

25 NOV 1991 BOSTON, MASSACHUSETTS

I WAS THERE: JAY MALONSON

I saw Tin Machine when I was 25 in November 1991 in Boston at the Orpheum Theater. It was simply the loudest thing I had ever witnessed up until that point in time or since. Bonecrushingly Loud!

LA BRIQUE

1 DECEMBER 1991 MONTREAL, QUEBEC, CANADA

I WAS THERE: ZENC BRILLIANT

The Tin Machine gig at La Brique in Montreal was quite memorable. First we waited outside for three hours at -15c because it was a general admission gig. Once inside, I'd never seen as many security personnel in my life, and we found ourselves stood right behind the mixing desk console and I could see the set-list. It was a very small place, quite rowdy and we were about 25 feet from the stage. At one point we lit up a joint, then a security guy just lifted it from my fingers ahah!

I remember the faces Bowie made during the song 'I Can't Read', he had really crazy eyes.

THE CONCERT HALL

3 DECEMBER 1991 TORONTO, ONTARIO

I WAS THERE: MATT SIMS

I met David Bowie once, when I was a young 23 year old, and in less than one minute he taught me something I'll never forget.

I was invited to a Tin Machine show in Toronto by a friend who worked for Bowie's record company at the time. After the show my friend brought me backstage to a room where the 'meet and greet' with the band would happen.

The room was filled with about 30–40 people, mostly industry heads by the sounds of the conversations going on around me. At some point the band (no Bowie) came into the room and started mingling with crowd.

About 10 minutes later, the energy in the room took a palpable shift straight up. 'He' had entered the room. Being tall, I could see over many of the heads and spot the centre of this energy as Bowie made his way slowly through the crowd.

I found myself unintentionally part of an ad hoc line, which had somehow formed near me. I saw Bowie being slowly taken down this line and introduced to various people, shaking hands and smiling politely each time. As he got closer, I could overhear the introductions, 'this is Steve blah-biddy-blah, our Senior VP of North American distribution. And this is X, our VP of (insert important title here).'

As he got closer, I started to feel a bit apprehensive he'd get introduced to me, the nobody in the room. Sure enough, a few minutes later there he was, standing in front of me. The handler looked at Bowie, then at me, and going into his routine said, 'and this is...?' trailing off with a quizzical look as if to say, 'So, yeah, who the hell are you?'

I smiled, took Bowie's extended hand and said 'I'm Matt. Matt, from Oakville.'

And then the coolest thing happened. Bowie lit up, and gave me what seemed like the biggest smile he'd given all night. He elevated our handshake by reaching forward and touching my elbow with his left hand. Realizing I was not yet another record executive, and just a real fan, he said in his charming British accent, 'I'm so glad you came tonight, please tell me Matt — how did you like the show?'

I sputtered some unintelligible gibberish about how much I enjoyed it, and he beamed and said, 'I'm SO glad you had fun, and thank you again for coming.'

And just like that, he let go of my hand and was gone, off to the next person, leaving me standing there, feeling a bit dumbstruck by the whole thing.

That night David Bowie taught me just how impactful, and meaningful, a little grace and humility can be, especially from those in perceived positions of power.

You and your music will be missed dearly, Mr Bowie. Thank you for all you gave us.

1992 **The Freddie Mercury Tribute Concert.** The concert was a tribute to the life of Queen lead vocalist, Freddie Mercury, who had enjoyed a lengthy friendship with Bowie dating back to 1972. Held before an audience of 72,000, the concert was broadcast live on television and radio to 76 countries around the world, with an audience of up to one billion. The profits from the concert were used to launch The Mercury Phoenix Trust, an AIDS charity organisation.

The first half of the show featured short sets from bands that were influenced by Queen, including Metallica, Extreme, Def Leppard, and Guns N' Roses.

The second half featured the three remaining Queen members – John Deacon, Brian May and Roger Taylor, along with guest singers and guitarists, including Elton John, Roger Daltrey, Tony Iommi, James Hetfield, George Michael, Seal, Paul Young, Annie Lennox, Lisa Stansfield, and Robert Plant. Via satellite from Tacoma, Washington, U2 dedicated a live performance of 'Until the End of the World' to Mercury.

David Bowie along with Mick Ronson (and backed by Queen), performed 'Under Pressure' with Annie Lennox, 'All The Young Dudes' with Ian Hunter,

Mick Ronson, Joe Elliot and Phil Collen, and 'Heroes'. At the end of his set, David also recited 'The Lords Prayer, Sleep In Heavenly Peace'.

WEMBLEY STADIUM

20 APRIL 1992 LONDON

I WAS THERE: STEVE MALIN

As soon as we heard the announcement of the memorial concert myself and three friends decided we had to go. We travelled from

Manchester to Wembley in an old transit minibus and arrived the evening before the show with no accommodation planned (the intention was sleeping in the queue).

We were sitting by one of the entry gates on the flat area at the top of the stairs by the turnstiles, when we heard the sound check for 'Under Pressure' and were transfixed. We got about two hours sleep that night, singing Queen songs with the others on the stadium steps. I was fifth through the gate the next day and was about 20-30 feet from the stage for the whole show. One of the better days of my life.

I WAS THERE: MATT LOVELL

My first gig at 16, the first band I saw live was Metallica at this concert. Still have my programme and ticket. David Bowie was one of the many, many highlights, a fitting tribute to Freddie Mercury and probably the best concert that has ever been staged.

I WAS THERE: CARL BIRKMEYER

I traveled from the US to the Freddie Mercury Tribute Concert at Wembley in order to pay my respects to Freddie Mercury, an artist whose music and personality had a huge impact on my life. I was looking forward to a wild and touching ceremony and I wasn't disappointed. There were so many stars there and from the moment Brian May started the opening chords to 'Tie Your Mother Down', it was a huge love-fest of rock. Joe Elliot, Guns N' Roses, Tony Iommi, Paul Young, and others came out and were wonderful. And then came David Bowie and Annie Lennox. I wasn't a huge fan of either but I enjoyed their music. You couldn't be a rock

Carl Birkmeyer

fan at the time and not enjoyed some of Bowie's music.

Many of us were surprised when we heard that he was even performing, as we knew there had been conflict between him and Queen over 'Under Pressure', and other songs, and that Bowie had even forced the band to remove his backing vocals from 'Cool Cat.'

The rumor was that Bowie hated the song and refused to ever play it live and he did refuse to do a video for it. I was anxious to see how this rendition would go. When Queen did it in concert, they had Freddie do both parts and the song lost a lot of its energy when it no longer was a duet.

Bowie and Lennox came out and just killed it. I was blown away at how good it sounded live and the passion both singers put in the song. Here it is, almost 25 years later and I still remember what David Bowie did next. He asked for applause for Annie Lennox and then said, 'And where did she get such a fabulous dress?' All 72,000 of us burst into laughter. Then, after taking a moment to remember another friend of his who had been diagnosed with AIDS, Bowie asked us all to pray and he knelt down and recited the Lord's Prayer. It was a deeply touching moment. You could feel the raw honesty and pain that Bowie was feeling from having lost friends to this disease and he translated it to us in a way we could feel. It was as if we all became one with him, asking for hope, asking for relief, asking for love. It was the perfect thing to do and it increased my admiration for the man, not the singer. He bared his soul to us for a minute and the result was an outpouring of love.

He somehow tapped into what we all were feeling and put our sadness into reflection and hope. I remember just standing there feeling the love, and feeling a tear fall down my face. I don't remember what he said next because I was still in the moment, but he brought out part of Mott The Hoople and performed 'All The Young Dudes.' It was a great song for that moment and brought us all back to that time when we were young and filled with hopes and dreams. Bowie's reflections before the song, helped make it okay that we no longer were those young dudes. As Bowie played the sax and did backing vocals, I remember thinking about how Bowie, as one of the biggest stars in the world, could have demanded to sing but instead he was content to join the band and just take part.

A lot of people have said that George Michael was the star of the day, and his vocals were superb, but to me, David Bowie's performance was the most meaningful. I never met him, but I felt like I now knew him and I cared about him and he cared about us.

I think that's what made Freddie Mercury such a powerful performer – when you saw him, you believed that he was doing the show for you. David Bowie made me feel like he was performing for me, and expressing the pain, love, and hope that I felt that day.

That memory has stuck with me since that long-ago concert. Every time that people ask me what the highlight was for me, it's not a specific song. It's David Bowie expressing what we all felt and singing for all of us, not to all of us. When I heard that David Bowie had died, I didn't think back to his music. I thought back to the man from that day and felt sad that we had lost such a good, caring man. I thought back to the feelings of sadness from that day that he turned into joy and hope and I wished that his friends and family could receive that comfort that he gave us that night in England.

I WAS THERE: MATTHEW THOMAS

Bowie singing 'Heroes' with Mick Ronson on slide guitar was fabulous and Ian Hunter singing 'All The Young Dudes', was awesome and of course George Michael singing 'Somebody To Love' was outstanding.

I WAS THERE: ANN MARTIN

I was fortunate enough to be there, althrough from my position in the stadium, I could not get perfect view of the stage. But I do have this lasting memory of the event involving David Bowie. My biggest memory was how sharp David looked in his green suit, and of him playing the saxophone and singing with Annie Lennox on 'Under Pressure'.

I WAS THERE: DANIELE SEMENZATO

I Travelled from Italy and found the ticket thanks to the editor of the Queen fanzine *Princes of the Universe*. David was just unbelievable but the real highlight (at least for me) was Mick Ronson playing guitar and Ian Hunter. If I remember well, Mick had been diagnosed with liver cancer but he looked mega cool that night. Since English is not my first language, I didn't understand David's prayer. What I remember is sudden silence from the crowd and an eerie atmosphere in the stadium. It was a glorious day. The sun was shining and everybody was in great spirits that special day. I cherish every single minute of it and I'm happy I was there. God bless you Dave, you really made my day special.

I WAS THERE: PAUL WARD

I was there. He looked great in his green suit and effortlessly cool. I Loved him playing sax on 'All The Young Dudes'. His Lord's Prayer wasn't expected but a wonderful mark of respect.

I WAS THERE: PAULA GORDON

By the end of it I was crying. David Bowie, George Michael, a line up that was incredible but for such a sad occasion. I still have my ticket and the poster is mounted up on my wall. It is a concert I will never forget.

I WAS THERE: RODNEY MARKS

Myself and my wife were there with our four children, the youngest being only three. He's now an accomplished drummer. Bowie on the night was one of the standout performers and seemed to have an aura surrounding him on stage in that green suit. It was an amazing night and a very suitable tribute to Freddie's life and music.

I WAS THERE: MARILYN McCULLOCH

I was there and saw my heroes – Bowie and Annie Lennox not forgetting Queen. Bowie and Annie were amazing together! I took my son to the concert as Freddie and Queen were his heroes. There were many tears. It was such an emotional time for both of us but worth going. I won't ever forget it. I saw a Freddie lookalike in the queue as well. My son thought the real Freddie would appear at the end in a spaceship and not be dead!

I WAS THERE: RICHARD OGGY OGDEN

I remember the build up to the event and waiting outside and buying the banner and programme, while a Freddie look-alike was in the queue. George Michael, Metallica and Bowie were the standout acts for me.

Bowie: you couldn't miss him in that suit even where I was halfway back in the old Wembley. It was a rather odd atmosphere when he recited the Lord's Prayer, but it seemed weirdly right. 'Heroes', a song I had not known of before, caught my ears, and made me realise how good he was. 'Under Pressure' with Annie Lennox in that big dress, which was surprising went down well I thought, and of course 'All The Young Dudes', a classic. Whoever was there I would think would never forget that day.

I WAS THERE: PATRICK DE NEKKER

I was there when Bowie, dressed in his fabulous green suit, created his own sub-universe at the centre of this massive galaxy of stars. Suave as only Bowie could be. I will never forget the haunted expression on the face of Roger Taylor, who sat, fidgeting, behind his drum kit, feeling the pressure of the star-studded line up, while Bowie kneeled in front of the 72,000 enchanted Queen worshippers to say his prayer. Rumour has it that Guns N' Roses were forced to cut their set short. No 'Sweet Child O' Mine'.

I WAS THERE: ALISON LIEBERMAN

I was there, stuck against the front barrier. My photo was centre page of *The Sun* newspaper the following day!

BLACK TIE WHITE NOISE

JUNE 1992 RECORDING SESSIONS

I WAS THERE: STERLING CAMPBELL, DRUMMER

In 1988, I received a call from Duran Duran to tour and eventually join the band. That's where I met Nile Rodgers. We stayed in touch, and after my time with Duran Duran ended in 1993, I received the call: Nile wanted to know if I was available to do David Bowie's new album *Black Tie White Noise*. I was over the moon!

My first meeting with David was wonderful. I was finally

meeting my hero and he was so inviting, smiling; he seemed excited to make a new album. He basically had demos of new songs and it was pretty simple: play. He didn't yet know I was from the school of Dennis Davis. I studied both David's music and Dennis's drumming. So I did me, but added some sprinkles of Dennis.

David for me was like a university with an incredible alumni. Part of his genius was his uncanny ability to cast talent, not only musicians, but producers, fashion designers, filmmakers, art designers, photographers, and everyone else. And we became family.

David's last big tour was the Reality tour. It was my personal favorite and the one that will stick with me forever. We covered so much of his catalogue. We learned over 50 songs, if memory serves me right. We played around the world - over 100 cities in 9 months - and we laughed a lot.

1995-1996

The Outside Tour opened on 14 September 1995 at Meadows Music Theatre – Hartford, Connecticut. Support during the US leg of the tour was provided by Nine Inch Nails, who segued their set with Bowie's to form a continuous show. The two bands played together with both Nine Inch Nails and Bowie and his band performing 'Subterraneans', 'Hallo Spaceboy' and 'Scary Monsters (and Super Creeps)', followed by two Nine Inch Nails songs 'Reptile' and 'Hurt' after which Bowie continued with his own set alone.

In a 2012 *Rolling Stone* reader's poll, the tour (pairing Nine Inch Nails with Bowie) was named one of the top 10 opening acts in rock history.

The opening of the concert tour preceded the release of the *Outside* album, which was released on 25 September 1995. Bowie told *USA Today*: 'How do you commit commercial suicide? Well, you do this: play songs from an album that hasn't been released yet, and complement it with obscure songs from the past that you've never done on stage.'

The stage resembled a building site, with paint splashed crumpled sheets draped about, and included an old-fashioned table and chair in one corner, onto which Bowie would occasionally climb during shows.

Bowie had a few outfits for the tour (which varied between the European and US shows), but included three jackets designed by Alexander McQueen.

Morrissey was slated to be the opening act of the European tour, but he unexpectedly quit just before the Aberdeen Exhibition Centre performance on 29 November 1995. The support slot was filled on later dates by The Gyres, Echobelly, Placebo and a variety of local bands.

I WAS THERE: GAIL ANN DORSEY, BASSIST AND SINGER

He just called out of the blue one day. I had no warning or anything. He tracked me down and asked me if I would like to be a part of the

Bowie and bassist/singer Gail Ann Dorsey in 2002

Outside band when they were touring for that album with Nine Inch Nails. Quite an initiation!

He had seen me on television in the UK many years ago with my solo work. I was on a major label and 25-years old and on TV a lot promoting the record. And he said he was in a hotel in London once flipping through channels and I came on the television and he thought that I was really interesting. I was singing and I went on the couch and talked to the host of the show and I did another song or something, and he was really impressed. And he said he thought that one day, when he's putting together the right ensemble, that he would want to work with me. And this must have been like five years later, and I just thought to myself whatever I did on that night, I must have been really on.

SKYDOME

20 SEPTEMBER 1995 TORONTO, CANADA

I WAS THERE: HELEN LYON

Two friends, my husband and I arrived early for this show. We decided to grab dinner at the restaurant that is right there in the upper deck of the venue. Our waiter comes over to take our order and says 'Are you guys here for the Bowie concert?' We tell him 'Yes' and that we are huge fans and can't wait to see him again. The waiter leans over and in a hushed tone says that if we stick around for a few more minutes that Mr Bowie would be here to participate in a radio interview. Oh My God !!!

Right there in the restaurant there was a 'studio' behind glass and soon David would be only feet away from us. We were hanging out at the bar, anxiously waiting, when there appeared to be some commotion coming from the hallway leading into the side entrance of the restaurant. I immediately walked to the edge of the glass surrounding the 'studio' and there he is! I almost passed out at the fact that he was sitting casually in a chair speaking to the interviewer like he was in my living room. The show that night was absolute perfection (as usual). We went home with great memories and an even greater story to tell.

NISSAN PAVILION

6 OCTOBER 1995 BRISTOW, VIRGINIA

I WAS THERE: DUSTIN STUMP

I was lucky enough to get to see Bowie in 1996 on his Outside Tour with Nine Inch Nails in Bristow, Virginia. The venue was fairly close to where I lived, maybe an hour away. A buddy and I got there early enough for the opening act, a new band called Prick that had just signed on to Trent Reznor's Nothing label. Nine Inch Nails were touring for their album *The Downward Spiral* and Bowie had just released his album *Outside*.

After a fantastic set by NIN, Bowie came onstage with no intermission or break in between and joined them for a few songs, three of his own and two with NIN, the last of which 'Hurt' was a big single at the time and was truly amazing, and one of the highlights of the many shows I've seen over the years. Bowie's set focused mainly on the *Outside* album, with some covers, a few *Low* tracks as well as some others. It was truly a fantastic night and one that still gives me bragging rights 21 years later.

THE SET LIST
01. Subterraneans (with NIN)
02. Scary Monsters (and super creeps) (with NIN)
03. Reptile (with NIN)
04. Hallo Spaceboy (with NIN)
05. Hurt (with NIN)
06. Look Back In Anger
07. I'm Deranged
08. The Hearts Filthy Lesson
09. The Voyeur of Utter Destruction (As Beauty)
10. I Have Not Been to Oxford Town
11. Outside
12. Andy Warhol
13. Breaking Glass
14. The Man Who Sold the World
15. We Prick You
16. Joe the Lion
17. A Small Plot of Land
18. Nite Flights (Scott Walker cover)
19. Under Pressure
20. Teenage Wildlife

KING'S HALL

5 DEC 1995 BELFAST, UK

I WAS THERE: MICHAEL MCALEER

This was the only time Bowie appeared in Northern Ireland. Posters advertised The Outside Tour for Thursday 23 November 1995 – but the show was actually postponed to 5 December. Morrissey had been touring with Bowie as his warm up act to promote his *Southpaw Grammar* album. But two weeks into the tour The Smiths front-man pulled out.

Four of us got free tickets, it was the Nineties so we were ah... chemically refreshed. Carlos Alomar and Hunt Sales (not Robert fuckin' Quine as my mate kept saying). 'Hang the DJ' was in the set, then 'Moonage Daydream', which blew my head off even more. I'm so glad I got to see him as I missed the Glass Spider Tour at Slane Castle, Dublin in 1987 due to a broken down motorcycle, but that's another story.

THE BIG TWIX MIX SHOW

13 DECEMBER 1995 NEC ARENA, BIRMINGHAM

I WAS THERE: TONY BRIGGS

This was an odd gig all round really. You had to apply for tickets with the wrappers of what seemed like around 40 Twix bars. Obviously consumed by us with consequences that still seem to survive to this day...

We managed to fulfill the sweet eating requirements and duly received our tickets. So with much excitement off we went from Leicester, a friend driving so we could have a few drinks. When we arrived we had standing tickets and had a fantastic view, as the standing area was quite small.

The opening act, and I think I have this in the right order, was Alanis Morrissette, mainly performing the *Jagged Little Pill* songs. She was excellent despite dancing like Joe Cocker performing 'With a Little Help From Our Friends'. Alanis was followed by The Lightning Seeds who were performing the *Jollification* album which I had really liked. Unfortunately I am not sure whether Ian Broudie had an off day or whether he was just a terrible singer but I am afraid they were appalling. This dampened the proceedings because you couldn't wait for it to be over.

Obviously following this was David Bowie. The First two songs, 'Look Back In Anger' and then 'Scary Monsters'. Wow this is brilliant but then the *Outside* songs started coming and I am afraid it is just one of those albums I don't like; despite having 'Strangers

When we Meet' on it, one of my favourite Bowie songs of the post *Let's Dance* era. So unfortunately I had an hour of ups and downs.

The *Outside* songs just didn't do it for me and they spoilt the rest of the songs in a way. After about an hour and a quarter, it was over which was also very disappointing. I may not have been having the time of my life but such short sets by headlining acts I thought had become a thing of the past. I don't know if this day was just not 'my day' but it wasn't the blow away, up close and personal night I was excited about. It is fair to say I probably wish I could have the chance to relive it to see if I was on an off day or whether others felt the same way.

Even though this wasn't the best, it didn't dampen my passion for all things Bowie nor live music in general. That is why I like whole tours. You get to see the really good shows and sometimes the really bad can be as entertaining in their own way. Life's rich tapestry and all that.

PRINS VAN ORANJEHALL

28 JANUARY 1996 UTRECHT, NETHERLANDS

I WAS THERE: ERIC SLIM

It happened after his concert in Utrecht, the Netherlands. After the concert my wife, her sister and I walked at the back of the Oranjehal, where the concert had taken place and waited to see a glimpse of him. Besides our three there were only three or four persons more waiting.

After 10 minutes a big touring car drove out of the hall and away from it. We did not have a chance to look inside it, but we were sure that Bowie was in it and that we'd missed our chance of seeing him. After the car left, three people walked out of the hall. One of them told us that Bowie was in the car. He saw that we were very disappointed and then told us that Bowie was spending the night in the Golden Tulip Hotel in Amsterdam (about 50 kilometers from Utrecht).

This was our second chance! We had no idea where this Golden

Tulip Hotel was in Amsterdam, but we could drive faster than his car, so I had only to track him down on the highway and follow him to the hotel. This was a great (and simple) plan but it didn't work because we joined a massive queue of cars, from all the other fans who had seen the concert.

After 40 minutes we arrived in Amsterdam but we had not seen his car again. This hotel could have been near the airport, near the highway or in the centre of Amsterdam. I guessed he would be in the middle of Amsterdam. After we arrived, I drove through a few streets. We were all looking if we could see a sign for the Golden Tulip hotel but we didn't. When I came to the central station, I passed at the left but we didn't see one hotel, so I turned and drove to the other side. And then we drove past his car, which was parked before a hotel that had another name (later we found out that this hotel was attached to the Golden Tulip). I parked my car right in front of the tour bus and we jumped out of it.

I saw guitarist Reeves Gabreles walking to the entrance of the hotel. I shouted his name and he stopped. I ran to him and asked him for his autograph. My wife told me after this that I had run right along Bowie, but I didn't see him. Especially for this occasion I had brought my beloved promo-CD of *Outside* (the 10 inch booklet with text and the CD of course) with me. At the moment that Reeves signed it someone came standing beside him and when I looked it was Bowie himself. Although my heart was beating in my throat, I did not think twice and gave him my hand and asked him also to sign my promo-CD. He was very friendly and did put his autograph beside the one of Reeves. Then I asked him if my wife could take a photo of us and he agreed.

Then the most terrible moment of my life came! I was standing beside a big smiling David Bowie waiting for the moment that my wife would press the button on the camera, but nothing happened. The camera jammed. It was a freezing 10 degrees outside and because of the great difference of temperature from inside the car and the temperature outside the camera had probably frozen.

Fuck, there I was standing beside my idol and my camera would not work!! Bowie was a little bit impatient because it was very cold. Then Bowie himself came up with the solution. He proposed that someone else could take our photo and that he/she could send it to me. Beside us there were four other fans outside the hotel. A German girl, who was standing beside my wife, took her camera and took the photo. After I shook hands with Bowie and thanked him, he said goodbye and entered his hotel. I gave the girl my address, and totally stunned we walked back to our car. Inside the car we looked at our hands and mumbled that Bowie had touched these hands. We were totally happy!

After four or five weeks I received my photo from the German girl (It was a pity that the girl only sent me the photo and not the negative). Bowie was looking great! He had a very big smile on his face. And I... I was standing sheepishly laughing beside him.

Outside Summer Festivals Tour
Following on from the earlier, David Bowie Outside Tour, which ended on 20 February 1996, the Outside Summer Festivals Tour opened at the Budokan Hall in Tokyo, Japan on 4 June 1996. With a slimmed-down tour band (Bowie, Reeves Gabrels, Gail Ann Dorsey, Zachary Alford and Mike Garson), the tour embarked to Russia and

Iceland, followed by a string of performances on the European Summer festivals circuit.

The Kremlin Palace Concert Hall performance on 18 June 1996 was recorded and a 50-minute broadcast was later shown on Russian Television.

KREMLIN PALACE CONCERT HALL

18 JUNE 1996 MOSCOW, RUSSIA

I WAS THERE: ALEXIS ROWELL

The most bizarre Bowie concert I ever saw was in the Kremlin in 1996, when I was working in Moscow as a BBC correspondent. The Russian capital was awash with money and violence as the KGB and the mafia fought over the spoils of the Soviet Union. Bowie landed like an alien in the middle of it all. And the new Russian rich came flocking to hear the Western star play in a concert hall inside the walls of the Kremlin. But it was clear that none of them knew anything about him or his songs. They came because he was a global rock star. They were totally bemused, stunned, transfixed. Those of us in the cheap seats at the back, the real fans, sang along and danced, when the bouncers weren't trying to keep us in our seats, but the front 30 rows were glued to their seats in silence. It was a characteristically bizarre moment in the life of the most eclectic and brightest star of them all. Now sadly dark. RIP Blackstar.

P.A.O. STADIUM

1 JULY 1996 ATHENS, GREECE

I WAS THERE: GOGO THEOPHANOPOULOU

Although Bowie was and is my 'first in class musician', the concert was average. He came as part of the Athens Rocking Festival along with Elvis Costello and Lou Reed. It was very hot weather, the stadium had bad acoustics and the only song I remember was 'The Man Who Sold the World'. Sitting far away from the stage we couldn't see his costume, which was designed by Alexander McQueen. At least I can say as a big fan, 'I was there'. I am very very sorry that he never again visited Greece.

PARK HAYARKON

3 JULY 1996 TEL AVIV, ISRAEL

I WAS THERE: TIFANY MILOSEVIC

I saw David Bowie perform in Tel Aviv in 1996 as part of the Outside Tour. I was 17 and fearless, and my friend and I snuck backstage after the show and basically went up to him, talked to him, shook his hand and got an autograph. He was beautiful and nice, and his handshake was strong. It was a short encounter since the security guards threw us out pretty quickly, but those were five minutes to last a lifetime.

By the time of the concert, I had been obsessed with Bowie for about three years. I was 14 when I first came across Bowie, stealing one of my big sister's mix tapes, which happened to have 'Space Oddity' on it. I remember how I felt listening to it (over and over). It brought tears to my eyes, and I didn't know music could do that to you. I just had to find out more about this guy, and I began collecting every single piece of music and visual I could find (mind you, not an easy feat in the pre-internet, pre-digital world). I was completely and utterly in love.

None of my close friends caught the Bowie bug like me, and so I was all alone in my obsession. Bowie is exactly my father's age, and I can't tell how many times I was told, 'He's old, why are you so interested in him?' I didn't give a shit. You can't explain Bowie to someone who doesn't get it. I collected any Bowie stuff I found. I also have a lot of vinyl records, some quite rare.

The concert itself was beyond amazing. I was pretty close to the stage, and I couldn't believe I was looking at him, real size. He was wearing his Outside-style garb, long coat and fire-orange hair, and at one point took the coat off, to reveal his sexy arms in a sleeveless black top. He shone. I was in another world.

The show ended too quickly, and we started making our way out of the park, when my friend came running up screaming, 'I saw him! I saw him! He was in a white robe backstage!' Turns out he managed to sneak behind the stage into the VIP area. Of course I had to try too. We went back in, ducked under the stage construction and somehow managed to break in to the enclosed VIP area. From afar I spotted something orange, and we darted straight towards it.

He was standing there, talking to members of Massive Attack (they were the opening act), smiling. He had changed his clothes, sadly no longer wearing a robe. I was out of breath by the time I reached him. The encounter itself is a bit of a blur… I actually went up and tapped him on the shoulder and said, 'David?' He stopped talking and looked at me with a surprised look. Then I said something like, 'Great show!' and he broke into a wide smile and said 'Thank you'. I whipped out a pen and a piece of paper (which was a bit damp because we were sprayed with water during the show). I apologized and explained why it was wet, but he didn't respond to that and asked if he could sign it and he said, 'sure', but he had nowhere to place the paper so I turned around and he signed it on my back. Then I asked if I could shake his hand and he put his out and I shook it! Actually touched him. Then he signed my friend's shirt, and then the guards came up and politely showed us the way out.

He was more beautiful then I expected, and he was nice and seemed outgoing although we rudely interrupted him, two sweaty, out-of-breath teenage fans. Looking into his eyes up close was so weird. You don't know which one to look into and it truly gives you an other-worldly vibe.

I couldn't sleep for days after I was so pumped. Then I experienced a sort of low, because I felt like nothing in my life could ever match this experience. I was going over the whole thing in my head again and again, kicking myself for not asking him questions and not telling him I loved him.

The thing is, you really are in love with him. Your heart flutters at the mere mention of his name, and you can't get enough of him. Since he is unattainable, it only makes you love him more. You feel like no man could ever come close to making you feel like he does, and it isolates you. I didn't let myself really fall in love with anyone for a long time, and even when I did it never worked out, my love life was quiet a mess for years (yes, David, I blame you. Damn you for setting such high standards). There is a happy end – eventually I did find love, I have a wonderful husband and a beautiful daughter (whom I seriously considered naming Zowie. Thank God I didn't). I really hope she'll appreciate him too when she grows up.

Loving Bowie is chronic, it never goes away.

THE PHOENIX FESTIVAL

18 JULY 1996 STRATFORD UPON AVON

I WAS THERE: CHRIS STOCKIL

Being 16 was tough. GCSEs were the most important thing in life to everyone except yourself. Suddenly you were finished with high school and the world opened up to throw everything it can at you without the protection of the classroom and daily routine. I recall

being in a graphic
design class in
the spring of '96.
I was only there
because I'd ticked
the wrong box on
the selection form
the year before
and mistakenly
missed out on
the woodwork
class. It became

Chris Stockil and Dom

obvious quite quickly that anyone who had an ounce of sense
was not in the woodwork class and was with me in graphics. I
couldn't draw but decided to stick it out. Who needs a wooden
fruit bowl in the Nineties anyway? (I now draw for a living).
Going round the class was a full-page newspaper ad. It was
slightly larger than a normal newspaper and was an attractive
purple in colour. It was the Holy Bible of the time, the *NME*.
To this day I'm not sure if it was ever meant to reach me,
but when it did my life changed forever. It was the line up
for Phoenix '96, the UK's first four-day festival. At the time I
don't think I'd even been to a gig let alone a four-day festival
200 miles from home. One of the indie girls asked if I fancied
going. I paused, read the line up over and over, David Bowie,
Neil Young, The Prodigy (the only group you could like if you
were a dance fan or a Mosher), then I saw it, The Sex Pistols!

Like any decade, if you were in it, the music was the best. We were
in a post grunge, indie booming, dance booming pop mainstream
playlist. I had started high school owning only a few albums, *Bad*
by Michael Jackson, *Queen – Greatest Hits* and the *Blues Brothers*
soundtrack. I also owned a large collection of ex jukebox 45s and
the odd single from my childhood. I still remember buying my first
record from the local Gateway supermarket, it was 'Star Trekkin' by
The Firm. I still own this and am convinced if you hold it up to the

light you can see straight through the groove, One more play and it would be a coaster.

One record always stood out from the rest. It was the one I would play the loudest, sing along to, or shout and send drifting over the fields from my isolated farmhouse bedroom window. The sound of horse hooves, a bugle-call then thundering bass followed by the crash of drums and ripping guitar riff. I never really understood why 'Swords of a Thousand Men' by Tenpole Tudor appealed to me back then but I certainly do now!

Christmas 1995 had arrived and to this day I don't know how I came to own it but I'd acquired *Kiss This – The Best of the Sex Pistols*. The songs were raw, angry, loud and offensive - everything a 15-year old needs from music, Indie music was good, looking back it was really good, but I always seemed to pick out the heavier songs from the likes of the *Shine* compilations or recording Willey and Lamacq off the BBC Radio 1 evening session.

I realised quite slowly that I liked punk. The adrenaline rush I would get listening to 'Oo ra oo ra oo ra ay' was definitely here to stay.

On seeing the Pistols were playing Phoenix as part of their *Filthy Lucre* comeback tour I didn't hesitate to sign up to the festival with a group of people who would be my closest friends for years to come. The cost was astronomical at the time, £65 for a four-day festival. Looking back that's less than dinner for two with the wife! What a steal!

I started listening to other bands on the bill so I didn't look stupid down the front humming along rather than singing each song word for word. Having dipped into grunge for a year or so, Nirvana had made 'The Man Who Sold the World' a very familiar song to me, the opening riff inspired hours of playing an out of tune warped acoustic guitar. I never really grasped the guitar at this age, lessons were uninspiring and the other people in guitar lessons at school were girls. I took some stick for that I'll tell you, being a teenager and the only boy in an all girl class is prime real estate for bullies.

I recall staying awake late one night watching *The Man Who Fell To*

Earth, and at the time all I could think was that it was a bit weird but the music was good and was David Bowie actually an alien?

The morning of the festival arrived. It was hot, I mean really hot, the hot you feel when you get off a plane in Majorca hot. I wasn't around to feel the heat of the summer of '76 but this was my '76.

Three lions, GCSEs , Fosters £1.40 a pint and embarking on the first of 24 festivals (to date). What a time to be alive!

Inexperienced in festival etiquette our group of nine had packed enough food and clothes for an arctic expedition. The tent myself and Dom were to share was steel posted double linen lined heavy duty. It weighed a ton.

Nervously we all met outside Rebecca's house in the village of Kirk Hammerton. We sat waiting for Geoff. Geoff was Becks' dad. He was a great guy, very funny, and would let us have parties in the loft, playing loud music and not going to sleep till the sun came up. Somehow, and I still don't know why, Geoff had agreed to drive us all from North Yorkshire to Stratford-upon-Avon by minibus for the festival. What a guy!

We were off in good time, bags packed, adrenaline rushing and our festival virginity about to be torn apart by four days of legendary artists climaxing with Rotten, Cook, Jones and Matlock doing what they were born to do, swear!

By midday we were well on the way, to nowhere. We had reached the outskirts of Stratford and hit traffic. We were sat for ages. Looking back at festival footage there was an interview with the band Dodgy. When asked if they were stuck in traffic the drummer responded 'Yeah, but not as bad as Steve Winwood, he was in Traffic for years!' This would be one of only a handful of memories I have from the festival. And a joke I still use when faced with tail lights on the M1.

We sat in the van, we sat on the van, we sat on the verge. The heat was intense; it was the furthest south I had ever been bar my one holiday to Majorca aged 10. I thought we were going to melt. We had nearly finished all our pop and crisps and were beginning to ration the bourbons, which are only good if they are heated with Yorkshire tea, not the midday sunshine. Whilst progress was slow, looking back I felt we bonded more as a group, grew closer through experience and made new lasting friendships.

In the distance we could hear the sound-check. We hadn't moved for hours but we must have been close. People had been walking past us, in their hundreds, leaving their cars and making the final few yards (or so we thought) on foot.

The music in the distance was unrecognisable, bass heavy with the odd lyric being called out. None of us knew who was on but we were close, so close. We debated for ages on if we should walk on or stay with the van. Geoff had sat calm and motionless at the wheel, unphased by the heat, the teenagers or the frustration of motionless traffic. What a legend.

The vote was cast, we mounted up, shared the loads and set off with the walking masses to get to the site. Most of the group wanted to see The Prodigy, who were at their peak. Still engaged with the club scene crowd and now following the release of 'Firestarter' and 'Breathe' they had now attacked the ears of indie and rock fans alike. This was new territory for any band. To have fans waving glow sticks next to fans moshing and crowd surfing was completely unheard of.

I wanted to see David Bowie!

The walk was quickly relegated to a crawl, the heat was getting to us and the night was drawing in. There was a level of unity, not just in our group, but throughout the many hundreds of others who had chosen to walk the last leg. Comments of 'Not far now' and 'Worse things happen at sea' were common phrase.

The last leg turned out to be 13 miles. There was no direct route to the site from where we were. We could see the lights, hear the bass but were so far away.

Walking through Stratford town centre carrying enough supplies for a small army was not fun. Festivals were meant to be fun, a time of joy, celebration and liberation. This was fucking torture!

Then the music stopped. It was still well above 25 degrees and the night was still. The noise of the wandering crowds had subsided as people's hopes of arriving on day one were fading fast. We had no choice but to press on and hope we could get our tents pitched before breakfast.

On turning a corner I recall being hit with a slight breeze, a cool breeze that reinvigorated the desire to get to the site. It was like a cold drink on the air. They say memories stay longer in the mind if there is emotion linked to them. This emotion was relief, the weight of our supplies, the hunger, the thirst all went away with those few breaths of cool air. Then I heard it.

The speakers fired up. I cant recall exactly the sounds coming out, I could look on YouTube but the memory is mine and is such a part of what I believe to be one of the best times of my life that don't want it tarnished with reality, I don't want that sound to be some fat roadie blurting out, 'One, two, testing, one, two.'

To me I heard stars, I heard planets, I heard all the sounds you can imagine when you look up into the starry sky at night. I heard light years of silence with the intermittent soft beeping of alien transmission then...two words that will stay in my mind forever... 'Hallo Spaceboy'

I never got to see Bowie. We arrived at 3am, bought a crate of Oranjeboom lager, poured some on some bread and got my mate Duncan to pretend he was Jesus by throwing slices of wholemeal at passers by saying, 'There is enough for everyone.' This is what 16 year olds did in the Nineties.

Aged 36 I now look back at the experience of that festival as a rite of passage. It was more about the journey than the music and Bowie was there playing St Peter at the pearly gates.

The Pistols were awesome if a bit intimidating and 20 years on I'm definitely a punk at heart.

MADISON SQUARE GARDEN

9 JANUARY 1997 NEW YORK CITY

I WAS THERE: LEE RANALDO

In 1997, we in Sonic Youth were amazed when we got word from

Sonic Youth

David Bowie, inviting us to perform with him onstage at Madison Square Garden in celebration of his 50th birthday. That he even knew who we were was amazing to us! We had been so inspired and influenced by his music for so long, and it was a huge thrill to join him in performance. Hanging out with him leading up to the concert, it was clear that he was still fully engaged and informed about all kinds of music and art going on around him, curious and open to new influences. Not many of his generation were tuned in to the kind of thing that we were doing, but he certainly was.

A few days before the show, we all trooped up to Connecticut for rehearsal. David had rented the Hartford Civic Center arena for the day so we could rehearse and get comfortable in a venue with a stage the same size as Madison Square Garden! He had asked our friend Tony Oursler to do some of his video projections as the stage set for the concert. Tony was a fellow artist-traveller who had directed our 'Tunic' video a few years prior. David impressed us with his focus and his friendly and positive demeanor throughout a long day. He was excited, and certainly we were! We were only halfway through our thirty-year career as a band at that time, while he was already past that mark, and obviously still going strong. A Radical Adult.

1997 Bowie and his band began rehearsing for The Earthling Tour in April 1997, and expected it to last from May through Christmas (1997). The Earthling Tour opened on June 7, 1997 at Flughafen Blankensee in Lübeck, Germany continuing through Europe, and North America before

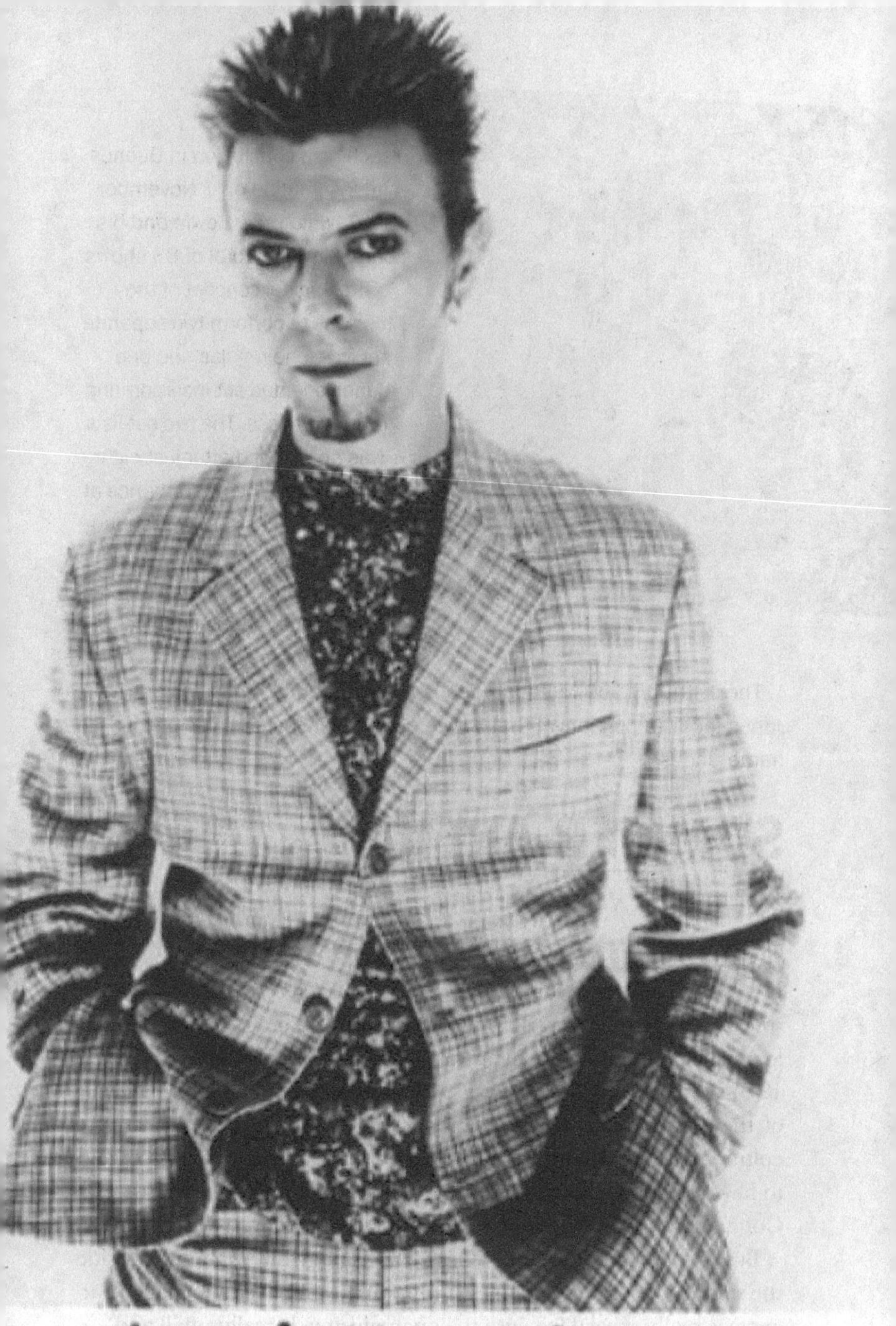

davidbowie

Photocredit: Nina Schultz

I WAS THERE

reaching a conclusion in Buenos Aires, Argentina on 7 November 1997, which saw Bowie and his band playing a total of 83 shows.

The original concept of the tour was to perform two separate set lists, one regular, and one dance-oriented set incorporating drum and bass. The two set-lists was abandoned after just eight shows (after the performance at the Muziekcentrum Vredenburg in Utrecht, of the Netherlands on 11 June 1997), due to the media critics and audiences' apathy for the idea.

The 19th July 1997 Phoenix Festival performance was billed as Tao Jones Index (a psudonym that Bowie used which includes his birth last name 'Jones').

SOMMER ARENA

24 JUNE 1997 VIENNA, AUSTRIA

I WAS THERE: FLORIAN BAUER

It was a big surprise when I heard about this gig. The Arena is a spectacular venue famous for its punk, rock and indie-gigs. It was a former slaughterhouse, which was supposed to be demolished. In 1976 it was occupied by activists, who were campaigning for a rescue of the area and its use as a location for youth culture, alternative culture and counterculture. More than 200,000 people are purported to have visited the premises during the occupation and Leonard Cohen described the area as the 'best place in Vienna.'

Bowie seemed to love this venue with its huge brick chimney beside the stage and commented a few times on how he liked the place. The gig was really special because the open air-area is really small and

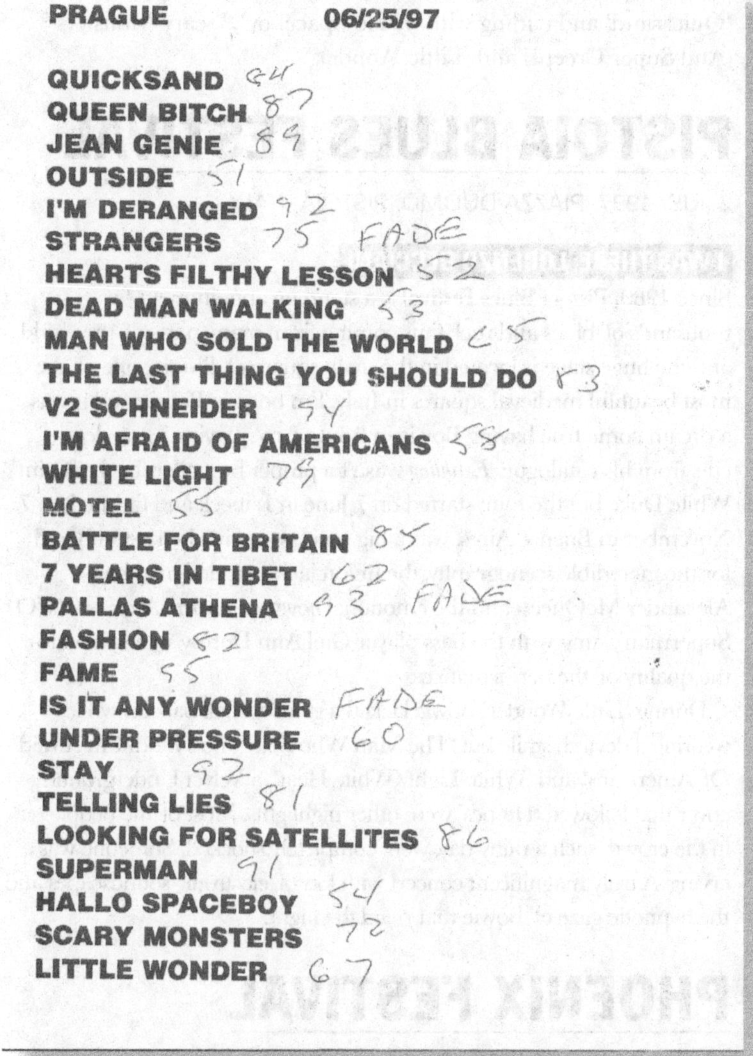

PRAGUE 06/25/97

- QUICKSAND 94
- QUEEN BITCH 87
- JEAN GENIE 89
- OUTSIDE 91
- I'M DERANGED 92
- STRANGERS 75 FADE
- HEARTS FILTHY LESSON 92
- DEAD MAN WALKING 93
- MAN WHO SOLD THE WORLD 95
- THE LAST THING YOU SHOULD DO 83
- V2 SCHNEIDER 94
- I'M AFRAID OF AMERICANS 98
- WHITE LIGHT 79
- MOTEL 95
- BATTLE FOR BRITAIN 95
- 7 YEARS IN TIBET 92
- PALLAS ATHENA 93 FADE
- FASHION 82
- FAME 95
- IS IT ANY WONDER FADE
- UNDER PRESSURE 90
- STAY 92
- TELLING LIES 81
- LOOKING FOR SATELLITES 96
- SUPERMAN 91
- HALLO SPACEBOY 94
- SCARY MONSTERS 72
- LITTLE WONDER 67

Set list from The Congress Centre Prague 25 June 1997

the atmosphere was magic. He played a 26-song set starting with 'Quicksand' and ending with 'Hallo Spaceboy', 'Scary Monsters (And Super Creeps)' and 'Little Wonder.'

PISTOIA BLUES FESTIVAL

2 JULY 1997 PIAZZA DUOMO, PISTOIA, ITALY

I WAS THERE: LORENZO BECCIANI

Since 1980, Pistoia Blues Festival is a standing appointment for thousands of blues and rock fans coming from many parts of the world and the huge stage is located in the main square of Pistoia, one of the most beautiful medieval squares in Italy. I'm born in Pistoia and it was a dream come true having Bowie in front of me playing some deep cuts from his catalogue. *Earthling* wasn't a proper bestseller for the Thin White Duke but the tour, started on 7 June in Lübeck and finished on 7 November in Buenos Aires, was a big success and it'll be remembered for the incredible scenography, the union jack coat designed by Alexander McQueen and the emotional cover of Laurie Anderson's 'O Superman', sung with the bass player Gail Ann Doresy, in addition to the quality of the performances.

During 'Little Wonder' Bowie kicked a giant eyeball balloon while wearing a devilish smile but 'The Man Who Sold The World/I'm Afraid Of Americans' and 'White Light/White Heat', a Velvet Underground cover that followed 'Heroes' were other highlights. Most of the people in the crowd, such a rainy day, were completely shocked. Someone was crying. A truly magnificent concert with lots of electronic soundscapes and the hypnotic gaze of Bowie that ruled the night.

PHOENIX FESTIVAL

20 JULY 1997 STRATFORD UPON AVON

I WAS THERE: GARY LEVERMORE

My first opportunity to see Bowie live was on the Serious Moonlight

Tour in 1983. For some reason, I turned a ticket down, thinking it might be a bit naff, even though I enjoyed a good fifty per cent of the *Let's Dance* album released that year. More fool me.

As it turned out, the only time I saw him live was at the Phoenix Festival in July 1997, when I happened to be working with another act on the bill. I wouldn't have gone otherwise. But, it was great.

My work duties done by late afternoon on a gorgeous summer day, I got to enjoy sets by Faith No More and Orbital ahead of Bowie.

Aside from starting with 'Quicksand', I really can't remember much of his set (in fact, I just had to check it on setlist.fm for what he played). But he and his band sounded great. I'm glad I saw him... even if it wasn't 1973 or 1978 vintage!

I WAS THERE: CURTIS McFEE

There has been an almost apocryphal memory that has stewed at the back of mind for the last 19 years. A long time ago. It was three years before the Millennium and pretty much nothing seemed wrong with the world, not like today. It seems an age away and as I look back the distance seems to stretch away into some kind of youthful haze.

In 1997 I went to a music festival and I didn't watch David Bowie live. That is the thought I have kind of chewed over since then. Of course, for a long time, it didn't even register. Then in the last ten years, long enough for the actual long-term memory to fade into half-truth, it has bugged me more and more. For a long time, I even thought it was the V Festival of 2000, so any attempt to go back and check ended up with confusion and less recall than ever. The story I have told, to myself, and others, was that I went to a festival and saw a number of bands – one of the acts was David Bowie. I watched a little bit but decided that I would rather go and see Sinead O'Connor.

From the more recent perspective, I kick myself every time I think that I had a chance to see the great man in performance and didn't recognise the opportunity set before me. Now, there is nothing wrong with Sinead; for at that time she was in a kind of 'Peak Sinead' state and I was very much into Irish folksy stuff. Also, Bowie was touring with the *Earthling* set and although I liked the record I was not yet fully cognisant of what David Bowie meant. This was before the impact of *Hours* and *Heathen*. This was a time when *Outside* received almost no press coverage and *Black Tie White Noise* was a little too close to the Eighties for anyone in the Nineties to offer any respect. Plus, there was the drum and bass connection which was a little too closely linked to some very poor bands at the time. Most just thought he had done a drum and bass album, so it didn't fully register on my internal landscape.

I have tried to justify this over time, thinking that it was so very hot that summer, pushing thirty degrees every day. I would tell myself that the crowd was too much and I couldn't see; that I would rather have a good position with a lesser act, than stand in the crush. Maybe that was the case, but my memory fragments are quite clear. I can remember the stage setting. I can remember the jacket. I can almost remember some of the songs... almost... remember... the only tracks that really set in my mind were 'Scary Monsters' and 'Little Wonder'. I saw myself listening to two tracks and then wandering off into a tent that smelt of weed and armpits to look at a bald lady.

This feeling has been with me. The idea of missing out. Looking left when history was happening to the right. You fool!

Some time ago, I spent the evening looking through a YouTube playlist of live performances and one of them caught my attention. It was Pheonix Festival 1997. Suddenly I remembered that it was not V Festival or anything like it. It was Pheonix '97. There was only a small clip but I remembered the set. I remembered the jacket. It gave me a keyword to search for more. I looked and I found out some things...

SET LIST FOR DAVID BOWIE – PHOENIX FESTIVAL 1997

01. Quicksand
02. The Man Who Sold the World
03. The Jean Genie
04. I'm Afraid of Americans
05. Battle for Britain (The Letter)
06. Fashion
07. Seven Years in Tibet
08. Fame
09. Looking for Satellites
10. Under Pressure
11. The Hearts Filthy Lesson
12. Scary Monsters (And Super Creeps)
13. Hallo Spaceboy
14. Little Wonder

Encore:

15. Dead Man Walking
16. White Light/White Heat (Velvet Underground cover)
17. O Superman (Laurie Anderson cover)
18. Stay

It's a helluva set. Do you see what I see? 'Scary Monsters' and 'Little Wonder' were not the first two tracks. They were among the last. This means I saw the whole thing and didn't stay for the encore. I saw the entire set. I saw David Bowie live.

I should be happy with this news and partly I am overjoyed. On one hand, I realise now that the narrative I had been telling myself was wrong and only made my own recollection that much more difficult. I had talked myself out of ever seeing him, erasing it from my memory bit by bit. On the other hand, I saw David Bowie live and have only a scant recollection of the event. I just didn't know I should be paying attention. Yet, it is also like waking up from a fog and suddenly seeing your own past clearly.

I still look back on that young self and think of what an arse he was, but that is the way of youth. I console myself with the idea, that perhaps if you can remember that summer, you weren't there. Mainly I am happy that I get to re-write the wrongs of memory and now I can say: I saw David Bowie live, and from what I recall, he was awesome.

I WAS THERE: CHRIS STOCKIL

Phoenix Festival 1996 and Bowie was headlining the first night. The traffic was chaos and our journey was already nine hours long when we decided to ditch the van and walk the remaining distance to the campsite. We never made it on time to see Bowie but we could hear all the great songs drifting across the fields on a red-hot night. Good times.

BARROWLANDS

22 JULY 1997 GLASGOW

I WAS THERE: RICHARD SAVAGE

He walked on stage with an acoustic guitar wearing a semi-transparent Jean Paul Gaultier outfit and played 'Jean Genie' to start. Then the band came on and played a blinding set starting with

'Scary Monsters (And Super Creeps)' followed by loads of *Earthling* stuff and many mid/late-era classics. His presence struck me as God - like and other worldly instantly. Overwhelming and awe inspiring in the flesh. One of my favourite concerts.

MANCHESTER ACADEMY

23 JULY 1997 MANCHESTER

I WAS THERE: TONY MICHAELIDES

Growing up in the Sixties was the perfect time to discover music and with an education like that it was no wonder I became a huge music fan. I was surrounded by the most amazing music from both sides of the Atlantic and one of my all time favorite artists and still to this day was David Bowie. Seeing The Spiders from Mars play the opening two nights at The Hardrock in Manchester in 1973 still remains as some of the finest shows I have ever seen. The atmosphere inside was electric and I don't think any of us there on those magical nights had experienced anything quite like it and probably never will. What made it even better was that the band looked like they were really enjoying it too. Nevertheless if you would have told me as an 18 year old back then that twenty five years later I'd be on the road working with him as his publicist, organizing all of his promotion, even sitting down and having my dinner with him I'd have said you were crazy!!

David Bowie will always be the most innovative artist of our generation. He was more than an artist he was a visionary. He saw things differently and although not a musician myself I could see the impact and inspiration he was to so many musicians. To me I was just happy to be a fan. Two years after see David Bowie and The Spiders From Mars I somehow landed myself a job in the music industry. I'd seen an ad in the local newspaper, the *Manchester Evening News* and for some reason I thought I'd apply for it. I had a pretty lousy job at the time and as I didn't have a job in the music industry I didn't think there was any harm trying for one. If I don't get it, then no big deal, I still didn't have a job in the music industry. Of course secretly, I'm a total liar. I'd have done anything to get the job but I couldn't set my sights too high in case I didn't get it. The 'what if?' would have been too much to bear. I began my career in the music industry in August 1974 selling records out of the back of a van for twenty-five pounds a week. My job had just become an extension of my hobby. Four years of utter bliss, could it get any better? It did, when in 1978 I landed a job at my all time favourite record label, Island. I'd been buying their records all through the Sixties and Seventies and now I was going to be working for them. The dream was getting bigger...and better. Here I was given the opportunity to work with people whose records I'd bought as a kid! Steve Winwood, Robert Palmer, Bob Marley, the list goes on.

Fast forward. It was July 1997 and one of my colleagues answered a call in the office, 'Roxy Meade's on the phone, do you want to take it?' I'd known Roxy for a few years because she was a publicist in London and had her own publicity company, Lipsey Meade, representing some of the biggest artists in the world. As they handled all the press, my company was responsible for the regional radio and television promotion. We handled a few of the same acts, so from time to time we'd speak and see how each other was doing. I took the call and from that moment on, even though I'd had a great many highs in the music industry my heart skipped a beat as we had a telephone conversation, I still to this day can't really believe. 'Hey Tony, we can't go on the road with Bowie, you're my first call, can you do it? Be his publicist for his Earthling Tour. PLEASE!' I hardly needed pleading with. 'You want me to go on tour with David Bowie?' To cut to the chase, I responded in the affirmative and although my company had promoted David Bowie's records for a good few years we had never had the opportunity to physically work with him. By that I mean take him into radio and TV stations. It was more mailing his records to regional radio and television and then try to get airplay and his videos on TV.

The following day I was summoned to the Manchester show as David always made a point of meeting every single person he directly worked with personally. I was flattered and fortunately DB gave me the heads up and I landed the job. And the very next day I was out on the road with...DAVID BOWIE. And no I still can't believe it.

I'll always regard working with David Bowie as an honour and something I will never forget. I still tell stories about it to this day and look forward to telling them to my grandkids when they're old enough! David was meticulous in the choice of the people he had around him and had a very big say on every part of his career. He virtually managed himself as he had done for several decades and the decisions he made regarding all of his promotion he made himself. I myself also liked to meet the people I would be working with but it doesn't always work out the way you hope. Working with artists on the road can be very draining for both them and you and you certainly need a lot of resilience. With Bowie it never seemed like work because the general atmosphere around all of his people is infectious and the work becomes pleasure. Over the next few weeks there would be a lot of conversations with David regarding media requests and I have to say he was so wonderful to work for, totally professional and very personable.

I remember one particular moment on the tour. Each day I would sit down with him and go through the promotion that was on offer. It wasn't rocket science; everyone wants to talk to Bowie! I mean he was a big star and they to be fair had ratings to consider; of course they wanted him on their shows. At a show in Nottingham I sat down with him and went through the requests. We had a guy from the BBC who'd put a request in and also someone from the independent TV network. David asked my opinion, 'Well, what do you think Tony?' I answered saying that the BBC guy was a huge fan and had followed him throughout his career and the other guy was just doing his job and reaching out to celebrities. I said it was up to him; he didn't have to do either but if I was to choose one it would be the BBC guy. He was clearly the more knowledgeable and likely to be the better interview. David looked at me and said in all sincerity, 'Well if you think I should do it Tony, then I will.' I walked out of the dressing room and down the corridor tightly clenching my hands.

> **I DON'T BELIEVE IT; DAVID BOWIE HAD AGREED TO DO SOMETHING ON MY RECOMMENDATION**

I don't believe it; David Bowie had agreed to do something on my recommendation. I was very flattered that he valued my opinion, I mean who wouldn't be.

David Bowie was one of the most humble and gracious people I had ever met. He also had a great sense of humour and treated everyone with the same respect. There was no us and them, he was a true star in every sense of the word. David Bowie was the story of my life. I mean getting to work with your childhood heroes just doesn't happen and it certainly doesn't happen to a kid from the North of England. Well luckily for me it did and there will always be one special part of it that I will treasure forever.

One of my tasks each night was to escort the photographers into the orchestra pit at the front of the stage where they were allowed to photograph the first three numbers before being politely asked to leave. Each night Bowie would walk out at the beginning of the show with an acoustic guitar draped over him, clad in a white linen shirt, white cotton trousers and barefoot and with a white spotlight shining down on him. With a chime of his guitar he would start each show with a song from either *Hunky Dory* or *Ziggy Stardust* and I would be stood there motionless looking up at him with my mouth wide open. Truly my rock and roll fantasy, a moonage daydream and I really did need to hang onto myself.

THE QUE CLUB

1 AUGUST 1997 BIRMINGHAM

I WAS THERE: BILL DOHERTY

The intimate Bowie gig. It was in a nightclub named The Q Club, set in an old Methodist Church dating back a hundred years or so. It stood in the shadows of Birmingham's Victorian Law Courts. I remember getting to the venue and the lines of fans stretched down the street. There was a bloke (a Bowie look-alike) walking up and down the crowd, dressed as Bowie would at this time, in his Alexander McQueen union jack over coat. We entered the venue. It was very grand place. I seem to remember having to climb up some very old but grand stairs. Our seats were on a balcony looking down onto the stage at the right hand side. The stage wasn't very big and the instruments seemed to be quite closely set up. There was cloth spread out all over the stage floor, a bit strange I thought but maybe something to do with the acoustics.

Bowie entered the stage on his own, very casually dressed in white shirt with his long trade mark cuffs open, dark trousers and sandals - yes, sandals - with straps so his toes were exposed. Not as flamboyant as you'd expect from the chameleon of pop. A short welcome. During this time he passed comment on his hair, running his fingers through it whilst throwing his head back and, 'How very Paul Weller it was' (I've heard a story where they say Paul Weller nicked Bowie's hairstyle from back in the late Sixties. As I'm also a big Weller fan I know this story carries some weight and I believe the two of them joked about it over the years), and he started with a song. I can't remember, just him and his acoustic guitar, part way through he was joined on stage by his band, with Gail Ann Dorsey taking up her usual space to David's right. We were sat above her.

Bowie's relaxed attire was a clue into the show, it was very relaxed. David seemed to be very happy playing to such a small audience, guessing a 1,000 people at most. About two or three songs with Bowie and his acoustic guitar gently strumming the strings to a certain rhythm that sounded familiar, David spoke about how it was the first record he had bought (Johnny Lee Hooker). As he strummed, he changed chords, the band joined in and then it became recognisable, 'Jean Genie'.

When Bowie was introducing the band, he also thanked his set up crew/roadies as they had to carry all the gear up all the stairs and it was on the first floor and there was no lift.

I remember the songs of the night were a mix of old classics, album tracks and songs from his *Outside* album, very techno, some say his rave years. There was a backdrop behind the band, just like a big sheet nothing fancy, I seem to remember a couple of large, balloon like things and at certain parts images of pornography films were projected up onto these (it was black and white, grainy and shaky but very explicit). I remember about five or six songs in, David was announcing the next song when he leaned over the crowd, where someone was smoking. David took the fag from him and had a few drags, saying, 'Man this takes me back' (not sure what exactly was in it, by Bowie's reaction). He went to return it, stopped and took another drag. As I've said, Bowie was very relaxed, very close to the crowd who if he stood at the edge of the stage could have touched him. During the show he did shake hands with a few at the front. I was happy just to see the great man at such close quarters. I'd seen him before in 1990 at the N.E.C. and I saw him again, which turned out to be his last show in Birmingham, at the N.E.C. Gail took lead on one song that I can't remember with Bowie joining in, at the end he stroked her head and I think he kissed her head. She was always with him over the past several years and she always joined him on

'Under Pressure'. He introduced the band. He returned and joked saying their would be two more encores. He played about four songs and it was all over. But I can say I was there.

RIVERSIDE

3 AUGUST 1997 NEWCASTLE UPON TYNE

I WAS THERE: ANDRE FANTARROW

The last show I saw him was the Newcastle Riverside Club, which is very small club. I got there as I always did early, very early, and after a while a roadie came out for something. We got chatting about the man (Bowie) and I told him I'd never met him but been close. I said to him maybe one day. Then the roadie said 'Come with me' and opened this side door and then took me though a few more doors and then opened a door to the stage. He said, 'Wait here and please don't move or talk, just sit.' After a bit of a wait the band came on the stage one by one. 'Mmmm,' I was thinking, 'this is good.' Then to my amazement Bowie slowly walked into the room jumped onto the stage and started his sound-check. I looked around and there was maybe about 15 people there, watching him perform, singing and joking. I Will never forget it and that kind roadie.

ROCK CITY

5 AUGUST 1997 NOTTINGHAM

I WAS THERE: NEIL COSSAR

Until his death, I hadn't really thought about how David Bowie had punctuated and influenced my life over the years, but thinking about this now, I've come to the conclusion that he was always there, in one way or another.

I first heard 'Space Oddity' on the radio in 1969 when I was 11-years old. At this point, I was a Beatles fan, mainly due to the fact that my elder sister would spend hours listening to their singles

Drummer Stu Burnett wonders how Cheaters guitarist Neil Cossar and singer Mick Brophy did that?

and albums. One single had captured my attention – 'I Am The Walrus'. I would listen to this over and over again, I didn't have a clue what the song was about, but it was magic to my ears. I'd never heard anything like it before. Listening to John Lennon singing 'sitting on a cornflake, waiting for the van to come', conjured up all sorts of theatre of the mind to me.

'Space Oddity' did exactly the same. I'd bought a copy from a second hand ex-juke box stall on Stockport Market, where my mum would take my sister and I every Saturday morning to by food for the week.

I played that single over and over again, I loved the weird sounds on the track, not knowing that one of the strange sounds was David playing a Stylophone. The mellotron and drifting guitar parts added to the mystery. Was Major Tom still up there? Floating in space? Also at this stage, I'd didn't know what David Bowie looked liked, so this all added to the mystery that surrounded the song and the singer.

By the time *Ziggy Stardust* was released I was 13 years old, and learning to play the guitar. I would spend hours locked in my bedroom, with my mono record player listening to *Ziggy* and playing along to it, 'Rock 'n' Roll Suicide' being the song I nailed best (or so I thought at the time).

I left school at 16 with my sights set on being a rock star, I mean, how hard could it be? I was already playing in a band called Zenith in various pubs around Stockport to sometimes 30 people!

The thought of working for a living didn't appeal to me at all, but I was forced into a compromise by my parents. They allowed me the summer off, as long as I starting looking for a job by September. Becoming a rock star was proving to be difficult, so I agreed I would take a job, as long as it was in a guitar shop or record store.

By the winter of 74, I was working at HMV records in Manchester, which at the time was the largest record store outside of London.

I loved it. I didn't really have to work behind the counter selling to the public, but instead I was working in the stockroom where I discovered I had the ability to work the shrink wrap machine faster than anyone else in the store (all albums would have a plastic film on them before going out in the racks).

The boss at HMV Manchester was a bloke called Pete Waddington, who himself had enjoyed a rather unsuccessful career as the lead singer in a group called The Amazingly Friendly Apple. Pete was a massive music fan and introduced me to so much new music. His party trick was when the shop was full on a Saturday afternoon, he would play one of several killer tracks by artists such as Randy Newman, Jackson Browne, Joni Mitchell, or The Eagles and watch to see how long it would take for someone to come to the counter and ask who was playing. It always worked within 30 seconds and they would buy the album.

Pete was Yorkshire man, and as tight as they come. He would never come to the pub with us after work in case he had to buy a round. He always struck deals with the reps from the record companies for the best deals, free tickets and in fact anything that might line his pockets.

One such opportunity arose when he was approached by some Manchester based concert bootleggers. It transpired they had a couple of thousand David Bowie bootleg albums ready to hit the market. The one thing missing before they went on sale was to have them shrink wrapped. Pete took me to one side and asked if I would work late for a few nights and he would pay me overtime. No problem, deal done, and the following week a very large van arrived as the store was closing

and we unloaded dozens of boxes of Bowie bootlegs ready for yours truly to shrink wrap.

The job was done over a few nights and the bootleggers returned to take the re-packaged albums away. What they didn't know was that the British Phonographic Industry's anti-piracy unit had been following the gang and arrested them all as they were loading up the van. Luckily for us, Pete somehow talked his way out of having any involvement with the gang and got away scot-free. I can't remember what the Bowie album was called and I never did find out what happened to the gang or the bootlegs!

I quit my job at HMV in 1978 to become a professional musician. Over the next 10 years, The Cheaters made three albums, played over 1,000 gigs and a good time was had by all, but we split after realising we'd taken our road to stardom as far as we could.

I ended up working at a radio station as the late night DJ who played great music, but nobody listened to. In fact to prove the point, one night after putting on a nine minute Van Morrison track, I ran out of the studio to the toilet, did my thing and ran back to the studio door, only to find I'd locked myself out. After much kicking and running at the door, I managed to break the lock and was back in the studio. The Van Morrison track had finished about 10 minutes ago and I was anticipating all 12 red lights on the phone lines to be flashing, with anxious listeners concerned that I had either fallen asleep or had suffered a heart attack. In fact, I didn't get one call, no one had noticed, or, no one was listening! To compose myself, I put on 'Space Oddity' and pondered maybe it was time for a new career.

Fast-forward to 1996, and I found myself working at the very successful UK promotions company TMP, which was run by my old friend Tony Michaelides. We were record pluggers and to me, this seemed like a dream job. And it was.

The following year Tony announced we had a very exciting new project. We would be working all the UK regional radio and TV promotion for David Bowie's new album *Earthling* as well as promotion around his forthcoming tour.

I would attend three shows on the tour, the first being the Manchester Academy show on 23 July 1997. On the night, a few of us from work met with a couple of RCA people (up from London) for dinner and drinks before the show to discuss the promotion around the tour. One of my co-workers was a young lady by the name of Liz, who although we were working together, didn't really get on or have anything in common. In fact I sensed she really didn't like me!

This was confirmed the year before when I was invited to a party at the very grand Manchester Town Hall to celebrate the boy band Take That, who were given the 'keys to the city'. After plenty of eating and drinking I found myself sat alone at a table with Liz and thought I would take the opportunity to come out with my best chat-up line. 'So, what's your story?' I asked. 'Far too complicated for you', came the reply. At which point Liz stood up, left the table and went off to dance with Jason Orange from Take That, leaving yours truly sat alone at an empty table for twelve.

On the night of the Bowie gig in Manchester, we arrived just as Bowie and his band took the stage, where they opened with 'Quicksand', followed by 'The Man Who Sold The World' and 'The Jean Genie'. With us arriving late, I found myself standing right at the back of the venue, with Liz. At the end of 'Jean Jeanie' we swapped thoughts on the show so far, and then I'm ashamed to say, continued to talk right through his set. With Bowie playing in the background I found to my surprise that Liz all of a sudden seemed more interested in me than watching David Bowie!

The next morning back in the office, our boss called a meeting to discuss the previous night's events and started off by saying how annoyed he was that two members of his staff (myself and Liz) had not really paid any attention to the show, drank too much and generally had behaved badly. He was really pissed off with us both and continued to tell us how unprofessionally we had conducted ourselves the previous evening!

Two weeks later I arrived at Rock City in Nottingham in the afternoon, which was my second show on the tour. I was working this night. My duties were to meet various radio and TV people who were on the guest list and also look after all the photographers for the night. All the snappers needed special passes to get to the front of the stage, but were only allowed to take photos during the first three numbers. They then had to either leave the venue or, take their cameras back stage (where I would meet them) and leave them in a secure room so they could then return to the venue and watch the show.

By early evening I found myself back stage looking for the tour manger (for some more passes) and was directed into the main dressing room. I walked in and was told to wait while someone went off to find him. The room looked amazing, leather sofas, candlesticks, rugs and large exotic plants, which had been brought in to brighten up the dressing room. Then it happened. A door opened and in walked David Bowie, and he was heading towards me. I stood there with a thousand

> **THEN IT HAPPENED A DOOR OPENED AND IN WALKED DAVID BOWIE**

thoughts going through me head. Should I stop him and talk? What would I say? He was getting closer, and closer, he looked straight at me. I looked at him and said 'Hi'. He replied 'All right?' and swept past and out a door. Fucking hell! I'd talked to David Bowie I thought! Well, once I'd composed myself, I thought what a dick, that was my chance to meet one of my all time heroes and all I could manage was, 'Hi'. Idiot.

I didn't really see much of the show with working, but when I did get the chance to stand and see the odd song I was really struck with how fantastic Bowie's voice sounded.

The following night was at the Town and Country Club in Leeds where I would see the full show. All I had to do for the evening as far as work was concerned was to meet BBC Radio 1 DJ's Mark Radcliffe and Marc Riley in Manchester, drive over to Leeds and make sure they were supplied with drinks for the evening. Both Radcliffe and Riley are top blokes so this was going to be a great night and it was. The Town & Country was a fairly small venue, with I would guess less than a 2,000 capacity. We had brilliant seats on the first row of the balcony and at last I was ready to see and enjoy a full show.

And I wasn't disappointed. 'Quicksand', 'The Man Who Sold The World' and 'Queen Bitch' for openers. Again Bowie's voice sounded truly amazing, and his band just brilliant. Bowie appeared to be really enjoying himself with lots of banter between songs. 'Under Pressure' with Gail Ann Dorsey was a stand out moment. 'White Light/White Heat', 'O Superman' and 'Look Back in Anger' closed the show. It was over so quickly. It also made me realise how good the songs from his latest album *Earthling* sounded live.

At last I'd seen David Bowie. And I'm also very pleased to say that after Bowie sprinkled a little of his magic stardust on myself and Liz on that hot Manchester evening, we really did hit it off and have now been together for 20 years. Thank you David.

OLYMPIA THEATRE

8 AUGUST 1997 DUBLIN, IRELAND

I WAS THERE: AUDREY HENNESSY

I was so lucky to see him in the Olympia in Dublin – a very small venue and I was in the first row of the balcony, amazing experience. When he played 'All The Young Dudes', how great it was to be able to belt out the chorus in the same space and with David Bowie. I still savour the memory. Wonderful amazingly talented man.

SHEPHERD'S BUSH EMPIRE

11 AUGUST 1997 LONDON

I WAS THERE: MIKEY GEORGESON

I saw Bowie at the Shepherd's Bush Empire in 1997. This is my time to see the legend in the flesh I thought. To put it in personal context somehow, having decided that I would be an illustrator after attending Chelsea School of Art, I found myself to be a flamboyant singer in an art-rock theatrical pop-combo championed by *Melody Maker* though not the *NME* who were, back then, suspicious of the art school penchant for pantomime (see The Clash vs The Sex Pistols).

The year 1997 was the tipping point of Britpop so it's weird to think that whilst the whole of Britain was celebrating all things vaudevillian and guitar-geezerish Bowie was deeply into drum and bass. The irony of course is that the Britpop shorthand view of British music sucked all the personality out if it and perhaps sensing this Bowie's one concession to the zeitgeist of cool-Britannia was his union jack tailcoat on the cover of *Earthling*. Ever the man to spot a niche and perhaps also aware of how cool guitars were at the time though, Bowie declared that the *Earthling* album is a real guitar album except that it's all processed through samplers. In fact it is Bowie's first completely digital album. Nowadays recording digitally is the norm but then it was cutting edge and a little bit of a risk. Still if I'm honest I always found this side of Bowie seeking to be cutting edge via technology a little bit cringy – like your dad trying to be down with the kids (see also Paul 'I invented looping' McCartney).

Having said this I was really into the *Earthling* album and my girlfriend (now wife) and I listened to it a lot in the car. The

intense isolation of listening to music in a car can have a weird effect of saturation and there was a brief period of time when it was *Our* Bowie album – so not *Hunky Dory*, not *Ziggy*, not *Heroes* but *Earthling*. The album somehow

SOLO PRESENTS

DAVID BOWIE

Monday
11th August

London
Shepherds Bush
Empire
SHEPHERDS BUSH GREEN
LONDON W12 8TT

Tickets:
£17.50
(incl Vat)
SUBJECT TO BOOKING FEE

Doors:
7.00pm

DOWNSTAIRS STANDING   000498

became my moment to really connect to Bowie through a current album.

As a child I had borrowed my sister's copy of 'Starman' and dutifully played it and played it not quite believing how unearthly it sounded and hoping the secret would reveal itself in our gloomy nylon-carpeted dining room. Then as I hit my teens *Let's Dance* brought an open secret to a wider audience. It was a massive album but I never found his cool kudos quota to go up for a while after that. Bowie remained slightly peripheral and a bit off the mark in terms of cool. It felt that *Earthling* was perhaps a return to a more idiosyncratic less try-hard approach. Perhaps the unhinged, stream-of-consciousness experimentation of *Outside* marked the beginning of Bowie being comfortable in his own skin?

This Earthling gig was irrefutably of its time in so much that most of the set list came from the *Earthling* album. The first encore of 'Moonage Daydream', was the only track from *Ziggy* and 'Heroes' didn't feature in the set at all. The point being this was a gig by a man who was still very much an artist who valued his current creative process. Which pretty much sums up what made Bowie such a great and authentic artist – always evolving always creating.

For that gig he's surrounded by great and empathetic musicians giving all of himself to his audience. If you watch it on YouTube you may see that, yes, there are some ersatz moments of theatrical dubiousness (billowy sea-island white shirt) but it's all from and of himself, and we his fans are completely connected to this vast creative vortex of openness.

CHILI PEPPER

7 OCTOBER 1990 FT. LAUDERDALE, FLORIDA

I WAS THERE: BELYNDA MORRIS

The last time I got to see David Bowie live in concert was the Earthling Tour in October 1990 at a little place in Fort Lauderdale called the Chili Pepper.

We waited in line outside for quite a while before they let us in. Parked on the side of the building were two tour buses, so who do we see coming out of the bus, but from behind, someone who looked just like David Bowie! I think my ex-husband told me, 'Oh it's probably a decoy, but you can go over there if you want to.'

Well I was too nervous and embarrassed, so unfortunately I didn't, and I could kick myself to this day for not doing it!

They finally let us in and we took our space standing on the floor about 10 to 15 feet away from the stage. So my (now) ex-husband decided to go to the back of the club, away from the stage, and watch some sport thing on TV. My former sister-in-law found the only seat in the place, on the second level. And me, I stood firmly in my spot on the floor in front of the stage, getting pushed a little further away from the stage by the time the show finally started.

(Which by the way, he was about an hour or so late. He apologised saying something about a flat tyre) and went on with the wonderful show which included giant eyeball balloons being tossed around the small venue.

I absolutely adored that place. It was small and quaint and it had that local club feel. I loved the vibe of the entire thing! I think this was the only concert that I did not know every single song, as I had been so busy the year before with planning my wedding, I hadn't heard the songs from *Earthling* yet.

The funniest thing to come out of the whole show was when we were leaving, and my (now-ex-) husband said, 'I didn't know David Bowie was afraid of Americans?'

I think the band weren't used to playing such a small venue, because they forgot to turn the amps down a notch or two and it felt like my ears were bleeding for about two weeks! Actually my hearing may be a bit off, from that concert, to this day! Such a memorable show! It was the time I finally got to see the wonderful pianist, Mike Garson, play after all these years. The band was so tight and I was very happy to get an up close and personal feel – type show.

FORO SOL

23 OCTOBER 1997 MEXICO CITY, MEXICO

I WAS THERE: DAVID BARCENAS

The first time I listened to Bowie was back in 1975. I listened to 'Fame' by Bowie/Lennon, it was superb, I was 14 and my life changed after getting the album *Young Americans*. I then came across *Diamond Dogs, Pin Ups, The Rise and Fall of Ziggy Stardust and the Spiders from Mars*. It was not easy, since some of them were not released in Mexico, so I had to buy them at special record stores, since these were imports. Not easy due to I was a student, so I had to save money to get them (I still have them). But for me it was sort of magical getting into the David Bowie world, I thought it was a dream finding out his music, which changed my life.

Then after 20 years the dream came true. Bowie was in Mexico on the Earthling Tour. I was in the middle of the audience, and Bowie was there just a few metres from me. I still remember the first song, 'Quicksand' from *Hunky Dory*. He was so theatrical and the concert was magical. He played Seventies hits and songs from the *Earthling* album. I will never forget it. He closed with the Mott The Hoople hit 'All The Young Dudes'. Bowie's music will last in my mind forever.

1999

The Hours Tour was a small-scale promotional concert tour comprising eight live performances in New York City, London, England, Dublin, Ireland and four other European shows) as well as numerous television appearances in support of the album *Hours*.

The Libro Music Hall, Vienna, performance on 17 October 1999, coinciding with the launch of *BowieNet* Europe was made available as a live webcast.

A new guitarist, Page Hamilton, the ex-Helmet founder member, was drafted to replace Reeves Gabrels whose final performance and association with Bowie ended at the *VH1 Storytellers* performance on 23 August 1999. Rumours of a split were denied by both parties, until a few months later the story changed as the guitarist admitted that he and Bowie had drifted apart.

BURLINGTON ARCADE

JANUARY 1999 LONDON

I WAS THERE: ANNA-MARIA PARASKEVA

Not on tour but in January 1999, Burlington Arcade (opposite The Ritz, London) – I went out for a stroll at lunchtime and walking towards me were David and Iman. I was so stunned, I just stood there staring as they walked past me. Wish I'd had the courage to ask for an autograph – no selfies back then!!

MANHATTAN CENTER

23 AUGUST 1999 NEW YORK CITY

I WAS THERE: DEAN WARDS, VH1 STORYTELLERS

I had been a member of *BowieNet* – Bowies online web community for a couple of years and had always entered into the online competitions to try and win a prize of some sort, in August 1999 I entered into a prize draw to go to the live recording of David Bowie's *VH1 Storytellers*.

12th August 1999, 'VH1 ticket giveaway, it's over, it's all over!'

Thursday night in the *BowieNet* chat room, the UltraStar crew put on their bingo hats and did and old fashion draw for the 50 lucky winners. I was shocked to see my name drawn out as a competition winner!

We had 24 hours to decide to accept our tickets and pledge to turn up in New York City for the event or return the tickets for a second draw, I wasn't going to miss out on this event. I called my wife to say I had won a ticket; she was excited, until I awkwardly explained it was only one ticket. She was OK about it and excited for me. I quickly booked a flight from London, England, to NYC.

The pre-event had a bit of a *Charlie and The Chocolate Factory* part to it; we got sent two emails from Ultrastar with instructions on what to do. We needed to turn up at a pre-arranged bar in NYC the night before the show, take along both emails; show our passports (to prove who we were) before we would be given tickets. My printer failed and I was only able to print one email off. On the flight to NYC I started to panic that they wouldn't allow me in.

I turned up at the bar at the arranged time and meet my fellow lucky *BowieNet* winners. The bar was a private bar for guests only, and inside everyone was really excited about the prospect of seeing Bowie in a small venue. One by one we all had to meet the *VH1* production team and the guys from Ultrastar. When it was my turn, I was in such a panic with only my one email, but they were OK about it and joked that they would have to think about letting me in. We had our IDs checked and pictures taken, told to turn up at the event the following evening with our newly issued tickets and to bring passports. They would check our photos before letting us into the event.

On the night of the show, I arrived at the set time. The event wasn't publicised, and the venue itself had no visible signs that

Bowie was playing. As we went through all the security checks we were warned over and over by *VH1* management not to speak to Mr Bowie, and not to try and get autographs or we would be removed from the venue, and we had to sign filming permission paperwork.

The seating was pre-arranged, so we got placed in our seats as the production team desired. I wore a black top which didn't please the production team as a black shirt apparently isn't good on TV. I sat just behind Mike Garson, so I had a stage side view, sat actually on the stage. It was amazing to watch Mike play from so close. Bowie stood behind me a few times as that was the side entrance to the stage, I wanted to say, 'Hi' but we had all been warned not to or else we would be removed! The guy sitting next to me high fived Bowie a few times. Looking back now I do wish I had just said, 'Hi'.

The show itself was special, after every song the audience rose as one and burst into loud applause. We seemed to be on top of him. He was a little overwhelmed and asked for a little calm. When he told his stories the room was deadly quiet. I am sure everyone has now watched the show, but at the time it just felt like he was in my living room, chatting away and playing my favourite tunes. I do remember admiring his jaw line and thinking how lucky I was to be doing this. After over three hours I began to believe that this was my life and I was part of his band! But then it was over and I found myself on the stage chatting with the backing singers, before security realised I wasn't part of the band and asked me to politely leave.

Outside the event I noticed Tony Visconti was mingling around, and now feeling brave, I went up to him and said, 'Hello' and could I shake the hand of the best Bowie producer. He was amazingly polite and friendly and proceeded to introduce me to some of the members of the B-52's. Like all good things it had to come to an end and the next day I returned to London, full of stories, which when I tell people they find hard to believe. I still have to pinch myself at times.

ASTORIA THEATRE

2 DEC 1999 LONDON

I WAS THERE: GLENN HILLYARD

I have to say, and it's no surprise, that trying to get tickets to see David at the Astoria wasn't easy. I eventually managed to find two tickets for sale on the internet – I ended up paying £250 for two tickets with a face value of £20 each! Was it worth it? Oh yes!!

The London Astoria, with a capacity of between 1,600 – 2,000, was a music venue, at 157 Charing Cross Road in London. It was closed on 15 January 2009 and has since been demolished. The venue is still seen today as an iconic music establishment, as it helped to launch the careers of many British rock bands and also played a part in the UK success of many international acts.

David also held a signing session at the Oxford Street Virgin Megastore just around the corner. I had my ticket number but decided not to queue. As it was such a high number I really didn't expect to get the chance to meet him (anyone wishing to 'meet and greet' with David and get a signed *Hours* album). David was only at the store for a fairly short time and I felt sure it wasn't worth queuing up for and being disappointed, so I kept my position near the front of the queue for the doors opening at the Astoria. As it transpired later there were other people with higher ticket numbers than mine that did get to meet him!

Considering that David had been suffering, and was still getting over a bout of the flu, it was still a superb evening.

I love the intimacy of small theatres – it was

almost like having David and his band playing in your living room. No theatrics, just a warm, funny and heady mix of old and new songs.

David was on sparkling form and some lucky person in the audience went home with a 'snot-filled' tissue'!

This was the last time I saw David live and it will remain as my favourite live experience – well worth forking out £250 for.

I WAS THERE: FLORIAN BAUER

I won the ticket in a *BowieNet* contest. I was really excited, booked a flight and hotel immediately and flew to London the next day. It was my first time in the city and I was hugely impressed. Not so much by the hotel near Marble Arch, that had bugs crawling in the carpet, but by the amazing pop culture references that were to be seen all over the city. The gig was awesome. I was blown away by the venue, which doesn't exist anymore unfortunately. My ticket was for the balcony and right beneath where I was standing was the VIP-Area. I could see The Pet Shop Boys sitting on a table, Boy George and Skin from Skunk Anansie, Placebo. Later I read that Mick Jagger, Pete Townshend and more celebrities attended, but I did not see them. After the gig, I met some fans who also won tickets and we tried to sneak in the after show party that was at a club behind the Astoria – we were not lucky. Instead I spotted Mike Garson sitting in a restaurant nearby and got my ticket signed. It Was a really nice trip to London!

ALCATRAZ

4 DECEMBER 1999 MILAN, ITALY

I WAS THERE: PAOLO BERTAZZONI

It was late November and, unexpectedly, the press announced that David Bowie was having a gig in Milan in just a couple of weeks. What a gift, I thought, until I realized it was already sold out the very moment I was reading the news. I still don't know if it was karma or any other kind of justice under the sky, but by chance, on a cold

November morning I stumbled upon five tickets, entering my favourite record shop. I don't think my brain has preserved any memories of the time I spent between that day and that crucial December 4th. Like living in a black hole until I'm at the club, the lights turn on and they start playing 'Life On Mars?' Just Mike Garson and him, nothing else. David's voice put everything under its spell: a smile, a quick glance at the audience and then his lips drawing the words, 'It's a god-awful small affair...', so gentle, warm, intense. It was years before 'mannequin challenge', and yet everyone was transfixed, and it was awesome, since the staging was so simple.

The days of big screens, kabuki and rock and roll super stardom were gone: only a few lights, a man wearing a yellow shirt and a superlative band, ready to play all of the songs left behind since the Sound+Vision Tour, back in 1990. Of course it was fun, singing along songs such as 'Thursday's Child', but having the chance to hear 'Always Crashing In The Same Car' was far beyond my imagination. It was real, it was happening in front of me, that very moment, just as in the 'Outside' lyrics. A man of words/man of music, but also a man of wit – I remember David laughing about his darkest days, telling us the reason why he had to read his own lyrics on a sheet – his irony and mind as beautiful as his body, always ready to make us smile. An evening culminated in a menacing, breathtaking version of 'I'm Afraid Of Americans', still 'haunting' my days. Some concerts don't finish when the music's over, they just keep on playing in your heart and soul year after year. This is definitely one of them.

2000 The Mini Tour was a four-date small-scale concert tour including two nights at Roseland Ballroom New York City, Glastonbury Festival in England and a concert for the BBC at the Radio Theatre in London.

GLASTONBURY FESTIVAL

25 JUNE 2000 PILTON

I WAS THERE: DOUGIE KILLEN

I was 30 years old. My first Glasto was in 1995, and I've been nearly every year since (I'm 47 now).

I'm from London, but at Glasto 2000 I went with two Bristol-based friends (one of whom happened to be a former girlfriend who I went to my first Glasto with, the other was her boyfriend at the time). I drove from London to their place in Bristol, and we decided that as rain was forecast for the Thursday night, we'd stay at theirs and make the short drive to Glastonbury in their car on the Friday morning. We actually had tickets (it was the first time I'd actually bought a ticket), but it was so crowded it took us a good two hours traipsing around trying to find somewhere – anywhere – to camp. Eventually we found a pitch just behind one of the First Aid tents.

Mobile phones were fairly common by 2000, but still not everybody had them. It was the last year before the 'superfence', and Glastonbury at the time was notorious for theft, so you'd only bring stuff that you were prepared to lose. The only remotely valuable thing I brought was a disposable camera, which probably explains why photos are few and far between despite the huge numbers of people that attended that year. Glasto still had a bit of a hippy vibe and the idea of getting away from the real world was quite appealing, so for that reason and the security aspect I'd left my mobile phone at home.

Being the 'third wheel', I spent quite a lot of the festival by myself, and I really enjoyed not having to compromise on anything while I was there (I remember at my first Glasto my girlfriend wasn't really into The Cure, so we had to leave about a third of the way through the set which was gutting for me!)

I was determined to get near the front for Bowie, and without too much difficulty (by simply wandering in halfway through the previous set), I got within touching distance of the front bar.

I remember Bowie came on wearing a big white coat. He said he'd worn it when he last played 30 years ago. He said we all looked like lucky people tonight, and then launched into a greatest hits set that few had dared to hope for (he had been notoriously disappointing live over the previous 15 years). 'Starman' and 'Heroes' were the standout moments, and there was a real sense that we were witnessing something unique and special that might never be repeated. There was warmth and a connection within the crowd and a feeling of elation that we were all so lucky to be there. The only other time I've felt anything remotely like this (without chemicals being involved) was during Blur in 2009 (of course Blur have played gigs since but at the time it felt like a one-off).

This was several years before huge flags were a thing, so you didn't actually need to be that near the front to get a good view, but that didn't stop the crowd surging forward every now and then (there were no crush barriers at the time), so I put my arms on the front bar either side of the girl standing in front of me, partly to protect us both from the surges and partly because I quite fancied her. There was a lot of spliff being passed around, and after a while we were snogging happily. This continued for a good while after the concert ended, and a great night was on the verge of becoming a perfect night.

However, it was at that point when I remembered I'd arranged to meet my ex-girlfriend and her boyfriend at his car at 1am for the drive back to Bristol. Without mobile phones, rearranging plans on the fly was impossible. If I stood them up, I'd be completely stuffed as my tent was packed up in his car, and my own car was parked outside his house in Bristol. Well I took the sensible option and headed back to the car and she headed back to her tent alone. I regret my decision to this very day.

I WAS THERE: MARK REED

When David Bowie first played Glastonbury in 1971, I wasn't born yet. You could argue he wasn't born either, but then, how many lives did David Bowie live? How many times was he born?

29 years later, when he took the stage at Glastonbury on a mediocre Sunday night in late June, he was born again. Having rotated through his many personas, this was probably the apex of his final live stage, where David Bowie first started playing a musician called David Bowie. This time around, being one of just a handful of shows to support the underwhelming *Hours* album, Bowie had, for the first time in ten years little active currency, and instead played his part as David Bowie, human jukebox. The new album was creatively dead in the water, and Bowie had shown little interest in promoting it. Reeves Gabrels had moved out of the Bowie band – claiming that David was about to become 'boring' (and Reeves was right).

Despite being there, my memories are now becoming confused with the television coverage. Glastonbury is often a long and punishing weekend without such indulgences as water, or sleep. By the time the 'Long Blond Haired Duke' came to his pyramid throne, I felt like I was surviving an endurance test. Having barely slept for three nights and not sat down properly for over half a week, even seeing David Bowie at Glastonbury was the type of experience where all I wanted to do was crawl up on a sofa and sleep. Not perhaps, the best way to experience his royal Bowieness.

This was the last of the 'great' Glastonburys that older people will tell you all about; where

Mark Reed masters the art of shaving in a field using his phone as a mirror

you could tunnel under – or drive through – an ineffectual fence. Where, on Sunday afternoon, they opened the gates to the public to come in for free. Where thousands of people would flood in smuggled in car boots. I remember, as the sun set, being surrounded by people as far as you could see – seemingly to the horizon. This, I imagined, is what a refugee camp of *Guardian* readers might look like. There were, by reports, over a quarter of a million people on site the day David Bowie took Glastonbury.

Sunday nights were traditionally the headline slot for the nostalgic 'Old Gods Almost Dead', the washed up, the past it, which were on their slow decline into a victory lap so they could buy new yachts. The kind of show that would boost the sales of a 'greatest hits' CD and the inevitable stadium tour next year. Where nobody wanted to hear any songs less than 20 years old. At the time, I was starting to tune out of Bowie; his music was veering to comfortable and lyrically there were less risks. I was too young to understand where he was creatively at this point. I'd adored the earlier stuff, particularly *Tin Machine/II/Outside/Earthling*: I was barely familiar with the material from his early Seventies as it sounded too new to be truly classic rock, and too old to be contemporary. I was, at the time, somewhat of a floating voter. And Bowie was just slightly too old for someone as young as I was then to fully understand.

So when Bowie came on with the longest hair he'd had since he was a teenager and a gold coat, I couldn't say I was impressed. His band was tight and clearly slick and well chosen. There were the smoothed over rough edges that comes with decades of experience, and Bowie was an accomplished crowd pleaser with both his songs, and his relaxed, settled approach. It was probably the moment where Sunday night at Glastonbury became the career-rejuvenating Indian summer. Every song was seemingly a hit; including many Bowie had barely played since his Sound+Vision Tour a decade previous.

By the end of the night, Bowie had silenced doubters and won over the critics and naysayers, by playing to his many strengths, and dropping any artistic pretense or facade – almost, in fact, an acceptance of one of his many roles: of a hero, just for one day.

In retrospect, it was amongst his defining performances: Michael Eavis still describes his performance as his best Glastonbury moment of all time.

At the top of a hill, about a quarter of a mile from the stage, a tiny dot stood in the darkness in a gold shirt, and sang 'Wild Is The Wind', and that I will remember for the rest of my life.

I never saw David Bowie again.

I WAS THERE: PAUL DREW

I had seen Bowie before in the Eighties and Nineties but was really excited when I decided to embrace middle age/relive my youth and get tickets for the first time at this famous festival and was over the moon when it was announced that Bowie would headline and close the weekend. Thing was, after four days of drink/sunshine and smoke, I wasn't in the best of states and can remember David singing for the first 15 minutes but little else. Everyone always says it was one of his best. Gutted!

2002

The Heathen Tour was in support of the album, *Heathen*, and was also notable for the performances of all songs from the 1977 *Low* album.

On 11 February 2002, it was announced that Bowie had accepted the role of Artistic Director at the Meltdown Festival, the annual music and arts event held at the South Bank in London, England. David Bowie's Meltdown 2002 ran from 14 to 30 June, with a schedule of concerts and events including performances by The Legendary Stardust Cowboy, Coldplay, The Waterboys and a London Sinfonietta performance of Philip Glass's *Low* and *Heroes* symphonies. The closing night was billed as The New Heathens Night with Bowie headlining the event.

The Heathen Tour proper began at the Meltdown Festival with Bowie embarking on a series of European performances including a link-up with Moby for the 12-date North America Area:2 Festivals with a return to Europe for a further six performances.

Before returning again to North America to perform a final seven shows with the first five in each of New York City's five boroughs, dubbed The New York Marathon tour by Bowie, who said, 'I could get home from all the gigs on roller skates.'

I WAS THERE: MOBY, MUSICIAN

David Bowie was my favourite musician of all time. In fact the first job that I ever had was as a caddy on a golf course at Wee Burn golf course in Connecticut. I was quite small so I could only carry old people's bags, as they didn't have as many clubs. I only took that job when I was 13 years old, so I could buy David Bowie records. I remember when I made my first $10 caddying I went to my local record store to buy *Low*, but *Low* was too expensive so I bought *Heroes*.

As a 13 year old in the suburbs, you heard a song on college radio, it was scratchy in the background, and the only way you could find out who did the song was to hang out in a record store. It was

my intention to buy *Low* because I had heard 'Sound and Vision' on some college radio station but I ended up buying *Heroes*, and I probably didn't hear *Low* in its entirety until 1979 or 1980. I think of *Low* and *Heroes* as brother-sister records. What was so remarkable about them, and what impacted me and a lot of other electronic musicians, was how wonderful the A-sides were, but also that this super successful, established artist would give an entire side of his record over to experimental, instrumental electronic music.

In the year 2000, David Bowie moved in across the street from me in New York and we became very good friends. We went on tour together. We had Christmas together. It was remarkable but very disconcerting to be neighbours and very good friends with a man who was my favourite musician of all time!

We would wave at each other from our balconies. I would go to the deli to buy soy milk and oats and he and Iman would be in there buying oranges and coffee. They were my neighbourhood pals. It started to seem normal but at the back of my mind I never forgot the fact that David Bowie was a demigod and a genius and the best musician who will ever live.

THE QUART FESTIVAL

3 JULY 2002 KRISTIANSAND, NORWAY

I WAS THERE: LARS-ANDRE TOKHEIM

As a Bowie fan since I was a kid, and growing up listening to *Ziggy Stardust*, I was delighted when Bowie around the time of the new millennium returned to a music style that to some extent resembled the sound of the Seventies, my favourite era. So when the news came that Bowie was going to play the Quart Festival, I did not hesitate a minute before buying tickets.

The Quart Festival was among the more popular festivals in Norway in the Nineties. They used to get many good international artists, but it was still quite an achievement to get Bowie as a headliner in July 2002.

In the company of my wife and four good friends I drove down to Kristiansand, a town nicely located on the southern coast of Norway, and entered the festival area on the Odderøya island, just outside the town centre.

When our man entered the stage around ten thirty it was about to get dark, and I will never forget the electric atmosphere among the 12,000 fans when he opened the show with 'Life on Mars?', one of my absolute favourites. Then – after throwing his jacket and getting ready to rock – he switched to the Nineties hit, 'Hallo Spaceboy', before the band played an energy-packed version of the rather unknown Neil Young tune 'I've Been Waiting for You'. This was also the first song from *Heathen*. The first surprise – and a very nice one as far as I was concerned – came in the form of 'Speed of Life' from another favourite album, *Low*. Then he played the 1983 monster hit 'China Girl', definitely an audience pleaser.

Kenneth, one of my friends that attended the concert, had smuggled in a pocket camera, and we managed to get a couple of shots of Bowie and the band, as well as some pictures of ourselves cheering happily in the crowd. Around halfway through the show there was some light rain, but strangely we never got wet – the heat flux from the packed audience seemed to evaporate the rain.

The band was just great, with Mark Plati as the band leader, Gail Ann Dorsey playing the bass and singing backing vocals, the jazz virtuoso Mike Garson on piano, the cool Earl Slick on electric guitar and the rock solid Sterling Campbell on drums; and in addition there was Gerry Leonard on lead guitar and Catherine Russell on keyboards and backing vocals – indeed an excellent lineup.

I can't remember whether Bowie played any guitar himself during the show, but I definitely remember him playing harmonica on 'A New Career in a New Town', another instrumental surprise from *Low*. Other songs from the Berlin era were 'Sound and Vision' and the majestic 'Heroes'. Bowie was in a very good mood that night and said a lot of nice things about the nature and the beautiful scenery surrounding the festival area.

As expected we got to hear several other tunes from *Heathen*, including '5:15 The Angels Have Gone', 'Afraid'(my favourite from *Heathen*), 'Cactus' – a cool version of the Pixies' original with Mark Plati playing the guitar intro 'Slip Away' and 'Everyone Says Hi', as well as the title track.

'Ashes to Ashes' and 'Fashion', two big hits from the *Scary Monsters* album, were not missed, and we also had the classic 'Changes' and 'Let's Dance' and 'I'm Afraid of Americans' as other hit examples. 'Stay' was the only song from *Station to Station*.

I have a very special feeling for the *Ziggy* album, as I used to play it over and over when I was a kid, learning by heart the lyrics that were printed on the German gatefold edition that was sold in the Norwegian record stores in the mid Seventies. And at the age of 50 I still play the album at least once a week and I do most of its songs in my own Bowie tribute band 'The Diamond Dogs' when we play gigs. So to me '*Ziggy Stardust*' was the perfect way to end the show.

SUMMER FESTIVAL

15 JULY 2002 LUCCA, ITALY

I WAS THERE: MATTEO TONOLLI

The man who once was an alien, then a duke and again a rock God landed in Italy for a concert for his Heathen Tour.

That day I drove from Verone across the Apennines to the

Matteo Tonolli treats his children to David Bowie tickets!

medieval city in Tuscany. My spirit was high but the weather wasn't good. It was raining heavily and I was a bit worried, because the concert would take place in the open air, in Piazza Napoleone – an ancient beautiful rectangular square in the heart of the town, where the Lucca Summer Festival usually hosts great stars of music.

When I arrived I visited the wonderful city and it seemed to be in Scotland, because the sky quickly changed several times, with short but heavy rain filling the streets of water. During the afternoon you could see many fans in the streets, but we all had to wait until they would open the barriers around Piazza

Napoleone. I really hoped to gain a good seat quite close to the stage. Fortunately I was able to get the second row, but the sky was still full of dark clouds.

After the set by Bluvertigo, a powerful Italian Bowie-devoted band, it was time for the man who once fell to earth. Before the show, I talked with some aficionados and I was surprised to hear that they were there for him, but they had never heard *Heathen*, an album that I considered, and still consider, bloody good.

Finally he arrived on the stage with great class, a blue Dior dress and his unmistakable smile. 14 years later, exactly 13th July 2016, I would observe the same dress inside the *David Bowie Is* exhibition in Bologna, in the final multi-media room. But my heart would be really sad and heavier, because a dummy, and not my hero, was wearing it.

However that day in Tuscany everything went in the right way. David started to sing his classic song 'Life on Mars?' The enchanted public sang with him and when the piano notes by the talented Mike Garson closed the god-awful small affair, David said something with a great self-confidence, something that pushed definitely away all my worries, 'There will be no rain tonight!' Then he introduced his band: Gail, Sterling, Gerry, Mike and Earl. He joked with the people who were looking from the windows of the historical buildings, pretending to know them and to be a friend of them, as five years before he filmed 'Il Mio West' in the countryside nearby.

15 years have since passed. I do not have any good photos of those two incredible hours. At the time smartphones didn't exist and my pocket camera didn't work very well. On the internet, I found a decent bootleg audio and a terrible video of the show. But I have a lot of wonderful memories, even if I do not remember all the details. Certainly the best of the three Bowie concerts I attended, also thanks to the magnificent set provided by Lucca and its Piazza Napoleone. I'm sure that some of those old fans bought *Heathen* after that live date. Oh, and obviously it didn't rain that night!

MAIDA VALE

18 SEPT 2002 LONDON

I WAS THERE: MARTIN LACEY

In September 2002 Bowie did a show at the BBC Radio 2 studios in Maida Vale, London. Prior to the show *BowieNet* and Radio 2 ran a competition to win tickets, which I entered with every person's email address that I knew with the proviso that they were mine should they win.

A couple of weeks later my wife Tracy gets a phone call at work. Caller 'Hello, is that Tracy Lacey?' Tracy, 'Yes, speaking',

Caller 'Hi, I'm calling from BBC Radio 2 and I'm pleased to tell you you've won two tickets for the Bowie competition that you entered'. Tracy, 'I don't know who you are but tell Martin to stop fucking about.' And then promptly puts the phone down! She then phoned me and started to have a go at me. I deny any knowledge of it. And then the penny drops. The other receptionist at Tracy's work called Radio 2 back and thankfully they hadn't given our tickets to someone less abusive.

The show? A tiny studio, with about 60 other people, ten feet from the man. Tracy was perched on the edge of the stage. A real, 'OK you can kill me now' moment. There's a recording of it on YouTube. If you ever listen to it you can hear someone constantly fingers in the mouth whistling at the end of every song. That's my wife that is. Bowie was filming the audience at one point with a small camcorder. It always amused me, that not only did I have videos of him, he had one of me.

MAX-SCHMELING-HALLE

22 SEPTEMBER 2002 BERLIN, GERMANY

I WAS THERE: HANS TETZLAFF

I was born in Hamburg, Northern Germany in 1962. David Bowie has influenced my life during five decades and still does. It all started in 1973 after *Aladdin Sane* was released. My older brother had a new friend, Oli, who invited the both of us round to listen to his record collection. My personal record collection at that time contained three albums; A *Greatest Hits Collection* of Little Richard, *The Best of Jerry Lee Lewis* and *The Very Best of Fats Domino*. Wow! He had almost everything by bands like Led Zeppelin, Deep Purple, ELP, Pink Floyd, Nazareth, Uriah Heep, Wishbone Ash, Slade, Status Quo, Genesis, Manfred Mann's Earthband, The Doors, Edgar Broughton Band, Hawkwind, Mountain. I hardly remember him having any single artists, but all bands. But he had entirely all the albums of a strange looking, really weird guy named David Bowie.

The first record I ever saw of his came with clear and useful instructions: 'To be played at maximum volume'.

We were German kids in the 70's and we followed instructions. The neighbors loved us. We simply were in another Universe.

Later when watching the Ziggy movie I found out that we were in the Bowie-Universe. I was an eleven year-old German kid and my English was, let's say, limited. My teachers would've been proud if they knew how many hours I was sitting with that thing, this *Oxford Advanced Learner's Dictionary for Current English*, the edition that does not contain *Hunky Dory*. And I really wanted to know where Ziggy came from or what's the story of the girl in 'Five Years.' I was sure she could have loved me.

Here I do need to admit, or more confess, I'm really not sure after all these years of floating in the Bowie-Universe if I ever got the meaning of any of his lyrics right, except maybe 'Don't Sit Down' but even here I'm not one hundred percent sure. So after spending hours and nights listening to 'Life on Mars?' and 'The Bewlay Brothers', without getting anywhere, I gave up. Since about 1974 I'm not trying anymore to find in there anything else that I hear. Sounds stupid? Maybe, but firstly it was a relief as I already felt haunted and please remember all this in pre-internet times, you had to know which books to ask for in the library. Secondarily, well what can I say, it is really fun to build stories around his lyrics. Honestly I love his voice, he could sing a software manual as long as he does it in his beautiful Bowie-way. I'd buy that recording.

I do remember it quite well, it was a Friday morning and as every morning on my way to work I got the local newspaper. I usually start with the sports section, which starts behind the pop-culture page, concert-reviews/previews interviews and announcements. So I was turning the pages to get to sports and my eye caught one word on this pop-culture page. Bowie!

Ok, got to get this clear, it was a very short announcement. David Bowie playing only three dates in Germany and one of them on Sunday in Berlin. Plans had to be worked out. I was at that time working for a PR agency and my monthly pay was decent. I was married, no kids, no cars, no insurances. So an over night trip to Berlin would work out fine.

I got to work and straight away called home telling my wife that I'd be going to Berlin on Sunday to watch David Bowie and what about her joining me? Unfortunately she didn't want to but confirmed it was OK if I go. So first point cleared, I got permission. I was a good husband. Next thing, who could accompany me and help with a lift? Quick email to the staff. One returned and said that she would be in Berlin on Sunday and would love to join in with her fiancé. Second point cleared, lift home booked, but now for the ticket.

I called the ticket hotline in Hamburg and asked if they had tickets for David Bowie in Berlin on Sunday? Yes!!!! "OK, I'll pick them up at lunchtime." Third point cleared.

To get to Berlin from Hamburg was actually simple and cheap. So by noon I had permission from home, a ticket for the show, bus ticket to Berlin and a lift at night home. I had the whole Saturday to prepare. I knew I had to get dressed properly. The choice for the show was as follows: a bordeaux red cap which is hard to describe, the closest description I found was 'cerevis' but in an oriental style, like a short fez but much shorter and without any cord. A white office shirt, a pale blue spencer and, well kind of colourful jeans, white ground with dozens of hand-palm wide red roses printed on. Socks in shock green and black front tapered shoes. You may not believe it but I looked gorgeous. Everything packed and done. Now for the sweet leaf and all done.

I set off on Sunday shortly after lunch and entered the bus with *Outside, Earthling, Hours* and *Heathen* on my Walkman. The 180 miles passed well and the only things I remember about the way to the venue is that I was in a hurry and had to change in the subway and that I did not find Hauptstraße 155 (where Bowie shared a flat with Iggy Pop in Berlin between 1976 and 1978). So this visit is still on my list.

I had a single seat not near my work colleague. I actually expected newer stuff but what I got was a great show with the *Low* album in its almost entirety. I do remember how surprised I was at what a great, great rockin' machine his band was when required and how beautifully they interpreted the *Low* section.

Since 1973 I have loved the music of David Bowie, and in '79 I gave up trying to predict what the next album would sound like. But in 2002 I was convinced that *Low* was his best work ever. I do remember that I was surprised to hear all the older tunes before and after the *Low* section. But the finest surprise and greatest gift I can imagine he could be giving to me, was to be really seriously performing *Low* in the city that he made his home as a lodger and created in. It was an experience of a lifetime. I still feel honoured to this day that I was allowed to attend.

I was absolutely overwhelmed and could not speak a word. After the last encore I felt like floating in the air and seriously could not talk. We arrived in the middle of the night back in Hamburg and in the morning I called work to say that I could not attend. I'm not sure if I've ever figured out what made it such a magic night in Berlin but it definitely changed my life.

LE ZÉNITH

24 SEPTEMBER 2002 PARIS, FRANCE

I WAS THERE: ALEXIS ROWELL

When I lived in Paris in the 2000s, I used to have vivid daydreams about meeting David Bowie, none of it the result of substance abuse!

He would come to Paris for a concert, such my all-time favourite at the Zenith in September 2002, then afterwards we'd meet up for a drink in a bar and he'd ask me what his next musical direction should be. Totally crazy, I know, but for years I couldn't work out if these meetings had happened or not. In the end, I realised that, like Bowie fans everywhere, I was caught in a spell, under the influence of the King of influence.

CARLING APOLLO

2 OCTOBER 2002 HAMMERSMITH, LONDON

I WAS THERE: CRAIG DANCY

2002 was quite a year to be a Bowie fan. He was riding high off the back of a now legendary appearance at Glastonbury in 2000 and *Heathen* was being recognised as an album of classic Bowie song writing. So when it was announced that Bowie would curate Meltdown, before moving on to a run of shows in Europe then returning to America, I knew that there would be some great opportunities to see him live again.

I'd managed to secure tickets at the Royal Festival Hall for the European live debut of *Low/Heathen* in June, then wangled myself into the Radio 2 Maida Vale gig in September, but levels got turned up to 11 when it was announced that the European leg would climax at Hammersmith Apollo on 2nd October. All that needed to happen now was to get my hands on tickets. This was pre-internet ticket scalping, so the odds were still vaguely OK. DavidBowie.com announced that the tickets would be

Craig Dancy (left) with his Bowie friend Rob McHarg

available to members and that any leftover would be first come/first served to fans with £50 in cash in person at Hammersmith on Saturday 28th September.

Although both I and my good friend Rob (another Bowie obsessive) managed to get great tickets via the website, rows one and eight, we thought that it would be nice to head down to Hammersmith at 5am on Saturday morning and spend a few hours to get a couple extras for friends to witness the master in action. So everything was set, tickets in hand, day off from work for the concert and a day off after so that my full attention would not stray on the night.

Due to the way the tickets were obtained, initially I was positioned eight rows back, but in front of Ben Elton, which pleased me no end. The atmosphere was electric, Bowie had been delving deeply into his back catalogue, we'd been treated to the first performance of

'The Bewlay Brothers' at Maida Vale, and the European set lists had included the whole of *Low*, a selection from *Heathen* and all the fan-favourites you could shake a stick at.

As the house lights dimmed, long term Bowie fans and BBC DJs Mark Radcliffe and Marc Riley took the stage to give Bowie an amusing introduction before Mike Garson graced the venue with his beautiful piano introduction of 'Life on Mars?' What a way to start! A venue rich in Bowie history (Ziggy and the Spiders' last performance in 1973), a song that has become recognised as maybe his ultimate classic. Mid way through the song the band joined in and it was clear that we had a whole evening ahead with an on form Bowie with his crack band of musicians. The song was greeted with rapturous applause and with barely a pause for some light banter we were straight into 'Ashes To Ashes', another song that represents everything that Bowie can be, will anyone ever write a number one hit so complex and multi-layered and melodic?

The songs came fast and powerful, 'Look Back In Anger', 'China Girl', 'Absolute Beginners', selections from *Low* and *Heathen* plus just chuck in an American number one with 'Fame'. Not only did Bowie sound great, he looked immaculate, a beautifully cut dark blue, three piece suit with gold watch chain, and hair as cool as ever.

There was barely any let up before the next wave of classics arrived: 'Fashion', 'Rebel Rebel' and 'Heroes' then 'Moonage Daydream' dedicated to Mick Ronson, 'Changes' and 'Starman'. It was a master-class in performance, Bowie clearly loving it; the band on fire and the crowd feeding energy back to the stage. I'd hoped it was going to happen and it did, with Bowie almost apologising for the lack of preparation and for digging out what he considered a song that would not appeal to a big crowd, the opening chords of 'The Bewlay Brothers'! The second time I'd heard this rarity in a fortnight and what a moment.

They finished off with 'Sound + Vision', another UK No 1 in 'Let's Dance' and a final triumphant 'Ziggy Stardust', 33 songs and nearly three hours of what I consider the most important British musician of all time.

SET LIST:
01. Life on Mars?
02. Ashes to Ashes
03. Look Back in Anger
04. Survive
05. Breaking Glass
06. Cactus (Pixies cover)
07. China Girl
08. Slip Away
09. Absolute Beginners
10. Alabama Song (Whisky Bar)(Kurt Weill)
11. Speed of Life
12. Be My Wife
13. Fame
14. I'm Afraid of Americans
15. 5:15 The Angels Have Gone
16. I've Been Waiting for You (Neil Young cover)
17. Afraid
18. Fashion
19. Rebel Rebel
20. Heroes
21. Heathen (The Rays):
22. Sunday
23. I Would Be Your Slave
24. Moonage Daydream
25. Changes
26. Starman
27. A New Career in a New Town
28. Everyone Says 'Hi'
29. The Bewlay Brothers
30. Sound and Vision
31. Hallo Spaceboy
32. Let's Dance
33. Ziggy Stardust

I WAS THERE: MARK RADCLIFFE

I first saw David Bowie on *Top of the Pops* in 1972 doing 'Starman'. To an adolescent grammar school boy, he appeared to have arrived from another planet and it seemed like a world worth visiting.

I bought his album, *The Rise and Fall of Ziggy Stardust and the Spiders from Mars*, the next day. Putting it on in my bedroom, it became clear from the opening bars of the first track, 'Five Years', that the future I had been waiting for had arrived.

And then there was the whole image thing. The Bowie look was intoxicatingly daring but presented problems for the pubescent imitator. Even if you were lucky enough to stumble across a Japanese-print jumpsuit in Bolton, you ran the risk of getting a good kicking if you wore it in Yates's Wine Lodge.

I got to meet Bowie years later and found him incredibly friendly – though heaven knows what he thought of our behaviour when Marc Riley and I compered his gig at Old Trafford cricket ground in 2002.

As 25,000 people waited in the rain for Bowie to appear, Marc and I – much the worse for wear and hardly able to string a sentence together – rambled about on stage for eight minutes.

Looking back, that was seven minutes and 45 seconds longer than we should have been there. We just kept repeating plugs for the show's sponsor, the *Manchester Evening News*, and pointing out that the paper now cost just 10p every Friday.

Despite that inebriated debacle, he mystifyingly invited us back that October to introduce his gig at Hammersmith Apollo, the venue of Ziggy Stardust's final appearance.

Turning up at the stage door, the signs were immediately good – among the signs was one saying 'Mark and Lard Dressing Room'. However, before we got to our billet, one of the greatest moments in my life occurred. As we sauntered down a gloomy corridor at the Apollo, we saw before us a figure in a cream-coloured jean jacket. David Bowie.

He greeted us as proper friends, not two drunkards who slurred their way through proceedings at Old Trafford, and invited us into his private dressing room. In a room containing fresh flowers, lots of fruit and some mid-priced hotel furniture was Marc Riley, me and the biggest rock star in our world. After a few moments of Bowie's trademark joshing, he pulled a handwritten list from the pocket of his caramel-coloured trousers. 'I was thinking of doing this tonight. What do you reckon?' Stunned, Marc and I cast our eyes down the list, which included 'Life on Mars?', 'China Girl', 'Rebel Rebel' and 'Heroes'. Then Bowie started to ask us about the running order: should 'Changes' come before 'Starman' or vice versa? It was one of the moments where life just seemed unreal. Of course we all fantasise about meeting our idols, but to be in the same room, and for him to be genuinely interested in my opinion, was too much to take in.

It seemed utterly surreal that David Bowie, who I'd grown up adoring and never expected to even meet let alone chat to, was asking me if his set list was any good.

We didn't meet again but I continued to follow his career closely and watching the video for his new song 'Black Star' was like hearing *Ziggy Stardust* for the first time as a 14 year old.

And although I was aware he'd had heart trouble, I had no idea his life was nearing its end.

Learning that he'd died of cancer on that January Monday morning stopped me in my tracks. I'm not a particularly emotional person but people were texting me saying, 'Are you alright?'

Although it's not a matter of personal grief it is peculiar knowing that there's never going to be another David Bowie record.

I know I only registered in a tiny way in his life but that's enough for me because it's far, far more than I ever expected.

2003-2004

The Worldwide A Reality Tour was in support of the *Reality* album, kicking off on 7 October 2003 at the Forum Copenhagen, Denmark, and continuing through Europe, North America, Asia, including a return to New Zealand and Australia for the first time since the 1987 Glass Spider Tour. This tour proved to be Bowie's final live shows before his death on January 10, 2016. At over 110 shows, the tour was the longest tour of Bowie's career.

As he walked on stage, Bowie would greet the audience each night with the flexible line, 'Hello, [city name], you crazy bunch motherfuckers.'

The set list included tracks spanning Bowie's from *The Man Who Sold the World* (1970) all the way to *Reality* (2003), along with collaborations such as 'Sister Midnight' (originally from *The Idiot* (1977) by Iggy Pop and 'Under Pressure.'

The 6 May 2004, a performance at the James L. Knight Center, Miami, Florida was cancelled after lighting technician Walter 'Wally Gator' Thomas fell to his death prior to Bowie going onstage.

The tour was curtailed after the Hurricane Festival performance in Scheeßel, Germany on 25 June 2004, as a result of Bowie being diagnosed with an acutely blocked artery that required an angioplasty procedure. In 2016, bassist Gail Ann Dorsey, recalled what happened at the end of the tour:

At the second-to-last show, in Prague, I remember we were playing the song 'Reality.' He was supposed to be singing at the very end of the song, and he wasn't. I was kind of watching him from behind. Everyone was soaking wet because it was really hot in there, but his shirt was just drenched. He was just soaking wet and holding the microphone out with his left hand straight out. And he was just standing there, posturing, but not singing. And I was thinking, 'Why is he not singing the last bit?

Then he looked over his shoulder at me and he was just white, pale, translucent almost. His eyes were wide and he was kind of gasping for air a little bit, having trouble catching his breath. And then I remember looking down at the audience, and I could see their expressions in the front row, looking up at him, had changed. They went from joy and dancing to looking kind of concerned. At that point, his bodyguard and helper guy saw the same thing. He ran onto the stage and took him off. We went back on and played a few more songs. He asked for a stool and he sat down. He just hated to cancel shows. There were some nights he was so sick he had a bucket on the side of the stage where he'd go between songs to puke, but he never wanted to cancel anything. And we didn't know he was having a heart attack until four or five days later.

At the last show, at the Hurricane Festival in Hamburg, Germany, I remember walking down the stairs behind him after we finished. When he got to the bottom, he actually collapsed. He was so tired and so sick. They rushed him to the hospital and we sat and waited in Hamburg for a few days, and that was the end. The last show.

HARTWALL AREENA

10 OCTOBER 2003 HELSINKI, FINLAND

I WAS THERE: ANNA KOLJANDER

The first time I saw David Bowie live was on my eighteenth birthday, October 10, 2003 in Helsinki. I started crying when he walked out on to the stage, and I never thought I would react like that. I remember that someone gave him a rose with all the thorns taken out and he seemed to really appreciate the effort.

Second time was I saw him as the next summer at the Provinssirock festival in Finland. It had rained all day, but when he came on the sun came out.

FORUM DI ASSAGO

23 OCTOBER 2003 MILAN, ITALY

I WAS THERE: ORDNASSELA ITTELIHC

I was born in 1971 and my sister bought *Ziggy* and *Aladdin Sane* when they came out. At this concert, I was at the front, on the second row. Bowie came on stage while the band were already playing the intro to 'Rebel Rebel'. As he walked along the front of the stage he shook hands with the audience in the front row walking on the extension of the stage. I stretched out my arm, but I couldn't quite reach him, although we did sort of touch with the end of our fingers. He looked at me and smiled as if to say, 'We tried' then he walked to his microphone and started singing 'Rebel Rebel'.

I WAS THERE: PAOLO BERTAZZONI

The chance to see David Bowie one more time was something I couldn't miss. Actually, by 2003 I was still angry about having missed the wonderful 2002 Lucca concert, so the very first day the pre-sale started, I went to Milan in order to buy my ticket (those were the last days before online ticketing became a standard). Anyway, that time I went to the concert with a totally different kind of curiosity, since I was working on my university degree, which was about the relationship between rock concerts, rituals and performing art. And finally, there he was, the man who once had become a rock and roll (leper) Messiah, officiating his sensual, mesmerizing ceremony.

The air was filled with electricity, rising more and more since The Dandy Warhols finished their set, making each and everyone of us count the seconds. Then the music started and soon images were taking shape on a screen: skylines, a band playing, turning out to be David's one. Adrenaline was ruling my thoughts and feelings: I already knew the first two or three songs of the setlist since a friend of mine (who is no longer a friend because of that) was the spoilering type, but I was glad to hear that 'Rebel Rebel' had a new, unexpected intro. Then, starting from 'Cactus', every song was such a surprise. Some sort of climax, reaching several peaks: I'm talking about 'Under Pressure', blessing us all by the chemical wedding between Gail Ann Dorsey's wild grace and David's charm, but also about 'Heathen', its dark, obscure mood spreading magic and tension all over the crowd. I still remember the way my skin started shivering, when I realized I was singing 'Heroes', it was like taking part in something special, a unique event, taking shape in that magical moment in time and in space.

Me as many others:

that was our personal 'Conquest Of Ubiquity', just to quote Paul Valery, the way David gave us back the 'aura', the aesthetic authority that only his music and his voice could create.

HALLENSTADION

24 OCTOBER 2003 ZÜRICH, SWITZERLAND

I WAS THERE: PHILIPPE ANTOGNINI

It was a foggy day in October 2003 when I took the train to Zurich to visit my friend Martin. It was a special day because David Bowie was announced to play the Hallenstadion that night. We had bought the tickets several months before and we were looking forward to that day for weeks.

After a warm opening show by The Dandy Warhols, David and his band took the stage in a very special, unconventional way. The band members were portrayed on a screen in an animated movie, playing an instrumental opening tune. Slowly the animated image was fading away and replaced by a movie showing the real band members on screen. Finally, the screen went up like a curtain and there stood the real band members in the exact same position as on the screen and were playing their instruments. David Bowie was playing the harmonica. It was breathtaking!

After this short intro of two to three minutes David grabbed his electric guitar and played the opening riff to 'Rebel Rebel'. An outstanding two and a half hour rock show was about to get started.

The setlist was a fine selection between new songs and greatest hits such as 'Fame', 'Heroes', 'Under Pressure' and 'Ashes to Ashes'. One of the highlights of the evening was definitely the song 'Slip Away' from the album *Heathen*. The lyrics were written on a big screen like on some kind of teleprompter and the whole crowd was singing along to it. Simply beautiful! The line 'Twinkle twinkle uncle Floyd' from the chorus is still ringing in my ears. Another song from the same album called '5.15 The Angels Have Gone' was also remarkable, very soft and delicate. The quality of the sound was incredible

An impressive encore of six songs! Closing the set with 'Changes', 'Let's Dance', 'Suffragette City' and 'Ziggy Stardust'. The night was unforgettable and David was in great shape. Hard to believe that this was one of his last concerts.

I'm very greatful to have attended this concert. It is a privilege to be part of David Bowie's history.

KÖLNARENA

31 OCTOBER 2003 COLOGNE, GERMANY

I WAS THERE: SUSANNE KRAUSE

I became a fan of Bowie in 1998 when I saw *Labyrinth*, and finally having the chance to see him was unbelievable! My mother managed to get two tickets on his A Reality Tour and I went with my Dad. We had seats but obviously I couldn't sit... I stood up for the entire concert, danced, screamed, sang and cried because of so much happiness. My Dad is not a fan but he had no problem listening to him...he is an open-minded person. I was fascinated and bought the *Low* album. Every time I had any spare money, I bought something by Mr Bowie.

MANCHESTER ARENA

17 NOVEMBER 2003 MANCHESTER

I WAS THERE: PHIL BRENNAN

Thirty-one years after my first Bowie gig at the Hardrock (Manchester) in December 1972 I saw him for the last time. Again it was in Manchester, at the MEN Arena in November 2003.

Throughout my teenage years and early twenties, I had attended hundreds of gigs but it was always Bowie that I would forsake any other artist for. Even after my marriage and becoming a father, I still went as often as I could to see my musical hero.

Luckily enough my wife Liz, even though she is a few years younger than me, is also a big fan of going to gigs and she loved Bowie too.

Having racked up thirty-two Bowie gigs up and down the country, and having seen more or less every tour in between my first and last, I took up my seat for what would turn out to be the great man's last ever Manchester gig.

The set began with a very moody version of 'Rebel Rebel', Gail Ann Dorsey's bass guitar giving the song a new slant, before the band played two recent songs 'New Killer Star' and 'Reality' from the latest album named after the latter track.

Bowie looked in good health and appeared a little perplexed by the fact that the audience, particularly at the front of the arena, hadn't as yet got to their feet. He shouted out, 'Come on Manchester, your grandad's up here dancing', as the band launched into the old classic 'Fame.' No second invite needed, there was a rush towards the stage.

With the majority of the crowd on their feet Bowie played two tracks from the *Heathen* album of the previous year, 'Cactus' and 'Afraid' before another old classic, 'China Girl', was given an airing.

Having raised the tempo, Bowie then brought a hush to the arena with the mean, moody and brilliant (in my opinion) 'The

Loneliest Guy' – you could have heard a pin drop as he sang with Mike Garson's piano the perfect accompaniment.

If there was a perfect song to follow it then surely it was the next track, a song I couldn't even remember the last time I had witnessed Bowie play 'live'. So rare was it that he actually mentioned that it had remained one of his favourite ever songs even though he had omitted it from his set list for so long. If the crowd were happy before, they were suddenly on a new level as the band started the opening bars of 'The Man Who Sold the World'.

In keeping with the show so far, Bowie then played a couple of lesser known songs, 'Hallo Spaceboy' and 'Sunday', before bassist Dorsey showed her vocal prowess as she duetted with him on the single that had seen him reach the top of the charts with the band Queen, 'Under Pressure'.

Having raised the roof with the last song, and obviously enjoying himself, Bowie treated his loyal subjects with two absolute classics – 'Life on Mars?' and 'Ashes to Ashes' before he slowed it down again with 'The Motel', 'Loving the Alien', 'Never Get Old' and 'Changes'.

The latter stages of the gig felt like it had been put together just for me as Bowie played several of my all-time favourite tracks, back to back.

Firstly came 'I'm Afraid of Americans' probably the outstanding track (along with 'Hello Spaceboy') from his albums of the Nineties. This was followed by the always brilliant, 'Heroes' following which Bowie and his band left the stage to great acclaim from the packed arena.

The three-song encore was a trip down memory lane for everyone as superb versions of 'Five Years', 'Suffragette City' and 'Ziggy Stardust' were belted out before Bowie, all smiles and applauding the crowd, left the stage for the last time.

It had certainly been one of my favourite ever Bowie gigs. In all the years I had seen him, throughout various guises, I can't remember seeing him look so happy. He had joked and laughed from the start of the concert until that last minute. The band had been unbelievably tight, and note perfect throughout as they had played a set list that showcased the brilliant back catalogue he had released over the previous four decades. It had been a night that I will never forget for the rest of my life.

NEC LG ARENA

19-20 NOVEMBER 2003 BIRMINGHAM

I WAS THERE: ELIZABETH DAVIS

I was 31 when I went to the concert. The NEC is only about 15 minutes from my house. I took my older brother (41 at the time), because he was the person that got me into Bowie. My main memory was of 'Under Pressure' as it is one of my favourite songs, and Gail Ann Dorsey was brilliant in the Freddie Mercury role. I also remember him singing 'Five Years' in the encore and my brother crying because it evoked memories of his early teens.

WEMBLEY ARENA

25 NOVEMBER 2003 LONDON

I WAS THERE: DARYL EASLEA

I deliberately waited to see David Bowie in concert. Although I attended my first London gig was when I was 11 in 1977 (a show which featured Bowie's ex-keyboard player Rick Wakeman in a band called Yes), I couldn't find an adult responsible (or irresponsible) enough to accompany me to 1978's Isolar II tour. By the time of the Serious Moonlight Tour, it seemed impossible to get a ticket, so swerve it. When I was 21, I could just sense that the Glass Spider was a wrong'un. Tin Machine? Full marks for puncturing your bubble DB, but not for me. The Sound + Vision hit disposal tour? Just didn't fancy it.

Bowie's renaissance began with *Black Tie, White Noise* in 1993 and continued apace with *1: Outside*, which although is now barely listenable, at the time was hailed as something remarkable – the reunion with Brian Eno. Its walls of industrial noise and opaque storyline was compensated by some beautiful songs, especially the revisit of 'Strangers When We Meet' that had first appeared on *The Buddha Of Suburbia* soundtrack. When I heard that Morrissey would be supporting Bowie on his first post-hits tour, I could not believe it – I had waited until exactly the right time to see him. Sadly, all the people around us at Birmingham's cavernous NEC that November in 1995 had gone at exactly the wrong time.

Audience expectation is a funny old thing – ticket sales are the lifeblood of any act, and to fill 15,386 seats you need more than a hard-core who were in attendance to hear *1: Outside's* non-linear Gothic Drama Hyper-cycle of the diary of 'Nathan Adler' (or, lest we forget, the art-ritual murder of 'Baby Grace Blue'). They wanted to hear 'Let's Dance'. After Morrissey played the sort of set that made him quit the tour several nights later, the audience in my tier were getting anxious. Bowie played what I'd been hoping for, a wilful connoisseur-only special – 'The Voyeur Of Utter Destruction (As Beauty)' was not 'Space Oddity'; the closest to whoppers that night were 'DJ' and 'Moonage Daydream'. It was all akin to a D-90 I'd made my future wife in 1984. By the time 'Under Pressure' came round as the encore, most around us had left in chattering disgust. Jules (the recipient of said D-90) and I had acres in which to dance; I felt truly righteous, a big back-slap for my wonderful taste versus populism.

By the time of the Phoenix Festival in 1997, Bowie had reconciled himself to his hits (he'd played the dance tent the night before as the drum and bass only Tao Jones Index to satisfy his art) – after all, the showbiz side of him could not resist a grandstand of 'The Jean Genie', emerging from a slow blues. Wearing his Alexander McQueen-designed union flag tailcoat, all spikes and goatee, Bowie glanced at the gorgeous full moon and said with childlike glee 'Look at the moon!'; 'Fame' and 'Fashion' softened the blow for some of *Earthling's* more testing moments. It was a stunning performance.

I was very fortunate to see Bowie twice on his 2003 Reality Tour, in Manchester and London. The Manchester show was on a Monday night, and my dear friend's Nick 50th birthday present. As a result, we rather over indulged and the show – with Bowie on bravura form – was a perfect marriage of old and new. By the time of the three-song encore from *Ziggy Stardust*, Bowie's embrace of his past was only matched by Nick embracing anything in the near-vicinity in floods of rapturous tears; 30 years earlier, this was the music he'd fallen in love with. He'd seen him at Hammersmith. This was his Bowie.

I went again to see DB two weeks later at Wembley with Jules. It was an emotional, nostalgic evening: neither of us realised that it would be his penultimate performance in the UK. It was an absolute pleasure to have been able to see David Bowie in concert – better late than never, you may think; but I remain a firm believer in his post-1993 catalogue, most of which stands up perfectly against anything from the glory period of 71-80. By these final shows, he was thoroughly comfortable being onstage again; chummy, chatty, dispensing art and memories at a rapid rate. He was a remarkable live performer.

I WAS THERE: DAVE HILLER

I saw him in London at the Wembley Arena when he did the Reality Tour in the early 2000s. My son and his then girlfriend, (now his wife and mother to our beautiful granddaughter) also came to the concert. My son is a big fan and this was a treat.

David seemed to genuinely enjoy the show. He talked about doing something like it again. Sadly, it was not long after that he had a heart attack and didn't tour again. A truly great talent. Always looking forward.

CSU CONVOCATION CENTER

7 JANUARY 2004 CLEVELAND, OHIO

I WAS THERE: NICK BROWN

I saw the Glass Spider Tour when it came to Lexington, Kentucky on September 14, 1987 and the Reality Tour in Cleveland, Ohio on 7 January 2004.

I live in Louisville, Kentucky so it was a 350 or so mile trip. I was 38 at the time and had been a fan of Bowie's for as long as I can remember, but I became a devoted fan upon release of the *Scary Monsters* album in 1980. The video for 'Ashes to Ashes' opened up my eyes and ears to a whole new world, so it was with jubilation that he played both this song and 'Fashion' that night along with many other favorites like 'Under Pressure' and 'Life on Mars?' That night, we also got treated with the rarely played 'Fantastic Voyage' and he called out an impromptu performance of 'Be My Wife.'

The A Reality Tour show was extra special, because the *BowieNet* ticket presale got me third row, center, seats and there was a *BowieNet* member meet-up at a nearby pizza parlor, where about a dozen of us met up. The concert was amazing and Bowie was directly in front of me...I felt I could almost touch him. My wife got some amazing pictures (shhhhh...don't tell). It was the day before his birthday, so we all sang 'Happy Birthday' to him. It was a magical night I will never forget.

PENGROWTH SADDLEDOME

21 JANUARY 2004 CALGARY, CANADA

I WAS THERE: CHERYL TOFFAN

It had been a while since Bowie had toured and the anticipation was very high! It was held at the Pengrowth Saddledome, I was 43 and tickets were $88.50. I remember vividly when he came on stage how healthy and you might say a little buff

Cheryl Toffan (seated)

looking and his big smile. It was an awesome show – I loved Gail Ann Dorsey on bass guitar. We had side view seats and pretty close to the stage so I was able to see him quite clearly. He began his concert with his classic 'Rebel Rebel'. We have the concert CD of that show and it's a keeper.

SYDNEY ENTERTAINMENT CENTRE

20 FEB 2004 SYDNEY, AUSTRALIA

I WAS THERE: KATHY CURRAN

My first David Bowie concert was in 1983 at the Sydney showground. I was 22-years old, and I remember my girlfriend and I sleeping out the front of the showground the night before the tickets went on sale, so that we wouldn't miss out. We were both so excited when we got those tickets, and headed straight home for a sleep. Sleeping on the footpath wasn't very comfortable, but getting tickets to see Bowie was worth it. Because it was quite some time ago, I can't really tell you what songs he played, but he could have played 'Baa Baa Black Sheep' for all I cared. What an amazing man he was. I do recall though, using the men's toilet at the concert. The line up for the ladies was ridiculous and there was no line up at the men's, so my friend and I headed into the men's. It turned a few heads at the time, and is funny to think back on it now.

I was disappointed to miss the Glass Spider Tour in 1987, but got to see the Reality tour with two friends and my husband in 2004 at the Sydney Entertainment Centre. There are so many songs that I love, but if I had to pick one as my favourite, it would have to be 'Sorrow'. He was an amazing entertainer and there will never be another like him.

I WAS THERE: MICHAEL TARRANT

I saw Bowie in 1983 at the Sydney Cricket Ground for the Serious

Moonlight Tour and thankfully saw him in 2004 at the Sydney Entertainment Centre for the Reality Tour. I remember being impressed with how personable and cheerful he seemed on the Reality show as well as being blown away by the visuals, the reinterpretation of his older songs and how tight the band was.

I WAS THERE: BRUCE BUTLER

When the Reality world tour was announced and, after a 17 year absence, it was confirmed Bowie would finally be returning to Australia, it was a no-brainer that I would be going to see the concerts in Sydney and Melbourne as I had on all three previous Australian tours.

For the first time tickets went on sale on-line instead of having to queue and, as a BowieNet member, I managed to get excellent seats for both shows in Sydney and the two Melbourne concerts.

Closer to the concert dates I was tipped off by an industry friend that Bowie would be staying at the exclusive Park Hyatt Hotels in both Sydney and my home town of Melbourne. My wife and I decided to book rooms in both cities and, as she received a corporate discount we upgraded to suites.

On arrival in Sydney for the first show we checked into the Park Hyatt and found we had been further upgraded to an Executive suite on the top floor with a view of the Sydney Opera House just outside our window. After dropping our bags we decided to go for a walk and as we walked out of our room Bowie, Coco Schwab and a minder were exiting the suite next to ours. We all met at the elevator, exchanged smiles and, when the elevator door opened we were ushered in first. We stood at the back facing the mirrored door making eye contact with Bowie who was smiling the whole time. When the door opened Coco and the minder stepped out but Bowie stepped aside saying, 'Ladies first', putting his arm around my wife and ushering her out and then saying, 'After you', holding the door open for me. They then jumped straight into a car presumably for soundcheck and we were left standing dumbfounded in the foyer.

Needless to say the shows were fantastic and we did see Bowie in the hotel a couple more times but each time Coco was keeping a watchful eye and it was obvious we were not to approach.

The following week back in Melbourne we were once again in the same hotel as Bowie but this time his 'Presidential Suite' was very segregated from ours and we didn't see him around the hotel at all. After the two extraordinary Melbourne shows it was time to check out of the hotel but at the last minute I got a message from a friend telling me the band's check-out call time and that if I was in the foyer I'd be able to see them all in one place. He also told me that Bowie would be checking out 45 minutes after the band, so if I was in the foyer he would suggest to Bowie's minder that I get to say hello.

The band gathered as scheduled, and were very approachable and I was able to chat a bit with each of them and get them to sign my Reality Tour programme. Then off they went to the airport and my wife and I waited for Bowie to appear. There was now another couple resident in the hotel who were also obviously waiting to see Bowie. After about an hour the minder came and checked us out and said if we waited just outside the foyer entrance Bowie would approach us to say hello. Soon after Bowie came out and walked straight up to me smiling. I asked if he'd mind signing my programme and handed him the pen I'd used for the band. He made a couple of attempts and scribbled on the top of the page but I'd left the lid off and it'd gone dry. He said, 'Well I won't be signing with this', laughing and handing it back. He moved on to the other guy and signed something of his with a hotel ballpoint. I asked if he'd try again with the pen and he obliged saying his goodbyes and off he went in the waiting car to the airport.

That was the last time I met Bowie and the only time there was any photographic evidence with a couple of hurried shots by my wife.

ROD LAVER ARENA

26-27 FEBRUARY 2004 MELBOURNE, AUSTRALIA

I WAS THERE: LUCILLE MCMILLAN

I saw David Bowie in Melbourne Australia in February 2004 on his Reality tour. I was 28 at the time so now feel so fortunate to have seen him. I'd always fantasised about seeing him in the Seventies during the Ziggy period! From the moment he arrived on stage, I was in awe as he exuded such warmth, style, vitality, humour and pure class. I kept thinking he looked better and younger and more energetic than ever! His singing voice we all know and love, but his talking voice was so beautiful and lilting to listen to; he charmed every single one of us I'd say being so cheeky and bloody funny. It felt like we were all just his mates and he chatted away to us throughout the show.

He began by laughingly pointing out a guy in the crowd (way up in the back row) wearing a red Christmas jumper with a giant reindeer on it. So the entire audience turns up to look and Bowie states, 'Ah, just joking' (or something to this effect), we all loved being the butt of his joke! The show was generous in quality and quantity with 'Life on Mars?' and 'All The Young Dudes' being highlights for me. He ended up playing for close to three hours and I finally needed to have a toilet break which I'd put off for fear of missing anything!

I finally went and I sometimes wonder if I dreamt this bit, as it's so weird. I went down to the loos, which were empty except for a lady cleaning the floors. The weird bit was that she had a Ziggy style orange mullet and told me to get back in there quick as he was about to finish with a *Ziggy* encore. So I rushed back in and sure enough, there was a *Ziggy* triple header ('Suffragette', 'Five Years', 'Ziggy'). Honestly such a bizarre moment I wonder if I either conjured it up or maybe Bowie planted her down there to ensure no one was wasting time in the toilets! Seeing Bowie was such a significant event in my life and I honestly thought I'd see him again one day given he has never stopped writing or producing new work. I'll have to content myself with the hope of seeing his musical *Lazarus* some day.

SUPREME COURT GARDENS

1 MARCH 2004 PERTH, AUSTRALIA

I WAS THERE: SHAUN EVANS

I bought a ticket for the Glass Spider Tour but my cover band at the time accidentally booked a show (on the same date), so I had to give my ticket away. I was gutted. I had to wait nearly two decades to see him again. The Reality tour 2004 in Perth did not disappoint. I Always remember he threw in 'Quicksand' introducing it saying, 'Oh this is old'. A rare performance I think, as it's not on the commercially available DVD. I would have loved to have met him. I don't see too many stars past or present that matched his talents. Nothing short of a messiah in my book.

Pete Carroll (3rd from left) behind Bowie after The Perth show March 2004

I WAS THERE: PETE CARROLL

The last time I saw Bowie was in Perth, Western Australia in 2004 during the Reality Tour. It was a hit filled set that also included 'All The Young Dudes'. I met him after the show; he looked remarkably fit and well. He was wonderfully accommodating, polite and surprisingly normal. I've worked in the music industry for many years and met many big name artists; from my experience Bowie, alongside the likes of Bruce Springsteen, Willie Nelson and Johnny Cash, stand out as artists who were grounded and hadn't lost touch with who they were. It's rare I bother to get a photo with an artist but the one I have with Bowie I'll treasure.

ROSE GARDEN ARENA

13 APRIL 2004 PORTLAND, OREGON

I WAS THERE: LEANN KAATTARI

I'd just started work at a law office as the receptionist. I deal with the mail and deliveries, and one morning, I took an envelope with some concert tickets for an attorney. I asked the delivery person who they were to and he said, 'David Bowie.' I immediately freaked, and took them back to the attorney. 'Are you fucking kidding me? DAVID BOWIE?' He said he'd gotten them for free from a friend, and if he could get better seats, he'd give me these. My then-husband's birthday was the day after the concert, and he was a fan, too, so this would be perfect. A couple of days after that, the attorney came and gave me the tickets! It was the most incredible show ever. Looking back, I'm so lucky to see him when I did, because it was the last time he came to Portland.

GREEK THEATRE

22 APRIL 2004 LOS ANGELES

I WAS THERE: BILLY GALLEGOS

I Saw him in 2004 and if I'm not mistaken, it was his last concert ever in Los Angeles. The Opening act was the Polyphonic Spree. I had planned on taking this one girl but she had been doing one too many stupid things to me that had been turning me off. Two days prior to the show, she didn't even know who we were going to see (she guessed Madonna?). So, one day prior to the show, I ran into a girl I had not seen in over a year. I asked if she'd like to come and see David Bowie, and she said 'yes', and the rest is history. We would end up spending the rest of 2004 traveling the country together. You could say the David Bowie concert brought us together that year.

The song me and my date sang together to was 'Under Pressure', (song of the night for us). I bought the programme (still have) and I bought her the DB coffee mug. We sat on the north wing (Greek Theatre). I was part of the Greek Theatre Concert Club, where you get tickets before they go on sale to the public. I usually would get section A seats thanks to my seniority but since this was David Bowie, I guess far too many members with more seniority than me loved him as well, which is why I had to settle with the north wing seating. I live in the San Gabriel valley so the drive was not bad. How nice it would be if this story got me back together with the girl I took. We lost touch in early 2005 and her whereabouts are unknown.

I WAS THERE: VERONICA LOPEZ

This was the one and only David Bowie concert I attended. I've been a fan since I was 5 and finally convinced my dad to buy tickets to see him in Los Angeles at the Greek Theatre. I was blown away by his performance and he covered songs from different eras of his long career. Sadly this was his last world tour before he subsequently backed down from live performances due to his heart attack overseas. I'm grateful I got to see him in my lifetime.

JAMES L. KNIGHT CENTER

6 MAY 2004 MIAMI, FLORIDA

I WAS THERE: KELLY JONES, STEREOPHONICS

It was quite a strange start because, when we started the tour in Miami, as we walked off stage a rigging engineer actually fell and died on stage, so David couldn't actually go on to do his performance.

The first time we met him is when he came into the dressing room to ask for a little nip of whiskey and we all got to know each other through tragic circumstances.

If he was doing a soundcheck he would shout over the mic, 'What do you think about that?' We couldn't believe he was asking us our opinion really. Watching him work different audiences with different styles of music across the many, very different states of America showed a huge range of work and I loved it.

He even dedicated 'Life On Mars?' to me one night after I'd asked for it the whole tour, and he also happily read a story I'd written while on tour and gave me his opinion – he'd just sit in our dressing room with us some nights, chatting away.

I remember we had a five-a-side tournament with him and his band and he'd heckle me from the touch-line. Then he'd lower a trophy down over our heads on a string when we lost the match and comically mock our poor football skills.

To see a man from that era to always be constantly moving forward artistically was an inspiration.

THE MARK OF THE QUAD CITIES

22 MAY 2004 MOLINE, ILLINOIS

I WAS THERE: MIKE SLODKI

He did 26 songs including the encore and I believe this was his

19th to last ever show. Welsh band Stereophonics were the opening act. Bowie started the show with 'Rebel Rebel', and my favorites that night were 'Cactus', 'New Killer Star' and 'Under Pressure'. Glad I saw him.

SHEA'S PERFORMING ARTS CENTER

25 MAY 2004 BUFFALO, NEW YORK

I WAS THERE: HELEN LYON

Next to Serious Moonlight, this was possibly the best show ever for me. Perhaps it was because it was right around the time he had his heart attack. The realization that this could be the final time I could see him was devastating. I heard he quit touring shortly thereafter. A few shows here and there, but none within my grasp.

After the show my husband and I waited outside to catch a glimpse of him. There were around 40 or so all jammed together trying to see the man we had become to love and idolize. A security person came out and said that Mr Bowie has, 'left the building' and we should all disperse. Yeah, right. After about 10 or 15 minutes, out he comes surrounded by a small army of security. He is jumping up over the heads of these guys and high-fiving the fans. My fingers brushed his very briefly and I was a happy girl. It was SO worth it.

BORGATA EVENT CENTER

30 MAY 2004 ATLANTIC CITY

I WAS THERE: LAURIE GREENER

It was Memorial Day weekend in New Jersey. Six of us David Bowie fans in our 40s from Bloomfield NJ headed on the NJ

Parkway South in the bumper-to-bumper traffic to head to the Jersey Shore for Bowie's Reality tour 100th performance at the Borgata. Our last glimpse of Bowie live was back in 1987 at the NJ Meadowlands Glass Spider Tour.

Being in a rather small arena, at once we knew we would be witness to one of the best shows of his career by the intro of the white magnifying spiritual surprise performed by The Polyphonic Spree. Nothing could have been more appropriate for setting the tone of what was yet to come.

Sporting a very much more distinguished look Bowie took the stage with the opening of 'Rebel Rebel'. All we had to hear was the first tone and we all were all on our feet singing along for the rest of the show.

My great memories of this performance includes an all around great delivery of his classics 'Fashion', 'All The Young Dudes, 'Panic in Detroit', 'Under Pressure', 'Changes', 'Fame', 'Let's Dance', 'Ashes to Ashes', 'Heroes...' and my husband's favorite 'The Man Who Sold the World' (who decided to use the rest room at this time).

The kicker was his encores of 'Diamond Dogs' and the great classic 'Ziggy Stardust'. After staying overnight at the casino we headed back up the Garden State Parkway for the anticipated two-hour ride. This turned out to be a gruelling four and a half hours due to the Jersey Shore traffic, But after seeing David Bowie perform one of his last and most exhilarating shows it was worth it! We hoped we could catch another performance by Bowie but unfortunately that thought was cut short by the news of his emergency heart surgery announced shortly afterwards.

FROGNERPARKEN

18 JUNE 2004 OSLO, NORWAY

I WAS THERE: ANN-SOFIE ANDERSSON

When Bowie announced his tour for 2003/2004 we decided that we would see as many as we could in Scandinavia, so for the summer tour 2004 it was Bergen and Oslo that were the closest to us.

We drove from Gothenburg up to Oslo and flew from there to Bergen for the show there, then flew back to Oslo for a festival called Norwegian Wood in Frognerparken. The show in Bergen, which we supposed would be in rain, actually got sunshine and wonderful summer weather. However, Oslo was not showing its best side. It started to rain as we arrived at our hotel but had stopped as we arrived at the park. We were early so we got great spots second row from the catwalk on the right side. The place was like a small amphitheatre, a smaller version of Milton Keynes.

The moment Bowie came on stage the rain started and didn't stop until the show was over, but we hardly noticed because we were into the show from the moment go.

Three songs in, it happens. Someone throws a lollipop on stage and manages to hit Bowie right in his eye! That's it we thought – show over. Bowie cursed and wondered who did this. No one confessed. (Some days later a girl showed up in the press confessing to it being her throwing it but it was an accident). Bowie then calmed down and joked that luckily it was his left eye which is already damaged, and 'Can you see the blood flowing' etc. He also later on threw a guitar pick into the crowd and wondered cheekily if it hit anyone in the eye?

After this incident something about the show changed and it just turned out to be one of the best shows I've ever seen with him, and Bowie himself said the same as he and the band took their bows.

It was raining and cold and Bowie was cold too, so halfway through the show he got a fleece sweater to warm him up. We thought we might get a shorter show because of the weather but he gave us almost two and a half hours with a great set list which included gems like 'The Supermen', 'Quicksand', 'Panic in Detroit' and 'Be My Wife' among others.

'All The Young Dudes' turned into a big sing-a-long and arm waiving song and 'Life on Mars?' was magical.

We were soaking wet and cold after the show but nothing matters when you get a show like this. I've seen him in 76, 78, 83, 87, 90 and 96, but I cherish these 2003/2004 as my favourites and really ending it all with this awesome show.

T-MOBILE ARENA

23 JUNE 2004 PRAGUE, CZECH REPUBLIC

I WAS THERE: DAVID MACKUU

I was at his Reality tour when he played in Prague. We had very heavy rain and Michael Hutchence was in the audience, INXS had played in town the day before. Unfortunately the start of the show itself signaled something wrong – the screen with the opening animation didn't work, but the music played on and musicians came to the stage as usual (one by one) – I saw the same show in Vienna Stadthalle few months before Prague.

But after some 15 or 20 minutes David left the stage, the band continued to play (looking surprised) one or two songs without him, one of the songs was sung by the keyboard player.

Then they all left and shortly afterwards David came back on and tried to sing 'Life on Mars?'. But then suddenly he apologised for being in pain and that was the end of everything.

I got a set list which one roadie gave me from the stage (A4 size paper with songs planned to be played) but shortly after that somebody else from the crew jumped in demanding it back. He wasn't polite at all and I just gave up and gave him it back.

ROYAL ALBERT HALL

29 MAY 2006 LONDON

I WAS THERE: MATT JOHNS

The 1990 Sound+Vision Tour came at a perfect time for me, and promised a greatest hits tour, partly informed by a fan vote for their favourites. The UK's weekly music newspaper the *NME* tried to subvert things a little with a 'Just Say Gnome' campaign, to get Bowie performing 'The Laughing Gnome' as part of the tour. Unfortunately he found out that there was a plot to get this novelty hit into the set, after seeing the high number of votes for it and mulled over 'playing it like the Velvets or something'. I still have – somewhere – the T-shirt the *NME* created with the Frankie Goes To Hollywood-esque campaign name on it.

The first of the shows on the tour I saw was at the Docklands Arena in London, a 15,000 seat venue, similar to Earl's Court, but much squarer in layout. Not fantastic, transport links tended to be a bit hit or miss, and the venue didn't last long – despite it being used by big acts such as Pink Floyd and Duran Duran, via things like the Great British Beer Festival. Anyway, I was sat just two seats away from some friends from work, coincidentally enough – causing a degree of panic for my girlfriend at the time and I; we worked together in the same office as those sat just along from us, and we were keeping it secret from anyone there!

The show suffered – I think – from something I witnessed a lot around that time...London audiences for shows with a big name could tend to be dominated by people who were fairly wealthy, had heard that the act puts on a good show, and went to the event so that they could say that they'd been there. A lot seemed to be bankers/ financial sorts, before the crash that happened that year. So, not fans, and often sitting waiting to be impressed. This was certainly the case for the show I saw at this venue – those in the decent seats at the front gave such little feedback and enthusiasm, the show felt really flat, and (unless my memory is seriously lacking), Bowie didn't

> **BOWIE DIDN'T COME OUT FOR AN ENCORE, CITING THE LACK OF ATMOSPHERE AND DESIRE**

come out for an encore, citing the lack of atmosphere and desire. The first time I saw David live, it was a bit of a disappointment – but not through lack of his efforts. It was a great example of how an audience can make or break a show.

Once the North American dates had taken place from April that year, through to the end of July (via a two-night excursion to Tokyo for some reason), the tour returned to Europe commencing with a pair of concerts at the Milton Keynes Bowl, at the start of August.

Memories of the show are fairly sketchy, despite me being very close to the front. However, overriding is the memory of just how wonderfully emotional the performance seemed – certainly from an audience's perspective, it felt like quite a pinnacle. I remember being in the middle of a crush of people, no more than ten feet from the stage, being lifted off my feet in time with the music as everyone reveled in the show. I also distinctly recall, in 'Young Americans', Bowie seeming to brush away a real tear as he sang the words, 'break down and cry...' such was the strength of the audience reaction.

Some 27 years later as I write this, but those two shows stick in the mind head and shoulders above many of the hundreds of shows I've seen since the early Eighties.

Fast forward to 2006. David Gilmour, Pink Floyd's guitarist, on a solo tour for his album *On An Island*, arrived at the Royal Albert Hall for a trio of shows to conclude the dates he'd done in Europe and North America. The first of the three nights saw a guest appearance of Robert Wyatt on the song 'Then I Close My Eyes', following shortly after David Crosby and Graham Nash who sang on the title track of the album, along with 'The Blue'. They were to return in the second half on 'Shine On You Crazy Diamond', but the big surprise came in the encores, when following another appearance on their own song 'Find The Cost of Freedom', Crosby and Nash left the stage to allow another David (the third of the night) to take over the microphone.

As he was a self-confessed Syd Barrett fan, the choice of 'Arnold Layne' was not a huge surprise as David's choice of song. Bowie fans will recall that Syd's ditty (one of Pink Floyd's earliest singles) 'See Emily Play' was covered on the *Pin Ups* album, so to hear him perform another from the early period of Pink Floyd was both a wonderful surprise, yet not particularly out of place.

Sitting a few rows from the front, virtually in front of Bowie, the incredible and unexpected appearance of the man was enhanced by the amusing sight of (what seemed to be) the entire staff of the Royal Albert Hall deserting doors, bars, and so on, to come into the hall itself, to stand by the exit doors and stairs watching Bowie appear on stage for his 'turn'. In all my years of concert going, I've never witnessed anything like this... I presume they knew he was to appear, or on hearing the ovation and his first few sung words, they hot-footed it to witness it themselves.

He'd been out of the public eye for some time before this appearance, due to his health issues, and this evening was also to be his final UK performance (not that we knew this), so to see him clearly having a ball as he knocked 'Arnold Layne' out of the park, before nailing the vocals in the finale of 'Comfortably Numb', was such a joy. At the time, with the power of his performance and obvious pleasure in collaborating with Gilmour for this very special appearance, we did wonder if it was a first glimpse of a proper return of Bowie to the stage. Sadly, not to be, but what a live swan song for a true legend...

2006 Bowie's final live performance took place on 9 November 2006, when he joined Alicia Keys at the Black Ball fundraiser at New York's Hammersmith Ballroom, where he sang three songs; 'Wild Is The Wind', (with Mike Garson on piano), and 'Fantastic Voyage' and 'Changes' with Alicia Keys.

2010-2012 *The Next Day* album was announced on Bowie's 66th birthday, 8 January 2013 when Bowie's website was updated with the video for the lead single, 'Where Are We Now?', and the single was immediately made available on the iTunes Store. His twenty-fourth studio album was released on 8 March 2013 on his ISO Records label. It was Bowie's first album of new material in ten years, since 2003's *Reality*, and surprised fans and media who believed he had retired. *The Next Day* was met with critical acclaim, and earned Bowie his first No 1 album in the United Kingdom since 1993's *Black Tie White Noise*. The album was nominated for Best Rock Album at the 2014 Grammy Awards and for MasterCard British Album of the Year at the 2014 BRIT Awards.

I WAS THERE: EARL SLICK, GUITARIST

He'd emailed me out of the blue to see what my schedule was and almost immediately we were in the studio, working. My favorite song from that album is probably 'Valentine's Day', because we cut it as a band, live in the studio. We'd worked together so long that we knew when something was working, and we generally worked really fast. But it was always really good. So it was great to reconnect, and it was great to see him looking so good and hear him sounding so good. It was a really special experience working with David again.

I WAS THERE: GERRY LEONARD, GUITARIST

David had a profound effect on my life, and I can see that now. He was a master and I was an apprentice and I learned a lot from him. But he was very generous with that relationship, and never treated you like the apprentice. When you were making music with him, he wanted it to be a level playing field. He wanted you to behave like an equal, or to try at least. That's an incredibly generous way of working with someone, to make them feel that they're wanted for what they bring to the table.

I WAS THERE: MIKE GARSON, PIANIST

He always had a vision, but he never micromanaged. Whatever it took to stretch the boundaries, no matter how wild it sounded, David was game. That's where his genius was, almost like a great casting director. In that sense he was like Miles Davis: He knew who to pick to work with, and he knew if he got out of the way and let them do their thing, he'd get the most out of them.

Some writer in England wrote a biography about me. He asked me to listen to 50 songs I'd played on with David that he felt had a lot of impact on his music. So I did that over the course of a few hours. That's not something I'd normally do and I was so blown away, because I was compressing 30 years into two hours. It was overwhelming. I wrote David an e-mail, immediately, saying I couldn't believe what we'd accomplished. He immediately wrote back, 'We did some great work together'. I can't begin to tell you how final that communication felt, though I didn't realize that was why he sent it. He knew we were never going to work again. But it was a beautiful note, because he knew.

2015

David Bowie's twenty-fifth and final studio album *Blackstar* was released worldwide on 8 January 2016, coinciding with Bowie's 69th birthday.

The album was largely recorded in secret between The Magic Shop and Human Worldwide Studios in New York City with Bowie's longtime co-producer Tony Visconti. Bowie recruited a local New York jazz combo led by Donny McCaslin as the backing band for the sessions

Two days after its release, Bowie died of liver cancer; his illness had not been revealed to the public until then. Co-producer Visconti described the album as Bowie's intended swan song and a 'parting gift' for his fans before his death.

Upon release, the album was met with critical acclaim, topping charts in a number of countries in the wake of Bowie's death, and becoming Bowie's only album to top the Billboard 200 in the United States. At the 59th Annual Grammy Awards in 2017, the album won awards for Best Alternative Music Album and Best Recording Package.

I WAS THERE: BEN MONDER, JAZZ GUITARIST

He was such a regular guy. We just had one rehearsal for the Maria Schneider session and he was very down-to-earth, very nice. He seemed to make an effort to make you feel like you weren't in the presence of a rock deity.

David and Tony Visconti were very accommodating, as far as being open to people's suggestions. I had some demos of the songs that David had done at his house, so I had some idea of what kinds of parts I was going to play, but we all came up with our own parts. I had lots of ideas. Some of them worked, some of them didn't. But when they didn't, nobody was watching the clock or vibing you about it. They were OK with anything when it came to experimentation.

OTHER SIGHTINGS

I WAS THERE: STEVE MASEY

Whilst working in London's West End in 1969, I popped down to the BBC Radio studios one lunch-time in Lower Regent Street and saw David Bowie dressed in his college gear with a scarf around neck, singing 'Space Oddity' on his acoustic guitar. I'll never forget it. I believe he had a light tanned jacket on at the time.

I WAS THERE: PAUL LOPICCOLO

I once saw David in *The Elephant Man*, front row, on Broadway. Whenever his part called for him to be upstage, there he was, spitting all over me, perfectly portraying the main character.

Years later, I happened to notice David and Iman sitting a few rows behind us at the *Motherfucker With the Hat*, also on Broadway. When the show was over, I wanted to tell David I owed him, lol, but they left a tad earlier.

I WAS THERE: LAURA ANDERSON

Two good friends and I went to see David Bowie in *The Elephant Man* at the Blackstone theatre when he portrayed life tortured Joseph Merrick. Without makeup, Bowie captured the essence of the character portraying the suffering and agony of his existence while undergoing treatment for his disease. It was incredible.

Afterwards we went outside to the exit and waited for Bowie. Upon exiting the theatre, I approached him with my programme and asked for his autograph, which he graciously gave. I was mesmerized by his eyes. He departed and we turned to see the limo door open. As he was getting in, who did we see in the back? Iggy Pop!! It was a great night.

I WAS THERE: LEWIS WHITE

My friend and his wife were waiting to eat lunch at a cafe in Santa

Barbara. David Bowie asked if they would like to eat with him and his wife, Iman. David said that he found that when he was with someone (not famous), people wouldn't approach him constantly. They had a wonderful time, and said goodbye.

I WAS THERE: CHRIS OSBURN

I was in Namibia cruising down a desert road miles from any living soul when I heard the news of David Bowie's death come on the radio. Or at least I assumed that was what the report was about. It was broadcast in German (a legacy of Namibia's colonial past) and sounded something like this to my ears:

German German German David Bowie German German German Iggy Pop German German German Berlin German German German ...

But, from the sombre tone of the announcer and not being able to figure out why else there'd be a news update about Bowie, I surmised the worst must have been true. I looked around – nothingness everywhere – and had something of a Major Tom moment.

> **I TOLD DAVID I WASN'T JUST A FAN BUT ALSO A MUSICIAN, INSPIRED BY HIM AND THAT I WOULD LOVE IT IF HE WOULD HAVE A LISTEN TO MY MP3s**

Then I started remembering how not even an hour before – and off and on over the past several days – I had been humming 'Starman' constantly (mostly because I'd watched the Matt Damon film, *The Martian*, on my flight down from London, and the song had featured prominently in the film), and how a few days earlier 'Life on

Mars?' had come to mind as I explored the otherworldly landscape of northern Namibia's Skeleton Coast. Of course, that wasn't really anything all that serendipitous or even coincidental: David Bowie's lyrics and music often had been near the forefront of my thoughts serving as an appropriate soundtrack as anything I'd ever listened to since I discovered his music for myself during my early teens.

Then I remembered the brief encounter I'd actually had with the artist about 15 years earlier at Newark Airport. I was with my then-wife waiting at a gate to board a flight. I don't remember where we were going, but it might have been Hawaii. A couple walked past toward an empty waiting area of the terminal. My ex chirped excitedly, 'That was Iman!' We looked and could see she was with her husband.

At that time I was still writing and recording music and playing gigs. The website MP3.com was a pretty big deal then, and I had my own profile page. So I scribbled out a note with my URL and email and headed over to greet the legend. David and Iman sat alone at a gate behind a sign. If we had not have seen them pass we would not have been able to tell anyone was at the gate. It was easy to tell the two were trying to hide. I imaged they'd fled a lounge as even from first and business class flyers they had been hounded for their fame. As soon as we approached it was easy to tell they just wanted us to go.

But I told David I wasn't just a fan but also a musician, inspired by him and that I would love it if he would have a listen to my MP3s. I gave him my scrap of paper. His face lit up. He beamed with a broad smile and accepted my note graciously. We let them go back to being unnoticed and returned to our gate to wait for our flight.

I was thrilled, to have met a legend and to be seen on the cusp of a new age by him. Of course, David Bowie never actually wrote me, but I did notice a slight bump in hits to my MP3 page soon after the encounter and started receiving email newsletters from davidbowie.com.

I WAS THERE: VAL KILMER

The last time I saw David Bowie was in Brooklyn, with some very very lucky people who got to hear Lou Reed play his dark glory, *Berlin*, live. He was sitting directly in front of me with Lou's wife, Laurie Anderson, who had recently visited my ranch in New Mexico with Lou. When we said hello he turned and I recognized him instantly. Instead of saying hello, I just started petting his shoulders.

> **'INSTEAD OF SAYING HELLO, I JUST STARTED PETTING HIS SHOULDERS'**

I can't describe it any more accurately. He was just so special it was the only way I seemed to be able to express my joy. I haven't petted that many men in my life. I'm so glad I got to do that. And more importantly, that he let me. He just smiled as I apologized for petting him. He seemed to not only understand, but accept the strange offering of gratitude and recognition. And suddenly, the spell was broken as he focused intensely on the stage, realizing before any of us, that the historic show was about to begin.

Berlin was a particularly important record to him as he said many times, and he prized his friendship with Lou, as Lou was a very very challenging dude. But we all wanted to be as cool as David. Even Lou. He was the always, always the coolest guy in the room. And he was a mastersinger – songwriter. God bless David Bowie.

THE STARS ARE OUT TONIGHT

IGGY POP

David's friendship was the light of my life. I never met such a brilliant person. He was the best there is.

DAVE GAHAN

Since I was in my early teens, Bowie had an extraordinary effect on me. He represented something that was a little different and he didn't feel comfortable going along with what was considered to be the norm. That really appealed to me and somehow comforted me, certainly as a teenager. His music has been with me throughout anything I've ever done. If you're backstage at a Depeche Mode gig, when you walk past my dressing room, you're probably going to hear a Bowie album before a show. Usually it's something from *Stage*, which was a live album recorded at a concert that I was very lucky to see when I just turned 16. Me, and a couple of my mates sneaked into the back of (the venue) and before we got thrown out, we saw a couple of numbers. It was mind-blowing to me at that age.

And I've seen him time and time again over the years. My daughter and his daughter went to the same school for a couple years, so I'd see him at these school functions. One thing I regret – of course when he passed away – is never telling him how much his music had meant to me all these years. I always thought it was kind of weird to do that, especially when we were at school together, just two dads with their kids.

JIMMY PAGE

Bowie was an innovator, a unique artist with a vision that changed the face of popular music. He is greatly missed.

PETER GABRIEL

I was shocked to learn of David Bowie's death this morning. He meant so much to me and to so many. He was a one-off, a brilliant outlier, always exploring, challenging and inspiring anyone who wanted to push the boundaries of music, art, fashion and society. There are so few artists who can touch a generation as he did, we will miss him badly. Long Live Lazarus.

YOKO ONO

John and David respected each other. They were well matched in intellect and talent. As John and I had very few friends, we felt David was as close as family. After John died, David was there for Sean and me. When Sean was in boarding school in Switzerland, David would pick him up and take him on trips to museums and let Sean hang out at his recording studio in Geneva. For Sean this is losing another father figure. It will be hard for him, I know. But we have some sweet memories, which will stay with us forever.

BRIAN ENO

David's death came as a complete surprise, as did nearly everything else about him. I feel a huge gap now. We knew each other for over 40 years, in a friendship that was always tinged by echoes of Peter Cook and Dudley Moore. Over the last few years, with him living in New York and me in London our connection was by email. I received an email from him seven days ago… It was as funny as always, and as surreal, looping through word games and allusions and all the usual stuff we did. It ended with this sentence: 'Thank you for our good times, Brian. They will never rot'. And it was signed Dawn. I realise now he was saying goodbye.

RICK WAKEMAN

As I'm sure you can imagine I'm gutted hearing of David's passing. He was the biggest influence and encouragement I could ever have wished for.

EARL SLICK

First and foremost, to Iman, Duncan and Lexi my heart goes out to you. To the man that had given me so much over the last 40 years I am beyond words at the moment. Good-bye David. Sleep tight my friend.

GENE SIMMONS

David Bowie, you will be sorely missed. Bowie's 'Changes' and the *Ziggy* story songs were a major influence for me.

BILLY CORGAN

When a true star blinks out, the sky looks different, and never feels the same.

PAUL McCARTNEY

David was a great star and I treasure the moments we had together. His music played a very strong part in British musical history, and I'm proud to think of the huge influence he has had on people all around the world. I send my deepest sympathies to his family and will always remember the great laughs we had through the years. His star will shine in the sky forever.

MICK JAGGER

David was always an inspiration to me and a true original. He was wonderfully shameless in his work. We had so many good times together... He was my friend. I will never forget him.

CHRIS CORNELL

140 characters will not suffice (nor would 10,000 words) #DavidBowie we love you and we will miss you...

KANYE WEST

David Bowie was one of my most important inspirations, so fearless, so creative. He gave us magic for a lifetime.

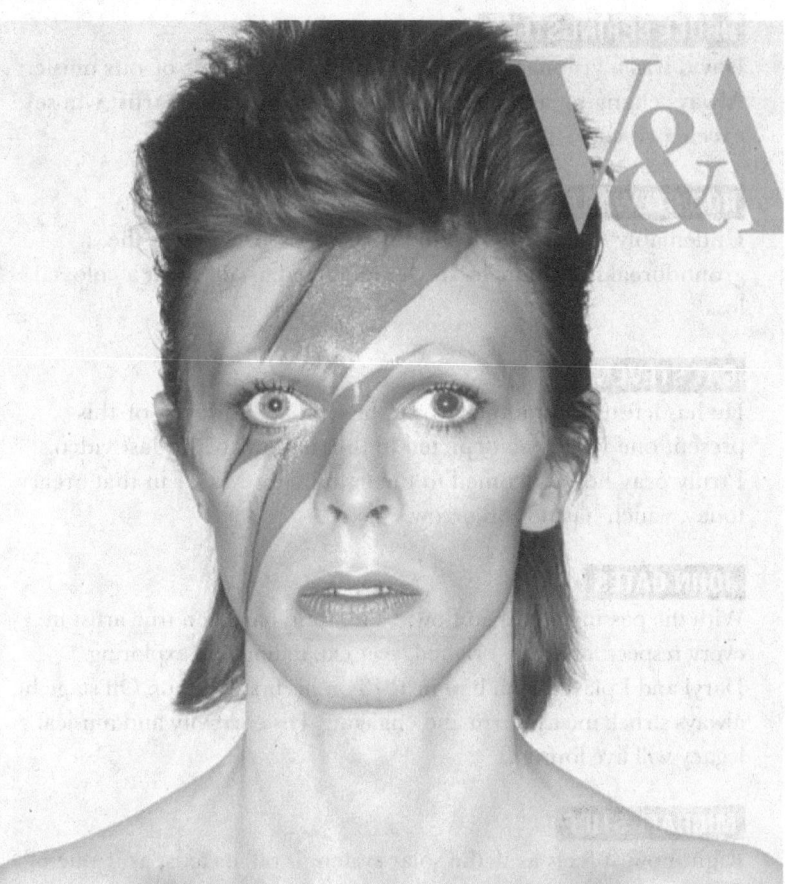

BRUCE SPRINGSTEEN

David was a visionary artist and an early supporter of our music. Always changing and ahead of the curve, he was an artist whose excellence you aspired to. He will be sorely missed.

ROD STEWART

Undeniably the fearless leader of the pack. David was the groundbreaking chameleon who impacted us all. Such a colossal loss.

CAT STEVENS

He has left us for another world, beyond the darkness of this present one vividly so depicted in the shadows of his last video. I truly pray he's welcomed to the light by his Maker in that great today, which has no tomorrow.

JOHN OATES

With the passing of David Bowie, the world has lost a true artist in every respect: uniquely original, ever expanding and exploring... Daryl and I played with him in 1973 on his first US tour. Off stage he always struck me as warm and engaging. His creativity and musical legacy will live forever.

MICHAEL STIPE

Right now, it feels as if the solar system is off its axis, as if one of our main planetary anchors has lost it's orbit. That said – I am certain that wherever Bowie is now – I want to be there someday.

ELVIS COSTELLO

The right words would be written in ink on card, not to be seen suddenly and brutally, like the news. In acknowledgement, the lights on this particular, peculiar little theatre will be lowered for a while. With deepest gratitude and respectful condolences to the family and friends of a truly great artist, beautiful melodist and elegant gentleman.

TINA TURNER

A piece of my heart has broken. Not only was David a passionate supporter of my career but more importantly a very special person in my life. An icon. Irreplaceable loving friend. I am missing him greatly.

LORDE

I've never met a hero of mine and liked it. It just sucks, the pressure is too huge, you can't enjoy it. David was different. I'll never forget the caressing of our hands as we spoke, or the light in his eyes. That night something changed in me – I felt a calmness grow, a sureness. I think in those brief moments, he heralded me into my next new life, an old rock and roll alien angel in a perfect grey suit. I realised everything I'd ever done, or would do from then on, would be done like maybe he was watching. I realized I was proud of my spiky strangeness because he had been proud of his. And I know I'm never going to stop learning dances, brand new dances. It's not going to change, how we feel about him. For the rest of our lives, we'll always be crashing in that same car.

TONY VISCONTI

His death was no different from his life – a work of art. He made *Blackstar* for us, his parting gift. I knew for a year this was the way it would be. I wasn't, however, prepared for it. He was an extraordinary man, full of love and life. He will always be with us.

ACKNOWLEDGEMENTS AND SOURCE NOTES

I am immensely grateful to everyone who has so generously helped with this project giving up hours in their busy schedules to talk to me about their personal experiences and providing insights into the world of David Bowie.

There are many people to thank in the course of researching and compiling this book. Firstly a big thanks to all the David Bowie fans from around the world who very kindly took time to send me their memories of seeing David live in concert as well as sending photo's, ticket stubs, flyers and posters to be included in the book.

Chris Charlesworth, for his introduction in this book. Chris has more rock 'n' roll stories than you can shake a stick at. Check out his site: justbackdated.blogspot.com

Soundman and singer, songwriter Robin Mayhew who sat at the mixing desk for every Ziggy Stardust concert performances around the world, between January 29 1972 and July 3 1973. Thanks for all the introductions and help. www.robinmayhew.co.uk

John 'Hutch' Hutchinson whose book Bowie & Hutch (Lodge Books) was used as a great reference in compiling this book.

George Underwood for the lovely photo and story.

I consulted the following television/radio networks, organisations magazines, newspapers, websites, and weeklists, some of which have now ceased publication and in some cases I extracted previously publish material and for this I remain truly grateful to: Jambase.com, ukrockfestivals.com, efestivals.co.uk, Guitar World, Today FM, Rock

ACKNOWLEDGEMENTS AND SOURCE NOTES

Cellar Magazine, Quartz Magazine, (interviews with Earl Slick, Gerry Leonard, Mike Garson, Carlos Alomar, Ken Scott), and thanks to Jeff Slate for arranging these. ©2016 Jeff Slate, as first published on Rock Cellar Magazine, Benjamin Chasteen/Epoch Times

The Morgan Fisher interview was originally published as part of an online tribute to David Bowie by The Japan Times in January 2016. Murray Scougall from The Sunday Post, Billboard.com, rockhistory.co.uk, manchesterbeat.com, News.com.au, Devononline.com, EW.com, UAL Alummi, justincaseofsunrise, Walesonline, Stuff.com, Radio X, The Telegraph Fashion Magazine, The Times, The Guardian, The Newcastle Chronical, Kentonline.co.uk, Bangkokpost, YouTube, Facebook, Twitter. Author, DJ and Music Consultant Daryl Easlea (www.sfob.co.uk), Vernon Dewhurst at Snap Gallery, Barbara Streun for her Bowie pics, Sonic Youth photo thanks to Michael Lavine, Alessandro Bottero from Classic Rock Italia.

Special thanks to Kris Needs, Pete Mitchell, Bob Harris, Mark Radcliffe, Marc Riley, Nick Weymouth from Queen on line, Photographer Peter Hince, Jez Lowe and the Northern Echo, Matt Sims from Quara, music and media historian Chris Phipps, Lee Ranaldo from Sonic Youth, Frank Henry, Mike Sauter, from 91.3 WYEP, Sam Coley, Roger Ferris, Charlie Dore, Tony Michaelides, Pete Carroll, Chris Phillips, Lisa Nelson Brown, and Phil Chapman.

Extra thanks to Liz Sanchez for photo research and support.

Carinthia West and the Hanging Out Archive, Craig Dancy, Val Kilmer and all the musicians Facebook, Twitter and YouTube feeds. And a very special thanks to author Richard Houghton for the idea for this series of books and all his help with guidance and contacts.

And a very special thanks to all the David Bowie sites: BowieLive.net, teenagewildlife.com, 5years.com, bowiewonerworld.com, Davidbowie.com, davidbowieblackstar.it, teenagewildlife.com, Bowiegoldenyears.

www.ingramcontent.com/pod-product-compliance
Lightning Source LLC
Chamberburg PA
CBHW011956090526

44590CB00023B/3744